Standard Catalog of
AMERICAN
Motorcycles
1898–1981

Jerry Hatfield

MW00442251

©2006 Krause Publications

Published by

krause publications
An Imprint of F+W Publications

700 East State Street • Iola, WI 54990-0001
715-445-2214 • 888-457-2873

Our toll-free number to place an order or obtain
a free catalog is (800) 258-0929.

All rights reserved. No portion of this publication may be reproduced or
transmitted in any form or by any means, electronic or mechanical,
including photocopy, recording, or any information storage and retrieval
system, without permission in writing from the publisher, except by a
reviewer who may quote brief passages in a critical article or review to
be printed in a magazine or newspaper, or electronically transmitted on
radio, television, or the Internet.

Library of Congress Catalog Number: 2005922934

ISBN 10-digit: 0-87349-949-2
ISBN 13-digit: 978-0-89689-949-0

Designed by Sandy Kent
Edited by Brian Earnest

Printed in The United States of America

ACKNOWLEDGMENTS

{M}ost of the pictures for this book were taken from period literature and magazines. From a copyright standpoint, such images have long been in the public domain. However, when enthusiasts have made period images available, I have credited them in recognition of their help. Likewise, current publications such as *The Antique Motorcycle, Motorcyclist, and Vintage Motor Bike Club* are cited for their reproduction of public domain period literature. In a few cases, these current publications have also been the source of other non-professional and non-copyrighted images. Thanks to the following non-professional enthusiasts who provided pictures and related information; large contributions are indicated: the late Sam Arena, Jack Armstrong, Peter Arundel, Butch Baer, Marv Baker, the late Earl Bentley (95), the late Dewey Bonkrud, Calvin Burnett, the late John Cameron, Ian Campbell, Earl Chalfant, Robert Cantrell (15), Pat Cramer, Frank DeGenero, Jim Dennie (45), the late Clyde Earl, John Eagles, the late Bob Finn (40), Grant Fish, the late Gene Grimes, George Hays, the late Bill Hoecker, the late Fleming Horne, Sam Hotton, Paul Huntley, Ronald Iannucci, the late Maldwyn Jones, Bruce Linsday (133), Robin Markey, Harold Mathews, the late Emmett Moore, Richard Morris, Ken Mullholland, John Nixon, the late Herb Ottaway, Tom Payne, the late Paul Pearce, Connie Schlemmer, Robert Scott, the late Bob Shingler, Pete Sink, Jeff Slobodian, Kevin Storey, George Stratton, Larry Struck, Jerry Turner, Ross VanEtten, Chuck Vernon, David Vittone, the late Red Woverton, Stephen Wright and George Yarocki (175). Thanks to the following professional photographers, totals indicated: Fred Crismon (4), Jeff Hackett (1), Sam Hotton (7), Bob Karolevitz (14) and Doug Mitchel (175). Thanks to Wheels Through Time museum curator Dale Walksler for extensive support (16 pictures).

I thank Stephen Wright. Steve rediscovered thousands of long-forgotten facts regarding pre-1915 American motorcycles. He published this information in his monumental work *The American Motorcycle, 1869-1914.* I've used a small part of that information, citing Steve in each instance.

Contents

ACE

America's motorcycling history includes the plots and subplots of three related four-cylinder marques: Henderson, Ace, and Indian Four. Designer William Henderson and his brother, manager Thomas Henderson, produced the Henderson luxury four-cylinder motorcycle from 1913 through 1917. From 1920 through 1926, William's design influence was carried forward in the Ace. William's ultimate impact was in the evolutionary years of 1927 through 1942, the period when his concept was continuously refined in the form of the Indian Four.

The Ace story starts two years before the first Ace rolled. In November, 1917, the brothers Henderson sold the design, manufacturing rights, and name "Henderson" to the Excelsior Motor Manufacturing and Supply Company, of Chicago, Illinois. The agreement stipulated that for the next five years William Henderson was to serve as the Excelsior factory superintendent, with an annual salary of $5,000. That was big money, enough to buy 10 top-of-the-line Henderson fours.

Both Excelsior and William Henderson hedged the bet, because the superintendent job could be terminated by either party upon 30 days notice. So much for the five-year job! But locked in place was the non-competitive clause. The Henderson brothers couldn't produce a competing design for two years, and further, any such future motorcycle couldn't bear the well known Henderson name. Buyer Ignatz Schwinn, the bicycle tycoon and builder of Excelsior motorcycles, was smart enough to know that William Henderson might become restless. Calendars had hardly flipped to the page exactly 24 months later, when William Henderson announced his intention to build another four-cylinder motorcycle.

Henderson motorcycles of 1912 through 1917 had proven fast and rugged, largely through long-distance record setting. Arguably the world's first super bikes, the early Hendersons had made their marks in runs from San Francisco to Los Angeles, Canada to Mexico, and from the Pacific to the Atlantic. A 24-hour record was also part of the legend. Henderson advertisements bragged

1920 Ace. This was the fastest production motorcycle in the world, topping out near 90 mph. This was about 5 to 10 mph faster than Hendersons and production Harley-Davidsons and Indians. The color of the Dupont Dulux enamel was Boatswain's Blue, coded 93-2063. The wheels were finished in a light cream—nearly white. (DOUG MITCHEL)

that if there was a long-distance record worth having, then Henderson had it.

William Henderson probably knew of, or even participated in, the emerging new Hendersons that would take the field simultaneously with the Ace as new 1920 models. From the beginning, Henderson engines had been F-heads, as explained later. But the new 1920 Hendersons would introduce side-valve (Flathead) engines to the four-cylinder field, while their overall construction appeared heavier and with emphasis on comfort and reliability. Clearly, William Henderson's new baby, the Ace, had to challenge the Henderson reputation. The new and more conservative Hendersons would leave an opening for a more sporting four-cylinder motorcycle. So William Henderson set to the task of building a go-fast four.

The muscle of the new Ace came from 1229cc packed into a design genre that is today almost forgotten. Though today's engines are almost exclusively of overhead-valve or overhead-cam design, most of us have either used or seen the occasional side-valve or Flathead-powered lawn mower, and know of the immortal Ford V-8 engines. But the F-head differs from all of

From 1912 through 1917, designer William Henderson had made his name with the Henderson marque of his creation. After selling out to Ignatz Schwinn of Excelsior, and working for Schwinn, William became unsatisfied with the evolution of Hendersons from sporty F-heads to conservative Flatheads (side-valves). The new Ace was said to embody William Henderson's best ideas. (GEORGE YAROCKI)

Though the F-head was not as efficient as the overhead-valve layout, the performance difference was marginal. Moreover, the configuration kept the exhaust plumbing down and away from the rider's thighs. The 1920-1924 Ace engines had a separate inlet manifold and inlet rocker-arms support. Later Aces had an integral manifold and rocker support. (MOTORCYCLING AND BICYCLING)

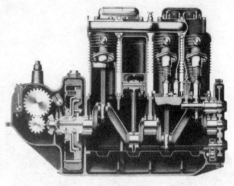

Some Ace engine components, such as the timing gears, remained in Indian Four production through 1942. The oil pump is keyed to the lowest gear. (BRUCE LINSDAY)

William Henderson's design was unusual. The four cylinder castings included most of the cylinder head structure. A single inlet-valves housing was secured to the four cylinders. A single inlet manifold was secured to the housing. Splash lubrication was employed. (BRUCE LINSDAY)

Keys to speed were the size and design. With four cylinders and a bore and stroke of 2.7 and 3.25 inches, the Ace displacement was 79.64 cubic inches (1305cc). The layout featured overhead inlet valves and side-mounted exhaust valves, and was termed inlet-over-exhaust, or I.O.E., and later, F-head. A multiple-plate steel disc clutch ran in the same oil used for the engine. The crankshaft was supported by three main bearings, standard for the era. The inlet rocker arms were hand lubricated, with the rider gaining access through spring-loaded "tobacco can" doors. (BRUCE LINSDAY)

Ace advertising once termed the luxury four "the Pierce-Arrow of motorcycles." Another ad intoned, "The speed of the Ace will astound you; its power will surprise you; its cozy comfort you will notice on your first half-mile...." (DOUG MITCHEL)

them. The F-head seemed to reflect a political compromise between advocates of Flathead and overhead-valve engines in that the inlet valves are indeed upstairs, but the exhaust valves remain on the side, operating within the cylinder blocks.

The compromise, of course, was an engineering one. Most American motorcycle engines were F-heads in the 1910s, including all Harley-Davidson and Indian V-twins. Exhaust valves were a big worry, because metallurgy was a young field. An F-head attraction was the situation of the relatively cool inlet valve directly above the hotter exhaust valve, the movement of the inlet charge thus serving to prevent excessive heat buildup in the exhaust valve. Even before 1910, theorists understood the drawback this presented. In cooling the exhaust valve, some of that heat went into the inlet charge. The hotter the inlet charge, the thinner the charge, and the lower the torque.

September, 1922: Erwin G. "Cannonball" Baker riding an Ace, en route to a new transcontinental record of 6 days, 22 hours, and 52 minutes. Over 90 percent of the ride was over dirt roads such as this one. (GEORGE YAROCKI)

November 19, 1923, near Philadelphia, Pennsylvania: Wolverton is riding XP-4 to a new unofficial American record of 129.61 mph. Nine days earlier, Britain's Claude Temple had set the official world's record of 108.85 on a British-Anzani. The American record was unofficial because it was run in one direction only, and the "trap" was only 1/10 of a mile long, and the engine was larger than 1000cc. (RED WOLVERTON)

This is a replica of the record-setting Ace XP-4. By the use of magnesium castings, the actual record-setter weighed only 325 lbs. (DOC PATT)

What sounds must have come from the record-setter's exhaust! (DOC PATT)

Steve McQueen was an enthusiastic collector of antique motorcycles. Fortunately, there wasn't an accident from the lowered side-stand at this early 1980s meet in California.

In its final form as a separate marque, the 1927 Ace was painted Sage Green, and offered first from the Detroit factory, and later from the Indian factory. Ace advertising from the Detroit operation claimed a pressure-fed lubrication system had replaced the simple splash setup, but longtime Ace test rider Red Wolverton asserted that only four or five Aces left the Detroit factory so equipped. (BOB FINN)

Saddle height was an important sales point and the Ace measured up at a commendable 20 inches. American marques tended to exaggerate this feature in sales literature. The saddle was pulled down and secured with wires, leaving it to an artist to brush away the wiring. (BOB FINN)

Theorists longed for the perfection of overhead-valve engines, but metallurgy problems were keeping that goal somewhere in the uncertain future. There was trial and error, and trial and error. Regardless of what was on paper, in motorcycles, F-heads were the practical reality, the design that worked, the accepted standard. At a time when the so-called squish principle had yet to invigorate Flathead design, F-heads were generally faster than Flatheads and were only slightly behind the pace of the few American overhead-valve motorcycle engines being built. Moreover, at the time, all overheads were exclusively factory racing department specials.

Maybe the solution was as much a matter of attitude as a matter of skill—damn the reliability "torpedoes"—full speed ahead! As to the design, what made the new Ace stand apart was the focus of all William Henderson's engineering skill toward a new goal—building a really fast production motorcycle.

The go-fast plot played out with outstanding performances rendered by the famous Cannonball Baker, and by hill climbing stars "T.N.T." Terpening and Charles "Red" Wolverton. Baker was well known for Canada-to-Mexico and transcontinental motorcycle records in the mid-teens on Indian motorcycles. In September, 1922, Cannonball rode from California to New York in 6 days, 22 hours, and 52 minutes, beating the Henderson record by over 17 hours. This feat was even more dramatic because only two days after Baker's departure, Henderson rider Wells Bennett rode east from California with the same goal, producing a near race between the two. But Bennett gave up when he realized he wouldn't be able to match Baker's performance.

Tragically, William Henderson was killed in a motorcycle accident in December, 1922. Arthur Lemon replaced him as chief engineer. With the goal of building the world's fastest motorcycle, Lemon was granted the considerable budget of $5,000 to purchase a dynomometer. He designed two special Ace competition machines, XP3 and XP4, which were used in the summer of 1923. Terpening and Wolverton won prestigious hill climbs, then perhaps more important than racing results. Wolverton won the overall Eastern States Championship, with the Ace beating out 1300cc twins as well as other fours. XP3 was a modified stocker, weighing 325 lbs.; XP4 was a one-off, benefiting from extensive use of magnesium.

The high point came in November, 1923, with Wolverton's unofficial solo record of 129.61 mph. Tracking the speed to 1/100 mph was a stretch; the trap was only 1/10 of a mile, and timing was via hand-held stop watch. Regardless, the motorcycle was likely the world's fastest, as the official world's record was 108.5 mph, by British-Anzani rider C. F. Temple over the Brooklands track in England. Only seven years later did the official world's record exceed Wolverton's run on the Ace XP4.

Despite the vigorous and successful Ace competition program, the company was unable to operate profitably. For a time, accounting errors were permitting the retail sale of new Ace motorcycles below factory cost! Two attempts were made to reorganize the company. XP4 was returned to Wolverton, but the three-year lapse in development proved XP4 uncompetitive. Now strapped for funds, Arthur Lemon was attempting engineering development without a dynomometer! Despite this handicap, Wolverton recalled to the author a definite seat-of-the-pants improvement, and Wolverton won a couple of late-season hill climbs. By late 1926, production was at a standstill. Ace design, the Ace name, Ace tooling, and all inventory were sold to The Indian Motorcycle Company of Springfield, Massachusetts. The following spring, Indian cataloged and sold green Ace motorcycles representing the final stage of development by the formerly independent company.

Circa 1902 Advance motorbike attachment. (JIM DENNIE)

Though details are unknown concerning the 1912-1915 AMC, the striking resemblance to period Harley-Davidsons suggests that either the maker copied the famous marque, that Harley-Davidson sold excess parts to AMC, or that both engines were assembled from castings made by the same foundry. (BOB KAROLEVITZ)

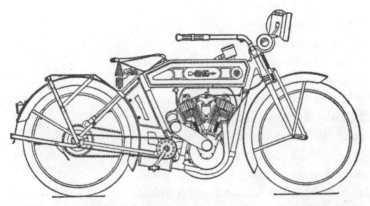

Another view of the AMC. Both chain- and belt-drive models were offered, using the same frame. The right rear fork tubes were bowed outward to allow room for the belt drive. (GEORGE YAROCKI)

ADVANCE

One of several motor bike attachments in the early 20th century, the Advance took the notice of a pioneer enthusiast, and was filed in his/her scrapbook of motorcycles. Unfortunately, no specifications were included. However, it can be seen that the engine was unusual for the time. In a world of F-head engines, the Advance was either a side-valve (Flathead) or a T-head. The latter features inverted valves on opposite sides of the combustion chamber.

AMC

AMC motorcycles were built from 1912 through 1915 by the Allied Motor Corporation, of Chicago, Illinois. These motorcycles appear to have been exact copies of the Harley-Davidson built in Milwaukee, Wisconsin. One wonders why anyone would have bought this Harley-Davidson clone instead of the real thing. The answer could only have been a lower price. But the buyers would not have enjoyed strong dealerships with good service and spare parts, and would not have been immersed in the clubs and informal associations nourished by Harley-Davidson dealerships. These after-sale factors, then as now, were strong points for "the real thing" made in Milwaukee.

AMERICA

The "America" was produced by the Great Western Manufacturing Company of La Porte, Indiana, in 1904 and 1905, but the marque may not have been built there. Like dozens of makes then on the market, the machine was a clone of the popular Indian brand. In fact, apart from the bizarre steering wheel, the America was an exact copy of the Indian. This marketing arrangement is discussed in the Indian and Thor sections.

Briefly, Indian contracted engine manufacture and perhaps some other services to the Aurora Automatic Machinery Company of Aurora, Illinois. Aurora used the same Indian-designed engines, frames, etc., in its own Thor brand. Aurora also sold either these components or, possibly, complete motorcycles to marketing outfits like America of La Porte. Aurora advertised the complete set of parts needed to build an Indian clone, so the general rule was probably that the buyers assembled these items.

AMERICAN *(Chicago, Illinois)*

"American" was the most frequently chosen name for several pioneering motorcycling companies in the U.S. Though billed as a Chicago firm, following a common practice of the era, the business address was merely that of the sales organization. This American was produced by the Theim Manufacturing Company of Saint Paul, Minnesota.

AMERICAN *(Connecticut)*

An American marque was part of the Pope family of pedal bicycles. When the company turned to motorcycle production, each of the several different bicycle brands were applied to a motorcycle design shown in the accompanying picture. As well as the American, other company marques included: Columbia, Crescent, Imperial, Monarch, Rambler, and Tribune. Some of these labels were also applied to Indian clones.

AMERICAN *(Louisville, Kentucky)*

The "American" horizontally opposed twin appeared in 1921 advertisements of *Motorcycling and Bicycling*. Such horizontally opposed twins were also termed flat twins (not to be confused with Flathead engines). At the time, Harley-Davidson was selling a 35.6-cubic inch (584cc) flat twin, and Indian had built a small 15.7-cubic inch

1910 American (Chicago) Model III. This re-badged Theim was part of the 1910 American lineup. Based on published Theim specifications, the engine had a bore and stroke of 3 1/4 x 3 47/64 inches, and a displacement of 31 cubic inches (508cc). Side-valve design was unusual for the era; industry leaders Indian and Harley-Davidson didn't switch to the "Flathead" layout until 1916 and 1929, respectively.

(BRUCE LINSDAY)

A 1904 or 1905 American (La Porte, Indiana). It had a steering wheel instead of handlebars; otherwise, these motorcycles were exact copies of the Indian. (JIM DENNIE)

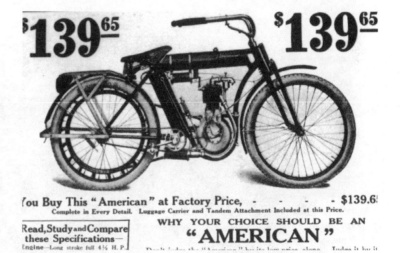

1910 American (Chicago). The American Motorcycle Company of Chicago purchased motorcycles from Armac, Theim, and Yale, then re-branded them as "American." This example is a re-badged Armac. The company touted the long stroke F-head (inlet-over-exhaust) engine. In addition to this battery ignition model, a magneto ignition job was also offered. In those days, batteries weren't very reliable and many riders of all brands opted for the extra-cost magneto option. (BOB KAROLEVITZ)

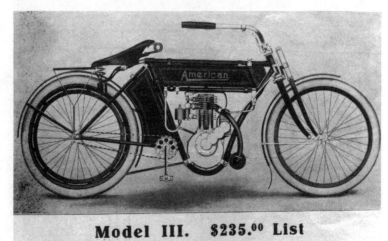

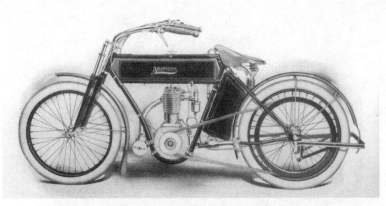

1911 American (Chicago) Model 51. Though belt drive was still popular, by 1911 the trend was moving to chain drive. The large box under the saddle housed the battery. Magneto ignition was more reliable in the era, but added up to 20 percent to the cost. The Model 51 was a hybrid of Theim components, as can be seen by comparing this illustration to Theim pictures. (BRUCE LINSDAY)

(257cc) flat twin. What worked for Douglas in Britain, and in Europe, didn't work in the United States. The V-twins of Excelsior, Harley-Davidson and Indian had captivated American motorcyclists with their classic "potato-potato-potato" sound. Consequently, the Harley, Indian and American flat twins didn't catch on.

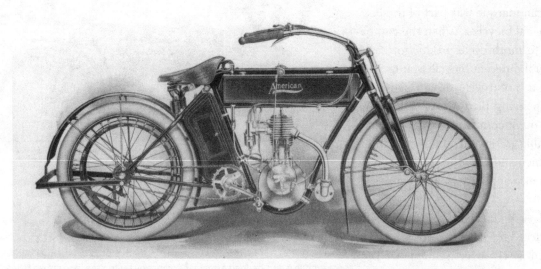

The 1911 American (Chicago) Model 51 had a maximum output of 5 horsepower, according to the industry custom of equating about 30.5 cubic inches (500cc) with this performance level. (BRUCE LINSDAY)

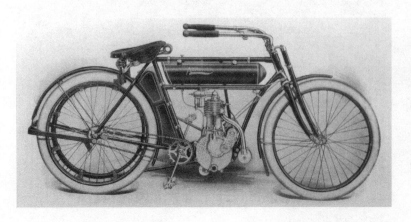

1911 American (Chicago) Model 61. The industry standard practice was to equate engine size with horsepower. A 5-hp motor, for instance, signified a displacement of about 30.5 cubic inches (500cc). Thus, this 4 1/4-hp model displaced about 27.5 cubic inches (450cc). The Model 61 was purchased wholesale from Yale, then re-badged. The Model 61 differed from the Yale only in the magneto arrangement, which was a relatively easy manufacturing change for Yale. (BRUCE LINSDAY)

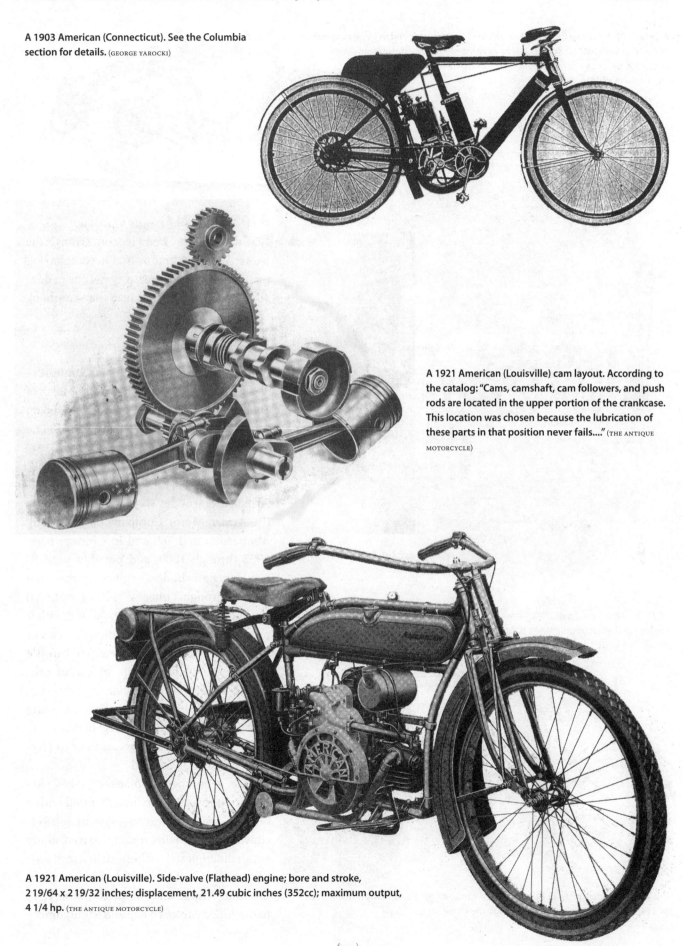

A 1903 American (Connecticut). See the Columbia section for details. (GEORGE YAROCKI)

A 1921 American (Louisville) cam layout. According to the catalog: "Cams, camshaft, cam followers, and push rods are located in the upper portion of the crankcase. This location was chosen because the lubrication of these parts in that position never fails...." (THE ANTIQUE MOTORCYCLE)

A 1921 American (Louisville). Side-valve (Flathead) engine; bore and stroke, 2 19/64 x 2 19/32 inches; displacement, 21.49 cubic inches (352cc); maximum output, 4 1/4 hp. (THE ANTIQUE MOTORCYCLE)

A Circa 1902 American (origin unknown). This image was found in the scrapbook of an early enthusiast." No specifications were listed. One wonders if some such circa 1900 pictures were concepts, rather than illustrations representing actual machines. (JIM DENNIE)

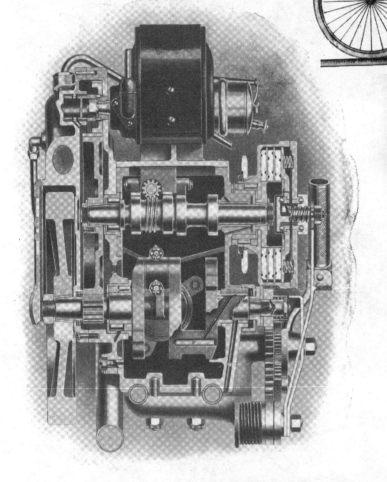

1921 The American (Louisville) , viewed from the front. The oil pump is in the upper center. On the left (motorcycle's right), is the combined flywheel and cooling fan. (THE ANTIQUE MOTORCYCLE)

The1907 Armac weighed in at 150 lbs., had a maximum speed, 40 mph, and a price of $145. The exhaust was routed through the frame. (BRUCE LINSDAY)

AMERICAN *(origin unknown)*

No details are known concerning the "American" machine in the accompanying picture (above). The picture was one of dozens of clippings pasted into the scrapbook of an early enthusiast.

APACHE

From 1907 through 1911, Apache motorcycles were the product of Brown and Beck of Denver, Colorado. The 1908 model used an Indian-designed "Thor" engine in a single loop frame, with a rigid front fork.

ARMAC

Armac motorcycles were manufactured by the Armac Motor Company of Saint Paul, Minnesota, in 1902, and in Chicago from 1902 through 1909, and possibly later. F-head single-cylinder engines transmitted power through either V-belt, or optional chain drive. Sidecars were sold with either rattan, or molded wood bodies. Armacs of 1908, and probably earlier, featured throttle control by left-hand grip, a feature otherwise used only on Indian motorcycles. Through 1908, Armacs used an unsprung front fork; in 1909 a leading bottom link fork, or parallelogram fork, similar to Harley-Davidson's, was used.

Like a number of pioneer makes, Armac motorcycles were initially fitted with a through-the-frame exhaust system. In 1911, conventional exhaust routing arrived, along with a different style of bottom link fork similar to that of Emblem motorcycles. At about this time, Armac sold complete motorcycles to the Allied Motors Corp and Montgomery

A 1908 Armac Model A. The one-piece cylinder and the left crankcase could be removed while the rest of the motor remained in the frame. The left-hand throttle grip was used only by Armac and Indian. The F-head single-cylinder bike had a bore of 3 inches, displaced 24.7 cubic inches (405cc); produced 3 hp at 1800 rpm; and cost $200. (BRUCE LINSDAY)

Ward. These bought-up bikes were labeled A.M.C. and Hawthorne respectively.

1905-1907 Specifications: 22¼-inch frame; 2-inch tires; 56-inch wheelbase; single-cylinder F-head engine; bore and stroke, 3⅛ and 3¼ inches; displacement, 24.92 cubic inches (408cc); automatic sight feed lubrication; belt drive; battery ignition; battery mileage, 1300 to 1500 miles; fuel mileage (distance to empty), 80 miles.

ARROW

The Arrow was a clone of the 1909 Marsh-Metz with cylindrical tank. These motorcycles were sold from about 1909 through about 1914, by the Arrow Motorcycle Company of Chicago, Illinois.

AUTO-BI *(also, Thomas Auto-Bi)*

The Thomas company began motorcycle production in 1900. According to *The Bicycling World and Motorcycle Review*, April 27, 1907: "The Thomas Auto-Bi, which, as a good many people do not know, was the first motor bicycle built in America..." The April, 1902, issue of *The Dealer and Repairman* said "The Auto-Bi was originally placed on the market by the E. R. Thomas Motor Co., of Buffalo, but last year the production of the motor bicycle was turned over to the Buffalo Automobile and Auto-Bi Co., the Thomas company wishing to limit its work to the production of motors. The motor sets of the Thomas company are still used exclusively, however, in the Auto-Bi and in the automobiles manufactured by the same company..."

There's some confusion as to the preferred name of the marque. Most references found by the author use the term "Thomas Auto-Bi." For that reason, further discussion and additional pictures are contained in the Thomas Auto-Bi section.

1902 Auto-Bi No. 5. This configuration is believed to be the same, or nearly the same, as the 1900 edition: engine, 2 1/4 hp, weight, 85 lbs., price, $200.

(BRUCE LINSDAY)

Circa 1913 Bailey Flyer. The 66.8-cubic inch (1095cc) engine was rated at 9 hp.

(MOTORCYCLE ILLUSTRATED)

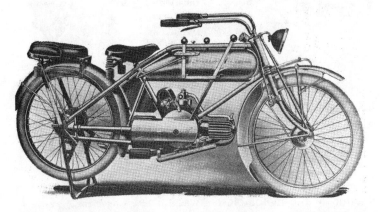

For 1914, the Bailey Flyer was made more attractive and functional with the introduction of a shorter frame and lower saddle. The more bulbous tank and refined fenders also added to the improved look. (BOB KAROLEVITZ)

A 1920 Baker De Long engine had a displacement of 73.06 cubic inches (1197cc) and a maximum output of 20 hp. (MOTORCYCLE ILLUSTRATED)

BAILEY FLYER

In 1913, the Bailey Flyer was built by the McLeod Manufacturing Company of Portland, Oregon. Later, production was moved to the Bailey Flyer Auto Cycle Company of Chicago. Limited production continued into 1917, then ceased. The Bailey Flyer was powered by a horizontally opposed F-head engine, laid out in line with the frame. Final drive was by shaft and bevel gears.

BAKER DE LONG

The Baker De Long engine has been erroneously described as a collaborative project of the well-known E. G. "Cannonball" Baker of Indianapolis, Indiana, and a Mr. De Long. Not so. As reported in the March 18, 1920, *Motorcycle Illustrated*, the venture was accomplished by C. E. Baker, C. E. De Long, and E. M. De Long, all of Hartford, Connecticut. The three enthusiasts designed and built this experimental engine over an extended period, completing the task in June, 1918. The engine was then installed in a modified Indian frame for road testing. Despite their creative work, no subsequent mention was made in the motorcycle press, and the project died. Incidentally, two years earlier, C. E. Baker and E. M. De Long had collaborated on the unusual Marathon marque, which went into production and is described later in the book.

Specifications listed for a 1920 Baker De Long engine included: Overhead-valve design with valves canted 90 degrees from bores; bore, 2 5/8 inches; stroke, 3 3/8 inches; displacement, 73.06 cubic inches (1197cc); maximum output, 20 hp claimed, compared to a typical industry quote of about 12 hp for this displacement; firing order, 1-2-4-3; camshaft, one-piece, removable by taking off side cover; connecting rods, one-piece; lubrication, by mechanical pump; four flywheels; ignition, magneto; drive, engine to shaft via worm gear.

BANKER

No details are known concerning the Banker, an illustration of which was found in a period enthusiast's scrapbook of motorcycle clippings. The machine is less crude than many of the 1900-02 motorcycles, and is therefore assumed to be of about 1903 vintage. The Banker had an F-head engine with automatic (suction operated) inlet valve, and battery ignition. Weight was probably in the 125-150-lb. range, the battery would have likely had about a 75-mile operating limit, and the top speed was probably in the 30-35 mph range.

BLACK DIAMOND

Black Diamond motorcycles were briefly manufactured by Reeser and Mackenzie, 1100 Betz Building, Philadelphia, Pennsylvania. The company was mainly a builder of air compressors and light machinery. Production may have been limited to the 1905 season, because no publicity has been found apart from the 1905 press release for April 1, 1905, *Cycle and Automobile Trade Journal*. The single-cylinder motorcycles were constructed with the increasingly popular features of loop frame layout and chain drive.

The 1905 Black Diamond had: a 22-inch frame; 2-inch tires; 52-inch wheelbase; single cylinder, 2 5/8-inch bore and 3 3/8-inch stroke, displacement 18.26 cubic inches (300cc); 2-hp motor; cup lubricator operated by lever near handlebar; and chain drive with friction clutch. Battery mileage (no generator) was rated at 500 to 600 and fuel mileage at 100. It had grip control, weighed 130 lbs., had a top speed of 40 mph and a price of $185.

A 1920 Baker De Long engine. Note the unusual valve arrangement. The valves were oriented 90 degrees apart from the cylinder bores. Valve actuation was by long enclosed levers. Valve adjustment was easy, access being by spring-loaded circular covers. But those long actuating levers must have significantly reduced the ability of the engine to spin fast. The design has the look of something done by steam engine technicians. (MOTORCYCLE ILLUSTRATED)

The Banker Motor Bicycle

A Circa 1903 Banker. This picture of the Banker motorcycle was found in an early enthusiast's scrapbook. (JIM DENNIE)

The 1905 Black Diamond's special features included speed control by throttling mixture (some marques used ignition timing for speed control), friction clutch and a superior oiling device. (JIM DENNIE)

BRADLEY TYPE B. PRICE $175.

A 1905 Bradley Model B. Specifications: 22-inch frame; 28 x 3-inch tires; 50-inch wheelbase; 2 3/4-inch bore x 3-inch stroke, 2 1/4-hp motor; sight feed and splash lubrication; belt or chain drive; fuel mileage to 125; single lever control; weight 94 lbs.; speed 35 mph; price $175. (THE ANTIQUE MOTORCYCLE)

BRADLEY TYPE C. PRICE $200.

A 1905 Bradley Model C. Specifications: 22-inch frame; 28 x 2-inch tires; 52-inch wheelbase; 3 1/4-hp motor; belt drive; fuel mileage 100; single lever control; weight 140 lbs.; speed 40 mph; price $200. (THE ANTIQUE MOTORCYCLE)

The 1914 Black Hawk had a keystone frame with the engine as a stress bearing member, a front fork with up-and-forward action, an F-head engine with bore and stroke of 3 1/4 and 3 34/64 inches, respectively, and displacement of 30.46 cubic inches (499cc).
(BOB KAROLEVITZ)

BLACK HAWK

The Black Hawk was built by the Black Hawk Motor Company of Rock Island, Illinois, from 1911 through 1914. The company produced only singles until a twin was announced for the 1914 season.

BRADLEY

The Bradley marque was produced from 1904 through 1912 by the C. E. Bradley Motor Company, 268 Diamond Street, Philadelphia. The 1904 Model A was similar to the 1904 Columbia. Three single-cylinder models were offered in 1905, the 17.8-cubic inch (290cc) diamond frame Model B, the 26.9-cubic inch (440cc) loop frame Model C, and the 38.48-cubic inch (630cc) single-cylinder Model D. For 1907, the Model B was dropped and the remaining $200 single (model designation unknown) featured a 3-hp engine, which, according to trade custom, signified a displacement of approximately 30.5 cubic inches (500cc). Likewise, the new $275 6-hp V-twin displaced about 61 cubic inches (1000cc). The twin was advertised as a 65-mph machine.

Single and twin engines could be bought separately for $100 and $175, respectively. All models through 1907 were of F-head (inlet-over-exhaust) engine layout. Later models were almost certainly F-heads, as this was the era's dominant type.

According to the April 1, 1905, *Cycle and Automobile Trade Journal*: "Special features of Bradley motorcycles are: mechanically operated valves; steel flywheel and shaft in one piece; cylinder and head cast integral; places for three separate spark plugs; exhaust valve lift and spark advance controlled by same lever."

BRIGGS AND STRATTON MOTOR WHEEL

In 1919, the Briggs and Stratton company of Milwaukee, Wisconsin, purchased the rights to the Smith Motor Wheel, from the A. O. Smith company, also of Milwaukee. Briggs and Stratton enlarged the bore from 2 1/4 inches to 2 1/2 inches, and the rated output increased from 1 hp to 1 1/2 hp. Production ceased around 1925. Incidentally, this was Briggs and Stratton's first commercially successful design. The company went on to become America's leading builder of small engines.

A 1912 Bradley, outfitted for racing. The overhead-valve configuration put the Bradley in the top tier of American motorcycle engineering. The engine capacity was about 30.5 cubic inches (500cc) to conform to period racing rules. (BOB KAROLEVITZ)

A 1920 Briggs and Stratton Motor Wheel. This cutaway shows the large drive gear that operated directly off the cam shaft. In order to achieve the desired 8-to-1 gear ratio, a four-lobe cam was fitted and the camshaft turned at 1/8 engine speed. This gear was secured to the bicycle wheel. (MOTORCYCLING AND BICYCLING)

A 1919 Briggs and Stratton Motor Wheel. Engine specifications: F-head single; bore and stroke, 2 1/2 x 2 1/2 inches; displacement, 12.3 cubic inches (201cc); maximum output, 2 horsepower. Fuel tank: 1/2 gallon, sufficient for 50 to 60 miles of running. Lubrication: wet sump, splash and pump. Weight: 60 lbs. 1919 improvements: larger cylinder with longer cooling fins. (MOTORCYCLING AND BICYCLING)

Buckeye Motor Cycle

Made by The Oscar Lear Automobile Co., 4th and Gay Sts., Columbus, Ohio.

BUCKEYE MOTOR CYCLE.   PRICE $140.

From the April 1, 1905, *Cycle and Automobile Trade Journal*: Specifications: price $140; 23-inch frame; 2-inch tires; single cylinder, 3¼ x 3¼ bore and stroke, 3-hp motor; lubrication by gravity from reservoir; chain drive; battery mileage, 1,000; fuel mileage, 150 miles; spark and throttle control; weight 115 lbs.; speed 35 mph-plus; **price $140.** (THE ANTIQUE MOTORCYCLE)

BUCKEYE

A product of the Oscar Leer Automobile Company, 4th and Gay Streets, Columbus, Ohio, the 1905 Buckeye was powered by a 27.46-cubic inch (450cc) F-head (inlet-over-exhaust) single-cylinder engine. The cylinder dimensions were unusual in that the bore and stroke were equal; almost all other engines of the era featured a stroke that was longer than the bore diameter. Frame layout was along pedal bike lines, and similar to the Bradley Model B, with the engine behind the seat mast. Special features: motor built in frame and strongly braced; friction disc in rear hub relieves strain on chain; one less chain than is usual on chain-driven machines. No information has been found for subsequent years, so production apparently ceased after 1905.

CALIFORNIA, SNELL-CALIFORNIA, AND YALE-CALIFORNIA

The histories of the California, Snell-California, Yale-California, and Yale marques, are entwined. In 1902 and 1903, California motorcycles were manufactured by the California Motor Company of San Francisco. From 1898 through 1903, the Kirk Manufacturing Company and the Snell Cycle Fittings Company were located at the same address in Toledo, Ohio. In 1903, Kirk and Snell merged into the Consolidated Manufacturing Company and purchased the California Motor Company. In 1904, two marques were offered: the Snell-California and the Yale-California. Both were built in the so-called Kirk factory in Toledo.

Apart from the names, the two marques were identical, as proven by the use of the same illustrations in both marque catalogs. In 1905, the Snell-California brand name was dropped. From 1906 through 1908, the company used the Yale-California name, but the motorcycles carried the Yale name on the tanks. Shown here are two illustrations under the "California" marque. Discussion of Snell-California motorcycles is in the later section of that name. Yale-California and Yale data are contained within the Yale section.

CENTURY

The Century lightweight was built in 1916 and 1917 by the Century Auto Cycle Company of Chicago. The company's rationale was that there was an untapped market among the 600,000 people who bought a bicycle in 1915.

A 1903 California. On such a motorcycle, branded as either a Yale-California or a Snell-California—take your pick—George Wyman completed the first motor vehicle crossing of North America. Wyman finished on July 6, 1903, three weeks before the first automobile crossing. The specifications were either identical to, or nearly so, to the 1905 model Yale-California shown later. (JIM DENNIE)

A 1903 California racer. From a magazine scrapbook clipping (name and date unknown): "We show herewith the 4 H. P. motor cycle racer made by California Motor Co., 2212 Folsom Street, San Francisco, Cal., which has never been defeated …The motor cycle is fitted with the California carburetor, which is also made for automobile use. The racers are built on order only, but the regular 1903 models are ready for delivery at any time." (JIM DENNIE)

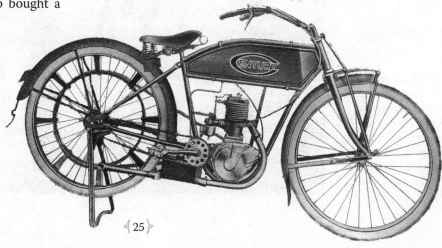

1916 Century. The Century got its name because it weighed 100 lbs., cost $100, and would run 100 miles in 3 hours on a gallon of fuel. (BOB KAROLEVITZ)

CHICAGO 400 MOTOR CYCLE. PRICE $150.

A 1905 Chicago 400: Specifications from the April 1, 1905, *Cycle and Automobile Trade Journal*: 22-inch frame; 2-inch tires; 62-inch wheelbase; single cylinder 3 1/8 x 3 1/4 bore and stroke; 3-hp motor; oil cup lubrication; belt drive; battery mileage 100; grip control; weight 150 lbs.; speed 30 miles. This machine was also furnished with a 23-inch frame; 2 1/4-inch tires; 68-inch wheelbase; two-cylinder, 3 1/8 x 3 1/8 bore and stroke, and 5 total hp. (THE ANTIQUE MOTORCYCLE)

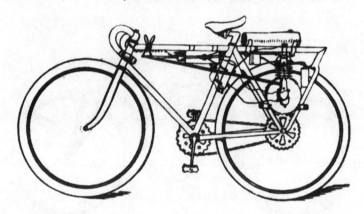

A Circa 1903 Clark motorbike outfit pictured in an early enthusiast's scrapbook. (JIM DENNIE)

A circa 1903 Clement power unit, attached to Columbia bicycle frame. As well as offering complete motorcycles, Clement sold this motorbike kit for $135. Restoration by Jeff Slobodian

CHAMPION

For a few months in 1913, the marque name "Champion" was given to an unusual half-bike half-car vehicle better known by its two other titles, "Militaire" and "Militor." This came about because the design was licensed by the inventors to The Champion Motor Car Company of Saint Louis, Missouri. Refer to the section on "Militaire, Militor" for information and illustrations.

CHICAGO 400

The 1905 Chicago 400 motorcycles were offered in two models: a 24.9-cubic inch (408cc) single, and a 47.9-cubic inch (785cc) twin. The motorcycles were made by W. Hoffman Motor Works, 1253 Halstead Street, Chicago. Previously, the same company had marketed an identical single under the trade name "Hoffman." There are no records of subsequent production.

CLARK

The author found no information on the circa 1903 Clark motorcycle pictured in an early enthusiast's scrapbook. The Clark was apparently a motorbike kit. A drawing was provided, rather than a photograph, it's possible that the illustration represented a concept rather than a reality. The picture is nevertheless provided, as its flavor speaks of the wide-open entrepreneurial environment of the fledgling industry.

CLEMENT

A French design, the F-head (inlet-over-exhaust) single-cylinder Clement was first exhibited in the United States at the New York City motorcycle show of 1902. As the motorcycle was well received, arrangements were made to produce it under French supervision at a factory in Hartford, Connecticut. The years of production are unknown, but the marque was surely brief in America because it wasn't exhibited in the 1905 New York City show.

CLEVELAND *(Connecticut)*

A product of the Colonel Alfred Pope conglomerate, the Hartford, Connecticut, "Cleveland" was built from 1902 through 1905. Initial production was by the American Cycle Manufacturing Company, and, apparently, later by the Eastern Department of Pope Manufacturing in Hartford. Except for the name, the 1905 Cleveland was identical to the 1905 Columbia. Other clones in this family tree included American, Crescent, Imperial, Monarch, Rambler, and Tribune. There were several brands because the company already sold pedal bikes under those labels.

CLEVELAND *(Cleveland, Ohio)*

The Cleveland Motorcycle Manufacturing Company was located at 7209 Platt Avenue, Cleveland, Ohio. From 1915 through 1925, the firm built lightweight two-stroke singles, in single-speed and two-speed configurations. In 1925, a brief attempt was made to market a four-stroke single with a three-speed gearbox, but this was aborted because Harley-Davidson and Indian were launching similar models. From 1925 through 1929, Cleveland built in-line four-cylinder F-head motorcycles.

In the September, 17, 1924, *Motorcycling and Bicycling World*, a Cleveland advertise-

A Circa 1903 Clement power unit attached to Columbia bicycle frame. Specifications:, F-head (inlet-over-exhaust); 2 1/2 x 2 1/4 bore and stroke; displacement 8.9 cubic inches (147cc). The overall construction is quite similar to the American marque Thomas Auto-Bi, which had already come on the market in 1900. Restoration by Jeff Slobodian

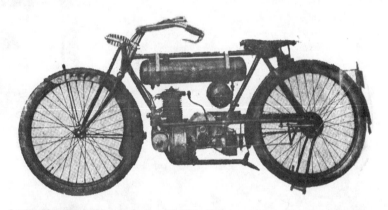

A 1915 Cleveland. This was the firm's initial offering, announced in the June 3, 1915 issue of *Motor Cycle Illustrated*. Rated output was 2 to 2 1/2 hp, and the bike weighed only 135 lbs. The short wheelbase and high saddle position were quickly abandoned. (MOTORCYCLE ILLUSTRATED)

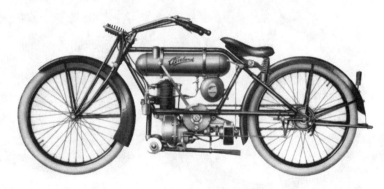

A 1915 Cleveland Model 1-A. Specifications: Two-stroke single-cylinder engine bore 2 1/2 x 2 3/4 bore and stroke; displacement 13.5 cubic inches (221cc); multiple disc dry clutch operated by left-hand lever; transmission shifted by right foot; transmission, 2-speed with chain final-drive; low gear ratio 9.5 to 1; high gear ratio 5.9 to 1; 1 1/2-gal. fuel capacity; 26-inch wheels; 26 x 2¼-inch tires; contracting band brake operated by left foot; finish, black with gray and nickel trimmings; price, $150.

(BRUCE LINSDAY)

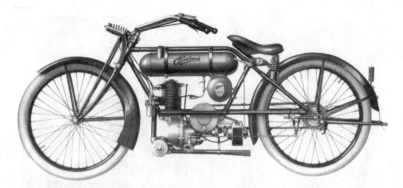

A 1915 Cleveland Model 1-B carried a price of $140. The Models 1-A and 1-B differed in clutch design. The $150 Model 1-A had a multiple disc clutch operated by a left-hand lever. The $140 Model 1-B had a sliding-jaw clutch operated concurrently with gear-shifting via the right-side pedal. Note that there's no kickstarter on either model. The rider used the compression release when push-starting the motorcycle. A mere walking pace was adequate for the low-compression-ratio two-stroke. (BRUCE LINSDAY)

A 1915 Cleveland cutaway engine. The "Swiss cheese" piston was avant garde at the time, whether two-stroke or four-stroke. The deflector piston was a standard two-stroke design feature of the era. (BRUCE LINSDAY)

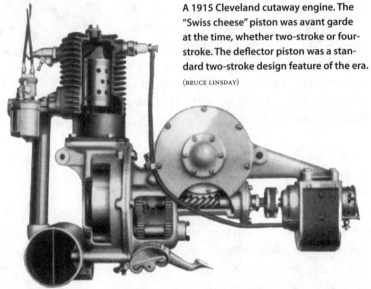

A 1925 Cleveland F-25 single. Launched in September, 1924, the early-1925 Cleveland four-stroke 21-cubic inch (350cc) single, other than the engine, was identical to the 10-year-running two-stroke two-speeder. When, at the same time, Indian announced the four-stroke 21-cubic inch three-speed Prince, Cleveland began planning for a three-speed update of the F-25. The latter work was then halted in order to launch a four-cylinder model. (GEORGE YAROCKI)

Early-1926 Cleveland Four with T-head engine. In late 1925, Cleveland brought out the first of its four-cylinder motorcycles. The unorthodox T-head engine featured side-mounted inlet and exhaust valves with each pair on opposite sides of the bore. The bore was 23/16 inches; the stroke, 27/16 inches; the displacement, 36.6 cubic inches (600cc). (DOUG MITCHEL)

The inlet side of the T-head Four. The inlet manifold doubled as a frame tube! Cleveland claimed the valves to be extremely large compared to the bore. This was possible because there were no constraints on valve size, since the valves weren't confined to the dimensions of a cylinder head (as in an overhead-valve engine) and the inlet and exhaust valves didn't compete for available space between the bores (as in a side-valve in-line four). In the low-rpm era, this seemed like a good idea.

ment proclaimed an improved two-stroke single, with twist-grip throttle control replacing the throttle lever. In the same issue, Indian announced their new Prince, a 21-cubic inch (350cc) three-speed four-stroke single, and with the same listed $185 price as the Cleveland. Cleveland knew its two-speed two-stroke couldn't match the competition from a major factory.

The company responded less than five months later. In the February 4, 1925, *Motorcycling*, Cleveland announced another $185 model, the F-25, to compete against the Indian Prince. The new Cleveland lightweight was a four-stroke single displacing 21.25 cubic inches (348cc). In all other respects, including the two-speed gearbox, the new Cleveland single was identical to the earlier two-stroke.

Still feeling the pressure, in the April 29, 1925, *Motorcycling*, Cleveland publicized the adoption of a three-speed transmission. Deliveries were projected for June, 1925.

Only a few of these Cleveland four-stroke singles were built.. In fact, the envisioned late-1925 three-speeder may not have gotten off the drawing board. No Cleveland four-stroke single of either type has to date surfaced.

With Indian now in the lightweight field, Cleveland management decided to abandon its 10-year lightweight program and enter the four-cylinder field. The result was the unorthodox 1926 T-head Cleveland Four, detailed in the captions. Announced in November 11, 1925, *Motorcycling*, the 1926 four-cylinder Cleveland sought a new market niche. Whereas the luxurious Ace and Henderson fours were big motorcycles, the Cleveland T-head was sized at about 37 cubic inches (600cc), the same size as the popular 1920-1926 Indian Scout V-twins.

Cleveland soon learned the T-head four-cylinder didn't have the pep motorcyclists would demand. So on April 14, 1926, a *Motorcycling* advertisement announced a

This F-head Cleveland update was apparently offered only for a few weeks, still in the original lightweight underslung frame. The exposed overhead rockers seem a throwback to the previous decade; however, Harley-Davidson still used exposed rockers on its twins. A conventional left-side frame tube replaced the combination left tube and inlet manifold.

(THE ANTIQUE MOTORCYCLE)

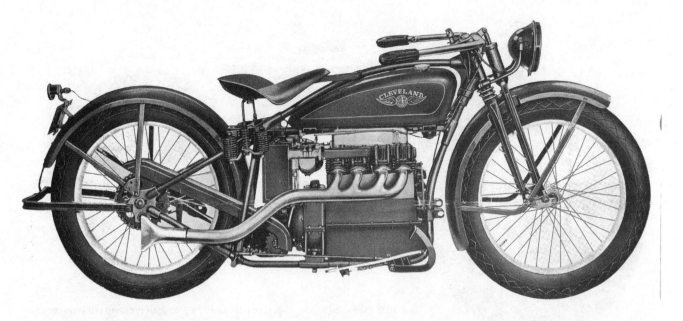

A 1926 Cleveland Model 4-45. The engine was a four-cylinder, F-head, with a bore and stroke of 2 1/4 x 213/16 inches, and displacement of 44.73 cubic inches (733cc). Ignition was by Splitdorf magneto. Unusual features included the one-piece combined inlet-manifold and rocker housing, and the one-piece cylinder block. Cleveland claimed the one-piece block provided better cooling than the use of four separate cylinders. (GEORGE YAROCKI)

companion 37-cubic inch (600cc) F-head four-cylinder Sports Model. The T-head four was soon phased out.

Then, in 1927, the Cleveland Sports model was enlarged to an advertised 45 cubic inches, or 750cc (actually 44.73 ci or 733cc). The redesigned F-head engine featured full valve enclosure, integral inlet manifold and head, and cylinders cast in a single block. A completely new fork and frame completed the revolution. To narrow the performance gap with the 80-cubic inch(1300cc) Ace and Henderson Fours, a sports configuration 4-45 was soon offered with a semi-racing camshaft, larger inlet valves, and polished ports.

Cleveland just couldn't seem to get it right. For the 1927 season, the new four was enlarged to a nominal 61 cubic inches (1000cc), and renamed the "4-61." This was the firm's fourth four in about 18 months! The new bike was capable of about 90 mph, bringing it up to Ace standards, both brands now being a bit faster than the more conservative Henderson. For once, Cleveland got ahead of the industry, by outfitting the 4-61 with a front brake. This was a year

Access to the Cleveland gearbox was simple. Transmission work on the rival Henderson and Ace fours required removal of the engine from the frame, and then splitting the crankcases! Because of both weight and various protruding items, Ace and Henderson engine removal typically meant first removing the inlet and exhaust manifold, the carburetor, the generator and the magneto!

(CLEVELAND SALES LITERATURE)

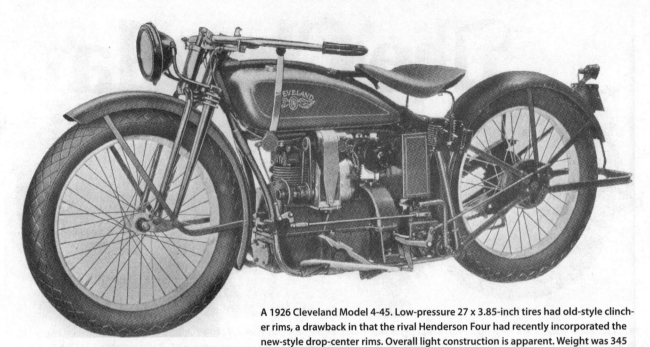

A 1926 Cleveland Model 4-45. Low-pressure 27 x 3.85-inch tires had old-style clincher rims, a drawback in that the rival Henderson Four had recently incorporated the new-style drop-center rims. Overall light construction is apparent. Weight was 345 lbs. Price was $350. (THE ANTIQUE MOTORCYCLE)

A 1927 Cleveland 4-61. The bore was enlarged from to 2 1/2 inches, and the stroke was lengthened to 3 1/16 inches. Displacement was 60.13 cubic inches (985cc). An industry first, was the fitting of a front wheel brake. Top speed of the 4-61 was about 90 mph.

(CLEVELAND SALES LITERATURE)

A 1929 Cleveland Tornado. Near-100 mph performance was achieved with the souped-up Tornado. The restyled frame and tank allowed the saddle to be lowered 2 1/2 inches in mid-season. (BRUCE LINSDAY)

before the rest of the industry brought out front wheel brakes as standard equipment.

The ultimate Cleveland was the Tornado Four introduced for the 1929 season. A new frame lowered the saddle 2½ inches, and accommodated a more shapely fuel tank. Dow metal (magnesium) pistons were 1 ounce lighter than previous aluminum pistons. A higher compression ratio, larger valves, and larger inlet ports increased the power and provided near-100 mph top speed. During the season, an even more potent "Century" version was offered, with higher compression ratio, larger inlet ports, and exhaust expansion chamber near the transmission, as well as a heavier front fork. Following an actual road test that verified 100 mph, a small brass certification plate was riveted to a valve cover.

Following the stock market crash of October, 1929, Cleveland ceased production. During its 15 seasons, the firm built about 40,000 motorcycles, according to the late

Ted Hodgdon, co-founder of the Antique Motorcycle Club of America.

COLEMAN

Coleman motorcycles were built by H. P. Coleman of Boston, around 1905. The single-cylinder was claimed to be exceptionally well cooled because of its forward sloping. The engine location was also described as "low in the frame." Any part of the machine could be bought separately.

The integral manifold and head, and the one-piece cylinder block were features of Cleveland fours from mid-1926 through the end of production in 1929.

A Circa 1903 Coleman: With a bore and stroke of 2 11/16 x 3 ¼ inches, the single-cylinder engine displaced 25.3 cubic inches (415cc). Claimed maximum output was 2 hp. Said the press release: "… Extra large valves are used. A single lever relieves the compression, advances the spark, and throttles the mixture. Sufficient fuel and oil for 80 miles running are carried. The total weight is 118 pounds, and the price is $135. Any part may be bought separately."

(JIM DENNIE)

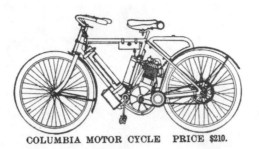

COLUMBIA MOTOR CYCLE   PRICE $210.

A 1905 Columbia. Specifications: 22-inch frame; 2-inch detachable tires; 54-inch wheelbase; single-cylinder 2 3/4 x 3 1/4 bore and stroke; lubrication by splash and sight feed; chain drive with spring sprocket; battery mileage 1000; fuel mileage 80; single lever control; weight 130 lbs.; maximum speed of road machine with regular gear, 35 mph; price $210. (JIM DENNIE)

COLUMBIA

The Columbia was built by the American Cycle Manufacturing Company in 1902. This firm was under the control of Colonel Albert Pope, president of the National Association of Manufacturers. Operating divisions were in Chicago, Illinois, and Westerfield, Connecticut. Colonel Pope eventually controlled a family of bicycles that included American, Cleveland, Columbia, Crescent, Imperial, Monarch, Rambler, and Tribune. When motorcycle production began, identical machines were sold under these various established brand names. As

Oddly, the 1905 Columbia production road model had no cover over the primary drive chain. The long forward slanting tube contained the battery (or batteries). The rearward sloping tube contained the ignition coil. The horizontal tube covered the carburetor. (GRANT FISH, RONALD IANNUCCI)

first offered in 1902, the single-cylinder 19.3-cubic inch (316cc) F-head (inlet-over-exhaust) Columbia was state of the art. But the design wasn't updated and by 1905 was obsolete.

The connection between Colonel Pope and the Columbia is evident from the mixed use of the terms in the following press release accompanying an illustration of the Columbia. From the April 1, 1905, *Cycle and Automobile Trade Journal:* "Their Cleveland and Tribune motorcycles have the same specifications and appearance as the Columbia and list at $210. Special features: automatic carburetor; single lever control; patent spring sprocket; Pope motor coaster brake; long wheel base."

COMET

Historian Stephen Wright (*The American Motorcycle*, 1869-1914), reports that a single-cylinder Comet was built in Milwaukee in 1909. This machine may have been related to a V-twin pictured in a 1911 advertisement.

CRAWFORD

The Crawford was a DeLuxe clone, powered by a Spacke engine built in Indianapolis, Indiana. Production and assembly of the frame, forks, etc., were carried out by the Excelsior Cycle Company of 166-168 N. Sangamon Street, Chicago, Illinois. The obscure company had no connection with the famous Excelsior firm of Chicago, which built the Excelsior motorcycle!

CRESCENT

The Crescent was one of the Pope family of motorcycles, a series of marques variously named for pedal bikes already distributed under the various labels. These included Columbia, Cresent, Imperial, Monarch, and Rambler motorcycles. The parent firm was The American Cycle Company, which had divisions in Chicago, Illinois, and Westfield, Connecticut.

A 1911 Comet. A real motorcycle or a concept drawing? Such line drawings surfaced occasionally from the very beginning of the American industry. Of interest, is that the machine is a "dead ringer" for the Flying Merkel racer campaigned by Maldwyn Jones in 1913. That Merkel layout was, in fact, a 1911-or earlier design. (BOB KAROLEVITZ)

A circa 1913 Crawford. The marque was an assembly operation combining standard frame and fork components used on the DeLuxe and other makes, with the proprietary Spacke engine. (BOB KAROLEVITZ)

A circa 1905 Crescent, which was not only an Indian clone (excepting the slightly different tank), but, as the advertising makes clear, was also identical to other marques produced by the same Pope management. (JIM DENNIE)

CROCKER

The Crocker marque is most widely known in the form of thundering V-twins of 1000cc-or-larger capacity, but the tiny firm earlier flexed its muscles with various forms of racing machines.

The man behind the machines was Albert Crocker, who first came into prominence around 1910 as a successful enduro rider on Thor motorcycles. In 1913, Crocker became the Denver Branch manager for Indian, operating both the shop and the area supply/service depot. In 1914, he moved to Kansas City as branch manager. There, he hired Roland "Rollie" Free in 1923. Free later set American speed records on Indians and Vincents. In 1928, Crocker sold the Kansas City business and reopened in Los Angeles as the city's new Indian dealer.

In the 1931 racing season, Crocker's ma-

chine shop built frames for speedway racing motorcycles. Incidentally, in the U.S. during that period, this sport was termed "short track racing." These early Crocker frames were built to house the popular Indian Scout side-valve (flathead) V-twin engine. Under American rules, these 45-cubic inch (750cc) flatheads were permitted to race in the same class as 30.5-cubic inch (500cc) overhead-valve machines.

In November, 1933, Crocker brought out his own single-cylinder overhead-valve racing engine, coupled with the proven Crocker frame and fork ideas. These overhead-valve speedway bikes were immediately successful in the hands of star riders such as Jack Milne, Wilbur Lamoreaux and Cordy Milne, who in 1937 finished 1-2-3 in the World Championships (on British J.A.P. bikes). In 1934, Crocker showcased two

This is a 1932 Crocker speedway racer powered by Crocker's overhead-valve conversion of the Indian 101 Scout engine. Thus configured, the displacement was reduced to 30.5 cubic inches (500cc). The previous year, Crocker sold the frames for use with the 45-cubic inch (750cc) side-valve (Flathead) engine. The Indian factory also built a few overhead-valve speedway racing twins that were very similar in appearance.

(STEPHEN WRIGHT)

A 1934 Crocker speedway racer. The overall engine layout was inspired by the successful Rudge (British) marque, but the Crocker featured a conventional two-valve head whereas the Rudge used four valves. Despite the appearance, the engine wasn't an overhead-cam unit, with the "tower" merely housing two push-rods. The neat cast-aluminum tank gives a hint of the craftsmanship later exhibited in the famous V-twin roadsters.

new overhead-cam racing singles, but these didn't benefit from continuous testing and refinement. The Crockers were increasingly outgunned by the J.A.P. bikes and, perhaps more importantly, Al Crocker was losing interest in this effort.

The most famous Crockers debuted in the 1936 season. These were the fabled V-twin roadsters. Under the headline "A New Crocker Comes To Town," the February 1936 issue of *Motorcyclist* said: "...Now the Crockers come to town again. This time it is in the form of the much discussed twin 61 o.h.v. Rumors and queries have been afloat for the past year. Actually, the designer did not know himself what the finished product was to be like in all its detail until recently. However, the first machine is now completed ... The job weighs 475 lbs. loaded with gas and oil. Wheelbase is 58½ inches. It packs a compression ratio of 7½ to 1 and develops 50 h.p. at 5800 r.p.m. ...An unusual feature of the Crocker is that, notwithstanding the sturdy design at places, the total weight is so low. For instance, an unusually strong gear box is used, that gear box being an integral part of the frame. Bearings in the transmission are carried by heavy steel plates fitted on the sides of the case. The transmission is three-speed constant mesh dog engagement and the gears are much wider than customary design. Because of the constant mesh design the teeth are a true 10 pitch and mesh much deeper than usual ... Cam design is such that both pushrods are enclosed in one tube.

"Entire accessibility is a special consideration on the Crocker 61, any part of the machine being removable without the necessity of removing anything else. Crocker is using

A Crocker single in action. Bo Lisman is the rider.

(SCHOLFIELD COLLECTION)

The Crocker (below) put out about 40 hp, compared to the 42 to 43 of the J.A.P. rivals. Albert Crocker had two overhead-cam racers built in 1934. These were not fully developed, thus not highly successful, when Crocker turned his attention to a new outlet, road-going V-twins.

To many, the rare 1936-1940 Crockers are the ultimate American collectors' bikes. Only about 60 Crocker twins were built, but the company skipped motor numbers to give the impression that more than 300 had been manufactured. These were the fastest American stock motorcycles of the era, and possibly the fastest out-the-door bikes in the world.

(DOUG MITCHEL)

The performance-enhancing overhead valves were intended to impress the American world of Flathead motorcycles. Unfortunately for Crocker, Harley-Davidson brought out its big overhead-valve twins the same year. Tanks were cast aluminum.

(DOUG MITCHEL)

The Crocker V-twins combined the best features of past and present marques. The cast-aluminum primary drive cover and the triplex primary chain were Indian inspired. Likewise, the Indian-style generator drive was a simple sprocket meshing with the middle row of the triplex primary chain. The cut-down fenders reflected the "California" look achieved on other machines with hacksaw and file. Likewise, the chrome-plated high-rise handlebars were a tip of the hat to the trend among west coast riders. The double-pad foot-clutch could be rigged for either Indian-style or Harley-style operation ; Harley toe-down to go or Indian toe-up to go. The throttle was on the right and the gearshift on the left with a Harley-style shifter gate. (DOUG MITCHEL)

his own carburetor, a development of racing experience, Edison Splitdorf magneto, and a built-in Corbin-Brown speedometer. The tanks are cast aluminum, held in place by through-bolts. Either style clutch (author's note; this means either Indian style toe-down for clutch disengagement or Harley style heel-down for clutch disengagement) is available through changing the fulcrum arrangement by moving one bolt. Gear shift is on the left side and throttle is in the right grip …English fork design is used, the forks being interchangeable and simple enough for an amateur to straighten. A three-ring piston is employed …In designing the new mount Crocker has drawn from both his experience in racing and as a dealer. The sturdy design is the purpose of meeting the hardest

kind of punishment and the clean simplicity is for complete accessibility.

"Thus far, with a heavy rider in the saddle, testing has been entirely in the field of cow trailing. Riding up and down fire breaks in the mountain and over all that rough trails have had to offer has brought forth no failures. Later, a break-down test is planned for Muroc (author's note: Muroc Dry Lake is now called Rogers Dry Lake and is part of Edwards Air Force Base) or some suitable place where the speed possibilities are to be determined …At present only 12 motors are going through the line of production. These are spoken for. Crocker does not plan to go into large scale at any time, but rather to stay closer to the field of custom built motorcycles. Later announcement will give details of price and other sales arrangements."

The first five engines were built with exposed valve rockers. These first five motors had hemispherical combustion chambers with the inlet and exhaust valves oriented 90 degrees from each other. The sixth and subsequent motors had enclosed valve rockers and parallel valves.

The timing of the V-twin Crocker was unfortunate. Harley-Davidson began development of its 61 OHV "knucklehead" motor in 1933 and, like the Crocker, the Harley knucklehead came on the scene in early 1936, just a couple of months after the Crocker. Prior to the Crocker V-twin, the only overhead-valve V-twins were the special racing and hill climbing jobs of the two surviving factories, Indian and Harley-Davidson. The big drawing card of the Crocker was to have been its overhead-valve layout. Thus, the overhead-valve Harley-Davidson knucklehead robbed the Crocker of an important advantage. Al Crocker's decision to give up the hemi-head in favor of parallel valves also left the Harley knucklehead with more development potential, though it would be some years before this potential was maximized.

The Crocker constant-mesh transmission with shifting by dog engagement was likewise intended to break new ground. Both Indian and Harley-Davidson had used sliding gear transmissions up to that time. Again, the advantage was lost because the Harley-Davidson knucklehead brought this same important improvement from a major factory. Moreover, Harley-Davidson upped the ante by adding a fourth ratio.

The remaining Crocker features, such as cast-aluminum tanks, rugged transmission gears in an integral housing, and oil bath primary drive, became the big selling points, instead of the basic engine and gearbox designs. To give the Crocker V-twin the intended performance edge over the knucklehead, Al Crocker quickly approved larger motors. Crocker cylinders were un-

The unique Crocker frame incorporated the transmission case.
(CROCKER SALES LITERATURE)

Though the first five engines were built with exposed rockers and hemispherical combustion chambers, all subsequent engines featured enclosed parallel valves.
(CROCKER SALES LITERATURE)

The primary drive system and the generator drive were inspired by the Indian arrangement in use since 1920.
(CROCKER SALES LITERATURE)

usually thick, so considerable over-boring was possible.

The late Gene Rhyne, former Excelsior hill climbing national champion, did most of the final assembly of Crockers. Rhyne recalled, "I bet I assembled every new bike that ever came out of Crocker. I'll say we probably made about 60 bikes—that's all. Yeah, some of these guys will tell you, well, I got so-and-so number—and they'll get in an argument with me, the guys that I've talked to that's got them ....Well, I don't care what you've got, I know. I assembled every bike but the last three. On the last three we were out of tanks and stuff, and the war was coming along. We couldn't get the foundries to do it, 'cause they were making other stuff. But the last three bikes had the engines in them and some of the transmission parts and stuff. Every one of those before that, I assembled—every one of them.

"The first batch we made was about 25 of them. Then we made 20 in the next batch ...There was only seven of us guys working in the place. And we made—God!—made everything there was for the Crocker except the rims, tires, spark plugs, and accessories. Those you'd buy out. Of course, we had the pistons cast. But we did all the machine work ...I figured it out one time. It cost us

$500 to build a machine you could buy for 550 bucks out the door.

"...We made 1000 cc's. So then, what happened, after the first 25 of the big Crockers, why, everybody wanted a special size, in a road machine, you know. So then we went up to a 68, and made some of them for certain ones. We made them up to 68 or 70 or 72 inches. Then somebody wanted so-and-so, so we did it. They were handmade then, you know. You could make them anything you wanted. And then somebody wanted a 4-inch stroke and 3 7/16-inch bore, and then somebody wants a 4 1/2-inch stroke.. and so on (author's note; a 4 1/2-inch stroke and 3 7/16-inch bore would make an 83.5ci, 1369cc, motor).

"...Toward the end we built some different colors. In fact, I think guys took them and had them painted themselves, and we put it together for them."

Al Crocker also built an attractive motorscooter that was sold in 1941. Probably less than 100 were built.

CROSLEY

The Crosley company, builders of small automobiles, developed some interesting prototype motorcycles for the U. S. Army in the 1940s. Their innovations included single-fork rear and front ends, and fuel tank integral with the rear fender. These were apparently unsolicited designs, because detailed Harley-Davidson wartime records make no mention of competitive trials involving Crosley motorcycles. There were two less-creative three-wheeler prototypes, one using a Harley-Davidson springer fork, and the other an Indian leaf spring fork.

CROUCH

Crouch motorcycles were built in Stoneham, Massachusetts, from 1903 through 1909. These were typical single-cylinder F-head machines of the era.

The front fork of this circa 1940 Crosley (below) is a copy of the BMW fork. Clear thinking is evident in the single-fork rear-end construction, which would have simplified tire changes. (COURTESY OF FRED W. CRISMON)

A later Crosley was even more advanced, with the front fork now a single-sided telescopic. (COURTESY OF FRED W. CRISMON)

A 1905 Crouch. A loop frame was fitted. (DOUG MITCHEL)

Crouch machines changed but little over the years. This 1907 example features the 1906-style frame with short twin lower frame tubes on either side of the crankcase.

(GEORGE YAROCKI)

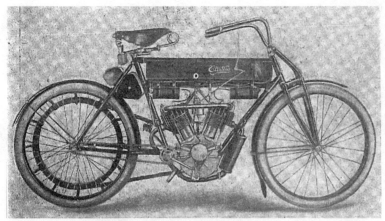

A 1907 Curtiss. This bike produced 5 hp and cost $275. Curtiss was one of the first to offer twin-cylinder models. Indian and Harley-Davidson first cataloged a twin in 1908 and 1911. (GEORGE YAROCKI)

A 1907 Curtiss racing twin. On February 9, 1907, at Ormond Beach, Florida, Glenn Curtiss rode this machine a mile at the rate of 77.6 mph while losing a race to a Peugot twin. The Peugot turned 80.5 mph for an unofficial world's record.
(BRUCE LINSDAY)

A 1909 Curtiss single-cylinder 3-hp with regular frame, battery ignition, and 28-inch wheel. It was the company's "general purpose motorcycle." (BRUCE LINSDAY)

CURTISS

Glenn Curtiss, a famed aviation pioneer, got his engineering start in the manufacture of Curtiss motorcycles. He manufactured Curtiss bikes from 1903 through 1912 at his factory in Hammondsport, New York. Curtiss offered the only serious racing competition to Indian during the years 1903 through 1907. At the New York Motorcycle Club road race of Labor Day, 1902, a Curtiss made the fastest time of "all regular stock or road machines." In May, 1903, Glenn Curtiss won the first American hill climb on one of his machines. That event was also sponsored by the New York Motorcycle Club.

In January 1904, Glenn Curtiss rode over Ormond Beach, Florida, to a 10-mile record, averaging 67.3 mph. The bike was a 1904, 42.4-cubic inch (695cc), V-twin. The 1904 Curtiss may have been the world's first motorcycle with twist-grip control. (Indian laid claim to this historic first in subsequent advertising, but the first twist-grip Indians were also 1904 models.) The single-speed belt-drive racer had a gear ratio of 4 to 1. The crankshaft was supported on ball bearings. Curtiss also offered a 21.2-cubic inch (347cc) single in 1904. These models were continued in the 1905 lineup.

The year 1907 saw Glenn Curtiss ride to a startling 136 mph at Ormond Beach aboard his amazing V-8 motorcycle. A broken shaft-drive universal joint and buckled frame brought these unofficial runs to a halt. This was the only time in history when a motorcycle was timed faster than any other vehicle in the world. Not until 1930 would the official world's motorcycle speed record exceed Curtiss's 1907 mark.

V-twin design stabilized by 1909 into a two-cam F-head layout. One camshaft was placed ahead of the front cylinder; the other camshaft was behind the rear cylinder. By 1912, another Hammondsport product, the Marvel, boasted of its Curtiss engine and Curtiss carburetor. The exact relationship between the two marques is vague, but it is

A 1907 Curtiss V-8 special. At the same Florida venue, Glenn Curtiss rode this monster shaft-drive through a 1-mile trap in 26.4 seconds, a rate of 136.3 mph! This was faster than any vehicle of any kind had been timed up to that point, and defined the only brief period when a motorcycle was the world's fastest vehicle. The engine had been built to order for an airplane, but Curtiss couldn't resist trying it in a motorcycle.

(MOTORCYCLE ILLUSTRATED)

The 1909 Curtiss 3-hp single. The engine displaced approximately 30.5 cubic inches (500cc). (BRUCE LINSDAY)

The 1909 Curtiss 3 1/2-hp single. According to the company, it had "Wehman-type frame, 26-inch wheels, magneto ignition. Lowest saddle position possible on a motorcycle." (BRUCE LINSDAY)

The 1909 spring fork. According to the company, the fork "Embodies the latest improvements.... applicable to all Curtiss motorcycles... does not interfere with the regular trussed fork construction." (BRUCE LINSDAY)

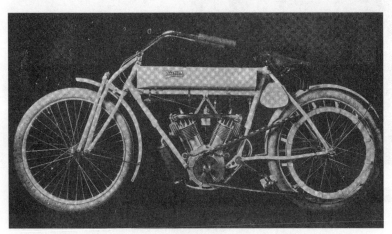

The 1909 Curtiss double-cylinder. Specifications: 6 hp, regular frame, battery ignition, 28-inch wheels, showing spring forks. "This model won perfect scores in both classes in the 1908 National Endurance Contest," according to the company. The motorcycle was wholesaled to the Geer company and re-labeled the "Geer Green Egg." (BRUCE LINSDAY)

A 1909 Curtiss "double-cylinder" engine. The engine was noted for "....numerous World's Records ....Roller bearings throughout ....Intake valves are made from a solid bar of high grade steel, and not from ordinary forgings." (BRUCE LINSDAY)

The 1909 Curtiss 10-hp triple. Specifications: 26-inch wheels, battery ignition, showing muffler and exhaust pipes removed. According to the company, "This is the most powerful regularly built motorcycle in the world." (BRUCE LINSDAY)

known that they were built in two separate factories. It appears that Glenn Curtiss was trying to divest himself of the motorcycle business in favor of aviation. Perhaps the Marvel marque was considered a tool in that management effort—a means of keeping a tie-in with the motorcycle world while reserving the Curtiss name for airplanes.

CUSHMAN

A thin gray line separates "motorcycles" from "motorscooters." Wheel size is part of the vague distinction. A "step-through" design is clearly another aspect of mainstream scooters. The thin line grew thinner in the 1940s with the introduction of small-wheeled straddle-style machines with the tank between the rider's legs. These half-breeds implied the slower and safer speeds of scooters, easing the task of selling to most of the real buyers—the parents of teenage boys. Concern was also lightened by the simplicity of operation. An automatic clutch enabled the rider to get off the line with nothing but a twist of the wrist.

The Cushman Eagle was the most successful of the scooter-cycles. Eagles went on sale in December of 1949. Hallmarks were the 17.9-cubic inch (293cc) side-valve engine, automatic clutch with foot-pedal over-ride for shifting, and both ignition and lighting provided by magneto. A rubber-belt primary drive, along with the automatic centrifugal clutch, made it difficult, if not impossible, for rowdy teens to break anything.

Only minor changes, like folding foot boards (1952), were made to these "barrel spring" Eagles from 1949 through 1954. Most Eagles were two-speeders, but a few single-speeders were offered. In 1955, Cushman gave the Eagle a telescopic fork, and this variant continued as the top of the Cushman motorscooter lineup through

A 1954-1958 Cushman Eagle. A telescopic fork defined the Eagle in this era.

(CUSHMAN SALES LITERATURE)

A 1949-1954 Cushman Eagle. About the only visible change during the era of the "barrel spring" models was the incorporation of folding foot boards in 1952. Maximum output of the "Husky" engine was 5 hp, but there was torque from idle on up, enough to move the 271-lb. bike quickly up to 30 mph. The 1952 price (California, plus tax and license), was $344.70.

(CUSHMAN SALES LITERATURE)

1958. To this point, all Eagles had been powered by a 5-hp, side-valve, single-cylinder fan-cooled engine. Beginning in 1959, buyers could opt for either the traditional 5-hp Eagle, or the new 7.95-hp Super Eagle with rather blocky body work over the rear portion of the machine. In 1960, the Silver Eagle was added, featuring an aluminum overhead-valve engine and extensive rear body work. The 1960 Super Eagle also got

the new engine, and was distinguished by traditional Eagle styling aft of the saddle.

In the early 1960s, Cushman faced the competition of a hoard of Japanese lightweight motorcycles. Cushman couldn't match the sophistication, performance, reliability and low selling prices of the Far East bikes. The last Eagles were built in 1965. A few leftovers were sold in 1966. The firm went on to be highly successful with commercial vehicles and golf carts.

CYCLEMOTOR

The Cyclemotor Corporation of Rochester, New York, built and sold motorbike attachments and complete motorbikes, from 1919 through 1924. Early units were sold under the name "Cyclemotor." During 1919, the name was changed to "Evans Power-Cycle," though the company name didn't change.

CYCLONE MOTORCYCLE SCOOTER

The name says it all. Like the Cushman Eagle, the Mustang, and the Powell P-81, the Cyclone Motorcycle Scooter was designed to soften the motorcycle image, rather than to replace it. Advertised in the December, 1947, *Motorcyclist*—and not thereafter—the marque surely had a brief existence. The machine was offered by the Clark Engineering Company of Pasadena, California.

According to *Motorcyclist*, the machine was "engineered around the parts of a popular low priced automobile: connecting rod, piston, valves, and timing gears." It weighed 250 lbs. and cost $272 plus tax. The history has been lost, but this machine is so nearly identical to the 1941 Powell Aviate Model A-V8 that there must have been a connection.

CYCLONE

Cyclone motorcycles were built from 1913 through 1917 by the Joerns Motor Manufacturing Company (previously, the Joerns-Thiem Motor Company) of Saint Paul, Minnesota. From 1903 through 1911, the

The 1960 Cushman Silver Eagle. On paper, the new aluminum overhead-valve engine, built by parent company Outboard Marine, was the great leap forward. In reality, these motors proved unreliable and were temporarily replaced by the in-house Husky engine while the bugs were worked out.

(CUSHMAN SALES LITERATURE)

A 1948 Cyclone Motorcycle Scooter. Features included: 60 mph top speed; 80 mpg fuel consumption; automatic clutch; automotive battery, ignition, and generator; automotive coil and cut-out; legal lights and easy starting. (MOTORCYCLIST)

A 1919 Cyclemotor kit installed in an ordinary pedal bike. According to historian Erwin Tragatsch, these were 119cc two-strokes. (BOB KAROLEVITZ)

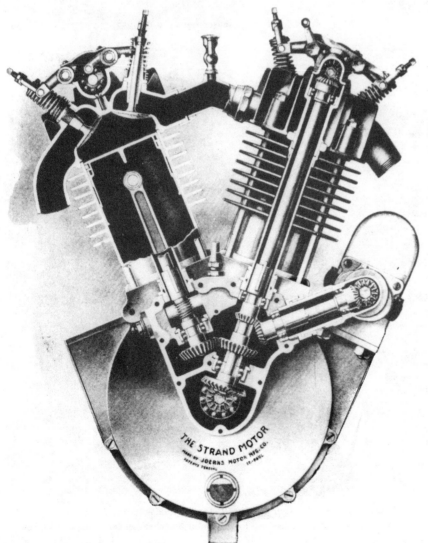

A 1914 Cyclone standard engine. Both road and racing engines featured shaft driven overhead cams and a shaft-driven magneto. Both had the unique "stirrup" rocker arms. Each was mated with an inverted "stirrup" that floated atop a valve stem. This setup minimized valve wobble and prolonged valve guide life. All engines featured ball bearings fitted to both cam drive shafts, both cams, and the generator drive shaft.

(CYCLONE SALES LITERATURE)

A 1914 Cyclone cylinder head. The included valve angle was 70 degrees. An arrow points to the rim or spigot, which was recessed into the cylinder barrel. (CYCLE)

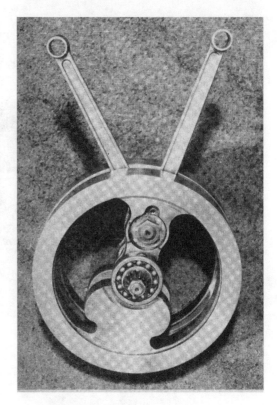

Circa 1914 Cyclone flywheels and connecting rods. Such "open" flywheels were standard for the era. (CYCLE)

A circa 1913 Cyclone standard engine, in racing frame. The hemispherical combustion chamber had an included angle of 70 degrees between the valves. The spark plug was equidistant from both valves, and as near to the combustion chamber center as permitted by the camshaft housing. The compression ratio was only 5.5 to 1.

A 1914 Cyclone road model. Road-going Cyclones were fitted with a trailing link front fork and a swinging-arm rear suspension, both operating via leaf spring.

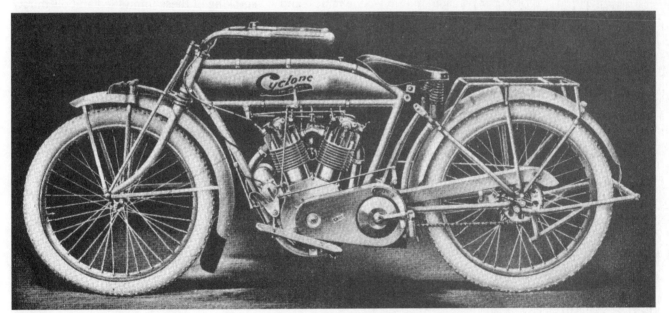

A 1914 Cyclone standard model, as depicted in the sales catalog. Specifications: overhead-cams driven by shaft and bevel gears; Bore and stroke, 3 5/16 x 3 17/32 inches; displacement 60.86 cubic inches (997cc); ignition, Bosch magneto; driven by shaft and bevel gears; carburetor Schebler; wheels 28 inches; tires 28 x 3 inches; Leaf-spring trailing link front fork; swinging-arm rear suspension; wheelbase 59 inches; price $250.

(CYCLONE SALES LITERATURE)

The 1914 Cyclone swinging-arm rear suspension.
(CYCLONE SALES LITERATURE)

company made motorcycle engines and complete motorcycles that were wholesaled to jobbers and large dealers, who then added their own brand name. Some Thiem motorcycles were sold to the American Motorcycle Corporation of Chicago. The Thiem company also built a two-speed rear hub that could be used on any motorcycle.

After marketing its own Thiem motorcycles in 1912 (and possibly 1913), in 1913 Joerns brought out its historic overhead-cam Cyclone 61-cubic inch (1000cc) V-twins. These soon proved to be the fastest motorcycles in the world.

The cam shapes were primitive by modern standards, with valve timing as follows: inlet valves opened 10 degrees before top dead center and closed 10 degrees after bottom dead center; exhaust valves opened 10 degrees before bottom dead center and closed 10 degrees after top dead center. Maximum engine speed was 5000 rpm. Cylinder breathing of the racing engines was enhanced by the use of a series of cylinder "ports." These were ¼-inch wide slots that vented crankcase pressure. When the pistons came within $5/16$ inch of bottom

dead center, these ports began to open, two-stroke style.

Not understood at the time was the additional benefit of more rapidly filling the combustion chamber with the next incoming charge—a sort of primitive supercharging. As well as helping in the go-fast department, the open ports made lots of racket and added spectacle, especially in night races when the flaming exhaust swirled around the engine. An unfortunate drawback was that riders' legs were invariably covered with oil from about the knee down. Another quirk was that the abundance of air gulped in by the open ports, called for a very rich carburetor mixture, and prevented effective throttling down. This was overcome by running the engines wide open, with the rider using an ignition cutout or "kill" button to regulate power. This, of course, added to the already considerable smoking of these unmuffled and oil-thirsty engines. Ported engine oil consumption was atrocious, running as high as 2.5 gallons in a 50-mile race!

Cyclone racing produced records and excitement, but the firm's brief life and limited resources resulted in insufficient development of this promising design. At Omaha, Nebraska, in 1914, rider J. A. McNeil sped over 111 mph, compared to the official world record of 93.48 mph. A number of half-mile and 1-mile horse track appearance demonstrated blazing speed but insufficient reliability. Failed items included exhaust valves, pistons, carburetor and control linkages. The 1915 Dodge City 300, the country's most prestigious race, marked a critical moment in Cyclone history. Dave Kinnie turned the fastest qualifying lap at 88.5 mph, besting the large factory teams of Indian, Harley-Davidson, and Excelsior. In the race, Cyclone rider Don Johns led laps two through 16 on the two-mile course. Johns ran one 1-mile lap at a pace of 97 mph, 10 mph faster than most rival bikes. According to *Motorcycle Illustrated*, "John's work was nothing short of spectacular and

The cylinder heads were cast iron. The cylinders were cast steel. On the drive side, the crankshaft was supported by four rows of caged 1/4-inch rollers. The tapered crankpin was shoulderless and carried three rows of caged rollers. Additional racing specifications: Rigid rear frame; wheels 28 inches; tires 28 x 3 inches, 28 x 2 1/4 inches or 28 x 2 1/2 inches; saddle, Troxel or racing model; improved standard roller chain; wheelbase, 53 inches.

it was generally understood that he was gaiting himself for a new 100-mile record. Johns resumed his lead on lap 24, but the Cyclone began to slow, and he dropped out after 70-plus laps.

Following Harley-Davidson's win of the 300, Cyclone made only two more splashes. Don Johns won the July 24, One-Mile National Championship at Sacramento, California. In the feature event, Johns' bike suffered magneto failure. In November, 1915, Cyclone rider Kinnie placed second Excelsior star Bob Perry in the 100-mile flat track race at Phoenix, Arizona.

During 1916, all Cyclone assets, including some partly assembled motorcycles, were purchased by a Chicago group. The Chicago group completed assembly of only a few motorcycles, but never resumed full production, before selling out to a group of investors led by misters Kennedy and Hineman. These men also purchased the remnants of the Thiem Motorcycle Company, Cyclone's predecessor. As the United States was entering World War I, the owners decided to sit out the conflict before resurrecting the Cyclone. In 1920, the Chicago group sold out to a firm in Cheboygan, Michigan, where a new factory was set up. Next, another firm took over and moved the Cyclone assets to Benton Harbor, Michigan. The Benton Harbor group hired Cyclone designer Andrew Strand. Strand brought with him a prototype three-speed Cyclone featuring Excelsior transmission components. Full-page magazine advertisements in 1921, heralded the return of the forthcoming Cyclone, but nothing came of it.

In 1923, the Reading-Standard company raced a re-badged Cyclone. Reading-Standard, it developed, had purchased all Cyclone assets. With that, the Cyclone name faded from the scene.

Rider J. A. McNeil ran his Cyclone 1 mile in 35.4 seconds, a rate of 101 mph in Omaha, Nebraska in 1914. He later turned the mile in 32.4 seconds, 111 mph. American records weren't recognized because the international rules required two one-way runs in opposite directions to account for wind. This was a technicality, of course, since one lap of a board track likewise neutralized the wind as a factor. The official world record at the time was 93.48 mph on an Indian.

(DAVE KINNIE COLLECTION)

On the Cyclone racing engines, reinforcing ribs were used on cylinders and crankcase. A series of open "ports" were spread around the circumference, near the lowest cooling fin. These vented crankcase pressure and achieved a super-charging effect. This accounts for the oil on the crankcase.

(DAVE KINNIE COLLECTION)

DAYTON

The Davis Sewing Machine Company of Dayton, Ohio, marketed the Dayton motorcycle from 1911 through 1917. Models were offered with the Spacke-built DeLuxe V-twin F-head engine. This Dayton series consisted of clones, there being no differences apart from name and colors from the DeLuxe motorcycle. Assembly of Dayton motorcycles was accomplished by the Excelsior Cycle Company of 166-168 North Sangamon Street, Chicago. This firm had no connection with the makers of the well-known Excelsior motorcycles.

From 1915 through 1917, alternative Dayton models were offered, with engines strongly resembling Harley-Davidsons of the era. Only single-speed models were sold during 1911, 1912 and 1913. In 1914, a two-speed model was added to the range. The 1913 Dayton fork was very similar to the Indian fork, but in 1914 a new fork design conspired to hide the spring action; the leaf spring was integral with the front fender. The company also built the Dayton Motor Bicycle attachment. It was similar in concept to the Smith (later, Briggs and Stratton) Motor Wheel, except that the Dayton device replaced the front wheel of the pedal bike, whereas the Smith and the Briggs and Stratton were attached just left of the rear wheel of the pedal bike.

The 1915 Dayton Model C7 two-speed with Spacke-built "DeLuxe" engine, sold for $290 stripped, as shown here. Other DeLuxe variants were a single-speed stripped at $265, a single-speed with electric lights and generator at $305 and a two-speed "electric" at $330. DeLuxe engines were cited as 9 hp. (THE ANTIQUE MOTORCYCLE)

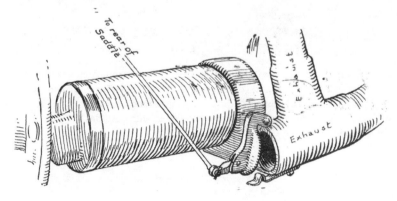

A Dayton muffler cutout. Such devices, fitted by almost all marques, were supposed to be used only for fast rural running, climbing steep hills or plowing through heavy sand or mud, in which cases a noticeable torque improvement resulted. Alas, motorcycling's bad reputation for noise had begun. Editorials in the motorcycling press periodically chastised riders who rode over city streets with the cutout open.

(PACIFIC MOTORCYCLIST)

This is a 1915 Dayton Model C-3, almost certainly a Harley-Davidson clone. One wonders if Harley was wholesaling some motorcycles to the Dayton company. The "Dayton" engine was claimed to produce 8 hp. This stripped single-speeder was listed at $240. (THE ANTIQUE MOTORCYCLE)

A 1915 Dayton Model C4. Listed at $305, this electric two-speeder was the flagship of the Dayton powered range. The strange front fork featured two different kinds of springing. At the base of the steering head, was anchored a leaf spring concealed in the front fender. The fork could rock up and forward against this spring. This was aimed at softening the wheels travel over holes. At the bottom of the fork was a short trailing link connected to the fender braces, which permitted an up and backward motion. This was intended to soften impact with obstacles like rocks. Exactly how the two motions combined much of the time is not apparent. (THE ANTIQUE MOTORCYCLE)

The 1915 Dayton oil tank was separate from the fuel tank. Rival makes such as Indian merely divided the single tank into fuel and oil compartments, an arrangement that could produce leaking of gasoline into the oil compartment. (THE ANTIQUE MOTORCYCLE)

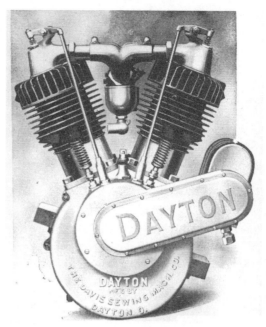

The 1914 Dayton engine strongly resembled the Harley-Davidson. The Dayton had the magneto in front of the engine, whereas the Harley had the magneto behind the engine.

(THE ANTIQUE MOTORCYCLE)

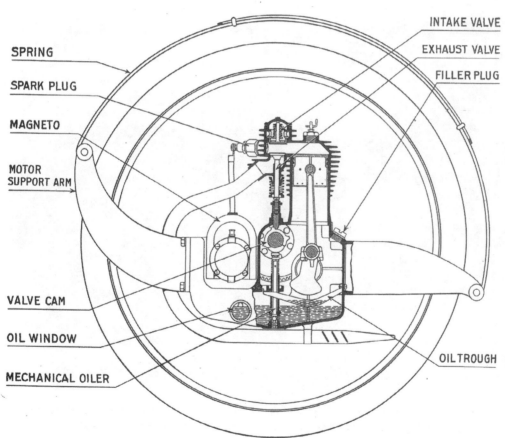

SPRING

SPARK PLUG

MAGNETO

MOTOR SUPPORT ARM

VALVE CAM

OIL WINDOW

MECHANICAL OILER

INTAKE VALVE

EXHAUST VALVE

FILLER PLUG

OIL TROUGH

Dayton Motor Bicycle Power Unit, Featuring Sturdiness and Simplicity

1918 Dayton Motor Bicycle details.

(GEORGE YAROCKI)

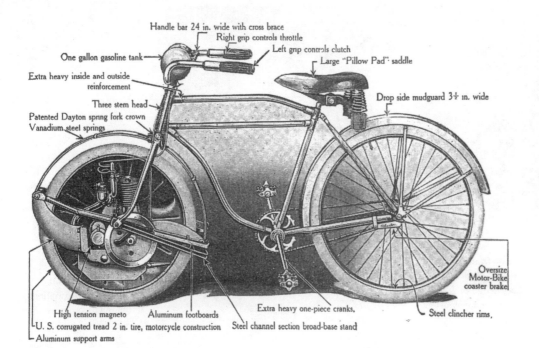

Handle bar 24 in. wide with cross brace
Right grip controls throttle
Left grip controls clutch
Large "Pillow Pad" saddle
One gallon gasoline tank
Extra heavy inside and outside reinforcement
Drop side mudguard 3¼ in. wide
Three stem head
Patented Dayton spring fork crown
Vanadium steel springs
Oversize Motor-Bike coaster brake
High tension magneto
Aluminum footboards
Extra heavy one-piece cranks.
U. S. corrugated tread 2 in. tire, motorcycle construction
Steel channel section broad-base stand
Steel clincher rims.
Aluminum support arms

A 1918 Dayton Motor Bicycle. The Dayton Motor Bicycle unit was attached to the front fork by a 180-degree leaf spring that doubled as a fender. The Dayton unit was inspired by the Smith Motor Wheel. A slotted disc wheel acted as a cooling fan. Four models were offered: M-18, men's type, compensator equipped, $110; F-18, men's type, clutch equipped, $120; L-18, ladies' type, compensator equipped, $110; and G-18, ladies' type, clutch equipped, $120.

(GEORGE YAROCKI)

This 1939 Delco prototype was a BMW clone. General Motors saw the opportunity for a vast order for three-wheelers, as this was before Jeep development. In movie theaters, newsreels of German army action invariably depicted motorcycles accompanying infantry and tank units. (COURTESY FRED W. CRISMON)

DELCO

At least one prototype motorcycle was built by General Motors. Identified as a "Delco," the shaft-drive tricycle competed with Indian and Harley-Davidson three-wheelers in Infantry Board tests conducted at Fort Benning, Georgia, in 1939. The machine was basically a clone of the BMW horizontally opposed side-valve (twin) used by the German army. As this test program was in advance of the development of the famed Jeep four-wheeler, General Motors rightly saw the potential for a vast order for the winning design.

DELONG

DeLong motorcycles were manufactured by the Industrial Machine Company of Phoenix, New York, around 1902. DeLongs followed the Indian layout, but differed in that the fuel and oil supplies were carried within the frame's approximately 2-inch diameter tubing. The electrical components were likewise concealed. The April, 1902, *Dealer and Repairman* termed the DeLong one of America's leading motor bicycles.

A 1902 DeLong. Two-inch frame tubes concealed much of the internals. Fuel was carried in the top frame tube, oil in the seat mast above the cylinder and the batteries and ignition coil inside the front down tube. Weight was 60 lbs. (JIM DENNIE)

The Delco (above) specifications included a Bantam automobile rear axle. Upon seeing this prototype at the Army trials, Harley-Davidson co-founder William S. Harley complained that the Delco was nothing more than a BMW, and so opined that the maker shouldn't be awarded a large development contract for a proven design.

(FRED W. CRISMON)

The 1913 DeLuxe. Clones of the DeLuxe were offered in several makes, including Crawford, Dayton and Sears. Spacke engines were used. (BRUCE LINSDAY)

The 1913 Detroit Bi-Car. (BOB KAROLEVITZ)

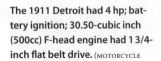

DELUXE

DeLuxe motorcycles were manufactured by the Excelsior Cycle Company of 166-168 N. Sangamon Street, Chicago, from 1912 through 1915. This firm had no connection with the makers of the Excelsior motorcycle, also located in Chicago. To add to the confusion, Excelsior Bicycle also termed its pedal bikes "Excelsior." DeLuxe used the Spacke proprietary engine. There were a number of DeLuxe clones, including the Crawford, Dayton and Sears.

The 1911 Detroit had 4 hp; battery ignition; 30.50-cubic inch (500cc) F-head engine had 1 3/4-inch flat belt drive. (MOTORCYCLE ILLUSTRATED)

DETROIT BI-CAR

A strange-looking hub-steering machine called the "Detroit Bi-Car" was offered for the 1913 season. Another unusual feature for the era was rear suspension. Aside from a republished picture, no information is known.

DETROIT

In 1911, these were distinctive-looking big singles featuring very large-diameter frame tubing that housed the fuel and oil.

DORSEY

F. F. Dorsey of Winchester, Massachusetts, built the parallel-twin Dorsey motorbike unit around 1902. It could be attached to any ordinary bicycle.

DRIVER

The Driver was manufactured around 1902 by Walter Driver and Son, of Philadelphia, Pennsylvania. The 1 ⅝-hp engine was said to be capable of climbing any ordinary grade without the use of the familiar "L.P.A.,"— light pedal assistance.

DYNO-MITE BIKE MOTOR

The Dyno-Mite motorbike attachment was sold by the Travis Products Company of Chicago. The period ad didn't state that Travis was the manufacturer. Later, the unit was advertised as manufactured by the Starbrand Corporation of Indianapolis, Indiana, and sold as the Travis Bike Motor. Possibly, Starbrand was the manufacturer throughout. The sequence of Dyno-Mite, then Travis, is clear because the respective prices were $69.95 and $79.95. These units appeared similar to the French-designed Velo Solex, yet were slightly different in shape and didn't have the long engage/disengage hand-lever on the French unit. Refer to the Travis section for photo.

The 1902 Dorsey parallel twin. The motor could be operated one cylinder at a time, with each cylinder skipping alternate power strokes, which was said to improve cooling. The crankcase pivoted on its mounting below the saddle. The arrangement of struts permitted the engine friction drive flywheel to engage or disengage the rear tire, the whole arrangement performing as a clutch. (JIM DENNIE)

A Circa 1902 Driver. Speed was regulated by a lever near the handlebar, at a rate of 5 to 20 mph. Price was $200. (JIM DENNIE)

A 1913 Eagle twin powered by the proprietary Spacke engine, which the builders branded "DeLuxe." (BRUCE LINSDAY)

EAGLE

The history of the Eagle motorcycle is about as complicated as it gets. The firm was originally called the Eagle Motor Works, and was located in Minneapolis, Minnesota, reports historian Stephen Wright (The American Motorcycle 1869-1914). Wright also provides the rest of the management details. In 1909 and 1910, Eagle sold its own design for a single-cylinder motorcycle. Next, it relocated to Chicago and began selling Marsh-Metz machines manufactured in Brockton, Massachusetts. These "M.M." motorcycles, as they had lately been termed, were "badge engineered" in Chicago to become "Eagle" motorcycles. In 1912, as well as the Marsh-Metz clones, Eagle offered V-twins powered by proprietary Spacke engines built in Indianapolis, Indiana. This was trickier, because Eagle had to buy the frames, forks, etc., from the Standard Welding Company of Cleveland, Ohio, then assemble and braze the frames in Chicago. This firm, Wright discovered, provided the tubing for three-fourths of the American motorcycle industry. At the end of 1912, the Marsh-Metz company, reformed as the American Motor Company, and still in Brockton, Massachusetts, bought out Eagle.

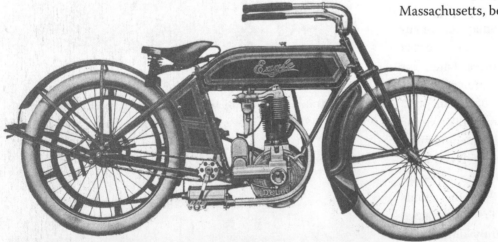

A 1913 Eagle 5-hp single. B based on industry terminology, we can conclude the displacement: 30.5 cubic inches (500cc). Incidentally, concurrent with Eagle sales, the parent company continued selling M-M machines. (BOB KAROLEVITZ)

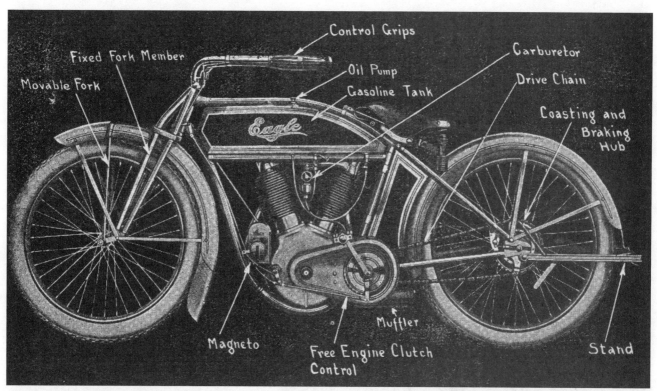

This 1915 Eagle was the last of the breed. Except for the name, the Crawford, Dayton, and Sears were identical motorcycles. (MOTORCYCLES AND SIDECARS)

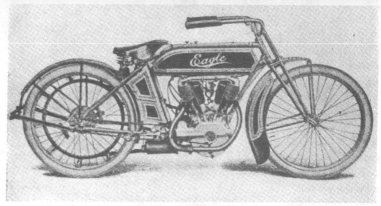

A 1913 9-hp Eagle Twin. From *The Bicycling World and Motorcycle Review*: "Motor, 9 hp; valves, mechanical; lubrication, sight feed and hand pump; speeds, one; fork, leaf spring; drive, flat belt; cylinders, two; ignition, magneto; clutch, disk on motor shaft; frame, rigid trussed keystone; brakes, one, band; tires, 28 x 2 3/4 inches; tanks, gasoline 2 1/2 gallons, oil 2 1/2 quarts." The engine displacement was approximately 61 cubic inches (1000cc). (BOB KAROLEVITZ)

1913 Eagle. This setup advanced the spark as the clutch was engaged.

(PACIFIC MOTORCYCLIST)

EMBLEM

Emblem motorcycles were built from 1907 through 1925 by the Emblem Manufacturing Company of Angola (near Buffalo), New York. The 1911 twins were offered with either V-belt or flat-belt drive, and an optional "free engine" (clutch) was featured. In 1913, the company brought out a 76.6 (1255cc) big twin, the largest on the market. The biggest Indians and Harley-Davidsons were 61-cubic inch (1000cc) jobs. In 1917, Emblem produced only one model, a 32.4-cubic inch (531cc) V-twin, with choice of single-speed or three-speed transmission. The Emblem was taken off the American market after 1917, but the marque continued to be offered in Europe through 1925.

Emblem was only slightly involved in American racing and record setting. In 1910, W. E. Gale set a New York to Chicago record of 35 hours, and racer Lee Taylor set a dirt-track 100-mile record for belt-drive singles. A year later, on the same Columbus, Ohio, track, George Evans raced a belt-drive Emblem twin to a dirt-track record for 100 miles, averaging 35.3 mph. As close as Emblem ever came to real racing glory was in the 1915 Dodge City 300 Mile National Championship road race, America's most prestigious event. An Emblem "team" was reported to have entered, but the race report cited only one rider who wasn't credited with a single lap.

A 1907 Emblem (above). This model was another of the many Indian clones. Certain details are identical to the 1907 Racycle. Refer to 1907 Indian section for applicable data, and to the Indian and Thor sections for the history of Indian cloning. (GEORGE YAROCKI)

A 1911 Emblem single. Color choices were carmine, French gray, and black.

A 1911 Emblem single. Along with direct belt drive, an optional "free engine" (clutch) was offered.

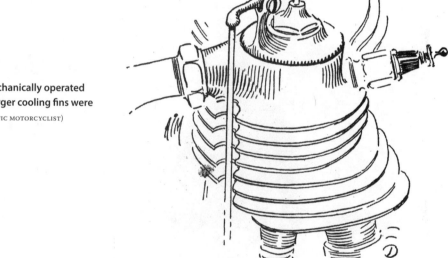

1913 Emblem. Mechanically operated inlet valves and larger cooling fins were new features. (PACIFIC MOTORCYCLIST)

A 1914 Emblem Model 108. The single-speed bike displaced 67 cubic inches (1098cc), had a free engine clutch, and costs $250.

(BRUCE LINSDAY)

The 1911 Emblem twin. (GEORGE YAROCKI)

A circa 1913 Emblem racer, and rider Lee Taylor. Taylor set a 100-mile dirt-track record for belt-drive singles of 48.7 mph. The engine displaced 38.5 cubic inches (630cc), and the model was offered either with belt or chain drive. (MALDWYN JONES)

A 1914 Emblem Model 110. This engine displaced 76.6 cubic inches (1255cc). The bike listed for $300. (BRUCE LINSDAY)

The 1914 Emblem Model 105 displaced 37 cubic inches (606cc). It was a single-speed with free engine clutch and either battery ignition or magneto ignition. (BRUCE LINSDAY)

A 1915 Emblem twin. This overall view shows the Emblem's good lines. (DOUG MITCHEL)

A 1915 Emblem. The wrist pins were secured by a single large piston ring. Typical of the era, two cam lobes moved four valves. Each lobe acted through two cam followers to operate both valves of the applicable cylinder. Magneto gear drive is evident. (EARL CHALFANT)

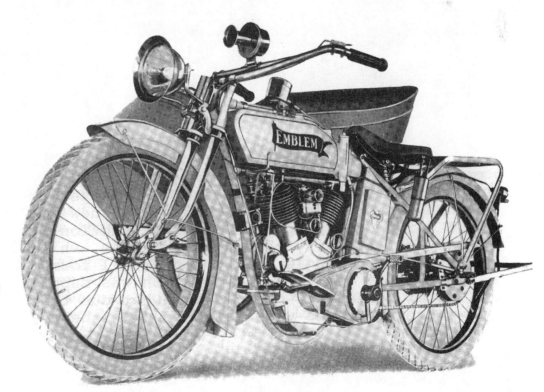

The 1916 Emblem Model 110. It displaced 76.6 cubic inches (1255cc), had 14 hp, and magneto ignition. The single-speed was $250; two-speed, $275.

(THE ANTIQUE MOTORCYCLE)

The 1915 Emblem. Engine removal and replacement were facilitated by horizontal motor-mounting platforms that were integral with the frame. The timing cover was secured with a single large hexagonal boss integral with the cover. In other words, the cover was screwed on like a jar lid.

(EARL CHALFANT)

A 1915 Emblem. The 76.6-cubic inch (1255cc) engine compared to the 61-cubic inch (1000cc) of Indians and Harley-Davidsons. In other respects, the F-head design was typical of the era. The company advertised this as "the Mighty Emblem." Double-row ball bearings were on each end of the crankshaft. (EARL CHALFANT)

The 1916 Emblem Model 108. Spec's included: 67 cubic inches (1098cc); 12 hp; magneto ignition; chain or V-belt final drive; single-speed, $225; two-speed, $250. Not apparent is the hinged rear fender that simplified rear tire maintenance. This was introduced on 1915 models. (THE ANTIQUE MOTORCYCLE)

The 1916 Emblem Model 105. In the clutch sprocket area, note the lever in the 2 o'clock position. This was the step starter introduced on 1915 models. The starter had a removable foot pedal so that the bicycle pedals could be used in the conventional manner. (THE ANTIQUE MOTORCYCLE)

A 1920 Emblem Model 106: three-speed, 50 cubic inches (819cc), free engine clutch, kick starter, $275. (BRUCE LINSDAY)

A 1920 Emblem Model 106 engine. According to the company: "The result of ten years of practical motorcycle construction. The most wonderful motor ever constructed, containing fewer parts and developing more power and speed than any other motor."

(BRUCE LINSDAY)

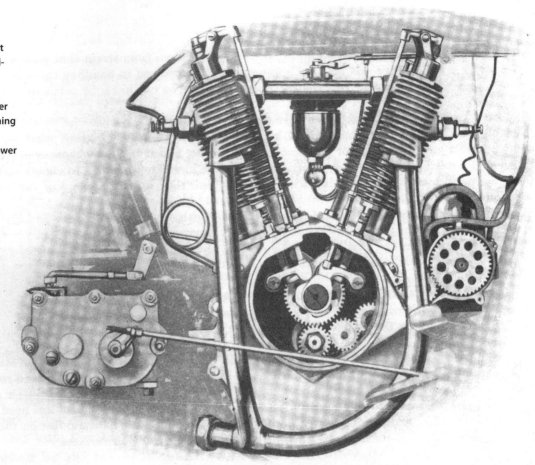

A 1920 Emblem Model 106, single speed. Something is amiss: bore and stroke were cited as 2 5/8 x 3 inches, and displacement was cited as 50 cubic inches (819cc); but those cylinder dimensions equate to 32.47 cubic inches (532cc)! $250. (BRUCE LINSDAY)

1906 Erie. Erie manufactured both complete motorcycles and motorbike attachments. Specifications: F-head engine, bore and stroke of 2 2/3 and 2 ¾ inches, respectively, displacement 15.4 cubic inches (252cc), 2 hp; frame offsets for drive pulley, idler pulley. (JIM DENNIE)

1909 Erie Lightweight Model. Though engine dimensions weren't provided by the catalog, an output of 2 1/2 hp was claimed. According to industry practice, this would have equated to about 15 cubic inches (250cc). Cited specification: speed, 4 to 30 mph; control, double grip; transmission, 3/4-inch Erie V belt; fuel range, 80 miles; oil range, 150 miles; wheelbase, 52 inches; frame height, 21 inches; wheels, heavy steel clincher; coaster brake, Morrow; tires, G & J clincher; handlebars, wide up-turned touring. (BRUCE LINSDAY)

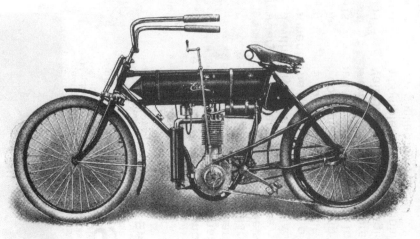

ERIE

Erie motorcycles were built from 1908 through 1911 by the Erie Manufacturing Company of Buffalo, New York. Previously, the firm was known as the Motor Bicycle Equipment and Supply Company, and then as the Motorcycle Equipment and Supply Company, MESCO (see Mesco marque). From catalog addresses and other sources, it seems that MESCO sold Reliance motorcycles in 1909 alongside Erie motorcycles, but dropped the Reliance name in 1910.

A 1906 Erie engine. This motor was sold as part of a motorbike kit. (BRUCE LINSDAY)

A 1909 Erie R.F.D. model. Motorcycles were popular with rural-delivery postmen. The R.F.D. (rural free delivery) model featured a two-speed gear and the so-called "free engine," which today is termed a clutch. This was the only Erie with a sprung front fork, though the fork could be purchased separately and fitted to the Model A or Semi-Racing Model. The motorcycle weighed 140 lbs. (GEORGE YAROCKI)

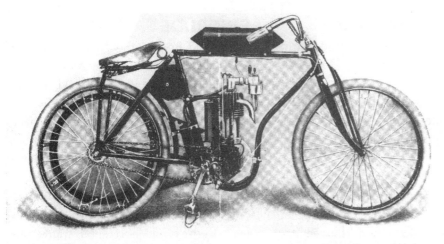

1909 Erie Semi-Racing Model. No extra output was claimed for this sporting job, so this was apparently a cosmetic exercise. This model weighed 105 lbs. (THE ANTIQUE MOTORCYCLE)

The 1909 Erie engine. From the catalog: "Mechanically operated intake valve which allows slower running, quicker picking-up and more speed. Both valves are operated by one cam. This is the most simple valve mechanism in use."

(THE ANTIQUE MOTORCYCLE)

1909 Erie Model A. The weight was 130 lbs. This was a single-speed model with a rigid front fork; other specifications were the same as the R.F.D. Model. (THE ANTIQUE MOTORCYCLE)

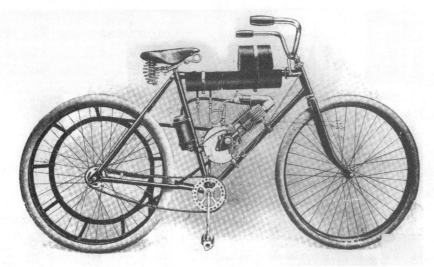

A 1909 Erie 2 1/2-hp attachment. The company's motorbike tradition continued with this kit, differing only in the details from the 1906 setup. (THE ANTIQUE MOTORCYCLE)

The 1909 Erie engine. From the catalog: "...The Intake Valve being directly over the Exhaust Valve, allows the incoming charge to cool the valve. This does away with so much burning and pitting and consequent grinding. This feature alone is worth many dollars to the Motorcyclist."

(THE ANTIQUE MOTORCYCLE)

EVANS POWER-CYCLE

The Evans Power-Cycle was produced by the Cyclemotor Corporation of Rochester, New York, from 1919 through 1924. The firm originally offered only a motorbike kit, under the trade name "Cyclemotor." During 1919, the product was renamed "Evans Power-Cycle." Advertisements showed a more substantial bicycle with twin top rails and a double-curved front down tube. It is unclear whether complete motorbikes were built up in this configuration. The mid-1919 power plant appeared identical to the earlier offering, except that a longer belt was required for the longer bicycle.

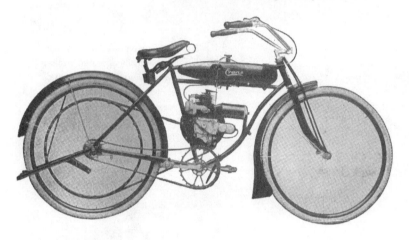

A 1919 Evans Power-Cycle. These were 119cc two-strokes. Ads implied the complete motorbike was offered, as well as a kit. (MOTORCYCLING AND BICYCLING)

The 1921 Evans Power-Cycle. According to historian Erwin Tragatsch, these machines were popular in Europe, and were built under license in Germany by the Stock firm. (MOTORCYCLING AND BICYCLING)

EVINRUDE SPEED BIKE

In 1936, famed outboard motor builder Evinrude came out with a motorbike kit. This was along the lines of the Velo Solex, but friction drive was via the rear tire, rather than the front. The engine was on a beam that pivoted from a fixture on the seat mast. Forward of the seat mast, the beam continued as a "jockey" shift lever. When the lever on the right side of the pedal bike was pushed slightly to the left, it could be stored beneath the lower (horizontal) frame tube. This kept the engine and small drive wheel suspended slightly above the rear tire. Moving the lever out of the stored position, and letting the lever rise up, through the fulcrum action allowed the engine driving wheel to lower against the tire. It was a practical but homely looking motorbike, and had none of the charm of the later Whizzer motorbike that made the rider feel some connection with conventional motorcycling.

EXCELSIOR

Motorcycles branded "Excelsior" were manufactured by the Excelsior Motor Manufacturing and Supply Company of Chicago. The company was formed and managed by Ignatz Schwinn, the bicycle builder. Production of Excelsior singles and V-twins spanned the years 1907 through 1924. In 1925, the V-twin range was completely redesigned, and marketed through early 1931 as the "Super-X" brand. Because the new genre represented a complete rethink as well as a different name on the tanks, Super-X motorcycles are presented later as a separate marque.

By the early 1910s, more than 100 small American motorcycle companies had come and gone. The industry had settled down into a two-tier arrangement, the "Big Three" and all others. The Big Three were Indian, Harley-Davidson, and Excelsior, and that was the pecking order. In 1917, the Excelsior company purchased the Henderson company and began production of these luxurious and expensive four-cylinder motorcycles. A few much smaller lower-tier firms continued until the U.S.A. entered World War I in 1917. Most failed to reappear after the War ended in late 1918. During 1917 and 1918, Indian made the colossal mistake of committing all its production to the Army. Indian fell into second place, well behind Harley-Davidson, and remained evermore in that status. With the ever-increasing presence of Ford Model T cars, American motorcycling completed its transformation from transportation alternative to sporting hobby.

Harley-Davidson continued to grow in the early 1920s, while Indian production and sales dipped. Harley's growth came at the expense of the smaller brands, the industry as a whole having leveled off. In this weeding-out era, the Excelsior company found its sales charts looking like the edge of a saw. Almost every above-average year was followed by a below-average year. In the boom period of 1920 through late 1929, Harley-Davidson and Indian averaged , respectively, 17,600 and 8,500 motorcycles per year. Combined Excelsior

A 1907 Excelsior. According to the Excelsior Motor Manufacturing and Supply Company, this machine was placed on the market after two years of design and development. The F-head single-cylinder engine was typical for the era, and had a displacement of about 30.50 cubic inches (500cc). On this example, battery ignition was used. The crankcase was a stress-bearing segment of the frame. In the United States, this was termed a "keystone" frame.

(BRUCE LINSDAY)

A 1910 Excelsior Model DM: F-head single-cylinder engine; displacement, 30.50 cubic inches (500cc); maximum output, 4 hp; automatic (suction operated) inlet valve; mechanically operated exhaust valve; ignition, magneto; belt drive; speed control, double-grip; wheels/tires 28 x 2 1/2 inches; wheelbase, 55 inches; saddle height, 21 inches; finish, gray with red panels and striping; price, $250. The $225 Model D was identical, except for battery ignition. (BRUCE LINSDAY)

A 1910 Excelsior Model EM. Specifications were the same as the Model DM, except wheels/tires were 26 x 2 1/2 inches and the wheelbase 53 inches. Price was $250. The $225 Model E was identical to the EM, except for battery ignition. (BRUCE LINSDAY)

and Henderson production averaged 3,000 motorcycles per year. Most American cities above 50,000 population had three dealerships representing the Big Three companies and the big four brands. Generally, a city's Excelsior-Henderson shop would be smaller than its Harley and Indian shops When an area could only support two motorcycle shops, the dropout was typically Excelsior-Henderson. There were some areas where Excelsior was stronger, around Chicago, for instance. But there were many areas where Excelsiors were seldom seen.

Through the 1910s, Excelsior engineering was abreast, or even ahead of its two principal rivals. But the company's economic struggles resulted in fewer and fewer technical updates. Fundamental Excelsior design did not change from 1915 through 1924. The same could be said of Harley-Davidson and Indian, but these firms did, in fact, inject many more detailed improvements than did Excelsior. Almost every year Harley and Indian announced new features and/or brought out entirely new models. Excelsior catalogs and press releases asserted that changes were few because the design had been so sound from the beginning.

Excelsior technology lagged more significantly in the limited production of special racing and hill climbing motorcycles. Though the brand had its wins and its records, at the national championship level Excelsior routinely fared third best among the Big Three.

A complicating factor was the Excelsior company's Henderson business. Dealers found it easier to sell Hendersons than Excelsiors. Buyers could feel that a V-twin is a V-twin is a V-twin, and that they would be better served by dealing with a more prosperous Harley or Indian shop. But from 1917 through 1921, Hendersons were the nation's only four-cylinder bikes. Often, dealers would have a Henderson on display, but would not have an Excelsior in stock. Even after Ace four-cylinder production began in 1922, that firm's production remained well under Henderson levels. The Excelsior company realized that its big V-twins faced the serious competition of their own fours. For this reason, the big V-twins were dropped at the end of the 1924 season in favor of a new line of middleweights branded "Super-X." Super-X models are treated later as a separate marque.

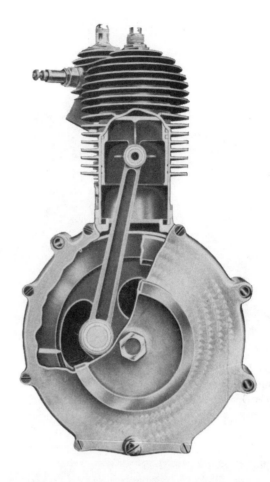

A 1910 Excelsior engine. The double-plunger oil pump is in the rear part of the timing case. In all F-head engines, exhaust valve cooling was enhanced by situating the relatively cool inlet valve directly over the exhaust valve. However, heat flowed from the exhaust valve directly into the inlet charge, which reduced the power. (BRUCE LINSDAY)

A 1910 Excelsior engine. The so-called "open" or "webbed" flywheel was typical for the era. The 1907 through 1912 Excelsiors featured spark plug mounting perpendicular to the cylinder bore. (BRUCE LINSDAY)

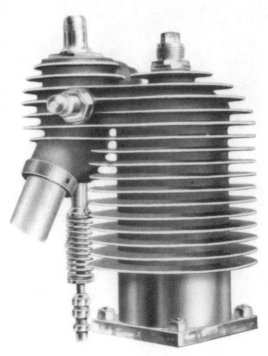

A 1910 Excelsior cylinder. The air space between valve chamber and cylinder wall was supposed to improve cooling.

(BRUCE LINSDAY)

1911 Excelsior Auto-Cycle Model F or G. These were the company's first twins. The "F" and "G" differed only in tire and wheel sizes, and wheelbase. The term "Auto-Cycle" was chosen by the firm because the term "motorcycle" was not yet universal. Specifications: F-head two-cylinder engine; maximum output, 6 hp; belt drive; speed control, double-grip; F wheels/tires, 28 x 2 5/8 inches; G wheels/tires, 26 x 2 5/8 inches; finish, gray with red panels and striping; price, F and G, $300. (GEORGE YAROCKI)

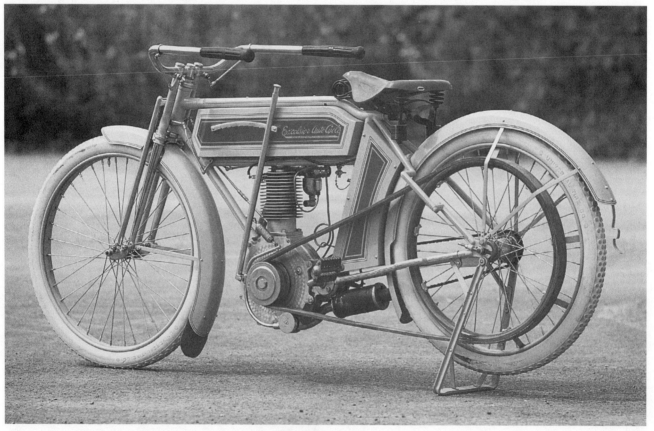

The 1911 Excelsior Auto-Cycle Model EM was unchanged from 1910. (DOUG MITCHEL)

The 1913 Excelsior twin was not significantly changed for 1913. Small wonder, as 1912 saw the introduction of this more shapely frame and tank, with lower saddle height, and the engine capacity increased from 50 cubic inches (819cc) to 60.90 cubic inches (998cc). (DOUG MITCHEL)

Excelsior clutch control in 1913 was accomplished through this linkage from the left twist-grip. (PACIFIC MOTORCYCLIST)

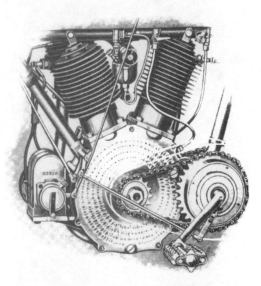

The 1913 Excelsior. Clearly shown are the Bosch magneto and the keystone frame with open lower area and crankcase filling the gap. The spark plugs are situated to be horizontal with the engine installed.

(EXCELSIOR SALES LITERATURE)

The 1913 Excelsior Model 7C. New features: new valve design; new valve lifter; improved inlet valve cage; magneto ignition exclusively; clutch control via left-hand twist-grip; heavier clutch cone; spark control via tank-side lever; gravity-feed lubrication; improved seat post; thicker tank plates; heavier fork springs; wider fenders with greater tire clearance; 7 to 10 hp; price $250. (EXCELSIOR SALES LITERATURE)

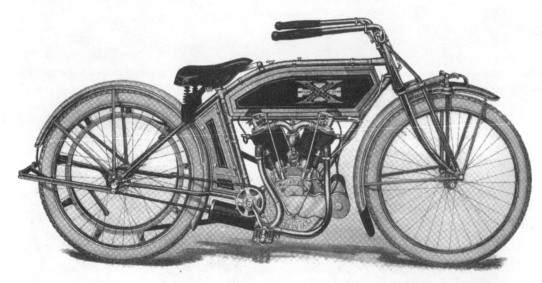

The 1913 Excelsior Model 7B: belt drive, 7 to 10 hp, priced at $250.

(EXCELSIOR SALES LITERATURE)

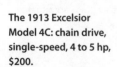

The 1913 Excelsior Model 4C: chain drive, single-speed, 4 to 5 hp, $200.

(EXCELSIOR SALES LITERATURE)

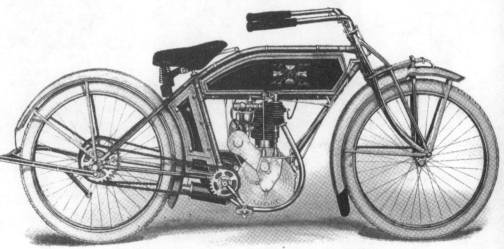

The 1913 Excelsior Model 4B, belt drive, single-speed, 4 to 5 hp, $200. (EXCELSIOR SALES LITERATURE)

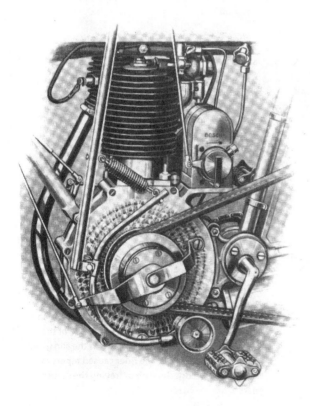

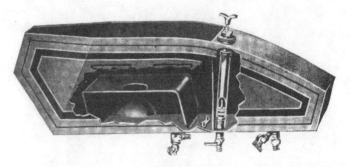

1913 Excelsior tank construction. Note how a baffle plate prevents fuel from sloshing in the area around the fuel tap. Typically in the industry, oil was carried within a compartment sealed off inside the tank. The oil section has within it a hand pump to supplement the drip feed that metered oil, according to average riding conditions. (EXCELSIOR SALES LITERATURE)

The 1913 Excelsior Model 4B. When the long lever was moved forward, the small idler pulley below the belt was drawn into contact with the belt, effectively tightening the belt. The lever was manipulated like a clutch, to gradually place the engine under load. (EXCELSIOR SALES LITERATURE)

MODEL 7—T.S. TWO SPEED CHAIN DRIVE, $260.00, F. O. B. CHICAGO

1914 Excelsior Model 7 T.S. The "T.S." denotes two-speed transmission. Said the catalog: "...particularly applicable to side car and commercial service. It combines all the speed qualities of the regular twin, with an enormous pulling power for special requirements."

(EXCELSIOR SALES LITERATURE)

The 1914 Excelsior engine. Bore and stroke, 3 21/64 x 3 1/2 inches; displacement, 60.90 cubic inches (998cc). The engine was rated at 7-10 hp, in accord with industry custom that related power to engine size, so "7-10" in trade-talk simply meant about 1000cc displacement. Actual output was 10 to 15 hp. There was no oil pump; instead, gravity oil flow was metered. A glass sight tube allowed the rider to verify oil flow.

(EXCELSIOR SALES LITERATURE)

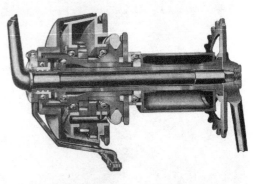

The 1914 Excelsior planetary two-speed clutch hub. All the major manufacturers launched two-speed models for 1914. Just visible is one of the eight planet gears mounted to the clutch hub. These gears meshed with a gear-set cut into the outside of the tapered clutch cone, the cone acting as the sun gear. By moving a hand lever, the rider caused tapers to wedge or un-wedge, locking or freeing the planet gears. (EXCELSIOR SALES LITERATURE)

A 1914 Excelsior. Because the Excelsior frame did not extend beneath the engine, it was necessary to design this involved footboard layout. (MOTORCYCLES AND SIDECARS)

The 1914 Excelsior cylinder. The spark plug is mounted 67 ½ degrees from the cylinder bore (22 ½ short of perpendicular). With the 45-degree V-twin engine installed, each spark plug was horizontal. Note the cooling air space between the exhaust port and the cylinder-proper. (EXCELSIOR SALES LITERATURE)

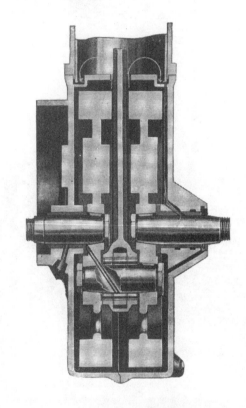

A 1914 Excelsior engine cutaway. Shown are the oil passages to the crank pins and crankshaft. (EXCELSIOR SALES LITERATURE)

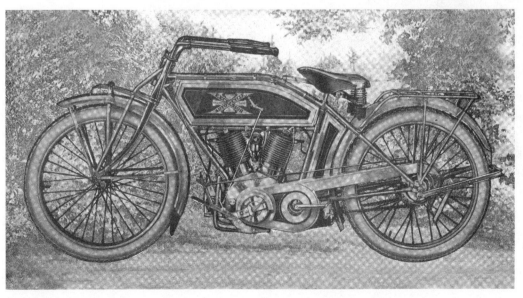

A 1914 Excelsior Model 7-C. The 1914 models were the first Excelsiors with footboards and a foot-pedal-operated brake. (EXCELSIOR SALES LITERATURE)

1914 Excelsior Model 7-B. At about this time, belt-drive was falling in popularity, but it cost Excelsior little to continue catering to this minority market.

(EXCELSIOR SALES LITERATURE)

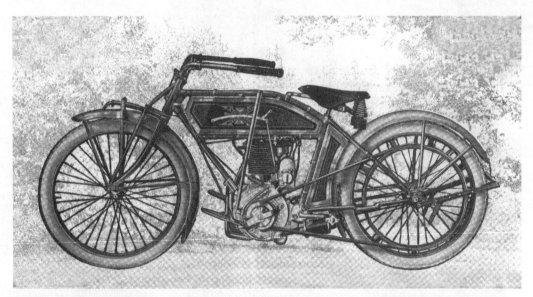

A 1914 Excelsior Model 4-B. At $190, this single-speed belt-drive was Excelsior's least costly model. There was also the minority viewpoint that belt drive was smoother, and easier on the engine and frame, because of the shock-absorbing nature of the drive belt.

(EXCELSIOR SALES LITERATURE)

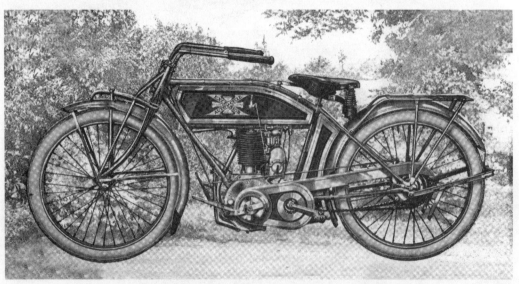

A 1914 Excelsior Model 4-C. Advertised at $200, the buyer would pay only $10 more for single-speed chain drive.

(EXCELSIOR SALES LITERATURE)

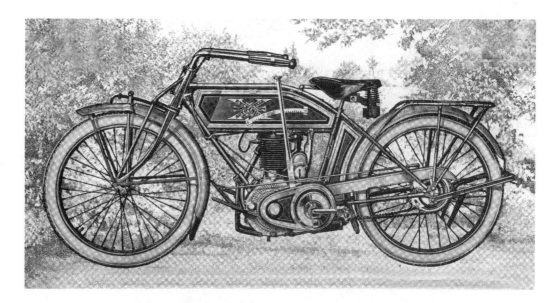

A 1914 Excelsior Model 4-T.S. The two-speeder went for $235.
(EXCELSIOR SALES LITERATURE)

The 1914 catalog hyped acetylene lighting. The following year Excelsior introduced its first models with electric lighting.
(THE ANTIQUE MOTORCYCLE)

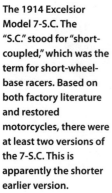

The 1914 Excelsior Model 7-S.C. The "S.C." stood for "short-coupled," which was the term for short-wheel-base racers. Based on both factory literature and restored motorcycles, there were at least two versions of the 7-S.C. This is apparently the shorter earlier version.
(EXCELSIOR SALES LITERATURE)

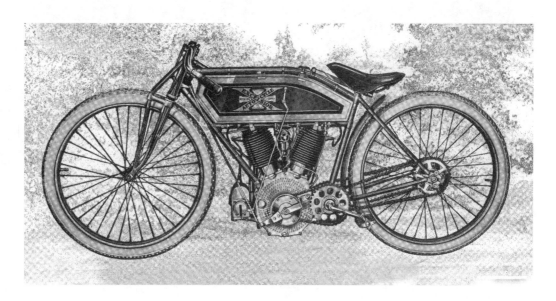

The 1915 Excelsior Model 15-3. This was the first year of the three-speed transmission; Harley-Davidson and Indian also brought out three-speeders that year. Uniquely, the Excelsior had dual clutch control, either by left-hand grip, or by left foot pedal.

(GEORGE YAROCKI)

A 1915 Excelsior Model 15-1. The year 1915 saw the introduction of the more pronounced sloping top frame tube (the 1914 models top tube had sloped only in the rear portion). The most important technical change was the fitting of an engine-driven oil pump mounted on the timing case. The single-speed option was continued with this model.

(BRUCE LINSDAY)

A 1916 Excelsior Model 16-3, electrically equipped. The MIDCO combination magneto and generator unit was new for 1916.

(GEORGE YAROCKI)

A 1916 Excelsior contracting band rear brake. A typical period brake, they were adequate for the slower speeds and mostly unpaved roads—until it rained! To get any stopping power when wet, riders continuously "stood" on the brake pedal, keeping the bands and drum hot enough to shed the water as steam. (GEORGE YAROCKI)

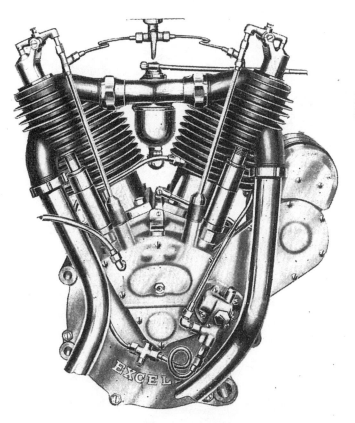

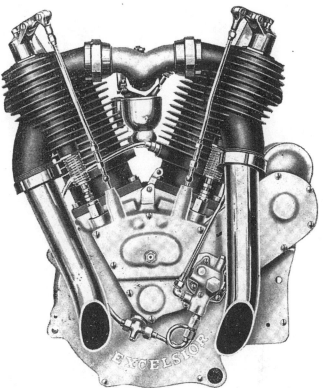

The 1916 Excelsior standard engine. New features: new horizontal inlet manifold, new cylinders with horizontal inlet ports, new enclosed exhaust valve springs, magneto in new 2 o'clock position, new timing case cover corresponding to new magneto drive setup, relocated spark plugs. (GEORGE YAROCKI)

The 1916 Excelsior "Big Valve" racing engine. The inlet manifold, valves, and inlet and exhaust ports, were larger. The push rods were slightly bent to clear the larger cooling fins. Customers could custom order the Big Valve engine for their road models. (GEORGE YAROCKI)

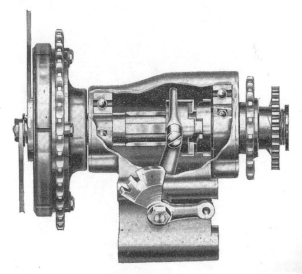

The 1916 Excelsior three-speed transmission. The single sliding gear had dogs on each side, so that dog-to-dog shifting was achieved when selecting first and third gears. Shifting to second-gear required finesse because of teeth-to-teeth engagement. The layout was better than both Harley-Davidson and Indian designs, which featured gear-to-gear engagement for first gear. (GEORGE YAROCKI)

A 1916 Excelsior single-speed transmission. (GEORGE YAROCKI)

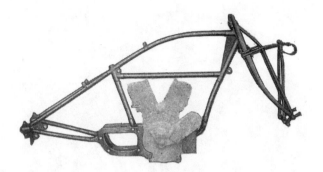

A 1916 Excelsior "keystone" frame. As in other motorcycles, the frame tube just above the engine is fixed solidly to the front and rear down tubes. This would change on 1917 models. (GEORGE YAROCKI)

A 1916 Excelsior starter. (GEORGE YAROCKI)

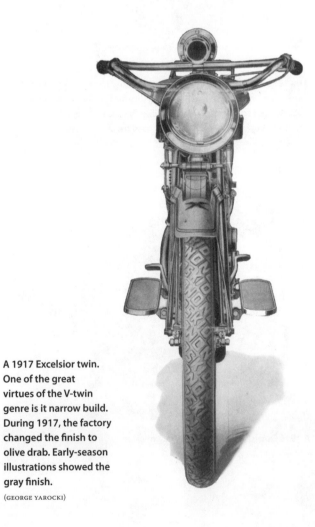

A 1917 Excelsior twin. One of the great virtues of the V-twin genre is it narrow build. During 1917, the factory changed the finish to olive drab. Early-season illustrations showed the gray finish.

(GEORGE YAROCKI)

A 1917 Excelsior twin. The combination of a right-hand throttle and a right-hand gear-shift lever slowed down the gear-shifting operation.

(GEORGE YAROCKI)

A 1917 Excelsior Model 17-3E. This top-of-the-line Excelsior was listed at $295. Without lights, the companion Model 17-3 went for $265. (GEORGE YAROCKI)

A 1917 Excelsior engine. Excelsior termed the 1917-1919 engine the "Ultra Power Motor." The new 1917 cylinders had more finning around the exhaust port, as well as larger valves. Excelsior claimed a power increase of almost 25 percent. An oil line was routed to the base of the front cylinder, because the front cylinder didn't receive as much oil sling as the rear cylinder. (GEORGE YAROCKI)

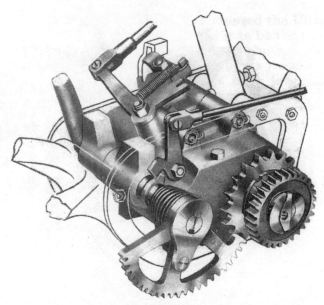

A 1917-1924 Excelsior kick starter with automatic compression release. A cam is on the right section of the starter shaft. When the engine was kicked over, the cam moved counter-clockwise, the rod moved forward, and a lever on the crankcase transmitted motion to an exhaust valve lifter inside the timing case. The exhaust valves momentarily opened to ease the kicking, but closed in time to seal off the next cylinder coming up on compression. This not only reduced starting effort, but also enabled the engine to be spun faster. (GEORGE YAROCKI)

A 1917 Excelsior Model 17-3E. Specifications: F-head twin-cylinder engine; bore and stroke, 3 21/64 x 3 1/2 inches; displacement, 60.90 cubic inches (998cc); lubrication, engine-driven pump with auxiliary hand pump for emergency use, independent oil feeds to front cylinder and right main bearing; saddle height, 27 inches; three-speed transmission. (GEORGE YAROCKI)

A 1916 and 1917 Excelsior Model 17-S.C. (the same picture was used in both years' catalog). From the catalog: "THE FASTEST MOTORCYCLE IN THE WORLD. Winner of the American National Championship, 300 Miles in 3 Hours, 29 Minutes, 51.4 seconds — 85.7 Mph. Holds World's Records for 1, 2, 5, 10, 50, 200, and 300 miles, 100-Mile Dirt Track, One Hour and other distances." From the 1917 catalog: "..the frame is shortened to give the short wheelbase of 56 inches." (THE ANTIQUE MOTORCYCLE)

1917-1919 Excelsior Model L-17, L-18, and L-19 "Light Weight." Some specifications: front fork, hinged coil spring moved wheel frame; single loop conventional (not a keystone as on larger models); tank, 13/4 gallons of fuel, 1/2 gallon of oil with measuring cup for preparing refuel mixture; brake (rear only), shoe against belt rim; wheels/tires, 26 x 2 1/4 inches; wheelbase, 51 inches. (BRUCE LINSDAY)

A 1917-1919 Excelsior Light Weight. The company jumped into the lightweight field after Indian brought out the 1915 Indian Featherweight two-stroke. Sales of the little Excelsior must have been very low for it to last but three seasons. (BRUCE LINSDAY)

The 1917-1919 Excelsior Light Weight engine. Specifications: single-cylinder two-stroke; bore and stroke, 217/64 and 23/4 inches; displacement, 11.09 cubic inches (182cc); lubrication, fuel/oil mist (no pump) via pre-mix; ignition, chain-driven magneto behind engine; kick-starter on left side; transmission, chain primary drive, two-speed counter-shaft gearbox, belt final drive. (BRUCE LINSDAY)

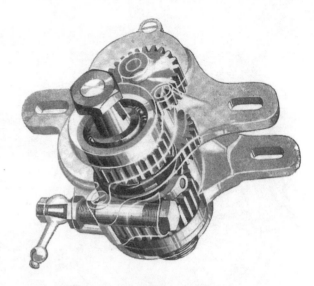

The 1917-1919 Excelsior Light Weight two-speed countershaft gearbox. The primary drive chain adjuster is beneath the transmission case. (BRUCE LINSDAY)

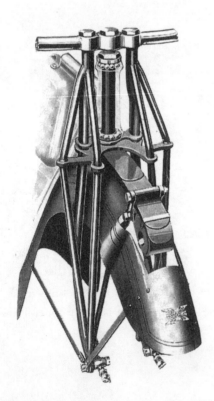

A 1919 Excelsior military style front fork with additional bracing.
(GEORGE YAROCKI)

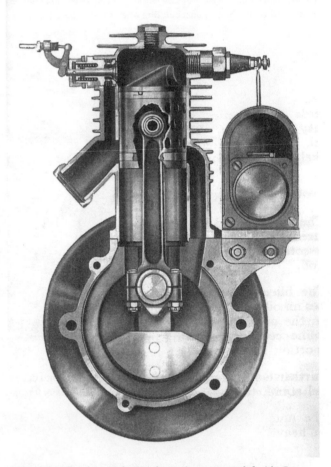

A 1917-1919 Excelsior Light Weight engine cutaway, left side. For easier starting, a compression release valve was fitted to the front of the cylinder. The deflector piston was typical of the era., as was the "Swiss cheese" piston. The outside flywheel was on the right side.
(BRUCE LINSDAY)

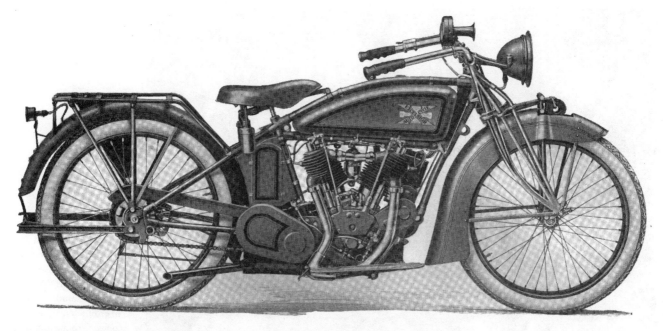

The 1919 Excelsior Model 19 (also referred to as Series 19). The machine was equipped with the military-style fork with additional bracing.

(GEORGE YAROCKI)

1919 Excelsior. On all Excelsior twins, the tank bottom was scalloped to provide clearance for the inlet rockers. Nickle-plated cylinders were an Excelsior hallmark.

A 1919 Excelsior. In 1918, the oil tank was made separate from the fuel tank, occupying the space formerly used for the toolbox. As this is an unlighted model, it has an ordinary magneto; compare to the following figure.

A 1919 Excelsior, fitted with MIDCO magneto-generator.

(GEORGE YAROCKI)

Excelsior Record Setting and Racing, 1907-1924

The highlight of Excelsior sporting achievements happened at the end of 1912, when rider Lee Hummiston became the first motorcyclist in the world to be officially timed at 100 mph. Hummiston and the "X" set American records for all distances from one through 100 miles. Previously, Indian had owned all these marks. In the 1910s, Excelsior fielded factory teams for all the more prestigious races, such as long road races and long board track races. In 1913, factory rider Bob Perry won the 300-Mile National Championship Road Race in Savannah, Georgia. In 1915, "X" rider Carl Goudy won the 300-Mile National Championship Speedway (board track) race in the factory's own city of Chicago, Illinois. Goudy averaged 85.8 mph.

Thereafter, as factory team bikes became ever faster, Excelsior seemed to lag about a year behind Indian and Harley-Davidson. In 1920, for instance, Excelsior's Paul Anderson finished the Marion, Indiana, 200-Mile National Championship Road Race in five minutes less than the 1919 Harley-Davidson winner. But Anderson's 1920 time was 13 minutes longer than the winning 1920 Harley rider! Excelsior's high-water mark in terms of factory commitment came in 1920. The customary several salaried riders arrived in Los Angeles for the 100-Mile National Championship (dirt track) with 61-cubic inch (1000cc) overhead-cam V-twins. Though the overhead-cam twins looked like world beaters, team rider Bob Perry was killed during practice, and the team withdrew.

For the balance of big-motor racing in the 1920s, Excelsior was sparsely represented. Harley-Davidson dominated, in various years winning all or nearly all the national championship races. Indian fell into second place in racing prestige, managing to win some of the shorter events. Excelsior competed well in local interest races and hill climbs, but stayed out of the winner's circle for all the big title races. Harley-Davidson riders were turning in impressive speeds on both eight-valve overheads and F-head racers. Indian gradually switched from eight-valves to side-valves, and wrote a remarkable story in some of the less prestigious shorter title races, which in fact were run at faster paces than the long haul races. For a while, Indian Flatheads ran faster than Harley's eight-valves. Excelsior never managed to develop F-head racers at the highest level, and, after the 1920 disaster, never pursued overhead-cam and overhead-valve racing development.

Something of a one-man band was Excelsior rider Wells Bennett, who specialized in long-distance records. His Excelsior records included: 1918 Three Flag (Canada to Mexico, or vice-versa) record, 1918 Los Angeles to Needles, 1919 San Francisco to Los Angeles, 1919 Los Angeles to Bakersfield on a side-car rig sealed in high-gear, 1920 Los Angeles to Bakersfield on a side-car rig sealed in high-gear, and 1920 San Francisco to Los Angeles on a side-car rig. Bennett was unlucky in racing. At the 1921 Dodge City, Kansas, 300-Mile National Championship Road Race, Bennett turned his fifth and sixth laps at a pace faster than winner Ralph Heburn's fastest lap, ran well during the second hundred miles, but was sidelined by a broken exhaust valve rocker. Bad luck also eliminated him from the 1921 Wichita, Kansas, 300-mile race. There are no further records of Bennett competing on Excelsiors. During 1922 and 1923, Bennett rode four-cylinder Hendersons to six new distance records.

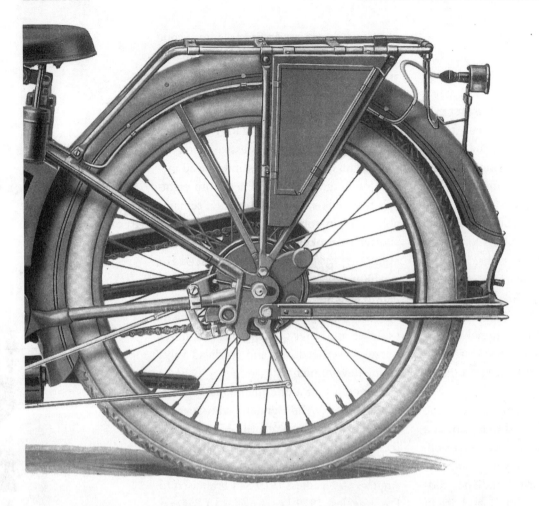

The 1919 Excelsior luggage rack and toolbox.

(George Yarocki)

The 1919 Excelsior Light Weight. The "bacon slicer" flywheel stands out. Two-strokes were weak engines in the era, and plagued by fouled spark plugs. The chore of measuring and mixing the oil each time the bike needed fuel was not a pleasant one.

At the 1919 Marion, Indiana, 200-Mile National Championship road race, Excelsior stars Bob Perry (left) and Carl Goudy (right) pose for the camera. Goudy, who had retired from racing, worked in the pits. Second in prestige only to the Dodge City (Kansas) 300-mile road race, this event saw Harley-Davidson finish 1-2-3. Excelsior's best effort was fifth place by Wells Bennet; Perry placed sixth, one lap behind the first five riders.

(JACK ARMSTRONG)

Excelsior star Wells Bennett shown on his way to a 1919 "Three Flag" record (Canada to Mexico) run, finished on July 26. Bennett's average speed of 32 mph was achieved through dirt, sand, mud, and, when lucky, stretches of gravel. It was in essence a 1,714-mile trail ride. (MOTORCYCLE AND BICYCLE ILLUSTRATED)

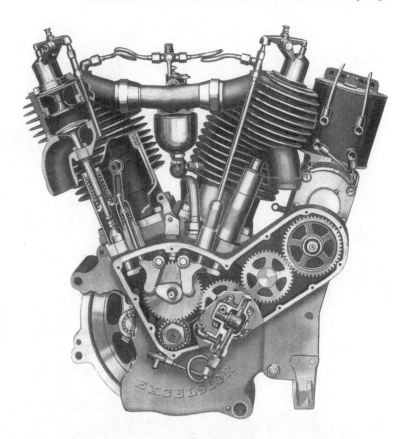

The 1919 Excelsior V-twin is representative of all the "Big X" engines, as these were changed only in minor details from 1917 through 1924. The "outside" cam lobe, visible here, served both inlet valves, and the "inside" lobe served both exhaust valves.

(GEORGE YAROCKI)

The 1919 Excelsior clutch. The company claimed their dry clutch was the largest and most efficient clutch in the industry. Actuation was via the left hand grip, which turned the worm gear to release or engage the clutch plates. Note the ball bearings.

(GEORGE YAROCKI)

The 1919 Excelsior "Kushion Sprocket." The device smoothed out the power pulses. (GEORGE YAROCKI)

The 1919 Excelsior three-speed transmission. The clutch drum (large left hub) and clutch plate areas have been widened considerably since the original 1915 design.
(GEORGE YAROCKI)

The 1919 Excelsior frame. In 1918, the frame was redesigned to include a removable frame tube. This greatly eased engine repairs. (GEORGE YAROCKI)

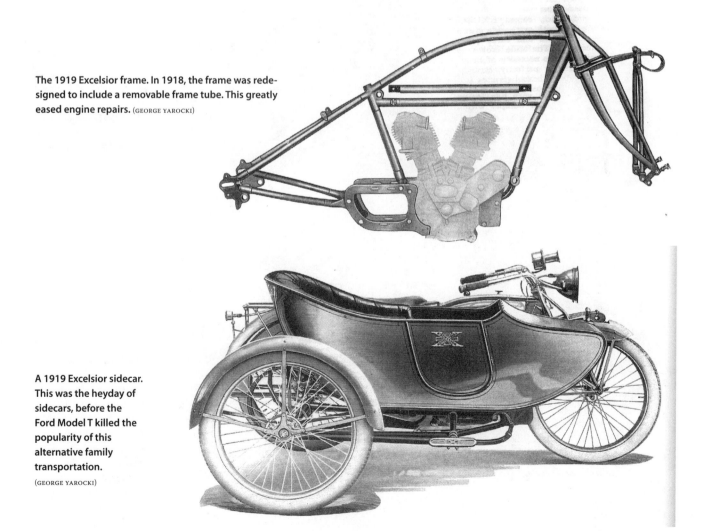

A 1919 Excelsior sidecar. This was the heyday of sidecars, before the Ford Model T killed the popularity of this alternative family transportation.
(GEORGE YAROCKI)

A 1919 Excelsior sidecar frame. The sidecar had an extendable axle, so that in heavily rutted roads the rig could ride in the car tracks. (GEORGE YAROCKI)

The 1919 Excelsior Commercial Van. Like rivals Harley-Davidson and Indian, Excelsior marketed commercial vehicles using the sidecar frame.

(GEORGE YAROCKI)

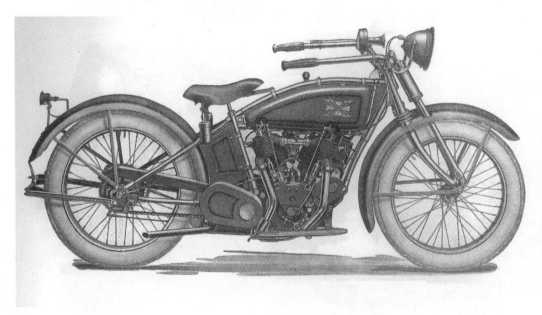

The 1920 Excelsior Series 20. Front fork design was changed to trailing link suspension via coil spring. The new front fork and the frame rear fork were wider to permit new wider (7 inches) fenders and the use of tire chains.

(GEORGE YAROCKI)

A 1920 Excelsior Series 20. The fenders had increased tire clearance, conforming to military specifications that prevented mud clogging under the most extreme conditions. During 1920, the MIDCO combined magneto-generator, shown here, was replaced by separate magneto and generator, shown in the 1924 illustrations. (GEORGE YAROCKI)

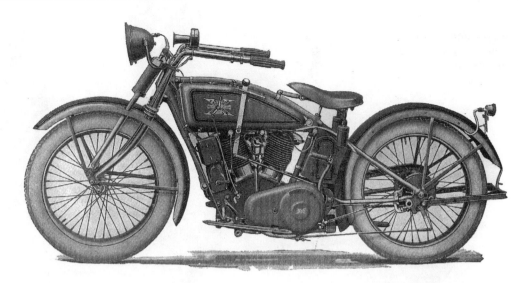

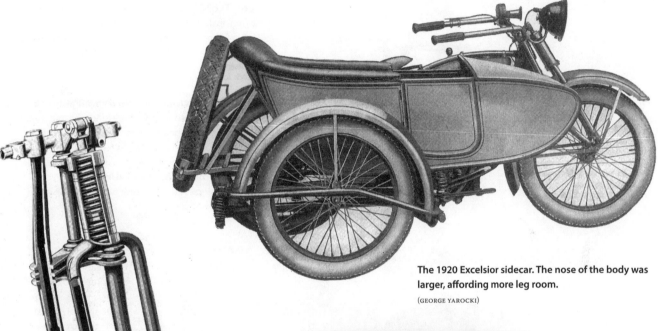

The 1920 Excelsior sidecar. The nose of the body was larger, affording more leg room.

(GEORGE YAROCKI)

A 1920 Excelsior front fork, cutaway view. The trailing link approach was maintained when coil spring action replaced the leaf spring arrangement. A trailing link suspension absorbed more road shock than did a leading link suspension. There was no front brake on any new domestic model of any manufacturer. (GEORGE YAROCKI)

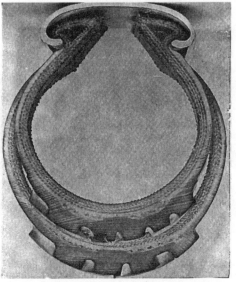

Comparison of 1919 28 x 3-inch tires and 1920 27 x 3 1/2-inch tires. (GEORGE YAROCKI)

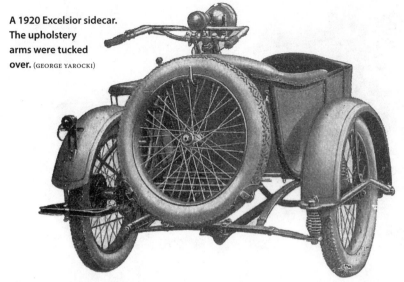

A 1920 Excelsior sidecar. The upholstery arms were tucked over. (GEORGE YAROCKI)

A 1922 Excelsior half-mile-track racer. Half-mile-track racing was popular, especially in the Midwest. These races were short, often 10 miles or less, and didn't carry national championship status like the 100-mile and longer races on board tracks and 1-mile dirt tracks. Excelsior fielded a two-man team for the 1922 season, including Paul Anderson, shown here, and Maldwyn Jones. During the season, Jones became the first racer to wear a steel-soled left boot.

(MOTORCYCLE AND BICYCLE ILLUSTRATED)

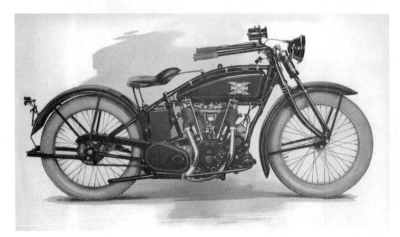

A 1924 Excelsior. A new brake and new Timken hubs were the only major new features since the mid-1920 incorporation of a separate generator (in front of the frame). The company had been plugging its four-cylinder Henderson marque in period magazines. The big "X" had come to be regarded by the factory and the dealerships as a competitor of the Henderson.

(EXCELSIOR SALES LITERATURE)

The 1920 Excelsior overhead-cam racer. Team rider Joe Wolters poses with one of the several special racers that came before the public at a Los Angeles dirt track race in early 1920. Teammate Bob Perry was killed while practicing for the 100-mile race, and the team withdrew. A false legend had grown, that president Ignatz Schwinn immediately destroyed the bikes with a hammer. A couple of riders raced these motorcycles at lesser events, before the machines passed from public view. (SAM ARENA)

Mid-1920 through 1924 electrical layout. The separate magneto and belt-driven generator came on the scene as mid-1920 changes.

(EXCELSIOR SALES LITERATURE)

1924 Excelsior details. From the catalog, "Details of the clutch mounting and operating mechanism."

(EXCELSIOR SALES LITERATURE)

The 1924 Excelsior brake. The new stopper had increased surface area, and was claimed less likely to lock the rear wheel with consequent sudden drop-off of braking effectiveness.

(EXCELSIOR SALES LITERATURE)

1924 Excelsior front hub. From the catalog: "Lubricant is retained and dirt and water excluded by the positive sealing glands of the new Timken Hubs."

(EXCELSIOR SALES LITERATURE)

1924 Excelsior details. From the catalog, "Mounting of the Excelsior power plant in the frame and details of clutch, drive chain, and generator drive housings."

(EXCELSIOR SALES LITERATURE)

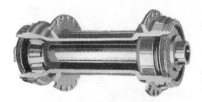

1924 Excelsior rear hub. From the catalog: "The new Timken Rear Hub. The roller bearings are interchangeable and of standard size obtainable anywhere."

(EXCELSIOR SALES LITERATURE)

1924 Excelsior. A final look at the final big Excelsior twin. The 60.9-cubic inch (998cc) F-head twin was replaced in 1925 by a 45.5-cubic inch (746cc) side-valve (Flathead) twin that was branded "Super-X." The Super-X is treated as a separate marque later in this book. (EXCELSIOR SALES LITERATURE)

FIELBACH LIMITED

Fielbach Limited motorcycles were also termed "Limited," which was the name on the tank. These were manufactured in Milwaukee, Wisconsin, from 1913 through 1915. Singles, and V-twins with either chain-drive or shaft-drive were offered.

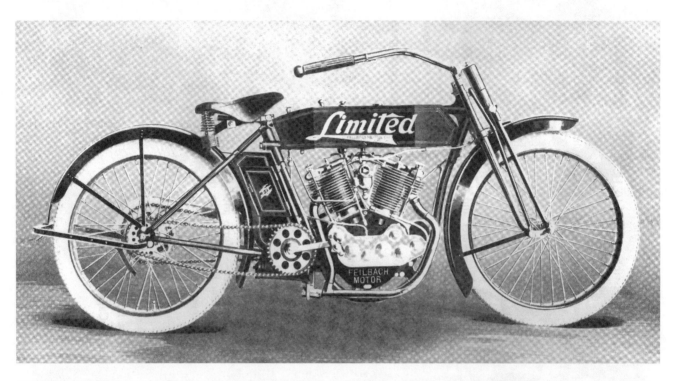

1914 Fielbach Limited Twin. Specifications: road clearance, 5 inches; brake, band operated by foot from footboards; handlebars, extra long with Rough Rider grips; saddle, Troxel; wheels/tires, 28 x 3 inches; tanks, fuel 2 gallons, oil, 1 gallon; wheelbase, 60 inches; weight, 285 lbs.; finish, Royal Coach Blue with white striping. (BRUCE LINSDAY)

1914 Fielbach Limited engine. Specifications: two-cylinder F-head with separate gear-driven camshafts for front and rear cylinders; bore and stroke, 36 5/16 x 4 inches; displacement, 68.9 cubic inches (1130cc); lubrication, splash automatic (total loss) with auxiliary hand pump; ignition, Berling magneto. (BRUCE LINSDAY)

1914 Fielbach Limited chain-drive twin. This is the single-speed model. The price was $275. (BRUCE LINSDAY)

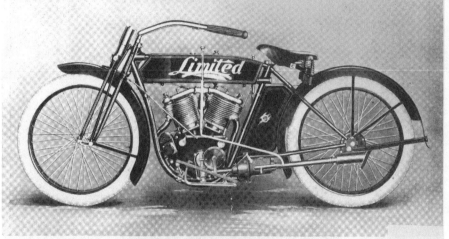

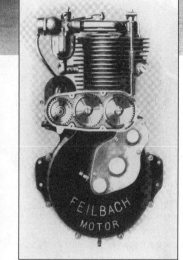

1914 Fielbach Limited single-cylinder engine. The single-cylinder chain-drive single-speed model was priced at $225. (BRUCE LINSDAY)

1914 Fielbach Limited shaft-drive twin. The fore-and-aft gearbox was worm driven, transmitting power through a two-speed sliding-gear setup, and the driveshaft drove the rear wheel through worm gears. Price: $310. (BRUCE LINSDAY)

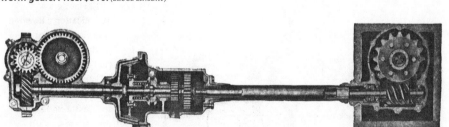

1914 Fielbach Limited transmission system. (MOTORCYCLE ILLUSTRATED)

1914 Fielbach Limited single-cylinder engine. (BRUCE LINSDAY)

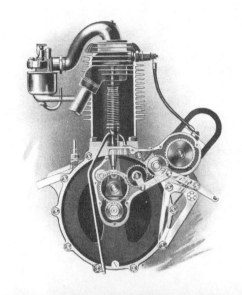

1912 Flanders 4
engine. Specifications:
F-head single-cylinder
engine, bore and stroke
of 3.25 x 3.6 inches,
displacement of 29.86
cubic inches (489cc);
carburetor, Schebler
Model H. Automatic
(suction operated) inlet
valve; Splitdorf
magneto.
(BRUCE LINSDAY)

FLANDERS

From 1910 through 1912 Flanders motorcycles were built in Pontiac, Michigan.
Production moved to Detroit for 1913 and
1914, then ceased. Through 1913, only typical F-head singles were built. For the 1914
season, a side-valve (Flathead) V-twin was
offered. Indian's first side-valve V-twin was
two years away, and Harley-Davidson's first
side-valve twin was five years distant. But
the Flanders company wasn't able to secure
sufficient dealers and orders with its "off
brand" motorcycles that offered nothing
else new.

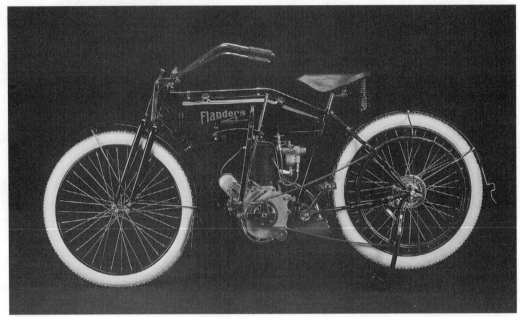

1912 Flanders 4, the
number referring to the
maximum rated output
of 4 hp. These were
conservatively designed
motorcycles featuring
the era's most typical
features: F-head engine
and single-speed belt
drive. (DOUG MITCHEL)

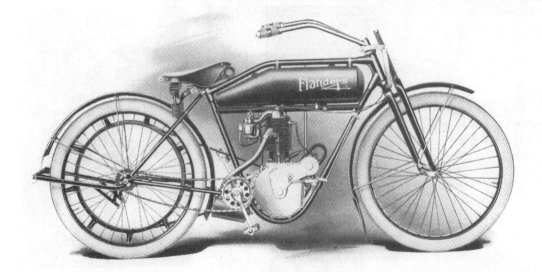

1912 Flanders 4.
Specifications: Bowden
wire controls, flat
leather belt drive, 2-gal.
fuel capacity, 2 1/2-quart
oil capacity, double-
spring (leading link)
fork, extra-wide
mudguards.
(BRUCE LINSDAY)

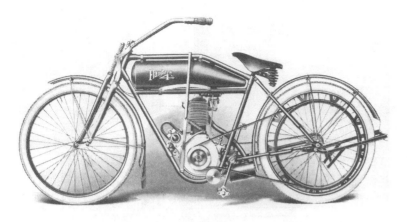

1912 Flanders 4. Standard tires were 2 1/2 inches; for $3 extra, 2 3/4-inch tires could be fitted. The retail price of $165 was appealing, but the company was unable to "buy into" the market. Dealer markup may have been insufficient. (BRUCE LINSDAY)

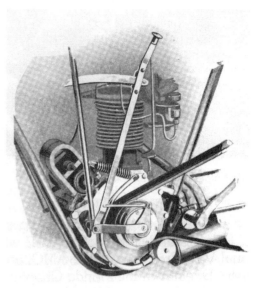

1912 Flanders 4. Typical idler pulley belt-slipping arrangement. (BRUCE LINSDAY)

1914 Flanders 4. The appearance was tidied up for 1914 by the fuel tank front being sloped to parallel the front frame down tube.

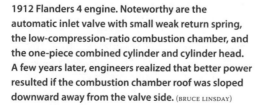

1912 Flanders 4 engine. Noteworthy are the automatic inlet valve with small weak return spring, the low-compression-ratio combustion chamber, and the one-piece combined cylinder and cylinder head. A few years later, engineers realized that better power resulted if the combustion chamber roof was sloped downward away from the valve side. (BRUCE LINSDAY)

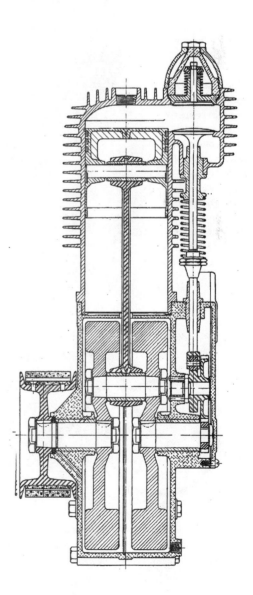

1914 Flanders "7-9" Twin. The fully enclosed drive chain prevented grime from accumulating, but the enclosure was likely considered unattractive by riders. The single-speed layout was a bad choice, as Indian, Harley-Davidson and Excelsior were all offering two-speeders, and in 1915 each would offer three-speeders. The $210 price was attractive, but proved insufficient for the company to firmly establish itself. (BRUCE LINSDAY)

1914 Flanders "7-9" Twin engine. Specifications: side-valve (Flathead) V-twin; "...enclosed valve springs and tappets, one cam to operate intake and exhaust valves, direct chain drive, transmission (chain) entirely enclosed, both valves in motor head, separate valve lift lever." Engine size was likely 61 cubic inches (1000cc). (BRUCE LINSDAY)

Circa 1902 Fleming. No information is available. (JIM DENNIE)

FLEMING

Filed in a period enthusiast's scrapbook was the following picture of the Fleming motorcycle. No information was on file.

FREYER AND MILLER

This was the first American motorcycle with magneto ignition. From *The Dealer and Repairman*, April, 1902: "Freyer and Miller of Columbus, Ohio, showed at the recent Chicago automobile exhibition for the first time a motor bicycle whose ignition apparatus is of the hammer break spark type, actuated by a magneto instead of with batteries. The machine is further unique in having not only a built-in crank casing (author: i.e., the crankcase was part of the frame), but a reducing gear in the crank box, so that the chain speed, and hence chance of chain breaking, is reduced." As no subsequent mention of the marque has been found, Freyer and Miller motorcycle production was brief.

1902 Freyer and Miller. From *The Dealer and Repairman*, April, 1902: "The motor does not have a single-lever control, but the two controlling levers (throttle and ignition timing levers) are both on the handlebar." (JIM DENNIE)

GEER

The Harry R. Geer Company of St. Louis, Missouri, operated from 1902 through 1911 as a mail order house. At first offering other marques under their own labels, around 1904 Geer began putting his name on the various makes of motorcycles that he purchased wholesale from manufacturers. Geer also sold almost all the components a buyer would require to assemble a motorcycle: carburetors, engines, engine blue prints, engine component castings, forks, frames, ignition breaker points, ignition coils, mufflers, wheel hubs and wheel rims. The Geer catalog didn't list batteries.

Circa 1904 Geer Blue Bird. This was a re-branded Mitchell. Specifications: "Engine, Geer, No. 2, 4 hp. Fork, Blue Bird type. Tires, G & J, 28 inch by 2 inch, detachable or Good rich. Coils, Dow or American. Carburetor, Kingston or Schebler. Saddle, Messenger type. Enamel, Blue Bird blue. Weight 140 lbs. Price, $200. (THE ANTIQUE MOTORCYCLE)

Circa 1904 Geer Green Egg. This was a re-branded Hercules. Specifications: F-head "5 hp, Geer double cylinder; width of crankcase, 4 inches; overall, 6 inches; height, 16 inches; bore of cylinders, 3 inches; stroke, 3 inches;" displacement, 42.4 cubic inches (695cc). "Speed, 300 to 3,500 revolutions per minute." There were two camshafts, one in front of the front cylinder and the other in back of the rear cylinder. The bikes were Enamel, Green Egg green, or black with red tanks." (THE ANTIQUE MOTORCYCLE)

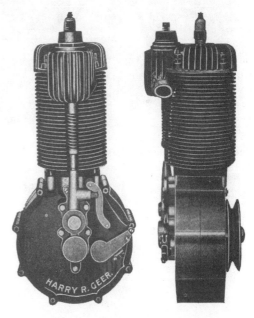

Circa 1904 Geer Model 4. The manufacturer of this Geer is not certain, but the motorcycle appears to be a re-branded Reliance. A rated 2 1/2 hp suggests a displacement of about 21 cubic inches (about 350cc). Weight was 125 lbs. Price was $150.

(THE ANTIQUE MOTORCYCLE)

Circa 1904 Geer 4-brake hp engine. The Geer company sold separately all the components a buyer would need to assemble a motorcycle. Bore and stroke, 3 1/2 x 4 inches; displacement, 38.48 cubic inches (631cc). According to the company, it was the "lightest engine on earth, considering its power. Air-cooled; weight, 61 lbs." (THE ANTIQUE MOTORCYCLE)

Circa 1904 Geer frame No. 301.

(THE ANTIQUE MOTORCYCLE)

Circa 1904 Geer Engine No. 2 castings, 4 hp.

(THE ANTIQUE MOTORCYCLE)

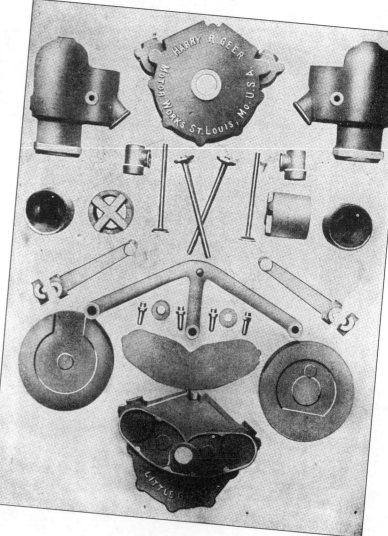

Circa 1904 Geer 5-hp water-cooled double-cylinder engine castings.

(THE ANTIQUE MOTORCYCLE)

GERE

Shown here is a circa 1902 Gere, built in Grand Rapids, Michigan. The illustration is from a period enthusiast's scrapbook. No other information is available.

GERHART

The Gerhart was an overhead-valve four-cylinder motorcycle offered in 1915 by the Gerhart Motor Cycle Company of Harrisburg, Pennsylvania. Only three illustrations have surfaced in the American antique movement. As no further illustrations or verbiage has been found past early 1915, and no Gerhart motorcycles have surfaced in the American movement, the marque probably didn't go beyond the prototype stage.

GREYHOUND

Greyhound motorcycles were built from 1907 through 1914 by the Greyhound Motor Company of Buffalo, New York. This firm was simply a name change for the old Thomas Auto-Bi company, which had built one of America's earliest commercially produced motorcycles. "Greyhound" was the new name for the pioneer company's motorcycles; originally, these had been termed "Auto-Bi," "Thomas Auto-Bi," or "Thomas."

Circa 1902 Gere. No information is available except manufacturer's city, Grand Rapids, Michigan. (JIM DENNIE)

1915 Gerhart, first configuration. The overhead-valve four-cylinder layout was decades ahead of its time. Engine dimensions weren't provided, but the rated output of nine hp suggest 61 cubic inches (1000cc). At the front of the engine was a housing for the magneto. The crankcase material was a combination of aluminum and tungsten. The large plate on the right side of the crankcase could be removed for inspection and maintenance activities. The front fork was a leading link leaf spring unit, and there was no rear suspension. (GOLDEN AGE OF THE FOURS)

1915 Gerhart, second configuration. The design was updated to include footboards and a swinging arm rear suspension very much like that of Indians. On the left rear of the tank was the gear-shift lever for the two-speed transmission. An interlock prohibited gear shifting without the clutch being disengaged. Fuel and oil compartments held 2 3/4 gallons and 8 pints. Wheels were 28 inches in diameter, and were fitted with 3 inch tires from Goodyear, U. S., or Empire. The wheelbase was 63 inches, and the price was $325.

(MOTORCYCLE ILLUSTRATED)

1909 Greyhound Model 48. Specifications: F-head, one-piece cylinder and head; bore 3 1/4 inches, stroke 3 1/4 inches, displacement 26.96 cubic inches (442cc); tires 2 1/2 inch G & J; front fork Auto-Bi Patent Cushion Spring; wheelbase 56 inches; batteries, three No. 6 dry cells; transmission, Auto-Bi Patent chain and leather belt; carburetor, Auto-Bi or Breeze. (BRUCE LINSDAY)

HAFELFINGER

Almost unknown today is pioneer engine builder Emil Hafelfinger, who, in January, 1901, exhibited his motorcycle engine at the New York City motorcycle show. The significance of the design, and of the date, is that the famous original Indian engine was closely pattered after the Hafelfinger.

Hafelfinger engine. Emil Hafelfinger built his first motorcycle in 1900, and displayed this engine at the January, 1901, New York motorcycle show. The engine was obviously the inspirartion and probably the pattern for Oscar Hedstrom's original 1901 Indian engine. Hafelfinger advertised his engine for sale to would-be motorcycle builders. (THE ANTIQUE MOTORCYCLE)

Emil Hafelfinger also built a complete motorcycle, as depicted in this sketch, including "1900" label, appearing in an early motorcycle magazine. The machine was similar to the period Royal. That's because, as historian Stephen Wright uncovered, Hafelfinger took his engineering skills to that company. (GEORGE YAROCKI)

In some early historical accounts of Oscar Hedstrom building the first Indian, much was made of Hedstrom working in absolute secrecy. No wonder. Just compare the picture of the Hafelfinger engine with any picture of an early Indian single, or compare it to an actual early Indian engine, and you will see that the resemblance is too strong to be a coincidence. But even Hafelfinger was probably not breaking entirely new ground, for his engine was likely a scaled-down version of motoring's first practical power plant, the French De Dion engine. Hedstrom rolled out his Indian Number One in late May of 1901.

HAMPDEN

Another period scrapbook photo without information shows the Hampden. How to mount the carburetor? The quick and dirty solution was to secure it to the crankcase. Thus, the ridiculously long inlet manifold!

Circa 1902 Hampden. (JIM DENNIE)

HARLEY-DAVIDSON
1903-1929, The F-head Era

Harley-Davidson borrowed one good idea and spent more than 25 years making it better. That idea was the F-head engine, also known as the inlet-over-exhaust, or i.o.e. engine. Outside the United States, motorcycle companies either gave up on F-heads, like Norton in 1911 and Rudge in 1924, or never even built them, like Triumph. The Isle of Man Tourist Trophy (T.T.) race was an international technical barometer. The last F-head T.T. victory was won by a Rudge in 1914.

Emerging as a prototype in 1903, and in true production in 1904, the first Harley-Davidsons had F-head engines that were typical except in one respect: Harley engines were larger than competitors' engines. That remained the case for several years. Novelty in the earliest Harleys was confined to the single-loop frame, designed purely for motorcycle use, as opposed to competitors' frames, which were beefed-up pedal bike frames. So, Harley-Davidson entered the field with the right combination, allowing it to evolve through detailed improvements in power, reliability and sophistication. Other companies wasted time and money in the wrong combinations before joining the mainstream that Harley-Davidson had pioneered.

After a decade of Harley production, some American motorcycle manufacturers tried to establish and grow by starting off with the latest technical features, like overhead-valve and overhead-cam engines. Though technically interesting, these innovative motorcycles were being offered by firms that were too far behind Harley-Davidson, Indian and Excelsior—the "Big Three." Rivals of the Big Three were too far behind in financing, too far behind in setting up large efficient factories, too far behind in the gradual process of building large dealer networks, and too far behind in gaining customer confidence.

The ultimate F-heads were the Two-Cam road models of the 1928 and 1929 seasons. These stock motorcycles would run in the high 80s (mph), and in the hands of adept dealers or rider-tuners, the bikes would run over 100. Harley-Davidson built other engine types in the 1903-1929 era, most having some degree of success, but it was the F-heads that put Harley on the map and helped the company become, by the early 1920s, the largest motorcycle manufacturer in the world.

Harley-Davidson stuck with the F-head formula as long as it could. While the Harley F-head parade marched on, the interna-

tional motorcycle world went through two changes, to side-valve (flat-head) engine in the mid 1910s, and to overhead-valve engines in the mid-1920s. Critics thought Harley's F-head adherence stubborn and unimaginative, but the critics were wrong. The F-head layout proved to have far more potential than was recognized anywhere outside the factories of Harley-Davidson and Excelsior. In walking down the apparently easy technical path—it wasn't actually easy—Harley-Davidson was able to concentrate on a continuous series of technical improvements—details piled upon details. These details that made Harleys go faster, run longer and sell better.

Equally important, the company realized, and practiced, the principle that dealers and riders wanted the whole "package," not just trendy motorcycles. The whole package meant prosperous dealers with good shops and ample spare parts, fast shipments of repair items not in stock, and the selling of a life-style through dealer-supported clubs. Sustaining the F-head range, helped prove the point to the factory and to the dealers.

The F-head remained Harley-Davidson's weapon of choice until the company was certain the F-heads had reached the limit. That certainty arrived in the engineering department around 1927, and on the show room floors in 1929 and 1930 with the arrival, respectively, of new side-valve middleweight and heavyweight V-twins. Considering that more than 100 American motorcycle companies went bust between 1900 and 1920, while Harley-Davidson was selling F-heads, these are arguably the most important motorcycles the company ever built.

1903 - 1908 Highlights

All models in this era featured a single-speed belt drive. 1907 brought the first front suspension, the long-running leading-link parallelogram fork. 1903-1908: Harley-Davidson Carburetors. 1908: carburetor options, Harley-Davidson or Schebler units.

Year	Model	Engine Data	New Features, Misc.	Cost
1903	first single	10.2 ci (167cc)	—	—
1903	second single	24.7 ci, (405cc)	11" flywheels, production prototype, top speed 35 mph, 178 lbs.	—
1904	single	24.7 ci, (405cc)	top speed 35 mph, 178 lbs.	—
1905	1 single	26.8 ci, (440cc)	top speed 35 mph, larger motor, 178 lbs.	—
1906	2 single	26.8 ci, (440cc)	optional hand crank, improved twist-grip, top speed 40 mph, 225 lbs.	$210
1907	3 single	26.8 ci, (440cc)	front suspension, leading link, top speed: 40 mph, 225 lbs.	$210
1908	4 single	26.8 ci, (440cc)	Removable valve stem steel cap, clearance adjusted by replacing and/or grinding cap, top speed: 40 mph, 225 lbs.	$210

1905 Harley-Davidson Model 1. The factory considered this the first production model, thus the designation "1." This example has been restored without striping. (DOUG MITCHEL)

1905 Harley-Davidson Model 1. From the beginning, Harleys were ahead of the game in two ways: motorcycle-specific loop frame was used instead of a beefed-up pedal-bike style frame, and Harley engines were larger than average. (DOUG MITCHEL)

Years	Models	Key Feature(s)	Engine Data	New Features, Misc.	Cost
1909-11	5, 6, 7	batt. ignition, 28" wheels	single, 30.2 ci (494cc)	Weight: 235 lbs., top speed: 45 mph	$210, $210, $225
1909-11	5A, 6A, 7A	magneto, 28" wheels	single, 30.2 ci (494cc)	Weight: 235 lbs., top speed: 45 mph	$250, $250, $250
1909-11	5B, 6B, 7B	batt. ignition, 26" wheels	single, 30.2 ci (494cc)	Weight: 235 lbs., top speed: 45 mph	$210, $210, $225
1909-11	5C, 6C, 7C	magneto, 26" wheels	single, 30.2 ci (494cc)	Weight: 235 lbs., top speed: 45 mph	$250, $250, $250
1909	5D	magneto	twin, 49.5 ci (811cc)	Automatic inlet valves, no belt slipping mechanism, weight (est.): 275 lbs., top speed 45 mph	$325
1910	6E	magneto "Stock Racer"	NA	NA	$275
1911	7D	magneto, 28" wheels	twin, (811cc)	Mechanical inlet valves, belt slipping mechanism, top speed 55 mph	$300

1910 Harley-Davidson Model 6. Displacement grew to 30.16 cubic inches (494cc) in 1909, which also saw the introduction of control by wires instead of rods and chains. (DOUG MITCHEL)

1905 Harley-Davidson Model 1 Specifications

Engine, F-head single-cylinder; bore and stroke, 3 1/8 x 3 1/2 inches; displacement, 28.84 cubic inches (440cc); compression ratio, 4:1 (estimated); maximum output, not specified. Transmission, single-speed; 1 1/4-inch belt; final drive, none. Brake, hub (rear only), activated by backward pedal pressure like an ordinary bicycle. Ignition, standard battery and coil. Frame, single loop, single down-tube. Suspension, "Sager" spring fork. Wheelbase, 51 inches. Weight, 185 lbs. (estimated). Fuel tank, 1 1/2 gal-lons. Oil compartment, 2 quarts. Tires, 28 x 2 1/4 inches. Finish: Renault gray with red double pinstriping; piano-finish black, ex-tra-cost option.

1909 -1911 Highlights

"5" Signifies 1909; "6" signifies 1910; "7" sig-nifies 1911. 1909: engine enlarged and wire control replaced rods and chains. Single-speed belt drive on all 1909, 1910, and 1911 Models. 1 1/4-inch belt on 1909 models; 1 3/4-inch belt on 1910 and 1911 models. On 1911 models, frame front down-tube changed from curved to straight. 1909: carburetor options, Harley-Davidson or Schebler unit. 1910-1932: Schebler carburetors.

1913-1917 Single-cylinder Specifications

The big singles, amounting to V-twins minus a rear cylinder, were offered through 1917, selling in dwindling numbers primarily for commercial use. For 1913, the bore remained 3 5/16 inches, while the stroke was increased from 3 1/2 inches to 4 inches, yielding a displacement of 34.47 cubic inches (565cc). These remained the engine dimensions for the duration of these models. Since the singles used the same frame and running gear as the V-twins, for other data refer to the applicable year of V-twin specifications.

1913 Highlights

All models fitted with magneto ignition and "free wheel" (clutch) rear hub.

The 1910 Harley-Davidson.
(DALE WALKSLER)

1911 Harley-Davidson Model 7A. This was the first year for vertical cooling fins on the cylinder head, for a straight frame front down-tube, and for broad tank striping. Apparently, the factory produced the striping in one or more of the following hues: gray, blue-gray, and dark blue. The $250 Model 7A was defined by magneto ignition and 28 x 2 1/2-inch tires. The $225 Model 7 had 28 x 2 1/2-inch tires and battery ignition. The $225 Model 7B had 26 x 2 1/2-inch tires and battery ignition. The $250 Model 7C had 26 x 2 1/2-inch tires. All were cited as 4-hp machines.

(DOUG MITCHEL)

1910 Harley-Davidson. From the beginning through 1929, the company built mainly inlet-over-exhaust, or F-head, engines. The inlet valve is directly over the exhaust valve. Inlet-valve action was automatic; on the inlet stroke the downward moving piston sucked the valve open; on the compression and power strokes the cylinder pressure closed the inlet valve. The exhaust valve was operated by the exposed valve spring. (DALE WALKSLER)

1910 Harley-Davidson. The long lever acts as a sort of clutch control by raising or lowering the idler pulley, thus tightening or loosening the drive belt. This motorcycle and others citing Dale Walksler's assistance are from Dale's Wheels Through Time Museum. (DALE WALKSLER)

1912 HIGHLIGHTS

All models with Ful-Floating Seat (spring seat post) and free-wheel (clutch) rear hub. First year chain drive offered.

1912 Models	Key Feature(s)	Engine Data	New Features, Misc.	Cost
8	batt. ignition	30.2 ci (494cc)	single-speed belt drive, weight: 235 lbs., top speed: 45 mph	$200
X8	batt. ignition, free wheel (clutch)	30.2 ci (494cc)	single-speed belt drive, weight: 235 lbs., top speed: 45 mph	$210
8A	magneto	30.2 ci (494cc)	single-speed belt drive, weight: 235 lbs. top speed: 45 mph	$225
X8A	magneto, free wheel (clutch)	30.2 ci (494cc)	single-speed belt drive, weight: 235 lbs., top speed :45 mph	$235
8D	magneto	49.5 ci (811cc)	single-speed belt drive, weight: 235 lbs., top speed: 50 mph	$275
X8D	magneto, free wheel (clutch)	49.5 ci (811cc)	single-speed belt drive, weight: 235 lbs., top speed: 50 mph	$285
X8E	magneto, free wheel (clutch)	60.3 ci (989cc)	first chain-drive HD, weight: (est.) 275 lbs., top speed: 60 mph	$285

1912 Harley-Davidson Model 8-A. The bicycle look began to ebb away with the new frame that had a sloping top tube near the saddle. This was also the first year for seat-post saddle suspension. (DOUG MITCHEL)

1914 Highlights

All models fitted with magneto ignition. New features on all models: enclosed exhaust valve springs, step starter, foot boards, padded front chain guard (to reduce noise) and tapered cylinder bores. First year two-speed transmission offered. Last year belt drive offered in the era (returned in 1980).

1911-1914 V-Twin Specifications

1911 engine: F-head; bore and stroke, 3 x 3 1/2 inches; displacement, 49.48 cubic inches (811cc); maximum output, 6 1/2 hp. 1912 engines: F-head, optional. 49.48 cubic inch, or 60.32-cubic inch (988cc) with bore and stroke of 3 5/16 x 3 1/2 inches, and maximum output of "7 to 8" hp. 1913-1914 engine: F-head, 60.32-cubic inch size only; maximum output; 8 hp. Transmission, 1911: belt-drive single-speed. Transmission, 1912: belt-drive single-speed or chain-drive single-speed with "free engine" control (clutch), and single-row chain primary drive. Transmission, 1913: chain-

1912 Harley-Davidson Model 8-A. The long hand lever and serrated lever gate were used from 1911 through 1914 on belt-drive models. On 1911 models, the lever adjusted drive-belt tension, in effect performing as a clutch. On 1912-1914 models, the belt pulley was independent of the rear wheel, and clutch action was through a "free wheel" device inside the rear hub. (DOUG MITCHEL)

1913 Models	Key Feature(s)	Engine Data	New Features, Misc.	Cost
9A	5-35 engine, magneto	single, 34.5 ci (565cc), 5-35 = 5 hp from 35 ci	larger engine, single-speed belt drive, weight: 245 lbs. , top speed: 50 mph	$290
9B	5-35 engine, magneto	single, 34.5 ci (565cc), 5-35 = 5 hp from 35 ci	Larger engine, single-speed chain drive, weight: 245 lbs. , top speed: 50 mph	$290
9E	magneto	twin, 60.3 ci (989cc)	Single-speed chain drive, weight: 275 lbs., top speed: 60 mph	$350

drive single-speed with free engine, and single-row chain primary drive. Transmission, 1914: chain-drive (single-row chain primary drive) single-speed (free engine) or hand-shifted two-speed rear hub (single-row chain primary drive). Ignition, 1911-1914, magneto. Brake (rear only), external contracting band. Frame, single loop, single down-tube. Suspension, leading link. Wheelbase, 59 1/2 inches. Weight, empty, 340-360 lbs., (depending on equipment). Fuel tank, 1.88 gallons. Oil compartment, 5/8 gallons. Tires, 28 x 3 inches. Finish, light gray with dark gray or blue stripe edged in red, centered in gold.

1913 Harley-Davidson Model 9B. Mechanical inlet valves were first used on the 1913 models. The inlet push rod exits the timing case! All 1913 Harleys were fitted with magneto ignition. (PERIOD POSTCARD)

1913 Model 9B. For 1913, the stroke of the single was increased from 3 1/2 inches to 4 inches, and with the continued 3 5/16-inch bore, this increased the displacement to 34.47 cubic inches (565cc). These singles were termed the "5-35," it being a point of pride that a 5-hp output was obtained from a 35-cubic inch engine. Harley-Davidson engines remained larger than those of most competitors. (DOUG MITCHEL)

1913 Harley-Davidson. Win a trivia bet: the famous "Two-Cam" V-twin racers arrived in 1919, and "Two-Cam" roadster V-twins in 1928. But this 1913 single uses the two-cam principle! It was easier to redesign the timing cover to include the push-rod guide than to redesign the right crankcase. An exhaust whistle is connected to the exhaust pipe.

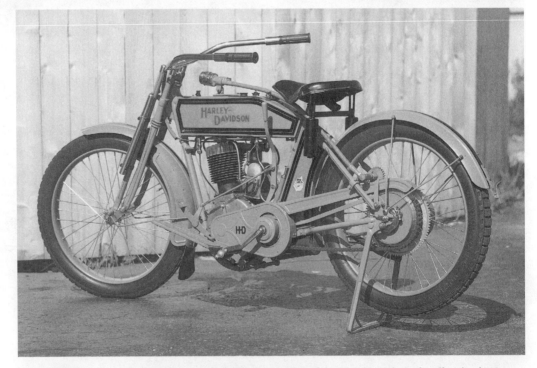

1914 Harley-Davidson Model 10C. This was the two-speed version of the 35-cubic inch single, offered at $245. Other singles were: the $200 10A 35-cubic inch belt drive, and the $210 10B 35-cubic inch single-speed chain drive. The 1911-1914 twins had a separate oil tank beneath the saddle. (DOUG MITCHEL)

1914 Harley-Davidson. In 1914 and 1915, the company offered a two-speed transmission. The small shift-lever is seen atop the tank. The water tank for the acetylene lighting is secured to the handlebars. The motorcycle is from Dale Walksler's Wheels Through Time Museum. Such unrestored machines are considered the ultimate collector bikes.

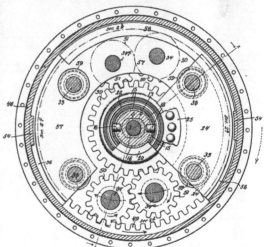

A patent drawing of two-speed rear hub submitted by William S. Harley. The patent became effective on December 20, 1910. (UNITED STATE PATENT OFFICE)

1914 Harley-Davidson Model 10C. The two-speed transmission was contained within the rear hub. This was a so-called planetary unit with a central "sun" gear, several small "planet" gears meshing with the sun gear, and a large ring gear surrounding and meshing with the planet gears. The planet gears were linked by a common support structure, the "hub." With the low-ratio (high engine speed, low road speed) selected, the planet gears spun freely and the gear-ratio within the hub was the ratio of the number of teeth on the ring gear to the number of teeth on the sun gear.

(DOUG MITCHEL)

Here, Dale Walksler is simulating squirting fuel through a primer cup and into the cylinder. This was the procedure for very cold weather. The purpose was not to enrich the mixture, but to loosen up the oil in the cylinder and on the piston. When not in use, the syringe was screwed back into the filler cap in the oil tank. The tank, not shown, is under the saddle.

(DALE WALKSLER)

Models	Key Feature(s)	Engine Data	New Features, Misc.	Cost
10A	5-35 engine, single-speed belt drive	34.5 ci (565cc) single	Last belt-drive HD, weight: 245 lbs., top speed: 50 mph	$200
10B	5-35 engine, single-speed chain drive	34.5 ci (565cc) single	Weight: 245 lbs., top speed: 50 mph	$210
10C	5-35 engine, two-speed chain drive	34.5 ci (565cc) single	First year of two-speed, weight: 255 lbs., top speed: 50 mph	$245
10E	Single-speed chain drive	60.3 ci (989cc) twin	Weight: 275 lbs., top speed: 60 mph	$250
10F	Two-speed chain drive	60.3 ci (989cc) twin	First year of two-speed, weight: 285 lbs., top speed: 60 mph	$285

1914 Harley-Davidson. Another 1914 Harley from the Walksler collection. The speedometer is labeled "Stewart-Warner Police Special." Beginning with the 1914 models, Harley-Davidson taper-bored cylinders and fit round pistons. The bore, rather than the piston, was designed to "round out" under heat stress. This practice, unique in motorcycling, would be continued through 1934.

(DALE WALKSLER)

1915

Models	Key Feature(s)	Engine Data	New Features, Misc.	Cost
11B	single-speed	34.5 ci (565cc) single	Weight: 245 lbs., top speed: 50 mph	$200
11C	two-speed	34.5 ci (565cc) single	Weight: 255 lbs., top speed: 50 mph	$230
11E	single-speed	60.3 ci (989cc) twin	Weight: 285 lbs., top speed: 60 mph	$240
11F	three-speed	60.3 ci (989cc) twin	Weight: 295 lbs., top speed: 60 mph	$275
11H	single-speed, electric lights	60.3 ci (989cc) twin	Weight: 305 lbs., top speed: 60 mph	$275
11J	three-speed, electric lights	60.3 ci (989cc) twin	Weight: 325 lbs., top speed: 60 mph	$310
11K	single-speed, "close-coupled," "stripped stock," production racer	60.3 ci (989cc) twin	—	$250

1915 Harley-Davidson Model 11F. Harley-Davidson, Indian, and Excelsior all launched their first three-speeders for the 1915 season. New cylinders with larger valves, larger inlet ports, and a new inlet manifold, increased power. The company boasted that it was the only one to guarantee a horsepower rating—11 hp on the twins—but added that dynamometer tests showed output as high as 16.7 hp. (DOUG MITCHEL)

1915 Highlights

All models fitted with chain drive. First year three-speed transmission offered. First year electric lights offered. Last year of two-speed models.

1915-1920 V-twin Specifications

Engine, F-head V-twin; bore and stroke of 3 5/16 x 3 1/2 inches; displacement, 60.32 cubic inches (988cc). Maximum output: 1915, 11 hp guaranteed, up to 16.5 hp on dynamometer tests; 1920, 16 hp. Changes in 1915: inlet valves cited as larger than previous (no dimensions provided); new four-row connecting rod big end bearings were 1 3/4-inch wide (previously, 1 3/8-inch); en-gine-driven oil pump (1915-1922) replaced drip-feed oil delivery; oil pump body integral with timing case cover. Transmission, chain-drive single-speed (with free engine) or three-speed counter-shaft layout (i.e., frame mounted), with hand-shift; primary drive, single-row chain. Brake (rear only), external contracting band. Ignition, magneto or battery (electrical models). Frame, single loop, single down tube. Suspension, leading link. Wheelbase, not specified. Weight, empty: stripped models, 370 lbs.; electric-lighting models, 398 lbs. Fuel tank, 2.75 gallons. Oil compartment, 1.25 quarts. Tires, 28 x 3 inches. Finish, 1915-1916, gray; 1917-1920, olive drab.

1915 Model 11F engine (at right). The company claimed a 31-percent power boost at 2500 rpm, and a 47-percent boost at 3000 rpm. With the new three-speed box and electric lighting, the F-head general concept was complete. The next 14 years, through 1929, would be years of refinements. (DOUG MITCHEL)

1916-1918 Highlights

1916: First year that the model numbers are the same as the model year, new tanks were curved along the edges instead of slab-sided, wider front fork and wider fenders, and singles used the same basic frame as twins. 1917-1927 road model twins: four cam lobes on one shaft. 1917: early-season models in gray with polished crankcases & unpainted trans. case; late-season models in olive drab with painted crankcases and trans. case.

1916 Harley-Davidson Model J. All 1916 models featured larger filler caps. On 1916 electric-lights models, the toolbox was relocated to the top of the tank. Behind the box, is the auxiliary oil hand-pump, for use in extreme conditions such as mud, sand, hill climbing, or prolonged high speed. Otherwise, the one-way oil pump metered the oil for average all-around conditions, typically over-oiling at slow speed and under-oiling at high speeds. (DOUG MITCHEL)

Typical F-head cylinder. There may have been significant foundry rejection rates on these complicated castings. Harley-Davidson F-head cylinders were cast with a non-removable head. This complicated periodic removal of carbon deposits, as recommended by the factory. However, these cylinders had the virtues of never blowing a head gasket and never leaking oil between head and cylinder.

1916 Harley-Davidson Model J and sidecar. The 1916 frame was reinforced below the steering head to better withstand sidecar stresses. The frames of singles and twins were standardized to reduce manufacturing costs. The front fork was wider, and there was more room between the fenders and the tires. Fender width was increased from 4½ inches to 5½ inches. More graceful gas tanks with rounded edges replaced the slab-sided tanks.

(DOUG MITCHEL)

Models	Key Feature(s)	Engine Data	New Features, Misc.	Cost
16B, 17B, 18B	single-speed	34.5 ci (565cc) single	Weight: 245 lbs., top speed: 50 mph	$200, $215, $235
16C, 17C, 18C	three-speed	34.5 ci (565cc) single	Weight: 265 lbs., top speed: 50 mph	$230, $240, $260
16E, 17E, 18E	single-speed	60.3 ci (989cc) twin	Weight: 285 lbs., top speed 1916 & 1917: 60 mph, top speed 1918: 65 mph	$240, $255, $275
16F, 17F, 18F	three-speed	60.3 ci (989cc) twin	Weight: 305 lbs., top speed, 1916 & 1917: 60 mph, top speed 1918: 65 mph	$265, $275, $290
16J, 17J, 18J	three-speed, electric lights	60.3 ci (989cc) twin	Weight: 325 lbs., top speed, 1916 & 1917: 60 mph, top speed 1918: 65 mph	$295, $310, $320
17R	"Speed Roadster"	60.3 ci (989cc) twin	—	$280
17S	single-speed "Stripped Stock Racer"	30.2 ci (494cc) single	—	$225
17T	single-speed "Stripped Stock Racer"	60.3 ci (989cc) twin	—	$280

1916 Harley-Davidson Model J. Engine, F-head V-twin, displacement 60.3 cubic inches (988cc); compression ratio (not specified); maximum output, 11 hp @ 3000 rpm. Transmission, three-speed hand shift; primary drive, single-row chain; final drive, chain. Brake (rear only), external contracting band. Ignition, magneto. Frame, single loop, single down-tube. Suspension, leading link. Wheelbase, not specified. Weight, 325 lbs. Fuel tank, 2.75 gallons. Oil compartment, 1.25 quarts. Tires, 28 x 3 inches. Finish, light gray with dark gray or blue stripe edged in red, centered in gold. (DOUG MITCHEL)

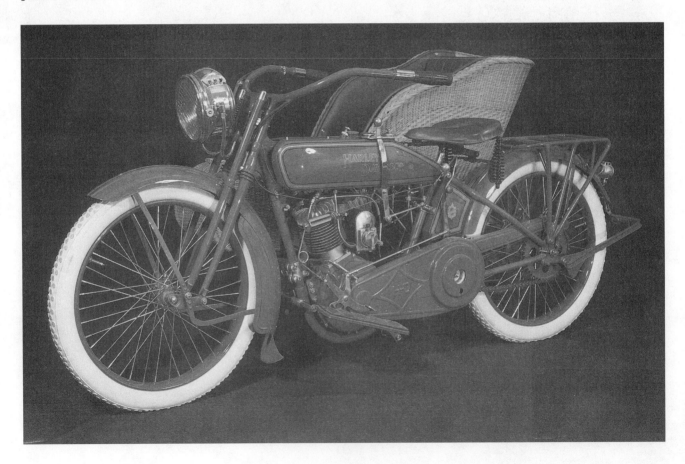

1917 Harley-Davidson Model 17F. Many fine restorations are finished with red striping, centered in gold, as shown in this and the following illustration. In the author's opinion, based on study of the factory photo collection of black and white prints, striping for 1917 through 1921 was Pullman Coach, a dark green, centered in black, edged in gold. (DOUG MITCHEL)

1917 Harley-Davidson Model C and wicker sidecar (at left). Engine, F-head single-cylinder; displacement: 34.47 cubic inches (565cc); compression ratio (estimated), 5:1; maximum output, 4 hp. Transmission, single-speed; primary drive belt; final drive, none. Wheelbase, 56.5 inches. Weight, 316 lbs. Fuel tank, 2.5 gallons. Oil compartment, 1 gallon. Tires, 28 x 2 1/2 inches. Price, $240. Finish, early-1917 model: Renault gray, with blue striping, edged in red, centered in gold, and polished crankcases. The finish on late-1917 models was olive drab. (DOUG MITCHEL)

1917 Harley-Davidson Model 17F. This year, the road models got the four-cam-lobe feature that had been used on racing engines. All four lobes were centered on a single camshaft. Because of the war in Europe, Bosch magnetos weren't available; Dixie magnetos were fitted instead. Other changes included increased valve clearances and increased valve overlap. (DOUG MITCHEL)

From the collection of the late John Cameron, comes this picture of an early 1917 8-valve racer. The timing cover appears the same as that of the road models. That's because the 1916-1918 eight-valves had the same single-camshaft layout as the standard models. "Half-twin" four-valve singles were also built, and were mainly used for half-mile dirt track racing that was popular in the Midwest. (JOHN CAMERON)

1919 Harley-Davidson Sport. Ironically, the Sport introduced features,that became the hallmarks of the long running Indian Scout series. These included: trailing link front fork, middle-sized side-valve (Flathead) engine, helical gear primary drive, and true unit construction of engine and transmission. Scouts were semi-unit, with separate engine and transmission, but bolted up as a single functioning power plant.

(DOUG MITCHEL)

1919 Harley-Davidson Sport. Among the user-friendly features were easy starting, exceptionally quiet operation, and silky smooth running. There was nothing cheesy about this middleweight, which surpassed the V-twins in technical sophistication (DOUG MITCHEL)

1919-1923 Models WF and WJ "Sport Specifications"

Engine: side-valve (Flathead) horizontally opposed twin; outside flywheel, bore and stroke, 2 3/4 x 3 inches; displacement, 35.6 cubic inches (584cc); compression ratio 3.75:1 (estimated); maximum output, 6 hp, rpm not specified. Transmission: three-speed hand-shift; helical-gear primary drive, chain final drive. Brake (rear only), external contracting band. Model WF Ignition, 1919, magneto. Ignition, 1920-1923, magneto in Model WF, battery in Model WJ. Electric lights on Model WJ only. Frame, keystone (engine as a stressed member), single down-tube. Suspension, trailing link. Wheelbase, 57 inches. Weight, 250 lbs. Tires, 26 x 3 inches. Ignition, Model WF, magneto; Model WJ, battery. Finish, 1919-1921, olive drab with Pullman coach (dark) green striping, centered in black, edged in gold. Finish, 1922-1923, Brewster (dark) green with double-line pinstriping.

1919 Harley-Davidson eight-valve racer. Note the timing case cover is different from the earlier view of a 1917 eight-valve. By 1919, these racing bikes were equipped with a two-cam valve operating system. (MOTORCYCLING AND BICYCLING)

1919 Harley-Davidson Sport. The Sport was a bold new concept. At 250 lbs., and with a wheelbase of 57 inches, the Sport was 70 lbs. lighter and 2 inches shorter than the V-twins. The idea was to appeal to people who were intimidated by the big V-twins. (DOUG MITCHEL)

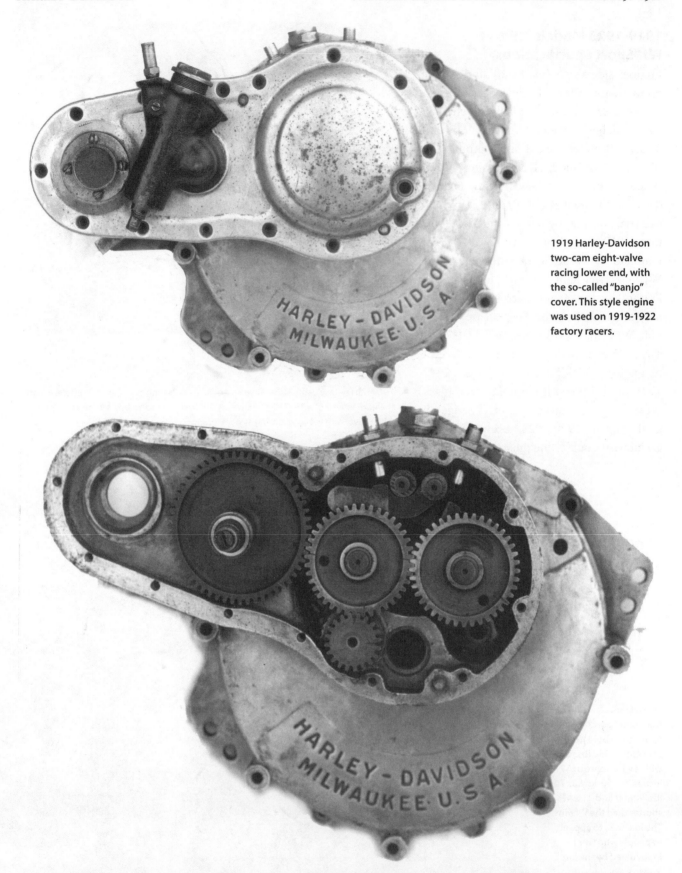

1919 Harley-Davidson two-cam eight-valve racing lower end, with the so-called "banjo" cover. This style engine was used on 1919-1922 factory racers.

1919 Harley-Davidson two-cam eight-valve racing engine. The two equal-sized gears are the cam gears, thus the term "two-cam." A two-lobe cam was driven by each gear, so there was a separate cam lobe for each cylinder's inlet valve and exhaust valve. The huge oil pump was driven at half the engine speed.

1919 Harley-Davidson two-cam eight-valve racing engine. Drilled connecting rods were the hot setup for racing. Even some early 1920s road models used drilled rods.

1919 Harley-Davidson two-cam eight-valve racing engine. The engine is oriented so that the rear is on the left side in the picture. Though this is a racing engine, the crankcase baffle system is typical of both roadsters and racers throughout Harley history. The closed-off portions at the base of the cylinders were termed "baffles." In this engine, the rear cylinder baffle is only on the rear side (nearest the magneto platform).

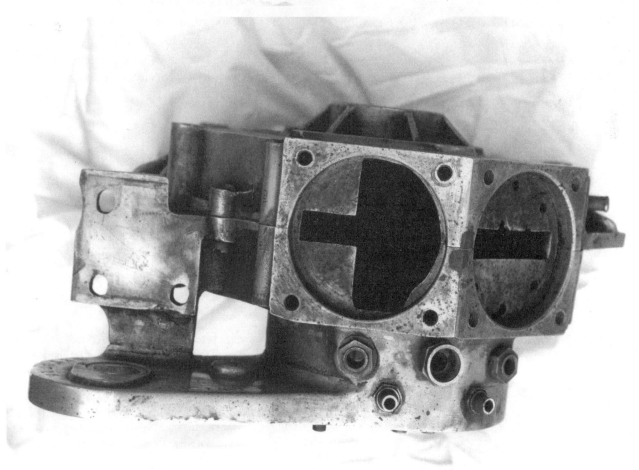

1920 Harley-Davidson Model (above). This was the last year of the "skinny" front fender without a valance forward of the front fork. (DOUG MITCHEL)

1919-1920 Highlights

1919: All models equipped with two-cylinder engine. 1919-1935: All models equipped with three-speed transmission. 1920: substantial V-twin engine redesign.

Circa 1920 Harley-Davidson hill climber. F-head construction is apparent in this unusual picture. From the 1910s through the 1930s, hill climbing rivaled flat track racing in popularity. All the motorcycle companies had factory-sponsored hill climb riders. The competitor is Doug Perkins, who, from the 1930s through the 1960s, sponsored several of the top Harley-Davidson racers on the national circuit.

(GEORGE YAROCKI)

1920 Harley-Davidson Model J Engine. New cylinders had a different fin pattern on the heads, and new inlet valve spring covers. The 1915-1922 oil pump consisted of an inclined slotted drum that was driven by a worm gear. At the base of the rotating vertical drum was a spiral cam that oscillated a spring-loaded vertical pumping piston. (DOUG MITCHEL)

Models	Key Feature(s)	Engine Data	New Features, Misc.	Cost
19F, 20F	magneto, regular engine	60.3 ci (989cc) twin	1920: new cylinders; new inlet pushrods	$359, $370
19FS, 20FS	magneto, sidecar engine	60.3 ci (989cc) twin	1920: new cylinders; new inlet pushrods	$350, $370
19J, 20J	battery ignition, regular engine, electric lights	60.3 ci (989cc) twin	1920: new cylinders; new inlet pushrods	$370, $395
19JS, 20JS	battery ignition, sidecar engine, electric lights	60.3 ci (989cc) twin	1920: new cylinders; new inlet pushrods	$370, $395
19W, 20W	magneto	35.6 ci (584cc), horizontally opposed side-valve twin, 35.6 ci (584cc)	—	$335, $335

1921-1923 Highlights

New for 1921: first 74 ci (1200cc) twins (both figures nominal); return of the large single; big twins termed the "Sixty-One" and "Seventy-Four;" solid (not spoked) flywheels on the "Seventy-Four." 1922 prices reduced 30 percent. 1922: color changed to Brewster (dark) Green with gold striping. 1923: price reduced 17 percent, big single eliminated.

1921, Other Matters

The V-twin front fender was given a full valance extending in front of the fork, whereas previous V-twin front fenders had a valance only in the rear half. The battery ignition Model JD "Seventy-Four" became the most popular Harley over the next nine years, leading to today's custom of referring to all 1921-1929 F-head twins as "Jay-Deez," except for the "Two-Cam" models of 1928 and 1929.

Models	Key Feature(s)	Engine Data	Cost
21CD, 22CD	single	36.8 ci (604cc)	$430, $315
21F, 22F, 23F	magneto, regular engine	60.3 ci (989cc) twin	$450, $335, $285
21FS, 22FS, 23FS	magneto, sidecar engine	60.3 ci (989cc) twin	$450, $335, $285
21FD, 22FD, 23FD	magneto, regular engine	73.7 ci (1207cc)	$485, $360, $310
21FDS, 22FDS, 23FDS	magneto, sidecar engine	73.7 ci (1207cc) twin	$485, $360, $310
21J, 22J, 23J	batt. ignition, electric lights, regular engine	60.3 ci (989cc) twin	$485, $365, $305
21JS, 22JS, 23JS	batt. ignition, electric lights, sidecar engine	60.3 ci (989cc) twin	$485, $365, $305
21JD, 22JD, 23JD	batt. ignition, electric lights, regular engine	73.7 ci (1207cc) twin	$520, $390, $330
21JDS, 22JDS, 23JDS	batt. ignition, electric lights, sidecar engine	73.7 ci (1207cc) twin	$520, $390, $330
21WF, 22WF, 23WF	magneto	35.6 ci (584cc) twin	$415, $310, $275
21WJ, 22WJ, 23WJ	batt. ignition, electric lights	35.6 ci (584cc) twin	$445, $340, $295

1923 Harley-Davidson. In 1922 and 1923 only, the standard color was Brewster green, a very dark hue, with double-line gold striping. Two late-1922 improvements were first advertised as 1923 advances: a manual ignition switch with an automatic alarm, and a double-plunger oil pump. New for 1923 were new cylinders on the Seventy-Four, and a hinged rear fender on all models, which simplified tire changes. (DALE WALKSLER)

Models	Key Feature(s)	Engine Data	Cost
24FD	magneto, regular engine	73.7 ci (1207cc) twin	$315
24FDS	magneto, sidecar engine	73.7 ci (1207cc) twin	$315
24FDCA	magneto, regular engine, aluminum pistons	73.7 ci (1207cc) twin	$325
24FDSCA	magneto, sidecar engine, aluminum pistons	73.7 ci (1207cc) twin	$325
24FE	magneto, regular engine, aluminum pistons	60.3 ci (989cc) twin	$300
24FES	magneto, sidecar engine, aluminum pistons	60.3 ci (989cc) twin	$300
24JD	battery ignition, regular engine, aluminum pistons, electric lights	73.7 ci (1207cc) twin	$335
24JDS	batt. ignition, sidecar engine, electric lights	73.7 ci (1207cc) twin	$335
24JDCA	batt. ignition, regular engine, aluminum pistons, electric lights	73.7 ci (1207cc) twin	$345
24JDSCA	batt. ignition, sidecar engine, aluminum pistons, electric lights	73.7 ci (1207cc) twin	$345
24JE	batt. ignition, regular engine, aluminum pistons, electric lights	60.3 ci (989cc) twin	$320
24JES	batt. ignition, sidecar engine, aluminum pistons	60.3 ci (989cc) twin	$320

1923 Harley-Davidson Two-Cam racing engine. These "Two Cams" still used the indirect valve action through pivoted cam followers. The production-style oil pump was driven at engine speed.

1924 Harley-Davidson Model FHAC. With a compression ratio of about 6:1 and special racing parts, the maximum output was about 35 hp. Transmission, single-speed; primary drive, single-row chain; final drive, chain; brakes, none; ignition, magneto; frame, "keystone" with engine mounting plates serving as lower frame structure, single down tube. Wheelbase, 51 inches; weight, 365 lbs.; fuel tank, 2.75 gallons; finish, olive drab with maroon tank striping edged in black and centered in gold.

(DOUG MITCHEL)

1924 Highlights

The Sport model was discontinued. Color changed back to olive drab. 1924 and later: in advertising and everyday discourse, the two big twins were referred to as the "Sixty-One" (or "61") and the "Seventy-Four" (or "74").

1925 Highlights

A new frame improved appearance and lowered the saddle height 3 inches. Aluminum pistons weren't offered. Cast-iron pistons were replaced with "iron alloy" pistons. All 74-ci models were re-designated to reflect new pistons; 61-ci models were not re-designated. Tire and wheel sizes changed from 28 x 3 inches to 27 x 3 inches.

1925-1927 Specifications

Engine dimensions were unchanged. "Sixty-One" models: bore and stroke of 3 5/16 inches x 3 1/2 inches; displacement, 60.32 cubic inches (988cc). "Seventy-Four" models: bore and stroke of 3.424 (advertised as 3 7/16) inches x 4 inches, for a displacement of 73.66 cubic inches (1207cc). The new 1925 frame had a curved top rail and lowered the saddle three inches. Tires were 27 x 3 1/2 inches (previously, 28 x 3). Weight was up to 405 lbs., empty.

Year	Model	Engine Data	New Features, Misc.	Cost
25	FDCB	73.7 ci (1207cc) twin	magneto, regular engine, iron alloy pistons	$315
25	FDCBS	73.7 ci (1207cc) twin	magneto, sidecar engine, iron alloy pistons	$315
25	FE	60.3 ci (989cc) twin	magneto, regular engine, iron alloy pistons	$295
25	FES	60.3 ci (989cc) twin	magneto, sidecar engine, iron alloy pistons	$295
25	JDCB	73.7 ci (1207cc) twin	battery ignition, regular engine, iron alloy pistons, electric lights	$335
25	JDSCB	73.7 ci (1207cc) twin	battery ignition, sidecar engine, iron alloy pistons, electric lights	$335
24	JE	60.3 ci (989cc) twin	battery ignition, regular engine, iron alloy pistons, electric lights	$315
24	JES	60.3 ci (989cc) twin	battery ignition, sidecar engine, iron alloy pistons, electric lights	$315

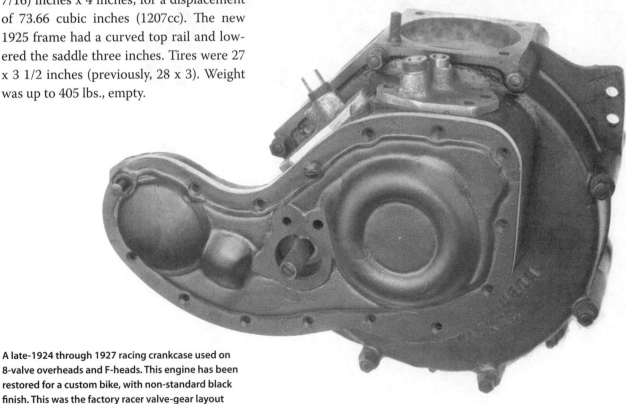

A late-1924 through 1927 racing crankcase used on 8-valve overheads and F-heads. This engine has been restored for a custom bike, with non-standard black finish. This was the factory racer valve-gear layout used on both F-head and eight-valve from 1924 through 1927.

1924 Harley-Davidson Model FHAC. This F-head racer has the late-1924 through1927 two-cam configuration. Harley-Davidsons were almost unbeatable in long races. This motorcycle is from the Dale Walksler Wheels Through Time museum.

1925 Harley-Davidson JD series, and sidecar. The biggest change on 1925 models was the more streamlined frame and tanks, with a 3-inch lower saddle. Commonly, collectors refer to all mid- and late-1920s 74-cubic inch (nominally, 1200cc, nominally) F-head twins as "JD" motorcycles. While there was a "JD" model, there were various other "Seventy-Four" F-heads depending on solo or sidecar engine, battery or magneto ignition, cast-iron or aluminum pistons, etc. (DOUG MITCHEL)

1925 Harley-Davidson JD series. The toolbox was relocated to the front fork. Softer cushion and recoil springs were fitted to the fork. The wider 1925 frame allowed the use of wider 27 1/2 x 3 1/2 -inch tires instead of 28 x 3 models. (DOUG MITCHEL)

1925 Harley-Davidson JD series. The 74-cubic inch (nominal, 1200cc) engines debuted in the 1921 season and immediately became the company's most popular power plant. Specifications: Engine, F-head V-twin, displacement 74.7 cubic inches (1207cc); compression ratio 3.8:1; maximum output, 22 hp @ 3200 rpm. Transmission, three-speed hand-shift; primary drive, single-row chain; final drive, chain. Weight, 405 lbs. Fuel tanks, 4.75 gallons. Tires, 27 x 3.85 inches. Finish, olive drab with maroon tank striping edged in black and centered in gold. (DOUG MITCHEL)

1926-1927 Highlights

The V-twin range was reduced to four models, all with battery ignition and electric lights. The 21-ci (350cc, both figures nominal) side-valve and overhead-valve singles were based on projected exports. The domestic singles market was a sideshow.

1926 Harley-Davidson Model B. Lightweight 21-cubic inch (nominal, 350cc, nominal) side-valve (Flathead) and overhead-valve singles were introduced for the 1926 season. These were planned for, and achieved, good foreign sales. Domestic sales were lukewarm, as anticipated. The aluminum cylinder head on this restored bike, was not shown or discussed in any sales literature or press releases. (DOUG MITCHEL)

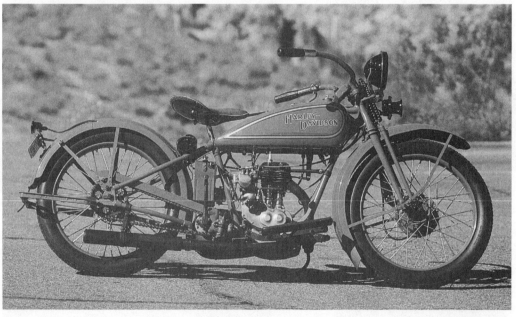

1927 Harley-Davidson Model B. Specifications. Engine, side-valve (Flathead) single, displacement, 21.10 cubic inches (346cc); Ricardo licensed cylinder heads with "squish" principle; compression ratio 5:1; maximum output, 10 hp (estimated). Transmission, three-speed handshift; primary drive, single-row chain; final drive, chain.

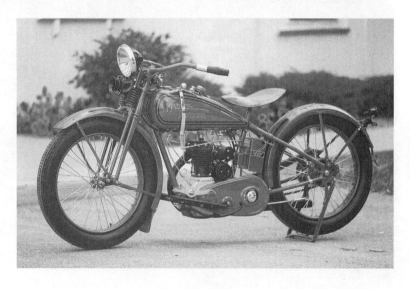

1927 Harley-Davidson B. 1927 Harley-Davidson Model B. The frames of all singles were reinforced at several points, although there was no change in part number. A heavier clutch spring and reinforced fuel tank were fitted. (DOUG MITCHEL)

Models	Key Feature(s)	Engine Data	New Features, Misc.	Cost
26A, 27A	side-valve single, magneto	21.1 ci (346cc)	Compression ratio 4:1, 8 hp	$210, $210
26AA, 27AA	overhead-valve single, magneto	21.1 ci (346cc)	Compression ratio 6:1, 12 hp	$250, $250
26B, 27B	side-valve single, battery ignition, electric lights	21.1 ci (346cc)	Compression ratio 4:1, 8 hp	$235, $235
26BA, 27BA	overhead-valve single, battery ignition, electric lights	21.1 ci (346cc)	Compression ratio 6:1, 12 hp	$275, $275
26J, 27J	twin, battery ignition, regular engine, electric lights	60.3 ci (989cc)	—	$315, $310
26JS, 27JS	twin, battery ignition, sidecar engine, electric lights	60.3 ci (989cc)	—	$315, $310
26JD, 27JD	twin, battery ignition, regular engine, electric lights	73.7 ci (1207cc)	—	$335, $320
26JDS, 27JDS	twin, battery ignition, sidecar engine, electric lights	60.3 ci (989cc)	—	$335, $320
26S, 27S	overhead-valve single, magneto, racer	21.1 ci (346cc)	—	$300, $300

1927 Harley-Davidson Model B. Specifications, continued: Brake (rear only), external contracting band. Ignition, battery and coil. Frame, single loop, single down-tube, forged plate beneath engine instead of tube. Suspension, leading link. Wheelbase, 56.5 inches. Weight, 269 lbs., Tires, 27 x 3.85 inches. Finish, olive drab with maroon tank striping edged in black and centered in gold.

1927 Harley-Davidson Model B. Although side-valve (Flathead) engines were the basis of the "Single," the company also built overhead-valve singles, some with two exhaust ports. The overhead singles were used for racing from the late 1920s through the late 1930s, because big V-twin racing had become too dangerous.

1927 Harley-Davidson Model JD. Minimal changes were incorporated on all Harleys for the 1927 season. The most important change on the twins was the elimination of the distributor, formerly mounted behind the rear cylinder. This eliminated potential failures. The so-called "wasted spark" or "double spark" system fired both plugs on every revolution, one for power and the other providing a harmless spark during the exhaust stroke. On V-twins, this remained a feature until 1961.

(DOUG MITCHEL)

1927 Harley-Davidson Model JD. The $320 JD was the most popular model, accounting for over half of the total production of over 18,000. (DOUG MITCHEL)

1927 Harley-Davidson Model JD. This is the typical mid- and late-1920s switch panel. (DOUG MITCHEL)

1928 Highlights

All models with battery ignition and electric lights from 1928 through 1940. First: front wheel brake on all models. First: throttle-controlled oil pump on all models.

1928-1929 Two-Cam F-head Production Road Models

The ultimate F-head roadsters were the 61-cubic inch Model JH and the 74-cubic inch Model JDH, affectionately known as "Two-Cams." These brought racing technology to the streets in the form of two-cam direct-action valve gear. Weighing around 408 lbs., the JDH "Seventy-Four Two-Cam" produced a maximum 29 hp at 4000 rpm, compared to the single-cam Seventy-Four JD maximum of 22 hp at 3400 rpm. According to varying accounts of old timers from the Harley and Indian camps, this either put Harley-Davidson abreast of, or ahead of, the surprisingly fast side-valve Indian Scout Forty-Five (750cc). While the ultimate F-heads were on the streets, the company was designing the next generation of roadsters that would be powered by side-valve (Flathead) engines. But it would be another decade before Two-Cam accel-

eration was bettered, and not by the much heavier (121 lbs.!) replacement Flatheads. It would take the third-generation roadsters, the overhead-valve "Knuckleheads," to improve on Two-Cam acceleration.

1928-1929 Harley-Davidson Two-Cam engine, motor number 29JDH12528H. Production Two-Cam models were equipped with a new valve gear setup. As well as featuring direct-action (no pivoted cam followers) valve lift, and removable lifter blocks, the lifter blocks had a raised section that routed oil back to the crankcase.

Models	Key Feature(s)	Engine Data	New Features, Misc.	Cost
28B	side-valve single	21.1 ci (346cc). 8 hp	controlled oil pump, new flywheels, wider fenders, hinged rear fender, longer bars	$235
28BA	overhead-valve single	21.1 ci (346cc), 12 hp	—	$255
28J	twin, regular engine	60.3 ci (989cc), 17 hp	throttle-controlled oil pump	$310
28JS	twin, s/c engine	60.3 ci (989cc)	throttle-controlled oil pump	$310
28JD	twin, reg. engine	73.7 ci (1207cc), 22 hp	throttle-controlled oil pump	$320
28JDL	twin, reg. engine	73.7 ci (1207cc), 26 hp	Dow Metal pistons, larger inlet valves	N/A
28JDS	twin, s/c engine	60.3 ci (989cc)	throttle-controlled oil pump	$320
28JX	twin, Sport Solo, reg. engine	60.3 ci (989cc)	narrower tanks, smaller (28 x 3.85) tires, lower saddle, shorter bars	$310
28JXL	twin, Sport Solo	60.3 ci (989cc)	Dow Metal pistons	$325
28JDX	twin, Sport Solo	73.7 ci (1207cc)	reg. engine	$320
28JDXL	twin, Sport Solo	73.7 ci (1207cc)	Dow Metal pistons	$335
28JDH	two-cam engine	73.7 ci (1207cc) twin	compression ratio, 4.6:1, 29 hp mid-season model, 2 camshafts, lower saddle, shorter bars	$370

1917-modified-to-1928 Harley-Davidson eight-valve racer. All the 1923-1927 factory team F-head and eight-valve bikes used two-cam valve gear. This engine, 1917 serial number 17 8V 1, is reputed to have been used by star English rider Freddy Dixon in 1923 at the Brooklands 2¾-mile concrete track in Surrey, England. The engine was subsequently fitted with a 1928 right crankcase with removable tappet guides. (SAM HOTTON)

The cylinders are also the type used on the earliest Harley eight-valve twins. In final factory-configured form (1927), each cylinder exhausted through twin stubby bean-shaped ports, and there were no exhaust pipes. (SAM HOTTON)

1929-1935, The Side-Valve Era

In the 1920s, while the rest of the motorcycling world was discovering the joys of overhead-valves, American manufacturers clung to the older F-head and side-valve (Flathead) engine configurations. Partly, this was due to the dominance of only three companies in the United States: Harley-Davidson, Indian, and Excelsior/Henderson. The three-player game either meant it was easier to sustain gentlemen's agreements to hold down engineering expenses, or the three companies figured they could quickly catch up in event any rivals' suddenly went to overhead designs. Another likely factor was the universal automobile, the Ford Model T, which to most Americans defined "standard" practice as side-valve engines, and perhaps cast doubt on other "experimental" layouts. Indeed, most American automobiles were powered by side-valve engines. Before World War I, some smaller American motorcycle companies had tried to break into the clear with engines of overhead-valve or overhead-cam design, or with shaft drive, or with other trendy innovations. But with the alsorans all but extinct, in the 1920s the Big Three had no worries on the technical front. Harley-Davidson felt little peer pressure.

While the Harley F-heads were winning races, along with their eight-valve overhead stable mates, the road model world was proving different. Increasingly fast road riding over improving highways was producing increasing reliability issues. The F-head valve gear, with the exposed inlet valve stems and rockers that were considered essential for cooling, was proving too messy at sustained high speeds. Oil got everywhere, and dirt with it, so that the goo formed an effective lapping compound that caused rapid wear. More wear also meant more noise.

The logical update, to modern enthusiasts, would have been a move directly to overhead-valve engines, skipping completely the American side-valve side-show.

But the practice of metallurgy was far from mature in the era, so that there were indeed overheating concerns with enclosed overhead valves. British and European overhead bikes continued to air out both the inlet and exhaust valves. As power output was greater in overheads, so, too, was heat build-up. This explained why the same manufacturers saw no inconsistency in the successful running of their own side-valve models with all enclosed valves. Their side-valve bikes were mostly slow-running under-stressed units.

There was a fly in the soup. In 1920, Indian won 17 national championship races, many of them with side-valve racers. These Flatheads were proving faster than the eight-valve overheads of both Indian and Harley-Davidson. Across the Atlantic, English engineer Harry Ricardo had developed patents concerning side-valve cylinder head design, the fabled "squish" principle that improved output while reducing consumption. Indian had been on to the same ideas.

From a business point of view, Harley-Davidson saw side-valve design as the next stage. The company, along with the rest of the planet, couldn't envision the rapid improvements in metals that would soon be at hand. Likewise, the emergence of tetraethyl lead as a "miracle" fuel ingredient was not all that clear. Indeed, the fuel situation was a factor in Indian Flatheads outrunning rival overheads—the overheads couldn't be run long at higher compression ratios that later made all the difference. So, side-valve engines appeared perfectly logical.

By this time, Harley-Davidson was selling two motorcycles for every one that Indian sold, and perhaps five or six for every one Excelsior/Henderson sold. That dominance sustained Harley-Davidson when, two years in a row, their heralded new side-valve models proved unreliable and unacceptable. First came the 1929 "Forty-Five" (45 cubic inches, 750cc), then the 1930 "Seventy-Four" (74 cubic inches, 1200cc). Production stoppage and rash re-engineering programs, along with free dealer labor support, converted these unacceptable motorcycles into worthy competitors. Had either Indian or Excelsior/Henderson committed these design sins, they may very well have gone bust.

After the initial bugs were worked out, the Harley Flatheads proved very reliable. The Forty-Five competed with "Forty-Fives" of Indian and Excelsior, the latter now termed the "Super-X." The Seventy-Four was up against the 74-cubic inch (1200cc) Indian Chief, and, to a lesser extent, the four-cylinder Indian and Henderson. In the everyday world of happiness per mile, Harleys were doing the job. Heavier than the preceding F-head big twins, the Flathead Seventy-Four had its detractors within the Harley community, because the excellent acceleration of the F-heads had been lost. But from the outset the Flatheads outlasted the F-heads, and with continuous engineering updates, hp and torque steadily improved and closed most if not all the gap. As to stop speed, the big Flathead roadsters had it all over the F-heads. Only one problem concerned the company. Again, as with the F-heads, average road speeds were increasing. Though the "noise level" was low, there were increasing reports of overheating pistons seizing up. By 1933, Harley-Davidson began drawing a new overhead-valve big twin roadster. Just in case.

1929 Highlights

All models equipped with four-tube muffler. "D" series "Forty-Fives" used the same frame as the singles. In advertising and everyday discourse a D-series motorcycle was termed a "Forty-Five" or "45," but never a "four-five."

Late-1929 through 1931 D Series "Forty-Five" Specifications

Engine, side-valve (Flathead) V-twin: bore and stroke , 2 3/4 x 3 13/16 inches; displacement 45.32 cubic inches (747cc); compression ratio, Model D = 4.3:1, Model DL = 5:1; maximum output, Model D = 15 hp @ 3900 rpm, Model DL = 18.5 hp at 4000 rpm. Transmission, three-speed hand-shift; primary drive, double-row chain; final drive, chain. Brakes, internal, conventional shoes. Ignition, battery and coil. Frame, single down-tube, forged plate beneath engine. Suspension, leading link. Wheelbase, 57.5 inches. Weight, 390 lbs. Fuel tanks, 4.6 gallons. Oil compartment, 2 1/2 quarts. Tires, 25 x 4 inches (4.00 x 18 in later terminology). Finish, olive drab with vermillion tank striping edged in black and centered in gold.

Early-1929 Harley-Davidson D-series "Forty-Five." Though the 45-cubic inch (750cc) Super-X had been around since 1925, Super-X sales were modest. The 1929 Model D was Harley-Davidson's answer to the popular 45-cubic inch (750cc) Indian Scout. Front brakes came to the Harley lineup in the 1928 season.

Early-1929 D-series "Forty-Five." The general lightness and the use of the same front fork and frame as the Single suggest that the initial design effort had been for a 37-cubic inch (600cc) unit. Indian's "45" came out in 1927 when the Harley middlweight was probably on the drawing board.

Early-1929 Harley-Davidson D-series "Forty-Five." Because of the "Single" frame with the straight front downtube, the generator was mounted vertically. Indian fans scornfully referred to the "D" as a three-cylinder Harley. In the Spring of 1929, "Forty-Five" production ceased while the model was being redesigned.

Models	Key Feature(s)	Engine Data	New Features, Misc.	Cost
29B	side-valve single	21.1 ci (346cc)	Compression ratio, 4:1. 8 hp	$235
29BA	overhead-valve single	21.1 ci (346cc)	—	$255
29BA?	Two-port overhead-valve single	21.1 ci (346cc)	export only, name unknown, power unknown	n/a
29C	side-valve single	30.1 ci (493cc)	—	$255
29D	all-new side-valve V-twin	45.3 ci (742cc) 15 hp @ 3800 rpm	—	$290
29DL	all-new, side-valve V-twin, high compression	45.3 ci (742cc)	19 hp @ 4000 rpm	$290
29J	regular engine	60.3 ci (989cc) twin	17 hp @ 3400 rpm	$310
29JS	sidecar engine	60.3 ci (989cc) twin	C. ratio 3.9:1, 1" inlet ports	$310
29JL	Dow Metal pistons	60.3 ci (989cc) twin	—	n/a
29JD	regular engine	73.7 ci (1207cc) twin	22 hp @ 3200 rpm	$320
29JDS	sidecar engine	73.7 ci (1207cc) twin	—	$320
29JDH	two-cam	73.7 ci (1207cc) twin	29 hp	$370
29JDL	Dow Metal pistons	73.7 ci (1207cc) twin	26 hp	n/a

Early-1929 Harley-Davidson D-series "Forty-Five." In this rider's view, one can see the distinctive tanks used on the singles and the early-1929 Forty-Fives. Late-1929 Forty-Fives used the same tanks as the forthcoming 1930 side-valve big twins. In early calendar 1929, Forty-Five production was halted in order to incorporate design changes. The late-1929 Forty-Fives were carried over unchanged as 1930 models.

1930-1936 Models V, VL, VD, and VLD Specifications.

Engine, side-valve (Flathead) V-twin, bore and stroke 3.424 (advertised as 3 7/16) x 4 inches, displacement 73.7 cubic inches (1207cc). Model V (1930-1933), 4:1 compression ratio, maximum of 28 hp @ 4000 rpm. Model VL (1930-1933), 5:1 compression ratio, maximum of 30 hp @ 4000 rpm. Model VD (1934-1936), 5:1 compression ratio, maximum of 33 hp @ 4400 rpm. Model VLD (1933-1936), 5.1:1 compression ratio, maximum of 36 hp @ 4600 rpm. Lubrication, total loss. Transmission, three-speed hand-shift, sliding gears ("crash" box); primary drive, double-row chain, oil-mist lubricated; final drive, chain. Brakes, front and rear, drum and shoe. Ignition, battery and coil. Frame, single loop, single downtube. Suspension, leading link. Wheelbase, 57 inches. Weight, 529 lbs. Fuel tanks 4 gallons. Oil compartment, 4 quarts. Tires, 19 x 4.00 inches. (Note: beginning in this era, wheel sizes referred to the diameter of the rim only; earlier quotes referred to the combined diameter of the rim and tire. Finish, a variety of colors; optional finishes listed in supplemental paint brochures but not in regular sales literature.)

1930 Highlights

First 74 ci Twins announced in August, 1929. All 1930 "D" series "Forty-Fives" had the late-1929 changes: a new frame, a new forged I-beam front fork, new tanks, higher motor mounts, and a new larger clutch.

1931 Highlights

The 21-ci "B" single was dropped for one year. Major mechanical changes were made to the 74-ci models early in the 1930 season. All models had a new wedge-shaped toolbox mounted on the front fork. Seventy-Four twins had a new muffler. Mid-season, on V series: optional 3-speed-with-reverse transmission. 1931 and later: "Special Sport Solo" appeared on dealer "Motorcycle Order" forms, but wasn't commonly used in advertising or everyday discourse.

1930 Harley-Davidson, V-series "Seventy-Four." For the 1930 season, the company replaced the long-running F-head big twins with all-new side-valve (Flathead) big twins. Apart from tires, spark plugs, and bits and pieces like clamps and brackets, no F-head parts were carried over. (COURTESY DALE WALKSLER)

1930 Harley-Davidson 30.50-cubic inch (500cc) racer, motor number 30SF505. Scarcely visible in the picture is the left side pipe of this four-port engine. Many Harley racing engines were numbered in the 500s. The generator is a restoration modification, as these were purely magneto-fired racers without lights.

(SAM HOTTON)

Models	Key Feature(s)	Engine Data	New Features, Misc.	Cost
30B	side-valve single	21.1 ci (346cc)	8 hp	$235
30C	side-valve single	30.1 ci (493cc)	—	$260
30D	side-valve V-twin	45.3 ci (742cc)	15 hp @ 3800 rpm	$310
30DS	side-valve V-twin, sidecar gearing	45.3 ci (742cc)	15 hp	$310
30DL	side-valve V-twin, high compression	45.3 ci (742cc)	18.5 hp	$310
30DLD	side-valve V-twin, high compression	45.3 ci (742cc)	20 hp (est.)	$325
30V	all-new side-valve V-twin	73.7 ci (1207cc)	28 hp	$340
30VL	all-new side-valve V-twin	73.7 ci (1207cc)	30 hp	$340
30VS	all-new side-valve V-twin	73.7 ci (1207cc)	28 hp	$340, $310

1931 Harley-Davidson V-series "Seventy-Four." Bikes of this genre are loosely termed "VL" today, but there were actually a variety of models that varied mostly in state of tune. The top speed of the early big twin Flatheads was about the same as the last of the big twin F-heads, with the best stock ones topping out around 80 mph. Flatheads were also more reliable, being able to run at sustained 60-plus mph without breaking down.
(DALE WALKSLER)

Models	Key Feature(s)	Engine Data	New Features, Misc.	Cost
31C	side-valve single	30.1 ci (493cc)	—	$260
31D	side-valve V-twin	45.3 ci (742cc), 15 hp	new rear brake	$310
31DS	side-valve V-twin, sidecar gearing	45.3 ci (742cc)	new rear brake	$310
31DL	side-valve V-twin, high compression	45.3 ci (742cc), 18.5 hp	new rear brake	$310
31DLD	side-valve V-twin, Special Sport Solo	45.3 ci (742cc), 20 hp (estimated)	new rear brake	$325
31V	side-valve V-twin	73.7 ci (1207cc), 28 hp	—	$340
31VL	side-valve V-twin, high compression	73.7 ci (1207cc), 30 hp	—	$340
31VS	side-valve V-twin	73.7 ci (1207cc), 28 hp	sidecar gearing	$340

1931 Harley-Davidson V-series "Seventy-Four." The 1931 model reflected changes made during the 1930 model year. This example is fitted with a 1932-style muffler; the correct muffler center section was can-shaped.

(COURTESY DALE WALKSLER)

Both Harley-Davidson and Indian had the nerve to term a key-and-ammeter panel as an instrument panel, calling up images of an aircraft cockpit with multiple gauges.

(DOUG MITCHEL)

1931 Harley-Davidson Model D. This motorcycle has been restored with the optional 1932-style tank panels. Optional colors and tank panels were explained in supplemental brochures, not in the regular sales literature. This panel style may have been offered during 1931. (DOUG MITCHEL)

1931 Harley-Davidson D series. Model variants were based on state of tune. Models D and DL were offered for 1929 through 1931; Model DLD was offered for 1930 and 1931. (DOUG MITCHEL)

1932-1933 Highlights

Pistons—R and V series. 1932, aluminum; 1933, magnesium alloy. 1933-1966: Linkert carburetors.

1932 Harley-Davidson R series. For 1932, the troublesome vertical generator was replaced by a conventional horizontal gear-driven generator—the same as used on the Seventy-Fours. A new frame with a bowed front down tube accommodated the generator. New cylinders featured an air space between the exhaust ports and the barrels. New crankcases housed larger flywheels. Aluminum pistons replaced Dow Metal (magnesium) pistons.

1932 Harley-Davidson R series. For the first time, the 1933 range included a variety of standard colors. This one is Delft Blue and Turquoise. A new oil pump had different internals, and a different mounting so it could be removed without also removing the timing case cover.

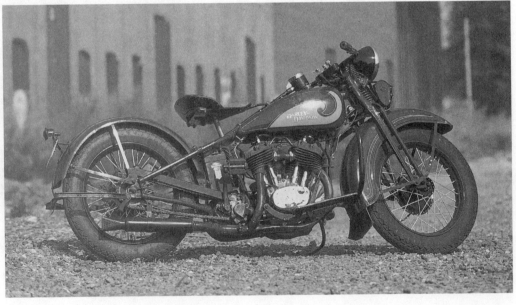

Models	Key Feature(s)	Engine Data	New Features, Misc.	Cost
32B, 33B	side-valve single	21.1 ci (346cc), 8 hp	1932: seat-post tube and saddle height lowered 1"	$195, $187.50
32C, 33C	side-valve single	30.1 ci (493cc), 10 hp	—	$235, $225
34CB	side-valve single	30.1 ci (493cc), 10 hp	same frame as 21 ci	$197.50
32R, 33R	side-valve V-twin	45.3 ci (742cc), 15 hp	1932: larger flywheels, new crankcases & clutch	$295, $280
32RS, 33RS	side-valve V-twin, s/c gearing	45.3 ci (742cc), 15 hp	1932: larger flywheels, new crankcases, new clutch	$295, $280
32RL, 33RL	side-valve V-twin, high comp.	45.3 ci (742cc), 18.5 hp	1932: larger flywheels, new crankcases, new clutch	$310, $280
32RLD, 33RLD	side-valve V-twin Special Sport Solo	45.3 ci (742cc), 20 hp	1932: larger flywheels, new crankcases, new clutch	$310, $290
32V, 33V	side-valve V-twin	73.7 ci (1207cc), 28 hp	compression ratio 4:1, 1932: aluminum pistons	$320, $310
32VL, 33VL	side-valve V-twin	73.7 ci (1207cc), 30 hp	compression ratio 4.5:1	$320, $310
32VS, 33VS	side-valve V-twin	73.7 ci (1207cc), 28 hp	compression ratio 4:1, aluminum pistons, sidecar gearing	$320, $310
33VLD	side-valve V-twin Special Sport Solo	73.7 ci (1207cc), 36 hp	compression ratio 5:1, "Y" inlet manifold	$320, $310

1932 Harley-Davidson R Series. Model R, RL, and RLD, had compression ratios of 4.3:1, 5:1 and 6:1. The R, RL and RLD had maximum hp of 15 at 3800 rpm, 19 at 3800 rpm and 21 1/2 at 4000 rpm, respectively.

1933 Harley-Davidson V series. This is either a Model V or a Model VL, because it continues with the "kitchen sink" inlet plumbing also used on Indians. A new Model VLD featured a "Y" inlet manifold for improved breathing, the return of Dow Metal (magnesium) pistons and a slight bump in the compression ratio to 5.1:1. VLD maximum output was 36 hp at 4600 rpm.

1934 Highlights

Last road-model singles. Aluminum pistons. No Models V, VL. Late-1934 bores changed from tapered to straight. R-Series clutch changed from 14 springs to 12 larger springs, the same as on the V-Series.

1934 Harley-Davidson V-series "Seventy-Four." The tapered fender panels were used on 1934 models only.

1934 Harley-Davidson V-series "Seventy-Four." On all models, the tanks got an art deco styling.

1934 Harley-Davidson V series. V-twin restyling included new front and rear fenders and a new paint scheme, as well as new color offerings.

Models	Key Feature(s)	Engine Data	New Features, Misc.	Cost
34B	side-valve single	21.1 ci (346cc)	—	$187.50
34C	side-valve single	30.1 ci (493cc)	—	$225
34CB	side-valve single	30.1 ci (493cc)	same frame as 21 ci single	$197.50
34R	side-valve V-twin	45.3 ci (742cc)	15 hp @ 3800 rpm	$280
34RS	side-valve V-twin, s/c gearing	45.3 ci (742cc)	15 hp @ 3800 rpm	$280
34RL	side-valve V-twin, high compression	45.3 ci (742cc)	19 hp @ 3800 rpm	$280
34RLD	side-valve V-twin, Special Sport Solo	45.3 ci (742cc)	22 hp @ 4000 rpm	$290
34VD	side-valve V-twin, low compression	73.7 ci (1207cc)	28 hp @ 3800 rpm	$310
34VDS	side-valve V-twin, low comp., s/c gearing	73.7 ci (1207cc)	28 hp @ 3800 rpm	$310
34VLD	side-valve V-twin, Special Sport Solo	73.7 ci (1207cc)	36 hp @ 4600 rpm	$310

1934 Harley-Davidson Model C. This was the last year for Harley singles. The two others were the 21-cubic inch (350cc) Model A, and the Model CB, featuring the 30.50-cubic inch engine in the frame of the 21-cubic inch model.

1934 Harley-Davidson Model C. Specifications: Engine, side-valve (Flathead) single, bore and stroke, 3 3/32 x 4 inches; displacement 30.1 cubic inches (493cc); compression ratio 4.2:1; maximum output, 10.5 hp @ 3400 rpm. Wheelbase, 57.5 inches. Weight, 365 lbs. Fuel tank, 4 gallons. Oil compartment, 4 gallon. Tires, 18 x 4.00 inches. Finish, Teak Red and Silver, or olive drab and black.

1934 Harley-Davidson V-series "Seventy-Four." To counter Indian's 1933-1934 dry sump (circulating) lubrication, a new oil pump varied delivery with throttle opening as well as engine speed. This was the same approach used on the 1931-1932 Indians. Harley-Davidson claimed the total-loss (delivery and consumption without return) system was better because the engine always had clean oil.

1935-1936 Highlights

RLDR engines were fitted with looser clearances in all major assemblies. The 78.9-ci Model 35VLDD was not included in sales literature, but was included in dealer order blanks. In advertising and everyday discourse, a 78.9-ci twin was termed an "Eighty" (or "80"). First "Knuklehead" E Series with overhead-valve (OHV) engines, dry sump (circulating) oiling, tubular fork, double-loop frame, new clutch, 4-speed constant-mesh transmission, and radically new styling. In advertising and everyday discourse, an E series bike was termed a "Sixty-One" ("61") or a "Sixty-One O. H. V." 1931 and later: the dealer "Order Blank" terms

1935 Harley-Davidson R-series "Forty-Five." These were the first Harley two-wheelers equipped with constant-mesh transmissions. The new transmission featured a rotating, slotted shifting drum (termed a shifting "cam" by the factory). Previously, this feature was offered only in the three-speed with reverse transmission of three-wheelers. Indian twins would remain in production for eighteen more years, yet never would get this important advance.

1935 Harley-Davidson Model VL. Maximum output was increased in 1933 for Model VLD: 36 hp at 4600 rpm. In 1935, Model VLH produced 38 hp @ 4500 rpm. These outputs were spurred by several steps, including increased compression ratios and the use of magnesium (Dow Metal) pistons. Top-speed performance was gradually restored to that of the fastest F-heads, though the heavier Flathead big twins never measured up to F-head big twins in acceleration. (DOUG MITCHEL)

Models	Key Feature(s)	Engine Data	New Features, Misc.	Cost
36E	OHV V-twin	60.3 ci (989cc)	37 hp @ 4800 rpm, 3.75-gal. teardrop tanks	$380
36EL	OHV V-twin	60.3 ci (989cc)	40 hp @ 4800 rpm	$380
36ES	OHV V-twin, s/c gearing	60.3 ci (989cc)	40 hp @ 4800 rpm	$380
35R, 36R	side-valve V-twin	45.3 ci (742cc)	15 hp @ 3800 rpm	$295, $295
35RS, 36RS	side-valve V-twin, s/c gearing	45.3 ci (742cc)	5 hp @ 3800 rpm	$295, $295
35RL, 36RL	side-valve V-twin, high compression	45.3 ci (742cc)	19 hp @ 3800 rpm	$295, $295
35RLD, 36RLD	side-valve V-twin, Special Sport Solo	45.3 ci (742cc)	22 1/2 hp @ 4000 rpm	$305, $295
35RLDR, 36RLDR	side-valve V-twin, Special	45.3 ci (742cc)	for 45-ci stock (Class C) racing. Full road equip.	$322, $320
35VD, 36VD	side-valve V-twin	73.7 ci (1207cc)	low compression, 33 hp @ 4400 rpm	$320, $320
35VDS, 36VDS	side-valve V-twin, s/c gearing	73.7 ci (1207cc)	low compression, 33 hp @ 4400 rpm	$320, $320
35VLD, 36VLD	side-valve V-twin, Special Sport Solo	73.7 ci (1207cc),	36 hp @ 4600 rpm	$320, $320
35VLDD	side-valve V-twin, Sport Solo	78.9 ci (1293cc)	38 hp @ 4500 rpm	$347
36VLH	side-valve V-twin, Sport Solo	78.9 ci (1293cc)	38 hp @ 4500 rpm	$340
36VHS	side-valve V-twin	78.9 ci (1293cc)	low compression, 34 hp @ 4500 rpm	$340

1935 Harley-Davidson V-series "Seventy-Four." The 1935 tank trim added the small contrasting color panel ahead of the tank transfer. Conventional straight cylinder boring arrived with the 1935 engines, along with cam-ground (out-of-round) pistons.

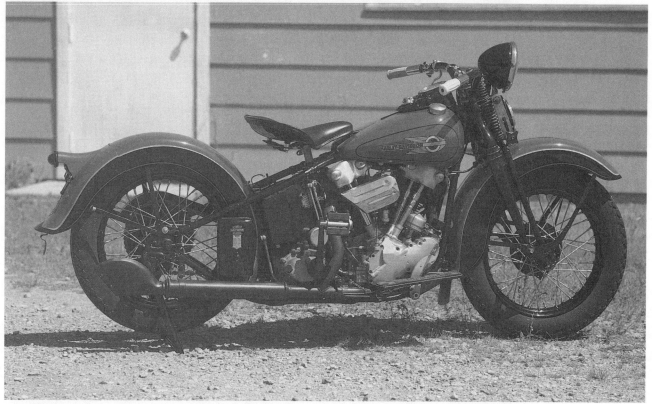

1936 Harley-Davidson E-series "Sixty-One," later nicknamed "Knucklehead." This is the motorcycle that finally put Harley-Davidson's engineering ahead of Indian's. The swooping top line, teardrop tank and, especially, the integrated tank-top instrument panel were all new. (DOUG MITCHEL)

"Sport Solo," "Special Sport Solo," and "Special" weren't commonly used in advertising or everyday discourse.

1936-1947, The Knucklehead Era

Twice burnt by the introductions of the side-valve 1929 Forty-Five and 1930 Seventy-Four models, Harley-Davidson cautiously introduced the overhead-valve "Sixty-One" as a mid-1936 model. Production was at a slow pace, so that any engineering problems could be solved without the hugely expensive cleanups experienced with the 1929 and 1930 Flatheads. The all-new Sixty-One was a styling revolution, as well as an engineering revolution, and this aspect, too, had to be evaluated. So, publicity was at a minimum, while the company gauged dealer and rider reaction. For months, magazine ads kept showing the old-style Flatheads, almost as if the company was keeping the Sixty-One a secret.

Management's worries proved unfounded, as the new Sixty-One met with overwhelming approval. Beyond the overhead-valve layout, there was a new dry-sump (circulating) lubrication system, a

big improvement over the old total-loss setup, and one that was overdue as Indian had performed this trick in 1933. Another big improvement was the four-speed constant-mesh transmission, instead of the traditional three-speed crash-box. In terms of big twin road models, the total Sixty-One engineering package put Harley-Davidson ahead of Indian for keeps.

The Flathead big twins continued to be the best sellers through 1940, with the 1941 Seventy-Four OHV finally putting sales supremacy in the "Knucklehead" camp. The side-valve range not only had a lingering popularity with street riders, but the Forty-Five model filled two other important needs: racing and military use. As with the F-heads, the company squeezed all the benefit they could from the Flatheads, and that squeezing process continued through the last side-valve big twins in 1948, primarily for police use, and into the late 1950s with models for road, track, police, and commercial use. But it was the "Knucklehead" range that ensured Harley-Davidson dominance in the American market.

1936 Harley-Davidson Model E or EL. The frame was originally designed for the side-valve (Flathead) big twins, but was first used on the E-series. This was a one-year-only frame, as it proved too light for the stresses. One unique 1936 feature is the absence of a forging at the bottom of each of the twin front down tubes, with the down tubes simply curving to become the twin bottom tubes.

(COURTESY DALE WALKSLER)

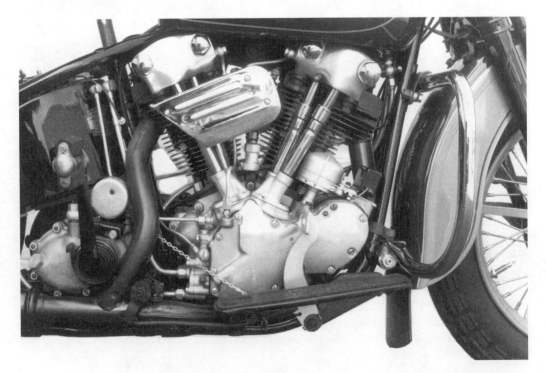

1936-1947 Overhead-valve Specifications

Overhead-valve V-twin, single four-lobe cam. "Sixty-One" bore and stroke, 3 5/16 x 3 1/2 inches; displacement 60.33 cubic inches (989cc); Model E compression ratio 6.5:1, Model IL compression ratio 7:1; Model E maximum output, 37 hp at 4800 rpm; Model EL maximum output, 40 hp @ 4800 rpm. "Seventy-Four" (1941-1947) bore and stroke, 3 7/16 inches and 3 31/32₂ inches; displacement 73.67 cubic inches (1207cc); Model F compression ratio 6.6:1; Model FL compression ratio 7:1; maximum output (F and FL) 48 hp at 5000 rpm. For 1936-1937, each valve stem was partially enclosed by a "two-piece baby food jar," but rocker shafts were exposed. For 1938-1947, valve stems and rocker shafts were fully enclosed by removable covers. Lubrication, dry-sump (circulating oil). Transmission, four-speed hand-shift, constant-mesh; primary drive, double-row chain, oil-mist lubricated; final drive, chain. Brakes, front and rear, drum and shoe. Ignition, battery and coil. Frame,

1936 Harley-Davidson V-series big twin. This fork spring shield was fitted to 1936 all side-valve (Flathead) models. The device wasn't fitted to subsequent side-valve big twins, but continued on the "Forty-Fives" through 1939.

1936-1937 overhead-valve cylinder head and valve gear. The "baby food jar" covers were designed as an afterthought on the original Knuckleheads. Though the covers leaked, it was an improvement over the British practice of completely exposing the inlet rockers and valve stems.

1936 Harley-Davidson V-series big twin. This is the tank styling used on all 1936 side-valve models. Listed for the first time in the sales literature, was the 1936 "Eighty," with either 5.3:1 or 5.5:1 compression ratio. The "Eighty" had appeared on dealer order blanks in mid-1935, and according to president Walter Davidson, had been built unofficially prior to that. Maximum "Eighty" output was 38 at 4500 rpm.

double-loop, double front down-tubes. Suspension, leading link. Wheelbase, 59.5 inches. Weight, 565 lbs. Fuel tanks, 3.75 gallons. Oil compartment, 4 quarts. Tires, 18 x 4.50 inches. Finish, a variety of colors.

1937-1948 Models U, UL, and ULH Specifications

U and UL engine: side-valve, bore and stroke of 3.424 (advertised as 3 7/16) x 4 inches; displacement 73.7 cubic inches (1207cc); U compression ratio 5:1; UL compression ratio 5.75:1; maximum U output, 32 hp at 4200 rpm; maximum UL output, 37 hp at 4100 rpm. ULH engine: side-valve, bore and stroke of 3.424 inches (advertised as 3 7/16 inches) and 4 1/4 inches; maximum ULH output, 39 hp at 4100 rpm. Lubrication, dry sump (circulating). Trans-

mission, four-speed constant mesh, hand shift. Clutch, dry, multiple-plate. Ignition, battery and coil. Wheelbase 59½ inches. Front suspension, leading link; rear suspension, none. Weight, 530 lbs.

1937-1938 Highlights

1937: U-Series and W-Series replaced, respectively, V-Series and R-series. 1937: 74-ci twin stroke increased to 4 9/32 inches—the same as on the 80 ci—and the bore decreased to 3 5/16 inches. 1937: New side-valve twins featured "Knucklehead" tubular fork, frame, styling, and dry sump (circulating) oiling. 1938: E-series, full enclosure of valves. 1937 and later: the dealer "Season Order Blank" term "Competition Special" wasn't commonly used in advertising or everyday discourse.

1937 Harley-Davidson UL engine. The big side-valve (Flathead) models got a double-loop frame the same as the 1937 "Knuckleheads." Side-valve big twins were fitted with larger flywheels, 8 9/32 inches in lieu of 8 inches, in order to smooth out high speed running. The pinion (right-side) gear bearing was changed from plain to roller design.

1937 Harley-Davidson UL (at left). All side-valve (Flathead) twins got the glamorous styling introduced by the 1936 overhead-valve "E" twins. The Flatheads also were fitted with dry-sump (circulating) oiling. For 1937 only (except one option in 1955), the oil tank on both the side-valve and overhead-valve big twins was painted in the same color as the tanks and fenders. Also unique to 1937 models was the fender striping inboard of the fender rib.

(DOUG MITCHEL)

1937 Harley-Davidson Model EL. The new air intake "horn" was the mirror image of the left-side air horn used on the 1936 side-valve (Flathead) twins. Unique to 1937 was the oil tank arrangement that combined the supply line with the drain plug. To drain the tank required removal of the supply line. A check-valve was supposed to prevent oil spillage when the engine wasn't running, so that the mechanic had time to open the drain plug. (DOUG MITCHEL)

1937 Harley-Davidson Model EL (below). Beginning in 1937, both side-valve (Flathead) and overhead-valve big twins used the same frame. For 1937, the frame was strengthened: an 11-inch reinforcement was placed between the seat post and the seat bar connection; the entire rear frame section was made of heavier tubing; forgings joined the twin down tubes and the twin lower frame tubes. (DOUG MITCHEL)

1937 Harley-Davidson Model WL. The right-side crankshaft bearing was changed from plain to roller design. Cam gears were changed to one-piece design, and oil passages in the crankshaft were changed. Horizontal cooling fins were added to the left side of the crankcase. Oil was carried in the right tank.
(DALE WALKSLER)

1938 Harley-Davidson factory hill climber. During the 1920s and 1930s, hill climbing was a popular as racing. The company built a wide variety of special hill climbers, some with overhead-valve engines as far back as 1930. Note the special frame. The front fork appears shorter than standard. Competition rules lumped 61-cubic inch overheads in with 80-cubic inch Flatheads.
(DALE WALKSLER)

Models	Key Feature(s)	Engine Data	New Features, Misc.	Cost
37E	OHV V-twin, med. comp.	60.3 ci (989cc)	—	$435
37EL, 38EL	OHV V-twin, Special Sport Solo	60.3 ci (989cc)	42 1/2 hp @ 5200 rpm	$435, $435
37ES, 38ES	OHV V-twin, s/c gearing	60.3 ci (989cc)	—	$435, $435
37WL, 38WL	side-valve V-twin, Sport Solo	45.3 ci (742cc)	high compression 22 1/2 hp @ 4700 rpm	$355, $355
37WLD, 38WLD	side-valve V-twin, Sport Solo	45.3 ci (742cc)	extra high compression, 24 1/2 hp @ 4700 rpm	$355, $355
37WLDR, 38WLDR	side-valve V-twin, Competition Special	45.3 ci (742cc)	29 hp @ 5000 rpm	$380, $380
37U, 38U	side-valve V-twin	73.8 ci (1209cc)	medium compression 33 hp @ 4400 rpm	$395, $395
37US, 38US	side-valve V-twin, s/c gearing	73.7 ci (1207cc)	33 hp @ 4400 rpm	$395
37UL, 38UL	side-valve V-twin, Special Sport Solo	73.7 ci (1207cc)	37 1/2 hp @ 4200 rpm	$415, $415
37ULH, 38ULH	side-valve V-twin, Sport Solo	78.9 ci (1293cc)	39 hp @ 4200 rpm	$415, $415
37UH, 38UH	side-valve V-twin, Sport Solo	78.9 ci (1293cc)	medium compression, 38 hp @ 4500 rpm	$340
37UHS, 38UHS	side-valve V-twin	78.9 ci (1293cc), low compression	—	$415, $415

1938 Harley-Davidson Package Truck. The company tried for decades to sell commercial rigs such as this cargo carrier. The three-wheeled Servicar ("meter maid" trike) sold well for police use, but other three-wheelers barely justified continued production. (DOUG MITCHEL)

1938 Harley-Davidson Model UL. Many detail changes were made to all side-valve and overhead-valve big twins. Examples: heavier frame tubing, thicker transmission mounting bracket, higher handlebars, stronger clutch releasing finger, and new clutch thrust bearing (late-1938). Hereafter, the term "big twins" will refer to all 61-, 74- and 80-cubic inch models of both Flathead and overhead layouts. (DOUG MITCHEL)

1939-1940 Highlights

1939: Model E discontinued; E and U Series clutch with 25 ball bearings (vice, 10); W Series with new valve springs and larger trans. shifter clutches (dogs); U Series with steel-strutted horizontal slot pistons. 1940: W Series tubular fork. 1940: 5.00 x 16 wheels/tires became optional; these low-pressure tires narrowed the comfort gap with the spring-frame big Indian Chief.

1939 Harley-Davidson Model WLDR factory racer. The company continually updated their Class C (stock) racing "Forty-Fives." Aluminum cylinder heads arrived in 1939. In accord with American racing rules for stock bikes, these motorcycles were delivered with full road equipment. This example is fitted with factory supplied over-sized tanks designed for the annual Daytona 200 road race. (DALE WALKSLER)

Models	Key Feature(s)	Engine Data	New Features, Misc.	Cost
39EL, 40EL	OHV V-twin, Special Sport Solo	60.3 ci (989cc)	1940: 1 1/4" crank pin	$435, $430
39ES, 40ES	OHV V-twin, s/c gearing	60.3 ci (989cc)	1940: 1 1/4" crank pin	$435, $430
39WL, 40WL	side-valve V-twin, Sport Solo	45.3 ci (742cc)	high compression	$335, $350
39WLD, 40WLD	side-valve V-twin, Sport Solo	45.3 ci (742cc)	extra high compression	$355, $365
39WLDR, 40WLDR	side-valve V-twin, Competition Special	45.3 ci (742cc)	racer with road equip.	$380, $395
39U, 40U	side-valve V-twin	73.8 ci (1209cc)	medium compression ratio	$395, $385
39US, 40US	side-valve V-twin, s/c gearing	73.8 ci (1209cc)	s/c gearing	$395, $385
39UL, 40UL	side-valve V-twin, Special Sport Solo	73.8 ci (1209cc)	—	$395, $385
39ULH, 40ULH	side-valve V-twin, Sport Solo	78.9 ci (1293cc)	—	$415, $410
39UH, 40UH	side-valve V-twin, Sport Solo	78.9 ci (1293cc)	medium compression	$415, $410
39UHS, 40UHS	side-valve V-twin	78.9 ci (1293cc)	low compression	$415, $410

1939 Harley-Davidson Model EL. The chrome fender strips became standard in the 1939 range; the strips were offered in 1938 as an accessory item. The gearbox featured a sliding gear engagement for second gear, an attempt to please riders who objected to the noisy but harmless "clunk" engagement of the constant-mesh feature. The neutral position was oddly placed between second and third gears! (DOUG MITCHEL)

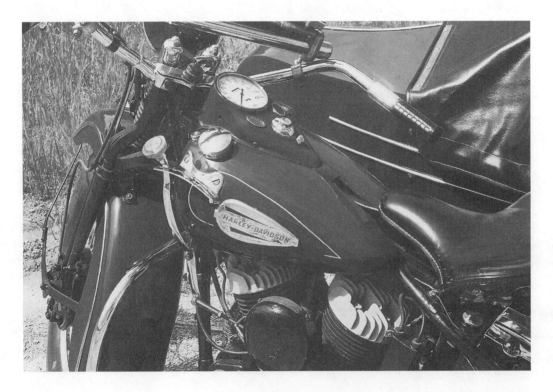

1940 Harley-Davidson Model UL. The "cat's eye" instrument panel was introduced in the 1939 range. The fuel reserve valve was moved to the top front of the left tank. The chrome nameplate and narrow tank stripe were new.

(DALE WALKSLER)

1941-1942 Highlights

1941: launch of F- Series 74-ci OHV twins; all models' prices unavailable; "E" reinstated; 80 ci twins discontinued. 1941 and later: in advertising and everyday discourse, a 73.7-ci OHV twin was referred to as a "Seventy-Four O. H. V." ("74 O. H V.") or "Seventy-Four overhead," while a 73.8-ci side-valve motorcycle continued to be termed a "Seventy-Four" ("74"). 1941: 5.00 x 16 tires became standard equipment.

1941 Harley-Davidson Model WR. In 1941, all road-model pretense was abandoned for the new racing model, which came stripped of lights and, since ignition was now via magneto, there also was no generator. This example is fitted with the special factory supplied oil tank, permitting greater fuel capacity and longer running at Daytona.

(DALE WALKSLER)

The big 1941 news was the arrival of the first 74-cubic inch (1200cc) Knuckleheads. The larger capacity was produced by increasing the Sixty-One's bore from 3 5/16 inches to 3 7/16 inches, and increasing the stroke from 3 1/2 inches to 3 31/32 inches. The Seventy-Four Knuckleheads had flywheels (two) that were each 4 lbs. heavier than the previous Sixty-Ones; the heavier flywheels were also put in the 1941 Sixty-Ones.

(DOUG MITCHEL)

Models	Key Feature(s)	Engine Data	New Features, Misc.	Cost
41E, 42E	OHV V-twin	60.3 ci (989cc)	medium compression	$425
41EL, 42EL	OHV V-twin, Special Sport Solo	60.3 ci (989cc)	—	n/a, $425
41F, 42F	OHV V-twin	73.7 ci (1207cc)	medium compression	n/a, $465
41FL, 42FL	OHV V-twin, Special Sport Solo	73.7 ci (1207cc)	48 hp @ 5000 rpm	n/a, $465
41WL, 42WL	side-valve V-twin, Sport Solo	45.3 ci (742cc)	high compression	n/a, $350
41WLD, 42WLD	side-valve V-twin, Sport Solo	45.3 ci (742cc)	extra high compression	n/a, $365
41WR, 41WRTT	side-valve V-twin, Competition Special	45.3 ci (742cc)	racer, stripped	n/a, n/a
41U, 42U	side-valve V-twin	73.8 ci (1209cc)	medium compression	n/a, $385
41UL, 42UL	side-valve V-twin, Special Sport Solo	73.8 ci (1209cc)	—	n/a, $385

1942 Harley-Davidson Model WLA. Some engines had a 5:1 compression ratio, others a 4.75:1 ratio. Maximum output was 23 hp @ 4600 rpm. Finish was olive drab matte (i.e., non-shiny or "flat") with no polished or brightly plated parts. The company built more than 80,000 military motorcycles during World War II, most of them variations of the Forty-Five.

(DOUG MITCHEL)

1939-1945 Military Models Highlights

A few OHV twins and 74-ci side-valve twins were supplied for military use; these aren't included. For essential civilian use, primarily police duty, OHV and side-valve big twins were supplied.

The XA was a BMW clone machined to American dimensions and fitted with H-D tanks and fork. In 1942, H-D supplied 1,000 XA models for U. S. Army testing. The army didn't award a full-scale production contract. H-D also built some XA-powered generators, and an XA-powered prototype light army car.

The company supplied a total of about 88,000 military motorcycles during World War II. A large majority of them were WLA and WLC models.

Models	Key Feature(s)	Engine Data	New Features, Misc.	Cost
WLA	side-valve V-twin	45.3 ci (742cc)	for American forces 1940-1945, 23 hp @ 4600, 576 lbs.	—
WLC	side-valve V-twin	45.3 ci (742cc)	for Canadian forces, 1942-1944	—
XA	s.v. flat twin, shaft drive	45.1 ci (739cc)	—	—

WLA "cockpit." The data plate, (not fully shown), provided lubrication instructions and cautioned that no additional equipment was to be added. Top speed on low-octane fuel was about 65 mph. (DOUG MITCHEL)

World War II, An Era Within An Era

In the war years of 1942 through 1945, state-of-the-art engineering—read "Knuckleheads"—took a back seat to fulfilling military requirements. Harley-Davidson produced nearly 90,000 motorcycles for military use, most of the army Forty-Fives. The military wanted short, medium-sized bikes with ample ground clearance, not the long, low, and heavy big twins. Flathead engines were good enough, as most riding would be done at slow speeds fueled by poor-grade gas. The company's military orders were hugely important because they kept the factory doing what it did best, building bikes.

Indian, on the other hand, sold no motorcycles to the U. S. Army and had modest sales to Allied government forces. Consequently, Indian struggled to stay afloat by doing a variety of non-motorcycle defense tasks. Thus, Harley-Davidson was poised to become even more dominant in the postwar American market.

With no concern for appearances, the Army bikes could be fitted with a large and well-functioning air cleaner. (DOUG MITCHEL)

1943 Harley-Davidson XA. On request from the Army, Harley-Davidson and Indian bid on a contract to build 1,000 shaft-drive motorcycles for testing purposes. The impetus for the XA and Indian shafty was the North African theater of World War II, where Harley's BMW clone and Indian's Guzzi-style transverse V-twin would more efficiently cool in the desert heat, while the drive shaft precluded extreme chain wear caused by sand. The German Army lost North Africa before there was any need for these desert motorcycles. (DOUG MITCHEL)

1942 Harley-Davidson Model XA. Specifications: Engine: side-valve (Flathead) horizontally opposed twin, displacement 45 cubic inches (738cc); compression ratio 5.7:1; maximum output, 23 hp @ 4600 rpm. Transmission, four-speed foot-shift; primary drive, gears, final drive, shaft. Brakes, front and rear, drum and shoe. Ignition, battery and coil, double-spark (no distributor). Finish, olive drab matt (i.e., non-shiny or "flat") no polished or brightly plated parts.

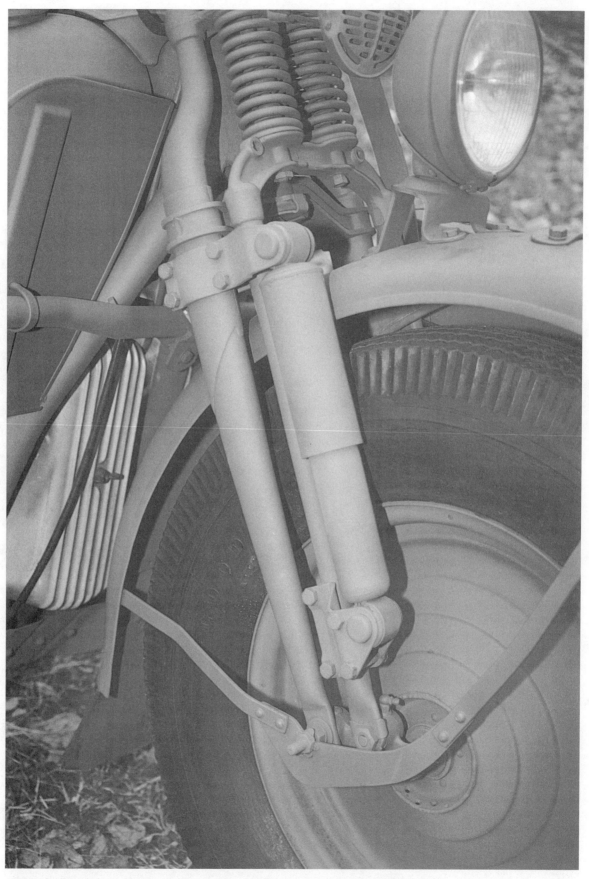

1943 Harley-Davidson XA. The time-honored leading-link fork was retained, with the addition of a large shock absorber. At least one prototype was built with a BMW-cloned telescopic fork. (DOUG MITCHEL)

1946-1947 Highlights

1946 and later: the dealer "Season Order Blank" term "High Compression Solo" wasn't commonly used in advertising or everyday discourse.

1946 Harley-Davidson Model UL. A view from the saddle.

1946 Harley-Davidson Model E. With pent-up demand after four years of war, would-be Harley buyers had to put their names on a list. In this seller's market, Harley-Davidson had no need to change the 1941 configuration, so all 1946 models were carry-overs. (DOUG MITCHEL)

1946 Harley-Davidson Model UL. A Tennessee Highway Patrol bike. The big Flatheads remained in production through the 1948 season, largely to satisfy police departments accustomed to this model.

1947 Harley-Davidson Model EL. In its final year of production, the Knucklehead (the nickname actually came later) was technically unchanged. One of the few cosmetic changes was the new ball-and-banner tank emblem.
(DOUG MITCHEL)

1947 Harley-Davidson Forty-Five. These bikes sported new nameplates, but were technically unchanged.

Models	Key Feature(s)	Engine Data	New Features, Misc.	Cost
46E, 47E	OHV V-twin	60.3 ci (989cc)	—	$464, $590
46EL, 47EL	OHV V-twin, Special Sport Solo	60.3 ci (989cc)	medium compression	$464, $590
46ES, 47ES	OHV V-twin, s/c gearing	60.3 ci (989cc)	medium compression	$464, $590
46F, 47F	OHV V-twin	73.7 ci (1207cc)	medium compression	$469, $605
46FL, 47FL	OHV V-twin, Special Sport Solo	73.7 ci (1207cc)	—	$469, $605
46FS, 47FS	OHV V-twin s/c gearing	73.7 ci (1207cc)	medium compression	$469, $605
46WL, 47WL	side-valve V-twin, Sport Solo,	45.3 ci (742cc)	high compression	$396, $490
46WR, 47WR	side-valve V-twin Competition Special	45.3 ci (742cc)	no brakes	n/a
46WRTT, 47WRTT	side-valve V-twin, Competition Special	45.3 ci (742cc)	no brakes	n/a
46U, 47U	side-valve V-twin	73.8 ci (1209cc)	medium compression	$427, $545
46UL, 47UL	side-valve V-twin	73.8 ci (1209cc)	high compression solo	$427, $545
46US, 47US	side-valve V-twin	73.8 ci (1209cc)	medium comp. s/c gearing	$427, $545

1947 Harley-Davidson Knucklehead and sidecar. (DOUG MITCHEL)

For 1948, new overhead-valve big twins arrived in 61- and 74-cubic inch versions. These were to a certain extent oil-cooled engines. A large aluminum cover fit over the entire upper end instead of only the valve area. Inside, cooling fins reacted to the copious oil supply, the latter necessary because of the lack of air flow over the heads. The 1948 Panhead combination was unique, combining the old springer fork with the new engine. To distinguish between the new engine and the earlier ones, enthusiasts coined the nicknames "Knucklehead" (for 1936-1947) and "Panhead" (1948 **and later).** (DOUG MITCHEL)

There was a new shifter gate for 1947, horizontal instead of arced, and the new black-faced speedometer was easier to read at night.

(DOUG MITCHEL)

1948-1949 Highlights

1948: Aluminum valve covers and hydraulic valve lifters. 1948: in advertising and everyday discourse the Model S was termed the "One-Twenty-Five" or "125" (never "one-two-five"). 1948: Model S price estimated. 1948 and later: the nicknames "Knucklehead" and "Panhead" came into use to distinguish the newer (Panhead) from the older (Knucklehead). 1949: telescopic "Hydra-Glide" fork on 61-ci and 74-ci twins. 1949: U Series discontinued. 1949-1957: in advertising and everyday discourse the term "Hydra-Glide" applied to all big twins, especially in the earlier years, to highlight the new fork.

1948 -1965, The Panhead Era

Again, as in the Knucklehead era, Harley-Davidson enjoyed significant business in other product lines. Unique American racing rules, created by Harley and Indian, continued to pit 750cc side-valve Harleys and Indians against 500cc overhead-valve imported bikes. Harley-Davidson entered the lightweight field with a 125cc two-stroke single built from expropriated German DKW drawings, and this business flourished for a few years.

As for the company's most popular line, the overhead-valve big twins, the new models, soon to be nicknamed "Panheads," addressed the messy subject of oil seepage

1948 Model WL. The new speedometer had the hash marks on the lower plate instead of the glass. (DOUG MITCHEL)

Models	Key Feature(s)	Engine Data	New Features, Misc.	Cost
48E, 49E	OHV V-twin medium compression, s/c gearing	60.3 ci (989cc)	1949: Hydra-Glide name for 61 ci and 74 ci twins	$635, $735
48EL, 49EL	OHV V-twin, Special Sport Solo	60.3 ci (989cc)	1949: Hydra-Glide name for 61 ci and 74 ci twins	$635, $735
48ES, 49ES	OHV V-twin, medium compression, s/c gearing	60.3 ci (989cc)	1949: Hydra-Glide name for 61 ci and 74 ci twins	$635, $735
48F, 49F	OHV V-twin, medium compression	73.7 ci (1207cc)	1949: Hydra-Glide name for 61-ci and 74-ci twins	$650, $750
48FL, 49FL	OHV V-twin, Special Sport Solo	73.7 ci (1207cc)	1949: name changed to "Sport Solo"	$650, $750
48FS, 49FS	OHV V-twin, medium compression, s/c gearing	73.7 ci (1207cc)	—	$650, $750
48WL, 49WL	side-valve V-twin, Sport Solo, high compression	45.3 ci (742cc)	—	$535, $590
48WR, 49WR	side-valve V-twin, Competition Special	45.3 ci (742cc)	no brakes	n/a
48WRTT, 49WRTT	side-valve V-twin, Competition Special	45.3 ci (742cc)	no brakes	n/a
48U	side-valve V-twin, medium compression	73.8 ci (1209cc)	—	$590
48UL	side-valve V-twin, High-Compression Solo	73.8 ci (1209cc)	—	$590
48US	side-valve V-twin, medium compression, s/c gearing	73.8 ci (1209cc)	—	$590
48S, 49S	One-Twenty-Five	7.6 ci (125cc)	3 hp	$283, $325

1948 WL. Except for the new speedometer, there were minimal changes on 1948 Forty-Fives. H-D realized that the model was nearing retirement. (DOUG MITCHEL)

that had been part of the Knucklehead experience. The entire head was covered with a stamped steel bonnet, under which copious cooling oil flow made up for the loss in air circulation. Although oil containment was improved with the Panhead layout, these engines were never as oil tight as had been hoped. This was partly because of the different thermal expansion rates of aluminum cylinder heads and the steel head covers. Riders and mechanics liked the new hydraulic valve lifters because they never had to fiddle with adjusting valve clearances. To tidy up the layout, there were no longer any external oil lines; oil now being routed through tunnels in the cylinders.

The 1949 season saw the arrival of telescopic forks in the Hydra-Glide (Panhead) range. Some unknown contracted artist proved his/her genius with the front fender design that managed to make the fat 5.00 x 16 front tire look "right." The esthetics of the front fork and headlight completed a masterful styling job. While the rest of the motorcycling world introduced rear suspension to their top models, Harley-Davidson faced no serious competition in the big twin field due to the end of major Indian production in 1949. In truth, the Panhead's telescopic fork, low-pressure tires, sprung saddle, and long wheelbase added up to excellent comfort over America's mostly paved highways. Rear suspension didn't arrive on the Panheads until the 1958 Duo-Glides replaced the Hydra-Glide range. Likewise, optional foot-shift transmissions arrived a bit late, in late 1951.

The mid-sized Models K and KH Flatheads of 1952-1956 appealed to a new generation of road riders who wanted lighter, shorter and nimbler motorcycles. The racing variants, mostly 750cc KR flat trackers and KRTT road racers, sustained Harley dominance in American racing. Growing out of the K/KH series was the overhead-valve 883cc Sportster. These bikes weren't the big money makers, but were strategically important.

This 1948 tank sports the horizontal shifter gate introduced on 1947 models. (DOUG MITCHEL)

1948 Harley-Davidson Model WR. Typical racer production was a few dozen, but factory records indicate an astounding 292 of these racers were built for the 1948 season! The side-valve Flathead V-twin displacement 45.3 cubic inches (747cc), produced 38 hp @ 5500 rpm, and weighed 360 lbs. (DOUG MITCHEL)

1948 Harley-Davidson Model S (above). The "125" had an engine that was a clone of the pre-World War II DKW 125. Rights to the DKW drawings were turned over to the Allied nations. The British BSA company produced its Bantam model as a mirror image, so that the British customary right-side foot shift could be achieved. Lubrication was via air/oil mist—you premixed the fuel and oil. (DOUG MITCHEL)

1949 Model FL "Panhead" (above). The new Hydra-Glide fork and the stylized front fender were hugely popular. Despite continuing the rigid frame, the super soft fork, softly sprung solo saddle or guitar-shaped buddy seat, and long wheelbase made these remarkably comfortable highway cruisers. Even today, out on the interstates, the ride would measure up. (DOUG MITCHEL)

1948 Harley-Davidson Model S, commonly spoken as the "One-Twenty-Five," or written as the "125." The 125 was a copy of the German DKW. Engine: two-stroke piston-ported single-cylinder, displacement 7.6 cubic inches (124.9cc); compression ratio 6.6:1; maximum output, 3 hp. Wheelbase was 50 inches. Weight was 185 lbs. Finish was black. (DOUG MITCHEL)

1950 Harley-Davidson WL . A big twin-style front fender was about the only new feature of this model, now very much behind times. Foreign middleweights with overhead-valve engines, telescopic forks, sprung rear wheels and four-speed foot-shifts were making it difficult to sell the Forty-Fives.

1950-1951 Highlights

1950: New E and F Series cylinder heads with larger ports. 1951: Models E, ES, F, and FS discontinued. 1951 E and F Series: late-season offering of optional foot shift and hand clutch.

1952-1953 Highlights

1952: A few W Series bikes built; K Series started. 1952 W prices estimated. 1952: K featured telescopic fork, swinging-arm rear suspension, hand clutch, four-speed foot-shift trans, unit construction. 1952-1953: KK version was a K with a dealer-installed kit. 1953: E Series discontinued. 1952: New KR-Series racers; these aren't shown in subsequent bi-annual tables but are presented later in one table covering all racing years. 1952-1953: in journalism and everyday discourse, but not in advertising, the term "K-Model" was popular. 1953: 165cc Model ST replaced 125cc Model S. 1953 and later: in advertising and everyday discourse a Model ST bike was termed a "One-Sixty-Five" ("165").

Models	Key Feature(s)	Engine Data	New Features, Misc.	Cost
50E	Hydra-Glide, medium compression	OHV 60.3 ci (989cc)	new heads, 10% power boost	$735
50EL, 51EL	Hydra-Glide, Sport Solo	OHV 60.3 ci (989cc)	new heads, 40 hp @ 4800 rpm	$735, $885
50ES, 51ELS	Hydra-Glide, medium compr., s/c gearing	OHV 60.3 ci (989cc)	new heads, 10% power boost	$735, $885
50F	Hydra-Glide, medium compression	OHV 73.7 ci (1207cc)	new heads, 10% power boost	$750
50FL, 51FL	Hydra-Glide, Sport Solo	OHV 73.7 ci (1207cc)	new heads, 48 hp @ 5000 rpm	$750, $900
50FS, 51FLS	Hydra-Glide, medium compr., s/c gearing	OHV 73.7 ci (1207cc)	new heads, 48 hp @ 5000 rpm	$750, $900
50WL, 51WL	side-valve V-twin, Sport Solo, high comp.	45.3 ci (742cc)	—	$590, $730
50WR, 51WR	side-valve V-twin, Competition Special	45.3 ci (742cc)	no brakes	n/a
50WRTT, 51WRTT	side-valve V-twin, Competition Special	45.3 ci (742cc)	no brakes	—
50S, 51S	One-Twenty-Five	two-stroke single, 7.6 ci (125cc)	—	$325, $365

1951 Harley-Davidson Servicar. Annual production was typically about 1,000. Most went to police departments. The model remained in production through 1973, for a total production life of 42 years! It was the last side-valve motorcycle built in large numbers.

1952 Harley-Davidson Model K. Designed to combat the flood of 30.50-cubic inch (500cc) British bikes being imported, the "K" stuck with American middle-weight tradition by countering with the historic 45-cubic inch (750cc) side-valve (Flathead) configuration.

Models	Key Feature(s)	Engine Data	New Features, Misc.	Cost
52EL	Hydra-Glide, Sport Solo	OHV 60.3 ci (989cc)	—	$955
52ELF	Hydra-Glide, Sport Solo	OHV 60.3 ci (989cc)	optional foot shift and hand clutch	$955
52ELS	Hydra-Glide, medium comp. s/c gearing	OHV 60.3 ci (989cc)	optional foot shift and hand clutch	$955
52FL, 53FL	Hydra-Glide, Sport Solo	OHV 73.7 ci (1207cc)	—	$970, $1,000
52FLF, 53FLF	Hydra-Glide, Sport Solo	OHV 3.7 ci (1207cc)	optional foot shift and hand clutch	$970, $1,000
53FLE	Hydra-Glide, Traffic Combination	OHV 73.7 ci (1207cc)	hand shift	$970, $1,000
53FLEF	Hydra-Glide, Traffic Combination	OHV 73.7 ci (1207cc)	foot shift	$970, $1,000
52FLS, 53FLS	Hydra-Glide, medium compression, s/c gearing	73.7 ci (1207cc)	optional foot shift, hand clutch	$970, $1,000
52K, 53K	side-valve V-twin, unit construction	45.3 ci (742cc)	—	$865, $875
52KK, 53KK	side-valve V-twin, unit construction	45.3 ci (742cc)	—	n/a
52KR, 53KR	side-valve V-twin, unit construction	45.3 ci (742cc)	racer w/o brakes	n/a
52KRTT 53KRTT	side-valve V-twin, unit construction	45.3 ci (742cc)	racer w/ brakes	n/a
52S	One-Twenty-Five	two-stroke single, 7.6 ci (125cc)	—	$385
53ST	One-Sixty-Five	two-stroke single, 10.1 ci (166cc)	—	$405
52WL	side-valve V-twin, Sport Solo	high compression, 45.3 ci (742cc)	—	n/a
52WR and 52WRTT	side-valve V-twin, Competition Special	45.3 ci (742cc)	only 8 built	n/a

1952 Harley-Davidson Model K. The K's unit construction was Harley-Davidson's first such design since the 1919 Sport. Yes, the 125cc two-stroke was a unit-construction, but that lightweight was designed by DKW. (CYCLE)

1952 Harley-Davidson Model K. The Model K was the company's most radical new design up to that time. New (for Harley) features were the four-speed foot-shift transmission, and swinging-arm rear suspension. On the left, Dick Hutchins of the Los Angeles Harley shop; on the right, *Cycle* editor and road tester Bob Greene. (CYCLE)

1952 Harley-Davidson Model K. Tester Greene tried every trick to flatter the home-grown brand with a 100-mph speed. He swapped carburetor jets, removed the muffler, and when those steps proved insufficient, he did the same on another K, a demonstrator with several hundred miles of action. At last, he achieved 100.5 mph. (CYCLE)

1952 Harley-Davidson Model K. Perhaps inspired by the era's flat-track racing motorcycles, such "spaghetti" bars commonly adorned custom cut-down "bobbers," and were also popular accessories for touring bikes. The factory simply followed fashion and produced the "California" look right there on the assembly line.

1952 Harley-Davidson Model K (right). Harley-Davidson had aimed at the wrong target. During the two-plus years of design work, Triumph and BSA had upped the overhead-valve ante from 30.50 cubic inches to 40 cubic inches (650cc). The new K couldn't hang with the British crowd it was supposed to rule, but the K series proved hugely successful as a racer, and as the roots of the later overhead-valve Sportster. (CYCLE)

1952 Harley-Davidson Model FLF. Overhead-valve (nick-named "Panhead") V-twin, displacement 73.7 cubic inches (1207cc); compression ratio 7:1; maximum output 48 hp @ 5000 rpm, four-speed foot-shift; primary drive, double-row chain, oil mist lubricated, final drive, chain, wheelbase, 60.5 inches, weight, 598 lbs., finished in a variety of colors. (DOUG MITCHEL)

1954-1955 Highlights

1954: K and KK replaced by KH and KHK with increased displacement. KHK version was a KH with a dealer-installed kit. KH racing variants with brakes were also built for so-called "TT" racing, the precursor of motocross racing. 1955: New high-performance FLH and FLHF with polished and flowed ports and "Victory" cams.

1955 Harley-Davidson Model FL. Detail changes included O-ring and hose clamp sealing of inlet manifold, tapered roller bearings, and larger crankcases. During the year, the Model FLH was introduced, offering a claimed 10-percent power increase through polished internals, new cam profiles and higher compression ratio. (DOUG MITCHEL)

1955 Harley-Davidson Model KH. Now in its second production year, the KH, with increased displacement, was putting Harley abreast or ahead in the street "wars" with 650cc British bikes. The KH engine dimensions were: bore and stroke of 2 3/4 inches (same as K) and 4 9/16 inches, displacement 54.94 cubic inches (900cc). The polished engines were standard on all KH models.

Models	Key Feature(s)	Engine Data	New Features, Misc.	Cost
54FL, 55FL	Hydra-Glide, Sport Solo	OHV 73.7 ci (1207cc)	hand shift	$1,015, $1,015
54FLF, 55FLF	Hydra-Glide, Sport Solo	OHV 73.7 ci (1207cc)	foot shift	$1,015, $1,015
55FLH	Hydra-Glide, Super Sport Solo	OHV 73.7 ci (1207cc)	hand shift	n/a
55FLHF	Hydra-Glide, Super Sport Solo	OHV 73.7 ci (1207cc)	foot shift	n/a
54FLE, 55FLE	Hydra-Glide, Traffic Combination	OHV 73.7 ci (1207cc)	hand shift	$1,015, $1,015
54FLEF, 55FLEF	Hydra-Glide, Traffic Combination	OHV 73.7 ci (1207cc)	foot shift	$1,015, $1,015
54FLS, 55FLS	Hydra-Glide, medium compr., s/c gearing	OHV 73.7 ci (1207cc)	hand shift	$1,015, $1,015
54FLFS	Hydra-Glide, medium compr., s/c gearing	OHV 73.7 ci (1207cc)	foot shift	$1,015, $1,015
54KH, 55KH	side-valve V-twin, unit construction	54.2 ci (888cc)	—	$925, $925
54KHK, 55KHK	side-valve V-twin, unit construction	54.2 ci (888cc)	polished ports, higher cam lift ('55)	$745
54ST, 55ST	One-Sixty-Five, two-stroke single	10.1 ci (166cc)	alum. alloy piston	$405, $405
55B	Hummer, two-stroke single	7.6 ci (125cc)	no-frills model	n/a

1956-1957 Highlights

1956: KHK was a dealer-kitted KH. 1957: Traffic Combination not listed, OHV X-Series Sportster replaced KH Series.

1956 Harley-Davidson Model KHK. On all K Series bikes, the rear suspension units were 9/16 inch shorter, and the frame was modified in both the steering head area and the rear shock area to achieve a lower saddle position. (DOUG MITCHEL)

1956 Harley-Davidson Model KHK. Like the KK of 1952 and 1953, the 1954-1956 KHK was the high-performance version. Special high-lift cams and polished ports were featured. All KH models got stronger second-gear and third-gear teeth. (DOUG MITCHEL)

Models	Key Feature(s)	Engine Data	New Features, Misc.	Cost
56FL, 57FL	Hydra-Glide, Sport Solo	OHV 73.7 ci (1207cc)	hand shift	$1,055, $1,167
56FLF, 57FLF	Hydra-Glide, Sport Solo	OHV 73.7 ci (1207cc)	foot shift	$1,055, $1,167
56FLE	Hydra-Glide, Traffic Combination	OHV 73.7 ci (1207cc)	hand shift	$1,055
56FLEF	Hydra-Glide, Traffic Combination	OHV 73.7 ci (1207cc)	foot shift	$1,055
56FLH, 57FLH	Hydra-Glide, Super Sport Solo	OHV 73.7 ci (1207cc)	hand shift	$1,123, $1,243
56FLHF, 57FLHF	Hydra-Glide, Super Sport Solo	73.7 ci (1207cc)	foot shift	$1,123, $1,243
56FLHS, 55FLHS	Hydra-Glide, medium compression, s/c gearing	73.7 ci (1207cc)	hand shift, replaced FLS and FLFS	—
56KH	side-valve V-twin, unit construction	side-valve 54.2 ci (888cc)	—	$935
56KHK	side-valve V-twin, unit construction	side-valve 54.2 ci (888cc)	—	$1,003
57XL	Sportster	OHV V-twin	45 hp	$1,103
56ST, 57ST	One-Sixty-Five	two-stroke, 10.1 ci (166cc)	—	$405, $445
56STU, 57STU	One-Sixty-Five	two-stroke, 10.1 ci (166cc)	—	$405, $445
56B, 57B	Hummer	7.6 ci (125cc)	1957: front brake	$356

1956 Harley-Davison S-165. For 1956, a larger tail light and 3.40 x 18 tires were new features.

(DOUG MITCHEL)

1957 Harley-Davidson Hydra-Glide (below). The rigid framed Hydra-Glide made its final appearance in the 1957 lineup. Technical changes were few, but included steel alloy inlet and exhaust valve guides and stronger valve springs.

(DOUG MITCHEL)

1956 Harley-Davidson S-165. The 10.1 ci (165cc) engine had a 6.6:1 compression ratio. Maximum output was 5.5 to 6 hp. (DOUG MITCHEL)

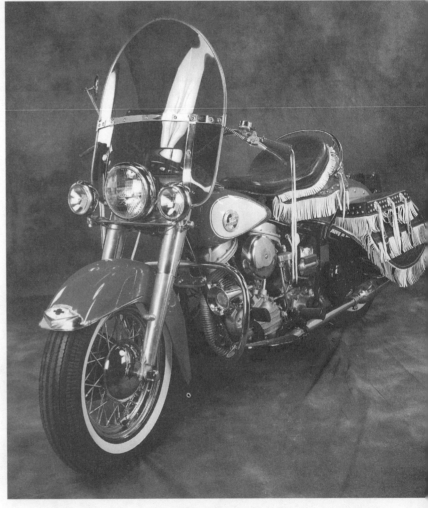

1957 Harley-Davidson Model XL Sportster. Without doubt, the new overhead-valve Sportster put Harely out front in the street "wars." Typically, only the mild "cooking" version was offered in the first year, but that was enough to impress. (DOUG MITCHEL)

1957 Harley-Davidson Model 165. At Dale Walksler's Wheels Through Time museum, a staffer demonstrated the refueling procedure: Fill the cup with oil; pour the oil in the tank; fill the tank with fuel; vigorously shake the motorcycle a few times. So-called "white" (unleaded) gasoline was recommended, but was sometimes hard to find during the era of tetraethyl lead.

(DALE WALKSLER)

1957 Harley-Davidson Model XL Sportster. Specifications: Engine: unit-construction overhead-valve V-twin, displacement 53.9 cubic inches (883cc); compression ratio 7.5:1; maximum output, 40 hp @ 5500 rpm. Transmission, four-speed foot-shift; primary drive. Wheelbase, 57 inches. Weight, 495 lbs. Fuel tank, 4.4 gallons. Oil tank, 3 quarts.

(DOUG MITCHEL)

1958-1959 Highlights

1958: "Duo-Glide" with rear suspension replaced Hydra-Glide. From 1958, there were no "Traffic Combination" models. Side-valve KR and KRTT models continued through 1969; these are not further listed. 1958-1964: in advertising the term "Duo-Glide" was used; in everyday discourse the term "Seventy-Four" ("74") was the favorite. 1957 and later: in everyday discourse the terms "Sportster" and "CH" were popular. From 1957, all road model twins (3-wheel Servicar excepted) were overhead-valve models; "o. h. v." not further listed.

1958 Harley-Davidson Model XLCH Sportster. The "CH" supposedly stood for "Competition Hot." The model was eligible for the unique American racing form called "TT," a term derived back in the 1930s from "miniature TT," a sort of miniature road race inspired by the trans-Atlantic Isle of Man TT. In the USA, TT racing typically was over a dirt course of 1/2 mile to 1 mile around, with at least one left turn, one right turn, and one jump. Brakes were permitted, along with overhead-valve engines up to 1000cc. (DOUG MITCHEL)

1958 Harley-Davidson Model XLH Sportster. Cam gears were integral with the shafts instead of keyed. A 1/8-inch-thicker counter shaft added strength. (DOUG MITCHEL)

1959 Harley-Davidson Model FL Police. Engine, overhead-valve V-twin, displacement 73.7 cubic inches (1207cc); compression ratio 8:1; maximum output, 48 hp @ 5000 rpm. Transmission, four-speed foot-shift standard, hand-shift optional. Ignition, battery and coil. Frame, double-loop, double front down-tubes. Suspension, front, telescopic, rear, swinging-arm. Wheelbase, 60 inches. Weight, 750 lbs. Finish, Police silver.

(DOUG MITCHEL)

Models	Key Feature(s)	Engine Data	New Features, Misc.	Cost
58FL, 59FL	Duo-Glide, Sport Solo	73.7 ci (1207cc)	hand shift	$1,255, $1,280
58FLF, 59FLF	Duo-Glide, Sport Solo	73.7 ci (1207cc)	foot shift	$1,255, $1,280
58FLHS	Duo-Glide, medium compression, s/c gearing	73.7 ci (1207cc)	hand shift, replaced FLS and FLFS	$1,320
58FLH, 59FLH	Duo-Glide, Super Sport	73.7 ci (1207cc)	hand shift	$1,320
58FLHF, 59FLHF	Duo-Glide, Super Sport	73.7 ci (1207cc)	foot shift	$1,320
58XL, 59XL	Sportster	53.9 ci (883cc)	—	$1,155
58XLCH, 59XLCH	Sportster "Competition Hot"	53.9 ci (883cc)	1958-1969: magneto ignition	1958: unknown 1959: $1,285
58ST, 59ST	two-stroke single	10.1 ci (166cc)	—	$465, $475
58STU, 59STU	two-stroke single	10.1 ci (166cc)	Modified carburetor	$465, $475
58B, 59B	two-stroke single	7.6 ci (125cc)	no-frills model	$375, $385

1960 Harley-Davidson Model FLH. Engine, overhead-valve (later, nicknamed "Panhead") V-twin, displacement 73.7 cubic inches (1207cc); compression ratio 7:1; maximum output, 60 hp @ 5000 rpm. Transmission, four-speed foot-shift standard, hand-shift optional, constant-mesh; primary drive, double-row chain. (DOUG MITCHEL)

1960-1961 Highlights

1960: Model XL discontinued. 1960: Super 10 lightweight consolidates Hummer and 165 specifications, replaced those models.

1961 Harley-Davidson FL. As usual, the annual model changes included a new paint scheme.
(DOUG MITCHEL)

Models	Key Feature(s)	Engine Data	New Features, Misc.	Cost
60FL, 61FL	Duo-Glide, Sport Solo	73.7 ci (1207cc)	hand shift	$1,310, $1,335
60FLF, 61FLF	Duo-Glide, Sport Solo	73.7 ci (1207cc)	foot shift	$1,310, $1,335
60FLHF, 61FLHF	Duo-Glide, Super Sport	73.7 ci (1207cc)	foot shift	$1,375, $1,400
60FLH, 61FLH	Duo-Glide, Super Sport	73.7 ci (1207cc)	hand shift	$1,375, $1,400
60XLH, 61XLH	Sportster	53.9 ci (883cc)	1961: New 3.75-gal. creased teardrop tank	$1,225, $1,250
60XLCH, 61XLCH	Sportster, "Competition Hot"	53.9 ci (883cc)	—	$1,310, $1,335
60BT, 61BT	two-stroke single	10.1 ci (166cc)	1960: Magneto ignition & lights	$455, $465
60BTU, 61BTU	two-stroke single	10.1 ci (166cc)	Modified carb	$465, $465

1962-1963 Highlights

1962: Three lightweight models, Pacer, Scat, and Ranger. 1963: Rear suspension on Pacer and Scat; Ranger discontinued.

1962 Harley-Davidson Duo-Glide (right). Except for a revised oil pump, all 1962 Duo-Glide changes were stylistic. The company shipped motorcycles with a wide variety of options, packaged in groups. For instance, there were six equipment groups in 1962. Group variances included such matters as chrome plated standard bits and pieces, additional bolt-on small accessories, three choices of seats, windshield or not, and white or black saddlebags. (DOUG MITCHEL)

1963 Harley-Davidson Duo-Glide (left). The new chain guard is evident. Other new 1963 features included: redesigned chain oiler, larger rear brake and external oil lines. The latter were deemed less leak prone than the internal oil passages routed through the cylinders. The considerable expansion and contraction of the large iron cylinders and the reaction with the aluminum crank-cases had proven a source of oil seepage. (DOUG MITCHEL)

Models	Key Feature(s)	Engine Data	New Features, Misc.	Cost
62FL, 63FL	Duo-Glide, Sport Solo	73.7 ci (1207cc)	hand shift	$1,335, $1,360
62FLF, 63FLF	Duo-Glide, Sport Solo	73.7 ci (1207cc)	foot shift	$1,335, $1,360
62FLH, 63FLH	Duo-Glide, Super Sport	73.7 ci (1207cc)	hand shift	$1,400, $1,425
62FLHF, 63FLHF	Duo-Glide, Super Sport	73.7 ci (1207cc)	foot shift	$1,400, $1,425
62XLH, 63XLH	Sportster	53.9 ci (883cc)	—	$1,250, $1,270
62XLCH, 63XLCH	Sportster Competition Hot	53.9 ci (883cc)	—	$1,335, $1,355
62BT, 63BT	Pacer, two-stroke single	10.7 ci (175cc)	1962: name-change to former Super-10	$465, $485
62BTU, 63BTU	Pacer, two-stroke single	10.7 ci (175cc)	carburetor restrictor	$465, $485
62BTH, 63BTH	Scat, two-stroke single	10.7 ci (175cc)	1962: off/on-road model	$475, $505
62BTF	Ranger, two-stroke single	10.7 ci (175cc)	off-road trail model	$440

1963 Harley-Davidson Scat. Engine, two-stroke single-cylinder, displacement 11 cubic inches (175cc); compression ratio 7.63:1; maximum output, 6 hp. Transmission, three-speed, foot-shift, primary drive, chain; final drive, chain. Brakes, front and rear, drum and shoe. Ignition, magneto. Frame, single-loop. Wheelbase, 52 inches. Weight, 220 lbs. Fuel tank, 1.9 gallons. Finish, a variety of colors. (DOUG MITCHEL)

1963 Harley-Davidson FL. New cylinder heads featured a drilled and threaded boss to support the new external oil lines. (DOUG MITCHEL)

1963 Harley-Davison FL. This speedometer style was new for 1962.

(DOUG MITCHEL)

1964-1965 Highlights

1965: electric-start Electra-Glide replaced kick-start Duo-Glide. 1965: BTU model discontinued.

1964 Harley-Davidson Duo-Glide: The last of the Duo-Glides received only minor updates. These included an improved front chain oiler, a new oil pressure switch for increased reliability, a new ignition switch and a side-stand with a bigger footprint.

(DOUG MITCHEL)

Models	Key Feature(s)	Engine Data	New Features, Misc.	Cost
64FL	Duo-Glide Sport Solo	73.7 ci (1207cc)	hand shift	$1,385
65FLB	Electra-Glide Sport Solo	73.7 ci (1207cc)	hand shift, "Turnpike" tanks or optional 3.75 gal.	$1,530
64FLF	Duo-Glide Sport Solo	73.7 ci (1207cc)	foot shift	$1,385
65FLFB	Electra-Glide Sport Solo	73.7 ci (1207cc)	foot shift, "Turnpike" tanks or optional 3.75 gal.	$1,530
64FLH	Duo-Glide Super Sport	73.7 ci (1207cc)	hand shift	$1,385
65FLHB	Electra-Glide Super Sport	73.7 ci (1207cc)	hand shift	$1,530
64FLHF	Duo-Glide Super Sport	73.7 ci (1207cc)	foot shift	$1,385
65FLHFB	Electra-Glide Super Sport	73.7 ci (1207cc)	foot shift, "Turnpike" tanks or optional 3.75 gal.	$1,530
64XLH, 65XLH	V-twin, unit construction	53.9 ci (883cc)	—	$1,295, $1,400
64XLCH, 65XLCH	V-twin, unit construction	53.9 ci (883cc)	—	$1,360, $1,396
64BT, 65BT	Pacer, two-stroke single	10.7 ci (175cc)	—	$495, $505
64BTU	Pacer, two-stroke single	10.7 ci (175cc)	carburetor restrictor	$495
64BTH, 65BTH	Scat, two-stroke single	10.7 ci (175cc)	—	$505, $515

1964 Harley-Davidson XLCH. Changes on both the XLH and XLCH models included: lighter, longer-wearing aluminum tappet guides, a new clutch seal and die-cast aluminum full width front hub. Since its inception, the CH Sportster had been King of the street wars. In 1962, Cycle World ran its test bike up to 122 mph. It must have been a cheater, because no other road test ever came close to this speed. But there was no disputing the kingship of the CH.

(DOUG MITCHEL)

1965 Harley-Davidson Model FLH Electra Glide. The electric starter and large 53-amp-hour battery resulted in weight increasing from 690 lbs. to 783 lbs. (each with half-tank of fuel). Primary drive, double-row chain, oil-lubricated. Electric starter and kick starter.

(DOUG MITCHEL)

1966-1980, The Shovelhead Era

Sportster-style cylinder heads arrived on the 1966 big twins, soon prompting the nickname "Shovelheads." The new heads flowed better, so maximum output increased from the last Panhead's 55 hp to the Shovelhead's 60 hp. The extra oomph compensated for the increased weight of the Electra Glide range, the initial 1965 machines having lacked the get-go of the kick-start Duo-Glides.

A landmark model arrived in the 1971 range, the Super Glide. The stripped-down genre, first seen in the 1958 Sportster, had now become part of the big twin scheme. This was the nucleus of the Harley-Davidson rebirth of the 1980s, needing but the new "Evolution" engine to complete the process.

In the sporting realm, American racing lost all pretense of using "standard" motorcycles, with the Gran Prix-style two-strokes beginning to take over road racing. Harley-Davidson bowed out of road racing in 1974. But, in dirt track racing, where mid-range torque counts more than maximum hp, Harleys remained dominant.

Near the end of the Shovelhead era, the FLT big twin appeared. The all-new frame, all-new steering geometry, and, most significantly, the rubber-mounted engine, positioned Harley-Davidson for unprecedented popularity. Just four years later came the Evolution "Blockhead" engine and, together with the rubber-mounted engine, such Har-

1967 Harley-Davidson XLH. The touring Sportster got an electric starter for 1967. The headlight nacelle and skinny CH front fender were also new.

(DOUG MITCHEL)

ley-Davidsons established new standards for smoothness and reliability.

1966-1967 Highlights

1966: New Sportster-style heads on Electra-Glides; soon nicknamed "Shovelheads." 1966-1969: Tillotson carburetor on all twins. 1966: last year of American-made lightweights (Bobcat Model). 1967: Electric-start XLH with new headlight nacelle.

Models	Key Feature(s)	Engine Data	New Features, Misc.	Cost
66FLB, 67FLB	Electra-Glide Sport Solo	73.7 ci (1207cc)	hand shift, Tillotson carb.	$1,545, $1,735
66FLFB, 67FLFB	Electra-Glide Sport Solo	73.7 ci (1207cc)	foot shift, Tillotson carb.	$1,545, $1,735
66FLHB, 67FLHB	Electra-Glide Super Sport	73.7 ci (1207cc)	hand shift, Tillotson carb.	$1,610, $1,800
66FLHFB, 67FLHFB	Electra-Glide Super Sport	73.7 ci (1207cc)	foot shift, Tillotson carb.	$1,610, $1,800
66XLH, 67XLH	Sportster	53.9 ci (883cc)	1967: electric starter	$1,415, $1,650
66XLCH, 67XLCH	Sportster Competition Hot	53.9 ci (883cc)	—	$1,411, $1,600
66BTH	Bobcat two-stroke single	10.7 ci (175cc)	integrated tank	$505, $515

1966 Harley-Davidson KR. These are the 750cc Flat-heads that ruled American racing from 1954 through 1968, when running against 500cc overhead-valve imports. Harleys won 65 percent of all national championship races during this era, and won 12 of 15 overall grand national championship seasonal titles giving them the No. 1 plate the following season.

(DOUG MITCHEL)

1966 Harley-Davidson KR. The skill and effort of America's premier Flathead tuner Tom Sifton, lead the way. Sifton's cam and porting secrets eventually were found out by the factory in 1954, and led to domination. (DOUG MITCHEL)

1966 Harley-Davidson Electra-Glide (above). New Sportster-style heads graced the Electra-Glides of 1966. The engine was soon nicknamed the "Shovelhead." Maximum output at 5400 rpm was increased from the Panhead's 60 hp to 65 hp. (DOUG MITCHEL)

1967 Harley-Davidson Electra-Glide. The premier Harley received only cosmetic changes for 1967.

(DOUG MITCHEL)

1968-1969 Highlights

1969: Last year of medium compression "FL" touring models; all later tourers are "FLH."

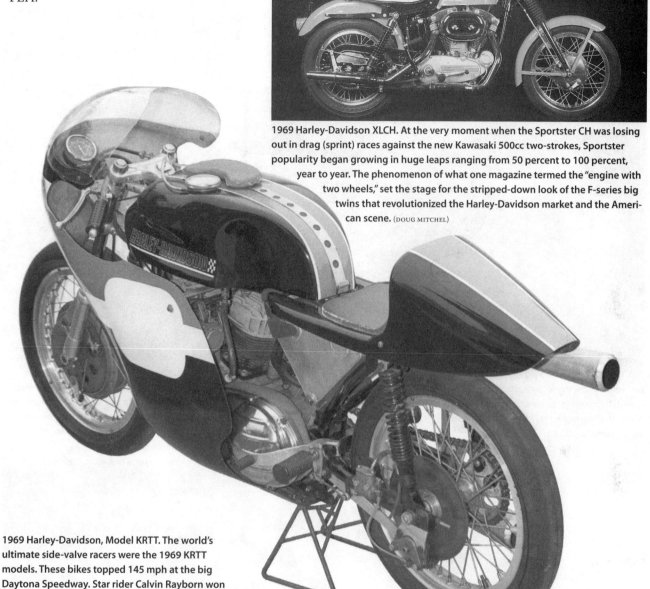

1969 Harley-Davidson XLCH. At the very moment when the Sportster CH was losing out in drag (sprint) races against the new Kawasaki 500cc two-strokes, Sportster popularity began growing in huge leaps ranging from 50 percent to 100 percent, year to year. The phenomenon of what one magazine termed the "engine with two wheels," set the stage for the stripped-down look of the F-series big twins that revolutionized the Harley-Davidson market and the American scene. (DOUG MITCHEL)

1969 Harley-Davidson, Model KRTT. The world's ultimate side-valve racers were the 1969 KRTT models. These bikes topped 145 mph at the big Daytona Speedway. Star rider Calvin Rayborn won both the 1968 and 1969 Daytona 200's on a KRTT.
(SAM HOTTON, STEVE WRIGHT)

Models	Key Feature(s)	Engine Data	New Features, Misc.	Cost
68FLB, 69FLB	Electra-Glide Sport Solo	73.7 ci (1207cc)	hand shift	$1,735, $1,885
68FLFB, 69FLFB	Electra-Glide Sport Solo	73.7 ci (1207cc)	foot shift	$1,735, $1,885
68FLHB, 69FLHB	Electra-Glide Super Sport	73.7 ci (1207cc)	hand shift	$1,800, $1,900
68FLHFB, 69FLHFB	Electra-Glide Super Sport	73.7 ci (1207cc)	foot shift	$1,800, $1,900
68XLH, 69XLH	Sportster	53.9 ci (883cc)	—	$1,650, $1,765
68XLCH, 69XLCH	Sportster Competition Hot	53.9 ci (883cc)	—	$1,600, $1,698

1970-1971 Highlights

1970: F-Series, alternator replaced generator; cone shaped timing case cover. 1971: FX Super-Glide is first of chopper inspired genre. 1970-1975: Bendix carburetor.

1970 Harley-Davidson Model XLH Sportster. Specifications: Engine: unit-construction overhead-valve V-twin, displacement 53.9 cubic inches (883cc); compression ratio 9:1; maximum output, 56 hp @ 6800 rpm. Transmission, four-speed foot-shift; primary drive, triple-row chain running in oil bath; final drive, chain. (DOUG MITCHEL)

1971 Harley-Davidson FX. Engine: overhead-valve ("Shovelhead") V-twin, displacement 73.7 cubic inches (1207cc); compression ratio 8:1; maximum output, 65 hp @ 5400 rpm. The cone-shaped timing cover had arrived on all 1970 big twins, along with an alternator in lieu of a generator. (DOUG MITCHEL)

1970 Harley-Davidson Model XLH Sportster. Specifications, continued: Brake front and rear, drum and shoe. Ignition, battery and coil. Electric starter (no kick starter). Frame, double-loop. Suspension, front, telescopic, rear, swinging-arm. Wheelbase, 57 inches. Weight, 510 lbs. Fuel tank, 3.75 gallons. Oil tank, 3 quarts. Tires, 19-inch front, 18-inch rear. Finish: a variety of colors. (DOUG MITCHEL)

Models	Key Feature(s)	Engine Data	New Features, Misc.
70FLP, 71FLP	Electra-Glide, police use	73.7 ci (1207cc)	hand shift
70FLPF, 71FLPF	Electra-Glide, police use	73.7 ci (1207cc)	foot
70FLH, 71FLH	Electra-Glide Super Sport	73.7 ci (1207cc)	—
70FLHF, 71FLHF	Electra-Glide Super Sport	73.7 ci (1207cc)	—
71FX	Super-Glide	73.7 ci (1207cc)	foot shift, all "FX" models 1971-1978, kick-start only
70XLH, 71XLH	Sportster	53.9 ci (883cc)	—
70XLCH, 71XLCH	Sportster Competition Hot	53.9 ci (883cc)	1970: battery ignition
70XR750, 71XR750	XR750 racer	OHV 45.5 ci (746cc)	de-stroked Sportster engine

1971 Harley-Davidson FX. Though the public went wild for the Super Glide's looks, this didn't include the unpopular "boat tail," which was not carried over in 1972.

(DOUG MITCHEL)

1971 Harley-Davidson Model FX Super Glide. This was the first of the factory-built custom or cruiser big twins. A new Harley image was on the way.

(DOUG MITCHEL)

1972 Harley-Davidson XR. Effective with the 1969 racing season, the old "mixed bag" rules were discarded, and a single 750cc class was established without regard to cylinder head design. The factory tried racing de-stroked iron-barrel Sportster engines in the 1970 and 1971 XR models, but the iron jug XRs overheated. The all-new 1972 engine, with aluminum cylinders and heads, returned Harley-Davidson to racing dominance.

1973 Harley-Davidson Electra-Glide. Front and rear disc brakes arrived on the 1973 F-series bikes.

(DOUG MITCHEL)

1972-1973 Highlights

1972: Last of FLP Series (police); last year F-Series listed as specific hand-shift and foot-shift models. 1972: First year of 60.9 ci X Series. 1972: Official model name "XLH 1000" was trimmed to "XL 1000" in advertising and everyday discourse. 1973: Front and rear disc brakes on F-Series; front disc brake on X-Series. 1973: Advertising switched to the terms "FLH 1200, FX 1200, XL 1000, XLCH 1000;" the public went along with using "FX 1200" (instead of "Super-Glide"), but continued to favor the terms "Electra-Glide" and "Sportster."

Models	Key Feature(s)	Engine Data	New Features, Misc.
72FLP	Electra-Glide, police use	73.7 ci (1207cc)	hand shift
72FLPF	Electra-Glide, police use	73.7 ci (1207cc)	foot shift
72FLH, 73FLH1200	Electra-Glide, also FLH1200	73.7 ci (1207cc)	—
72FLHF, 73FLHF1200	Electra-Glide, also FLHF1200	73.7 ci (1207cc)	—
72FX, 73FX1200	Super-Glide, also FX 1200	73.7 ci (1207cc)	—
72XLH1000, 73XLH1000	XL 1000, also, "Sportster"	60.9 ci (997cc)	—
72XLCH1000, 73XLCH1000	XLCH 1000, also "Sportster"	OHV 60.9 ci (997cc)	—

1974-1975 Highlights

1974 and later: no listings for hand-shift models. 1974: First year of the electric-start Super Glide. 1974 and later: Advertising favored the term "FLH 1200," but the public favored "Electra-Glide."

1975 Harley-Davidson XL. The tamer version of the Sportster now looked virtually identical to the hotter XLCH. The "engine with two wheels" was definitely "in." The single (front) disc brake first appeared on the 1972 X-series and the 60.9-ci (997cc) displacement debuted on the 1972 X-series.
(DOUG MITCHEL)

Models	Key Feature(s)	Engine Data	New Features, Misc.
74FLH1200, 75FLH1200	Electra-Glide, also FLH1200	73.7 ci (1207cc)	—
74FLHF1200, 75FLHF1200	Electra-Glide, also FLHF1200	73.7 ci (1207cc)	—
74FX1200, 75FX1200	FX 1200	73.7 ci (1207cc)	—
74FXE1200, 75FXE1200	FXE 1200	73.7 ci (1207cc)	electric start
74XLH1000, 75XLH1000	XL 1000, also Sportster	OHV 60.9 ci (997cc)	—
74XLCH1000, 75XLCH1000	XLCH 1000, also Sportster	OHV 60.9 ci (997cc)	—

1976-1977 Highlights

1976-1983: Keihin carburetor on twins. 1977: First year of Low Rider. 1977: First and only year of XLT touring Sportster.

1977 Harley-Davidson Model XLCR. Engine: unit-construction overhead-valve V-twin, displacement 60.9 cubic inches (997cc); compression ratio 9:1; maximum output, 68 hp @ 6200 rpm. Transmission, four-speed foot-shift; primary drive, triple-row chain running in oil bath; final drive, chain. Wheelbase, 58.5 inches. Weight, 515 lbs. Fuel tank, 3.75 gallons. Finish: black on black. (DOUG MITCHEL)

1977 Harley-Davidson XLCR. New for all 1977 X-series bikes was the left-side shift. With 68 hp @ 6200 rpm, the 1977 XLCR was billed the most powerful stock motorcycle the company had ever built. Cycle World ran a test XLCR up to 106 mph @ 6277 rpm, a far cry from its 1962 road test CH's 122 mph. With half a tank of fuel, the XLCR weighed 515 lbs. The 1962 CH was 35 lbs. lighter. Despite its visual appeal and subsequent collectible status, the bike was too foreign for Harley fanciers and too "Harley" for performance bike enthusiasts. (DOUG MITCHEL)

Models	Key Feature(s)	Engine Data	New Features, Misc.
76FLH1200, 77FLH1200	Electra-Glide	73.7 ci (1207cc)	—
76FX, 77FX	FX, also Super-Glide	73.7 ci (1207cc)	kick starter only
76FXE, 77FXE	FXE, also Super-Glide	73.7 ci (1207cc)	—
77FXS	Low Rider	73.7 ci (1207cc)	—
76XLH1000	XL 1000	OHV 60.9 ci (997cc)	—
76XLCH1000, 77XLCH1000	Sportster, also CH	OHV 60.9 ci (997cc)	—
77XLCR1000	XLCR 1000 cafe racer	OHV 60.9 ci (997cc)	—
77XLT	Sportster, touring version	OHV 60.9 ci (997cc)	—

1978-1979 Highlights

1978: First 80-ci Shovelheads; electronic ignition on all F and X Series. Second and last year of XLCR1000 "cafe racer." 1978: Two disc brakes on Sportster (formerly, front disc, rear drum). 1978: Last year of kick-start (only) FX Super-Glide. 1978: Advertising returned to favoring the term "Sportster." 1979: First year of "Ham Can" air cleaner.

1978 Harley-Davidson XL1000 (above). The 1978 Sportsters featured electronic ignition and, as part of the 75th anniversary package, a saddle top in genuine leather. (DOUG MITCHEL)

1978 Harley-Davidson FXS Low Rider. Specifications: Price, $4,180. Weight, 623 lbs. (with 1/2 tank of fuel). Fuel tank, 3.5 gal. Top speed, 98 mph.

(DOUG MITCHEL)

Models	Key Feature(s)	Engine Data	New Features, Misc.
78FLH1200, 79FLH1200	FLH 1200, also Electra-Glide	73.7 ci (1207cc)	—
78FLH80, 79FLH80	FLH 80, also Electra-Glide	OHV 81.8 ci (1340cc)	—
78FX1200	FX 1200, also Super-Glide	73.7 ci (1207cc)	final kick-start only model
78FXE1200	FXE 1200, also Super-Glide	73.7 ci (1207cc)	—
78FXS	Low Rider	73.7 ci (1207cc)	—
79FXEF1200	Fat Bob	73.7 ci (1207cc), 73.7 ci in 1979	—
79FXEF80	Fat Bob	81.8 ci (1340cc)	—
78XLH1000	Sportster	60.9 ci (997cc)	electronic ignition
78XLCH1000, 79XLCH1000	Sportster, also CH	60.9 ci (997cc)	electronic ignition
78XLCR1000, XLCR 1000	cafe racer	60.9 ci (997cc)	—
79XLS1000	Sportster Special, also Roadster	OHV 60.9 ci (997cc)	—

1980 Harley-Davidson FXWG. The flame tank decor was further evidence of the company following the market. (DOUG MITCHEL)

1980 Harley-Davidson FXWG. The Wide Glide featured a 21-inch front wheel, and a wider, longer, and more raked front fork. This was a factory chopper, as opposed to a custom. (DOUG MITCHEL)

1980-1981 Highlights

1980: Rubber-mounted engine/transmission and five-speed transmission on FLT Series. 1980: FXB80 series (Sturgis) was the first all-belt drive model. 1980: FXWG Wide Glide debuted and included: wide fork, dual front and single rear disc brakes, forward gear shift and brake, big teardrop tank with tank top instruments, flame tank trim and mini headlight.

1980 Harley-Davidson FTL. (DOUG MITCHEL)

Models	Key Feature(s)	Engine Data	New Features, Misc.
80FLH80, 81FLH80	Electra-Glide	81.8 ci (1340cc)	—
80FLHC80, 81FLHC80	Electra-Glide Classic	81.8 ci (1340cc)	with styling touches
80FLT80, 81FLT80	Tour Glide	81.8 ci (1340cc)	first five-speed transmission
80FLTC80, 81FLTC80	Tour Glide Classic	81.8 ci (1340cc)	with styling touches
80FXB80, 81FXB80	Sturgis	81.8 ci (1340cc)	—
80FXE1200	FXE 1200, Super-Glide	73.7 ci (1207cc)	—
81FXE80	FXE 80, also Super-Glide	81.8 ci (1340cc)	—
81FXEF80	Fat Bob	81.8 ci (1340cc)	—
81FXS80	Low Rider	81.8 ci (1340cc)	—
81FXWG80	Wide Glide	81.8 ci (1340cc)	—
81XLH1000	Sportster	60.9 ci (998cc)	optional shorter shocks in "Hugger" version
81XLS1000	Roadster	60.9 ci (998cc)	—

1912 Haverford. Big 4. This motorcycle was manufactured for Haverford by the American Motor Company, and was identical to one of the 1912 M.M. models. Specifications: Bosch magneto; Schebler carburetor; free-engine (clutch); flat-belt idler; aluminum crankcase; roller bearings; studded 28 x 2½-inch tires; Persons Champion Motorcycle Saddle; Nickname: the "Blue Beauty." (GEORGE YAROCKI)

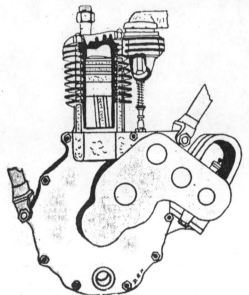

1911 Haverford engine. This illustration appeared in the December 8, 1911, Motorcycle Illustrated. Though the magazine termed this a Haverford engine, it was actually a Marsh-Metz product as used in several M-M clones such as the Peerless. Specifications: F-head (inlet-over-exhaust) engine; displacement 33.18 cubic inches (544cc).

(MOTORCYCLE ILLUSTRATED)

HAVERFORD

The Haverford was marketed by Haverford Cycle Company of Philadelphia, Pennsylvania, from 1909 through 1914. These machines were actually re-badged M-M (Marsh-Metz) motorcycles built by the American Motor Company of Brockton, Massachusetts.

HENDERSON

William "Bill" Henderson's design influence spread across three decades of American motorcycling, culminating in the 1942 Indian Fours that debuted 20 years after Bill's death. The first production Henderson arrived for the 1912 season. Preceded in the American four-cylinder field only by the 1909-1911 Pierce, the Henderson continued past the last 1913 Pierce models. The original factory was in Detroit, and the company was organized and controlled by Bill and his brother, Tom.

The original Henderson concept featured an unusually long wheelbase, so that a passenger was seated in front of the rider. The front fork was a leading link unit, and there was no rear suspension. Apart from the four cylinders, the F-head engine was otherwise a typical motorcycle power plant. In a "pocket" to the side of each cylinder, the inlet valves were situated directly above the

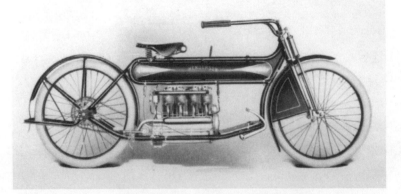

1912 Henderson. The 65-inch wheelbase, about 10 inches longer than necessary, was claimed to have an "easy riding effect." If a passenger was to be carried, the passenger saddle was in front of the rider's saddle! The F-head engine had a bore and stroke of 2 1/2 and 3 inches, for a displacement of 58.9 cubic inches (965cc). (BRUCE LINSDAY)

side-mounted inverted exhaust valves. Single-speed operation was featured until the 1915 models introduced a two-speed rear hub, along with an optional shorter conventional frame. The 1917 models introduced a three-speed sliding gear transmission contained within the crankcase.

In 1918, the Henderson brothers sold out to Ignatz Schwinn, who added the marque to his Excelsior lineup of singles and twins. Bill and Tom worked for Schwinn at the Chicago factory for two years before departing to start up another four-cylinder motorcycle, the Ace.

The 1920 Henderson range was drastically altered to feature all valves on the side, which had become the standard engine configuration in the American automobile field. Detail refinements continued through 1928. During this era, Henderson riders captured most of the American long-distance records. These included the 24-hour record, the "Three Flag" (Canada to Mexico) record, the Transcontinental record and city-to-city records with and without a sidecar.

For the 1929 season, Henderson reverted to the F-head layout. The 1929-1931 Henderson "streamliners" featured many improvements, as well as styling that was years ahead of its time. Beloved by police departments across the nation, and by connoisseurs in general, the expensive Henderson fours didn't sell in sufficient numbers to remain in production once the Great Depression began in late 1929. Production stoppage in early 1931 was influenced by Indian's entry into the four-cylinder field, with the Indian Four becoming the major competitor that the Ace had never been. Another factor in Henderson disappearing was the modest sales performance of the Super-X (formerly, Excelsior) twins. The Super-X was up against the recognized leader of the middleweight field, the Indian Scout. Moreover, neither the Super-X, nor the Scout, commanded the popularity of the Harley-Davidson big twins.

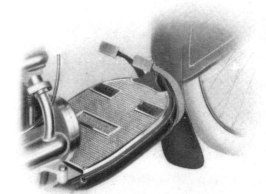

1912 Henderson. The floorboard was necessarily roomy, since a passenger might share it. (BRUCE LINSDAY)

The first motorcyclist to complete an around-the-world ride was Carl Stearns Clancy aboard his 1912 Henderson. (BRUCE LINSDAY)

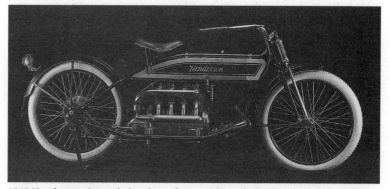

1913 Henderson. A restyled tank was featured. Though the long wheelbase was retained, the optional passenger saddle was fitted over the rear wheel. The front fork was made stronger. (DOUG MITCHEL)

1913 Henderson engine. The engine bore was increased from 2 1/2 to 2 5/8 inches, and with the continued 3-inch stroke, displacement grew to 64.9 cubic inches (1064cc). Crankcase oil capacity was increased. (BRUCE LINSDAY)

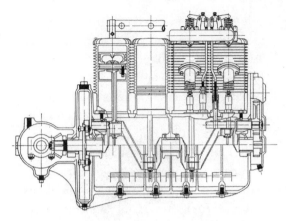

1913 Henderson engine details. Three crankshaft main bearings were fitted, which was typical automotive practice. (BRUCE LINSDAY)

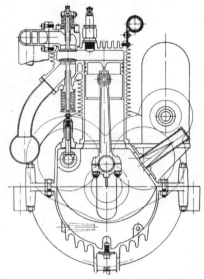

1913 Henderson engine details. The 1912-1915 Henderson engines had the spark plugs mounted on top of the cylinder head. Note the flat-topped combustion chamber "roof," resulting in a low compression ratio. This predated the "squish principle" achieved by a sloping combustion chamber roof with higher compression ratio. (BRUCE LINSDAY)

1913 Henderson engine. No explanation was provided for the two large tubes each secured to the crankcase by four fasteners. Apparently, this was done to lower crankcase compression. (BRUCE LINSDAY)

1913 Henderson cylinder. To improve cooling, an air pocket was placed between the exhaust valve guide and the cylinder proper.

(BRUCE LINSDAY)

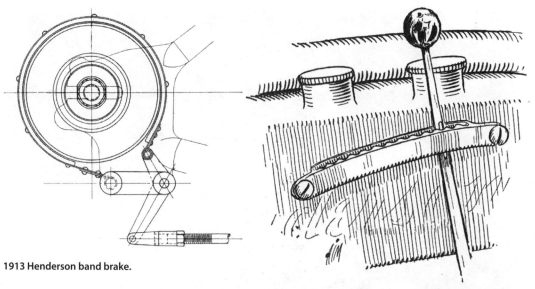

1913 Henderson band brake.

The 1913 Henderson clutch control, as captured by an artist at the 1913 New York City motorcycle show. (PACIFIC MOTORCYCLIST)

1914 Henderson passenger accommodation. An after-market two-speed rear hub was available from Eclipse.

(BRUCE LINSDAY)

1914 Henderson kick starter. (BRUCE LINSDAY)

1914 Henderson. A new saddle adjusting plate allowed the rider to adjust spring tension to his own weight. The saddle was 1 inch lower than in 1913. (BRUCE LINSDAY)

1914 Henderson engine. New pistons were 3 oz. lighter. New crankshaft bearings were bronze with babbitt inlay. Note the small pipe running from the carburetor to the exhaust manifold. This was not pictured in the sales literature. The rider could select warm air delivery to the carburetor for cold weather operation.

1915 Henderson engine details. (BRUCE LINSDAY)

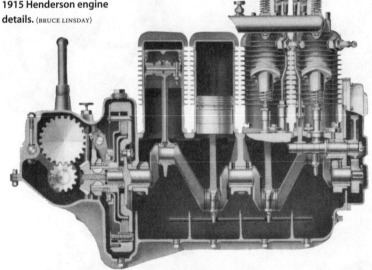

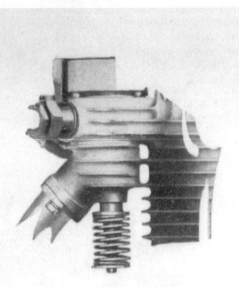

On the 1916 models, the spark plugs were moved from the top of the cylinders to the side. (BRUCE LINSDAY)

1915 Henderson two-speed rear hub. The marque was running a year behind Harley-Davidson, Indian, and even Henderson's brother marque, Excelsior. All these had introduced two-speeders for 1914 and three-speeders for 1915. (MOTOR CYCLING)

1916 Henderson. Only the short (58-inch) wheelbase was offered on the 1916 models. (BRUCE LINSDAY)

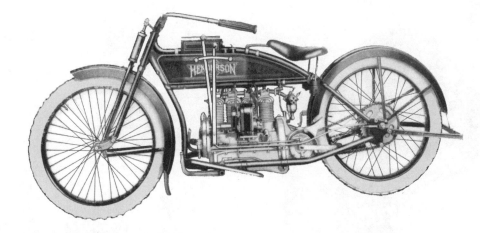

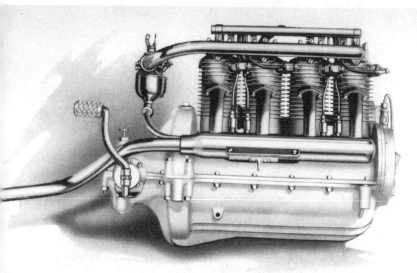

1916 Henderson engine. Only one large tube was fitted to the crankcase, apparently signaling a smaller crankcase compression reduction was required than in previous years. (BRUCE LINSDAY)

For 1916, the cylinder bore was decreased from 2 5/8 inches, to 2 17/32 inches. This yielded a displacement of 60.4 cubic inches (990cc). (BRUCE LINSDAY)

1916 Henderson engine. In general layout, the Henderson, Ace and Indian Four engines were the same. In each, the camshaft ran along the right side of the engine. In each, there was a greater gap between numbers two and three cylinders than between the other cylinders, in order to accommodate the center crankshaft bearing. (BRUCE LINSDAY)

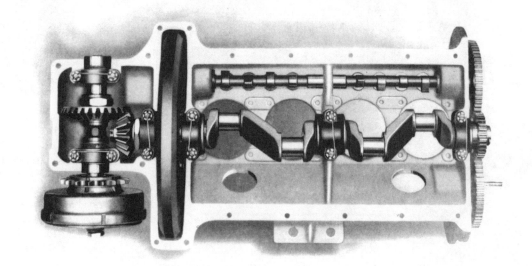

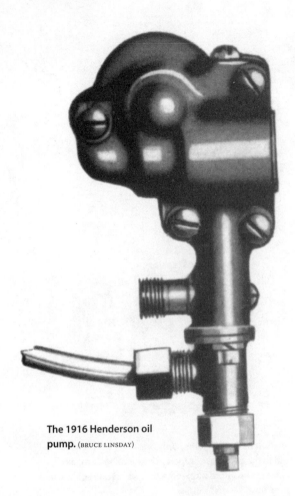

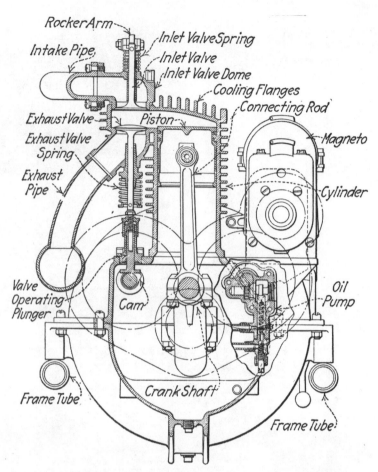

The 1916 Henderson oil pump. (BRUCE LINSDAY)

From 1916 through 1919, Hendersons were configured with a "squish" combustion chamber, formed by the reduction in cross-section progressing away from the valves side. (BRUCE LINSDAY)

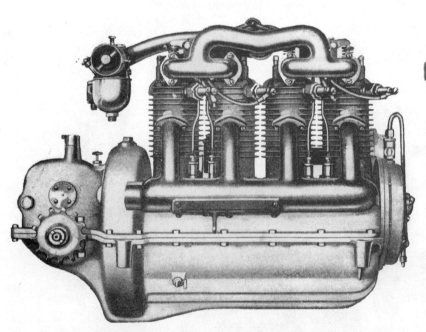

Early 1917 literature and press release photographs showed this double-branched inlet manifold that ensured equal distribution among all four cylinders.

(BRUCE LINSDAY)

According to historian Richard Schultz (*Hendersons, Those Elegant Machines*), this simpler inlet manifold was advertised beginning February 1, 1917. The carburetor was raised, eliminating the previous up-draft action. The exhaust manifold is depicted in phantom view, showing the long inlet air tube for preheated carburetor air. Carburetor heating was beneficial on cold days. With the long inlet manifold and no carburetor heating it was possible to clog the inlet manifold with ice. (BRUCE LINSDAY)

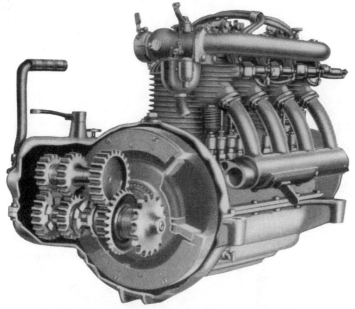

1917 Henderson. The kick starter was moved to the left side. (BRUCE LINSDAY)

1917 Henderson power plant in phantom view, showing the robust three-speed sliding-gear transmission introduced that year. A single sliding gear, with dogs (also termed "clutches") on each side, accomplished dog-to-dog engagement of first and third gears. Shifting into second gear was achieved by tooth-to-tooth engagement between the sliding gear and the middle cluster of the upper triple gear. (BRUCE LINSDAY)

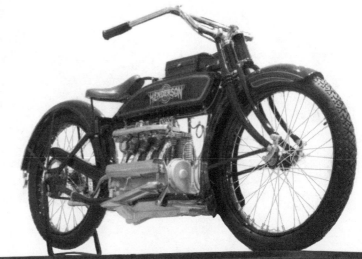

1917 Henderson. A new trailing link front fork graced the 1917 models. The fenders were larger on the 1917 models. The characteristic single front down tube frame is apparent.

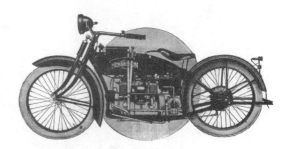

1917 Henderson. In the 1917 range came the first offering of an electrically equipped Henderson.

(GEORGE YAROCKI)

1917 Henderson. With the integral transmission, the unit was now more properly termed a "power plant," rather than an engine. (BRUCE LINSDAY)

1919 Henderson Model "Z." The model designation apparently was chosen because this represented the last of the Bill Henderson designed F-head fours. The bore was increased from 2.531 inches to 2.75 inches, and the stroke remained 3 inches, for a displacement of 71.3 cubic inches (1168cc). Fenders were widened to 6 inches. The Henderson-designed rear brake was replaced by the Excelsior rear brake, which required the fitting of a new hub and wheel. (GEORGE YAROCKI)

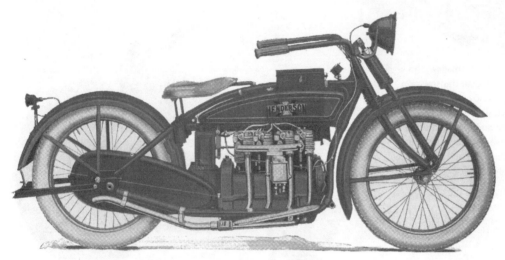

1920 Henderson, Model "K." After almost no changes on the 1918 and 1919 models, the 1920 Hendersons were completely redesigned. Most significant and visible was the new side-valve (Flathead) engine configuration. A new double-loop frame was aimed at improving sidecar operation. (HENDERSON SALES LITERATURE)

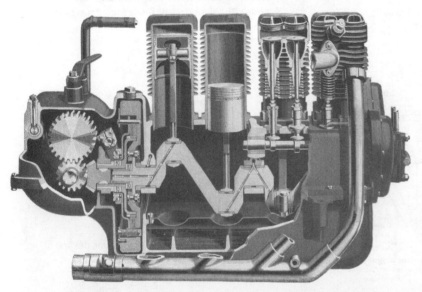

1920 Henderson power plant. The new engine was so compact it may have appeared less impressive than the F-head motor it replaced, but full enclosure of the valve gear was a big improvement. (HENDERSON SALES LITERATURE)

1920 Henderson three-speed-with-reverse transmission. This view is from the right rear of the motorcycle. The sprocket was secured to the main shaft, on the opposite end of which was a small gear. The other gears on this axis were free to rotate about the main shaft. When reverse gear was selected, the smallest gear, aft of the main shaft, engaged the small gear on the left end of the main shaft. This caused the main shaft to reverse its direction of rotation.

(HENDERSON SALES LITERATURE)

The 1920 Henderson Model "K" power plant. (HENDERSON SALES LITERATURE)

The 1920 Henderson was slender looking from the front.
(HENDERSON SALES LITERATURE)

1920 Henderson Model "K." The finish was deep blue with gold striping and gray wheels.
(HENDERSON SALES LITERATURE)

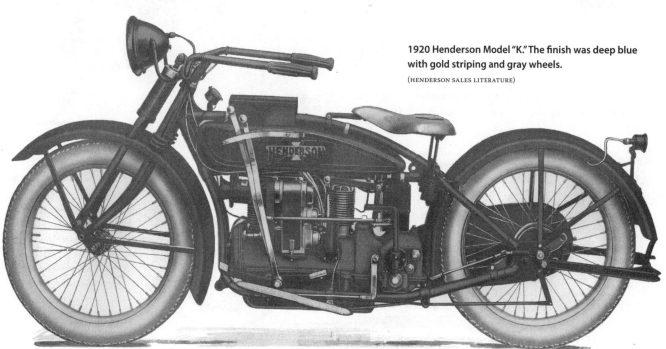

1920 Henderson Model "K" power plant. (HENDERSON SALES LITERATURE)

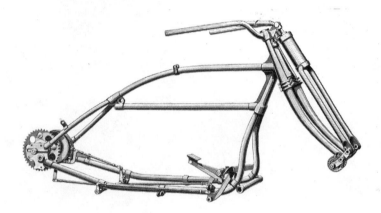

1920 Henderson Model "K" frame. The 1920 frame head was a solid forging brazed directly to a center tube and to the twin cradle tubes.

(HENDERSON SALES LITERATURE)

1920 Henderson Model K front fork. The new front fork had a straight spring "leg" instead of a curved one. The new fork had heavier cushion springs and heavier-gauge tubing.

(HENDERSON SALES LITERATURE)

1920 Henderson brake. As on the 1919 Model "Z," the 1920 Model K used the same brake as the Excelsior twin. As well as eliminating royalty payments to William Henderson, this standardization simplified production and spare parts management.

(HENDERSON SALES LITERATURE)

1922 Henderson De Luxe. Advertising tried to convey that the 1922 De Luxe was a much-improved model, but its changes were relatively few compared to the dramatic 1920 redesign. (MOTORCYCLING AND BICYCLING)

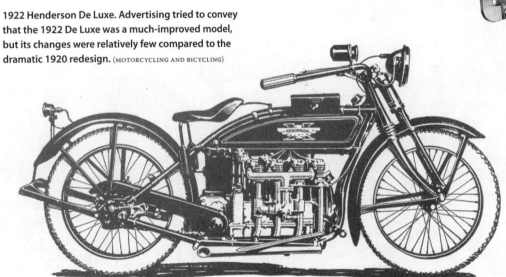

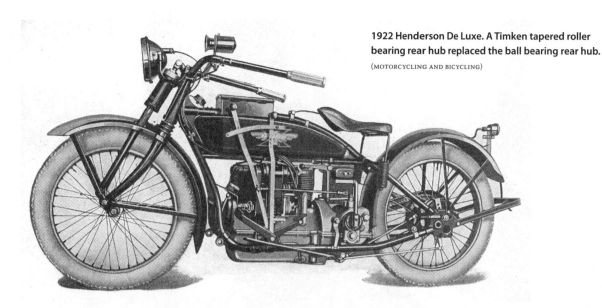

1922 Henderson De Luxe. A Timken tapered roller bearing rear hub replaced the ball bearing rear hub. (MOTORCYCLING AND BICYCLING)

Rider Wells Bennett is shown after his record-breaking transcontinental run made in October, 1922. His time was 6 days, 15 hours, and 13 minutes. (MOTORCYCLING AND BICYCLING)

This picture gives some idea of what passed for "roads" during the Henderson era. Wells Bennett made two other record runs in 1922: a 24-hour record of 1,562 miles over the Tacoma, Washington, board track, and a "Three-Flag" (Canada to Mexico) run of 1,650 miles in 43 hours. These records were important to the manufacturer, which had not fared well with racing Excelsior twins. For a while, the company boasted that if a long distance record was worth having, then Henderson had it. (MOTORCYCLING AND BICYCLING)

1923 Henderson. An advertisement for this machine proudly proclaimed "Judge the Henderson by its performance records," then cited a host of accomplishments.

(MOTORCYCLE AND BICYCLE ILLUSTRATED)

1925 Henderson. The fuel tank was shortened to provide a lower saddle position, and widened to retain the same capacity. The dark blue finish was continued on the major components, but the wheel styling was changed to cream with blue stripes. This style of front fender continued through the early 1927 models. (GEORGE YAROCKI)

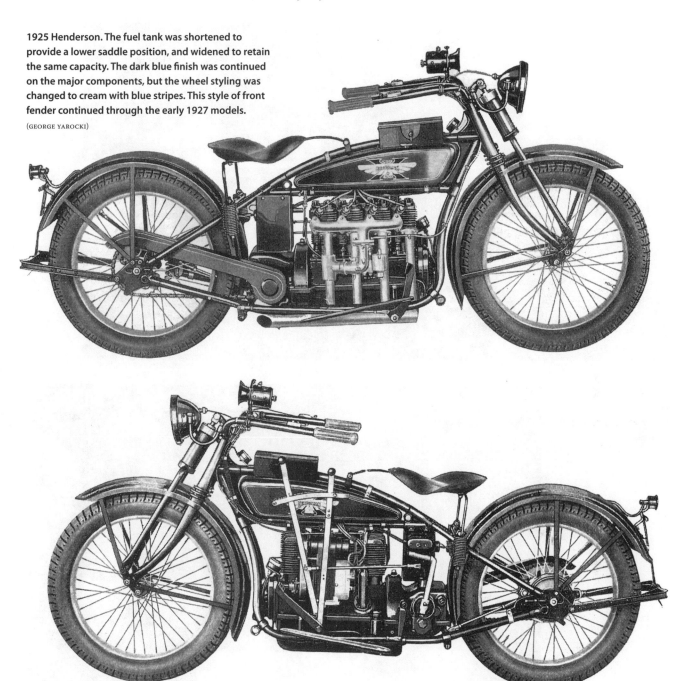

1925 Henderson. One of the shortcomings of Henderson management was lack of promotional pizzaz. While Indian and Harley-Davidson continuously proclaimed new features, Hendersons and Excelsiors were often advertised as having changed few or none at all. The idea must have been that the designs were so good that they needed little or no updates. (GEORGE YAROCKI)

1925 Henderson flywheel and transmission.

(HENDERSON SALES LITERATURE)

The 1925 Henderson engine (above) was favored by builders of light planes.

(HENDERSON PUBLICITY PHOTO)

This 1925 Henderson engine also found a home powering an airplane.

(HENDERSON PUBLICITY PHOTO)

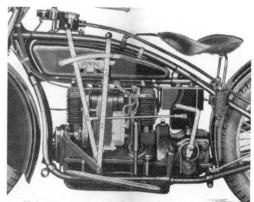

1927 Henderson. This is a typical left side view of the power plant for the years 1925-1928. (GEORGE YAROCKI)

1926 Henderson. Cleanliness was improved by the adaption of two-piece "clam shell" covers for the side-mounted exhaust valve stems and springs. (GEORGE YAROCKI)

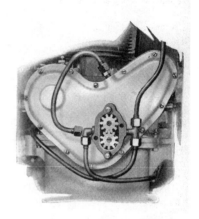

1927 Henderson oil pump. (BRUCE LINSDAY)

1928 and early-1929 Henderson. The new leading-link parallelogram fork was inspired by the Harley-Davidson fork. The rocker arms were longer than on the preceding trailing link design, so maximum fork travel was increased. The change was perhaps also aimed at improving the appearance. Also new were the 27 x 4-inch wheels and tires. This model continued unchanged through early 1929, as shown in early 1929 sales literature. (GEORGE YAROCKI)

Late-1927 Henderson. Henderson introduced the valanced front fender and fender-mounted horn in February, 1927. Earlier 1927 models were visually identical to the 1926 models. An improved Zenith carburetor was used on all 1927 Hendersons. The idling jet could be removed without disassembling the rest of the carburetor. In the advertisements, there was no visible difference from the previous Zenith. (GEORGE YAROCKI)

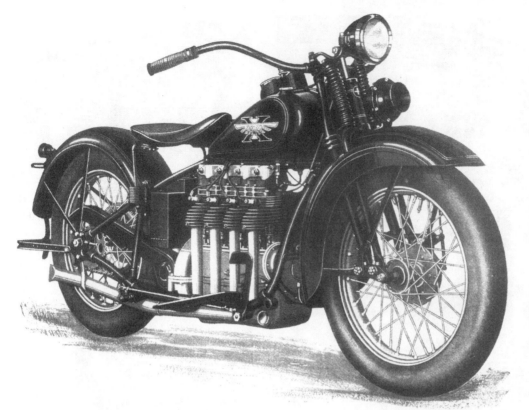

1929-1931 Henderson "streamliner." In February, 1929, the company brought out the "New Streamline Henderson." The basic specifications were not changed through the end of production in early 1931. Fifty-seven improvements were advertised.

(MOTORCYCLING)

1929-1931 Henderson Streamliner power plant.

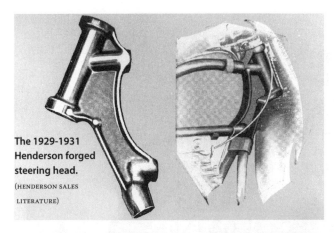

The 1929-1931 Henderson forged steering head. (HENDERSON SALES LITERATURE)

The 1929-1931 Henderson one-piece rear fender could be pivoted for simplification of rear tire maintenance. (HENDERSON SALES LITERATURE)

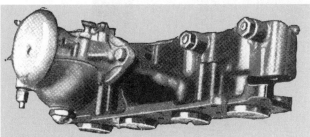

The 1929-1931 Henderson inlet manifold with integral rocker arms, valve springs, and valves. (HENDERSON SALES LITERATURE)

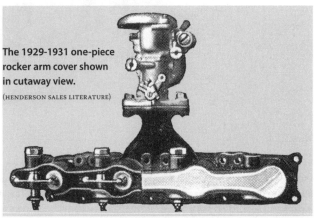

The 1929-1931 one-piece rocker arm cover shown in cutaway view. (HENDERSON SALES LITERATURE)

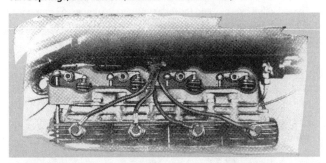

1929-1931 Henderson inlet valves with cover removed. (HENDERSON SALES LITERATURE)

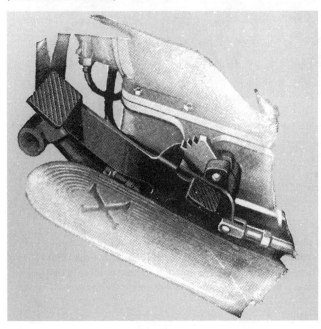

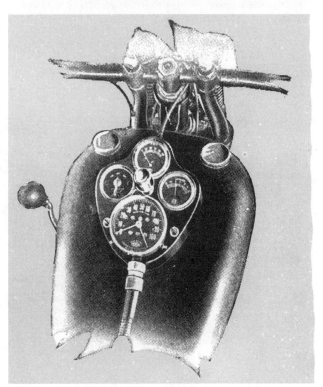

1929-1931 Henderson instrument panel (above)—seven years ahead of Harley-Davidson; eight years ahead of Indian.

The 1929-1931 Henderson clutch pedal (left) with toe-actuated lock-down and heel-actuated lock release. (HENDERSON SALES LITERATURE)

1930 Henderson "Special." The "Special" was announced with this picture and brief advertising copy that didn't explain the details. It can be safely assumed that the "Special" was fitted with some of the typical speed modifications of the era, such as larger carburetor venturi, polished inlet and exhaust ports, stronger valve springs, camshaft with higher lift and/or increased valve overlap, and looser assembly clearances. A companion magazine article reported that factory rider Joe Petrali was timed in April at 112.61 mph, a two-way average attained in Chicago. The article opined that the average new Henderson was good for 80 to 85 mph, and that the new "Special" would top out between 85 and 100 mph. (AMERICAN MOTORCYCLING AND BICYCLING)

A last look at the 1929-1931 Henderson Streamliner. Though the model was advanced for its time, and holding the allegiance of thousands of enthusiasts, company weaknesses couldn't be overcome. The companion 45-cubic inch (750cc) Super-X twin was priced above some Harley-Davidson and Indian 61- and 74-cubic inch twins. This suggests that either the Excelsior company factory wasn't as efficient as those of Harley and Indian, or that company boss Ignatz Schwinn was unwilling to operate with smaller profit margins. The failure of the Henderson was connected to the disappointing sales history of the Super-X middleweight. (AMERICAN MOTORCYCLING AND BICYCLING)

HERCULES

Aviation pioneer Glenn Curtiss is best known in motorcycling history as the creator of the Curtiss marque. But he also designed and built motorcycles bearing the names "Marvel" and "Hercules." The latter motorcycles were first produced in 1902, according to historian Stephen Wright (*The American Motorcycle, 1869-1914*), who also reports that Curtiss learned the trade name "Hercules" was previously claimed, and so re-branded his bikes "Curtiss" during 1903. All of the Curtiss-designed motorcycles were built in Hammondsport, New York.

1899 Herring. The extraordinarily long cylinder functioned with an equally extraordinarily small crankcase. Apparently, the connecting rod set some sort of record for length compared to bore. A shaft running from the crankcase to the top of the cylinder suggests an overhead-cam or rotary valves. The large spoked external flywheel was on the right side of the motorcycle. The double-tube frame construction testified to the heavy weight of the machine. (JIM DENNIE)

1903 Hercules single. Though the specifications are unknown, the single probably had the same engine dimensions as the twin. If so, the single displaced 21.2 cubic inches (348cc). (JIM DENNIE)

1903 Hercules twin. Glen Curtiss poses behind the first successful V-twin American motorcycle. This motorcycle was re-branded and marketed as the 1904 (and later) Geer Green Egg. Specifications: F-head "5 hp, double cylinder; width of crankcase, 4 inches; over all, 6 inches; height, 16 inches; bore of cylinders, 3 inches; stroke, 3 inches; displacement, 42.4 cubic inches (695cc). Speed, 300 to 3,500 revolutions per minute. There were two camshafts, one in front of the front cylinder and the other in back of the rear cylinder, and the valve pairs were correspondingly situated." (JIM DENNIE)

As the Hoffman was identical to the later Chicago 400, the Chicago 400 specifications are here repeated: From the April 1, 1905, *Cycle and Automobile Trade Journal*: "...22 inch frame; 2 inch tires; 62 inch wheelbase; single cylinder 3 1/8 (inch, bore) x 3 1/4 (inch, stroke) 3 H.P. motor; oil cup lubrication; belt drive; battery mileage, 100; grip control; weight 150 lbs.; speed 30 miles. This machine is also furnished with 23 inch frame; 2 1/4 inch tires; 68 inch wheelbase; 2-cylinder, 3 1/8 (inch, bore) x 3 1/8 (inch, stroke), 5 H.P." (JIM DENNIE)

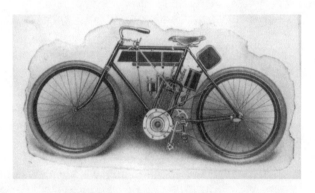

1902 Holley. 2 1/4 hp (approximately 21 cubic inches or 350cc) F-head (inlet-over-exhaust) engine; fuel capacity, 4 1/2 quarts; fuel range, 100 miles; belt drive; lubrication, gravity feed; oil range, 150 miles; weight, 104 lbs.; price, $200. (BRUCE LINSDAY)

HOLLEY MOTOR CYCLE. PRICE $210.

1905 21.2-cubic inch (348cc) Holley. From the April 1, 1905, Cycle and Automobile Trade Journal: "Holley Motor Cycle. Price $210. 22 or 24 inch frame; 28 x 2 inch tires; 51 inch wheelbase; single cylinder, 3 (inch, bore) x 2 (inch, stroke), 3 H.P. motor; splash lubrication; drive by 1 1/4 inch flat belt; battery mileage, 1,500; fuel mileage, 125 to 150; single lever control; weight 140 lbs.; speed 5 to 40 miles; price $210. Special features: Motor base brazed into frame at lowest point, making a rigid fastening for motor; automatic oiling device; detachable rear pulley." (THE ANTIQUE MOTORCYCLE)

HERRING

The Herring was built in 1899 by Augustus Moore Herring, according to historian Stephen Wright. Apart from a single illustration in a period scrapbook, and Wright's reportage, no further information was found by the author.

HOFFMAN

Hoffman motorcycles were built in 1904 by the W. Hoffman Motor Works, 1253 Halstead Street, Chicago. In 1905, the machines were re-branded "Chicago 400," apparently without any technical changes.

HOLLEY

Holley motorcycles were first manufactured by the Holley Motor Company, and later by Phillips and Hamilton, both firms of Bradford, Pennsylvania. Whether this was a name change only, a restructuring of the original firm, or a buy-out, is unknown. From the April, 1902, *The Dealer and Repairman*: "... one of the pioneers in built-in motor construction, and almost before any of the other makers has started to incorporate the motor in the frame, it had produced a machine with a construction which is unique in that the motor case is actually brazed into the frame and serves as the bottom bracket thereof." Access to the lower end was via removable crankcase side plate. Production ceased in 1911.

HUDSON

According to historian Todd Rafferty (*The Complete Illustrated Encyclopedia of American Motorcycles*), the Hudson company was located in Middletown, Ohio, and was in operation during 1911 and 1912. No further information has been discovered. However, it seems likely that there was a connection between Hudson and the Miami Cycle Manufacturing Company of the same city, makers of Racycle and Flying Merkel motorcycles, as explained in the captions.

Circa 1911 Hudson (above). The front fork, front fender and front fender braces of the Hudson appear identical to those same Racycle items.

Circa 1911 Hudson. The Hudson frame appears identical to the Racycle from the steering head to the rear of the tank. As the Hudson employed battery ignition and the Racycle had magneto ignition, the rear portion of the Hudson frame was longer in order to accommodate a battery box. The Hudson and the Racycle differ in the timing mechanism. The Hudson ignition components appear identical to those of the Indian, Indian clones and the Thor, but the Racycle ignition unit is not such a copy.

INDIAN

In 1900, former high-wheel bicycle racing star George Hendee was manufacturing Silver King "safety" bicycles in Springfield, Massachusetts. These were conventional bicycles with two equal-sized wheels, which in the 1890s had displaced the standard bikes that had a big front wheel and small rear wheel. To advertise his bicycles, Hendee promoted bicycle races in Springfield. Record setting was a popular activity at the Springfield Coliseum and at other tracks across the nation. These attempts were facilitated by crude one-off pacing motorcycles, each powered by a large, but primitive, single-cylinder engine. However, the pacing machines were unreliable, so many record attempts ended when the pacing motor quit. Hendee had seen this for himself in Springfield.

Then, in January, 1901, he heard of a seemingly never-fail pacer that was racking up large mileages in New York City. So Hendee arranged for the machine's builder, Oscar Hedstrom, to bring the better pacer to Springfield. Hedstrom's pacer impressed Hendee. The two men discussed the prospect of a reliably designed and expertly crafted series of road-going motorcycles

that might be sold to the public. Hedstrom agreed to build a prototype road model, at an available shop in Middletown, Connecticut. Hendee agreed to obtain investors—a process that he had already mastered in starting up his bicycle firm.

Six months later, Hedstrom arrived in Springfield via train, and off-loaded his machine. To those accustomed to the track pacers, the Hedstrom machine was surprisingly small. Yet, it was surprisingly peppy. Hedstrom rode the motorcycle up and down the steep hill on Cross Street, repeatedly showing that the prototype could be slowed to a crawl on the hill and then accelerate all the way to the top. The engine idled slowly and rock steady, and never overheated. Hendee captured the investors' dollars, and he and Hedstrom set to the task of launching their production machines.

Hendee settled on the name "Indian," as it was both romantic and symbolic of the machine's status as a pioneer. Incidentally, the emerging field hadn't completely settled on a name for powered two-wheelers. The term "motorcycle" was gaining favor, but the term "motocycle" had been used earlier. A still smaller minority favored the term "autocycle." Hendee liked "motocycle," and

Below is the pacer that Oscar Hedstrom designed and rode in New York City bicycle events of 1901. After seeing this machine and affirming its unusual reliability, bicycle manufacturer George Hendee arranged with Hedstrom to start up a motorcycle operation.

(BUTCH BAER)

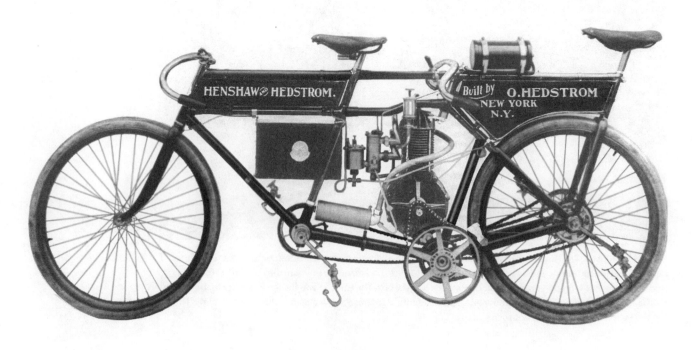

stuck with it long after "motorcycle"—with the "r"—became otherwise unanimous. Then, as now, copywriters had to rebut editors' so-called spelling corrections.

1901-1908 Diamond Frame F-heads

The earliest Indian design phase produced user-friendly machines to a public accustomed to pedal bicycles. Now, we would call such machines "mopeds." Then, Indian pushed the term "motocycle," suggesting that Indians were somehow fundamentally different from all other motorcycles. That was a smart tactic for Indian in the earliest years, and it's similar to Honda's highly successful image definition in the 1960s. The author, then a part-time salesman in a Honda shop, once sold a new Honda to a lady who insisted that her son could have a Honda, but not a motorcycle!

1901 Models

Only three Indians were built in 1901—the prototype and two others. Indian No. 1 was fitted with four cylinder hold-down studs, two on each side, as shown in the photos. In an interview four decades later, Hedstrom recalled that Indian No. 1 was parted out very early in the company's life. One four-stud motorcycle survived until 1922, and was pictured in the August 10th issue of *Motorcycle and Bicycle Illustrated*. However, this example may have been a 1902 model. With no subsequent sightings and/or applicable verbiage in the motorcycle press, this long-running four-stud bike evidently disappeared from the antique motorcycle movement not long after the magazine publicity. Neither, this nor any other early four-stud engine, has subsequently surfaced.

1901 Indian. The crude hand-written "1902" on the original Indian company file picture has been edited out, because the Yarocki study proves this is a 1901 model. Indian was often sloppy and/or forgetful concerning their photograph collection. The 1901 models were started by holding the exhaust valve open while pedaling bicycle style, then closing the valve. Because there was no clutch, stopping the motorcycle required killing the engine. Clutch-less design continued through 1910. Note the two securing studs on the left side of the engine; there are also two studs on the right side, making this a "four-stud" engine. (BOB FINN)

1901 prototype Indian. This is Hedstrom's first road-going "motor cycle" published in the *Springfield Sunday Republican* of June 2, 1901. This picture was republished in the 1902 catalog and was used as late as December, 1902, according to historian George Yarocki (*Early Indian Motorcycle History*). However, the 1902 models differed, as shown later. Among collectors, the nickname "camel-back" applies to the 1901-1909 Indians with the tank over the rear fender. (GEORGE YAROCKI)

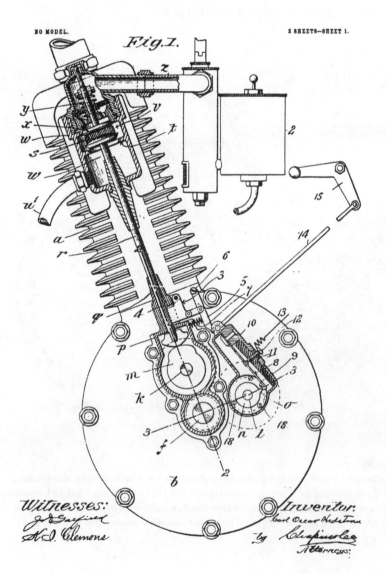

Technical details weren't provided, but based on subsequent years' data, the displacement of No. 1 was probably 13.7 ci (224cc). The engine is remarkably similar to that of Emil Hafelfinger, which he exhibited at the January, 1901, New York City motorcycle show. Indian builder Oscar Hedstrom obviously patterned the first Indian engines after Hafelfinger's, but the latter had basically scaled down the French built De Dion engine which was the world's first practical road-going engine. (GEORGE YAROCKI)

An early Indian valve lift mechanism and other details as shown in a patent application made by Oscar Hedstrom and approved on May 12, 1903. (GEORGE YAROCKI)

Early Indian engine cylinder head, viewed from the left side. From the first, Indian engines featured a removable cylinder head. This was quite unusual, as all other notable marques used a one-piece cylinder with integral head. Obviously the layout made it easy to accomplish the era's periodic task of scraping out carbon deposits. Rivals claimed that the Indian was prone to gas leakage. (STEPHEN WRIGHT)

All surviving 1902-1909 camel-back Indians have three-stud engines. After an exhaustive study, including Indian drawings filed with the U. S. Patent Office, historian George Yarocki has been unable to confirm with 100 percent certainty the situations for three-stud and four-stud engines. But his informed opinion, which the author of this book shares, is this: probably all production late-1902 through 1909 engines were three-stud units. Note that the exhaust pipe isn't readily apparent as in the previous figures; this is because the exhaust pipe exited sharply downward. So this picture represents a second configuration in the four-stud era. (EARL BENTLEY)

1901 or 1902 Indian. Just to remove any doubts that might linger, here is an un-retouched picture of an un-restored 1901 or four-stud camel-back Indian, flat tire and all. To date, there is only one other four-stud picture to have surfaced, that being an un-retouched magazine shot from the August 10, 1922 issue of *Motorcycle and Bicycle Illustrated*. The Indian company claimed to have built only three motorcycles in 1901. In October, 1902, Indian subcontracted engine production to the Aurora Automatic Machinery Company of Aurora, Illinois. Oscar Hedstrom stayed several weeks at the Illinois plant, supervising the start-up process. Yarocki opines, and this author agrees, that Aurora probably built only three-stud engines. There's one other puzzle: though this is a four-stud engine, the exhaust pipe exits downward like the later three-stud engines. (EARL BENTLEY)

Circa 1902 Indian and designer Oscar Hedstrom. For decades, Indian published this picture, always claiming it to be Hedstrom and the first Indian. However, at the earliest, the machine is a late-1902 model, because an identical machine is pictured in the 1903 sales catalog. (BOB SMITH)

The Thor Connection

Hendee and Hedstrom faced the enormous tasks of designing and building not just motorcycles, but also the jobs of designing and building a factory, and of building "The Hendee Manufacturing Company." To simplify the challenges, in October 1901, Indian contracted engine production with the Aurora Automatic Machinery Company, of Aurora, Illinois. As part of the arrangement, Aurora was permitted to use the Hedstrom-designed engine and the rest of the motorcycle parts.

As a result, Aurora marketed its own Thor brand motorcycles, initially differing from Indians only by the name on the fuel tank. Aurora also wholesaled engines, frames, forks, and accessories to jobbers who assembled them and placed their own name on the tank sides. Some of these Indian clones were: America, Crescent, Imperial, Light Thor-Bred, Monarch (Chicago, Westfield) and Thoroughbred.

1902 Models

As to the four-stud versus three-stud engine configuration, we simply don't know whether or not any of the Aurora-built bikes had the four-stud motor. The 1902 Indian catalog contains only a right profile view of the motorcycle, which is identical in the case of both four-stud and three-stud engines. No technical details were provided in the catalog, which, other than a single picture and generally worded description, was otherwise entirely devoted to bicycles, now sold under the "Indian" brand. Based on subsequent technical data, the author estimates that the 1902 engines continued in the same size as the 1901 prototypes, about 13.7 ci (224cc).

1903—1908

Technical details were at last published in the 1903 sales literature, and thereafter. These are highlighted in tables covering all production years. During the 1903-1908

Indian President George Hendee on a 1904 Indian. As with the Hedstrom picture, the company published this picture claiming it was the first Indian. However, it is a 1904 model as revealed by the right-hand twist grip speed control (via changing the ignition timing). Engine size was not stated, but the rated 1 3/4-hp output was based on an industry standard equating size to power. From this the conclusion is approximately 13.7 ci (224cc). (BOB FINN)

period, the basic Indian design remained intact with the continued use of the pedal bike style "diamond" frame. In 1908, when Indian began regulating speed conventionally, via throttle opening, the firm simply added a left twist-grip for this function, keeping the now occasional ignition timing a function of the right-hand twist grip. In other words, Indian "backed into" the unique left-hand throttle.

1903 Indian, as pictured in the 1903 catalog. Differences from the prototype and earlier production models include an exhaust pipe that exits downward and details of the timing apparatus. (GEORGE YAROCKI)

1904 Indian. Right-hand twist grip control was introduced, making Indian and Curtiss the world's only marques with this feature. However, Indian speed was regulated by varying the ignition timing, and the throttle hand-lever on the top frame tube was used only occasionally as a sort of gross adjustment. (EARL BENTLEY)

1903—1908 HIGHLIGHTS

Year	Engine Type, Model	Engine Data	Transmission	New Features
1903	Single cylinder, F-head, 1 3/4 hp	estimated 13.7 ci (224cc)	single-speed, all chain	1 3/4" tires, optional 2" rear tire
1904	Single cylinder, F-head, 1 3/4 hp	estimated 13.7 ci (224cc)	single-speed, all chain	right-hand twist-grip
1905	Single cylinder, F-head, 1 3/4 hp	estimated, 13.7 ci (224cc)	single-speed, all chain	cartridge spring fork, 2-inch tires
1906	Single cylinder, F-head, 2 1/4 hp	17.6 ci (288cc)	single-speed, all chain	steel cylinder, compensating sprocket, 2 1/4" tires
1906	"Double Cylinder Racer,"	details unknown	single-speed, all chain	steel cylinders, claimed 4 hp
1907	Single-cylinder, F-head, 2 1/4 hp	17.6 ci (288cc)	single-speed, all chain	cast-iron cylinder, optional roller-gear primary drive
1907	Twin-cylinder, F-head, 4 hp	estimated, 35.2 ci (577cc)	single-speed, all chain	cast-iron cylinders, Indian's first road twin
1908	Single cylinder, F-head, 2 3/4 hp	19.3 ci (316cc)	single-speed, all chain	double twist-grip control, longer spring in cartridge fork
1908	Single cylinder, F-head, 3 1/2 hp	26.96 ci (442cc)	single-speed, all chain	double twist-grip control, longer spring in cartridge fork
1908	Twin-cylinder, F-head, 5 hp	38.61 ci (633cc)	single-speed, all chain	double twist-grip control, longer spring in cartridge fork
1908	Single-cylinder racer, 4 hp	30.16 ci (494cc)	single-speed, all chain	rigid fork
1908	Twin-cylinder racer, 7 hp	60.32 ci (988cc)	single-speed, all chain	short-spring cartridge fork

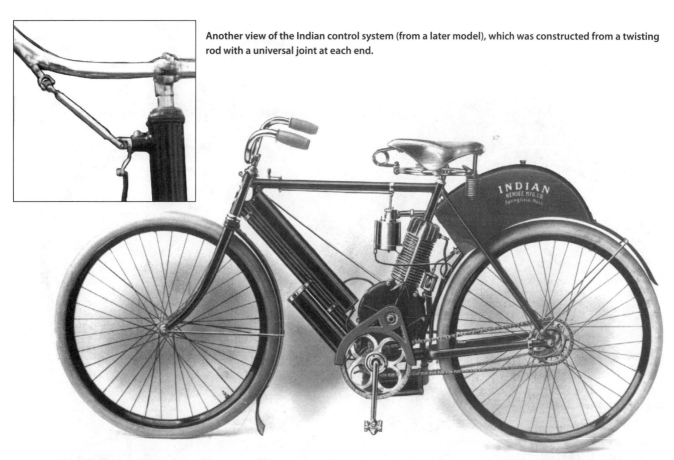

Another view of the Indian control system (from a later model), which was constructed from a twisting rod with a universal joint at each end.

1904 Indian. A front chain guard and a different pedal sprocket were featured on the 1904 models. For the first time, Indian Red finish was optional; a black finish was also offered. (EARL BENTLEY)

1905 Indian cartridge spring fork. When the tire encountered a road obstacle, the lower fork legs pivoted forward and up. (EARL BENTLEY)

1905 Indian. Front suspension arrived via a cartridge spring fork. The front fender was extended forward from the steering head. The top frame tube was longer. The pedal sprocket with 16 holes replaced the clover leaf design. The coil box with conical top end replaced the flat-ended coil box. As well as the standard royal blue finish, a dark green finish was optional. (EARL BENTLEY)

1906 Indian. In 1906 there were three significant mechanical changes. A "compensating sprocket" was a sort of clutch. This was adjusted to permit only the slightest possible slippage, effectively reducing shock loads from sudden stops, yet not slipping under normal running conditions. The device was set up by adjusting four nuts; it was not controllable while riding. The engine size was increased from approximately 13.7 ci (224cc) to 17.6 ci (288cc), while stated output increased from 1 3/4 hp to 2 1/4 hp. Detail changes were made to the contact breaker mechanism and to the exhaust valve support structure. (BOB FINN)

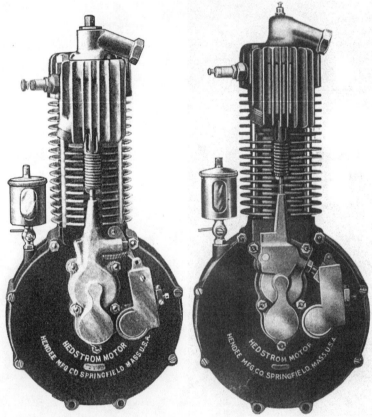

1905 (left) and 1906 (right) Indian engines. The support of the exhaust valve, and the bits and pieces of the contact breaker mechanism, were new for 1906. Also, the 1906 cylinder head studs passed through the cooling fins, rather than along a trough between the fins. (GEORGE YAROCKI)

1906 Indian "Double-Cylinder Racer." This was Indian's first cataloged twin. The displacement wasn't specified. (GEORGE YAROCKI)

1907 Indian. The oil compartment of the "camel-back" tank was replaced by the separate oil tank behind the cylinder. This 1907 single is fitted with the optional gear-driven primary drive. Rather than using conventional gears, the arrangement consisted of a driving wheel with pegs, the pegs then meshing with an ordinary sprocket. The setup, termed a "roller gear drive," was offered only in 1907. (EARL BENTLEY)

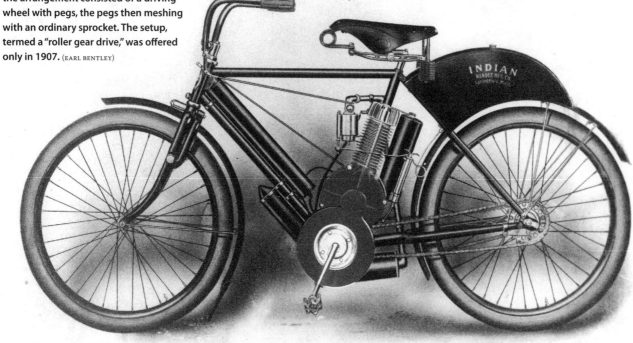

1907 Indian twin. This was Indian's first offering of a road model twin. The displacement wasn't specified, but it appears a double-up of the standard single, which would make it a 35.2-ci (576cc) unit.

(BOB FINN)

1908 Indian. This year, the fork spring was longer and a larger flap was fitted to the front fender. (BOB FINN)

1908 Indian engine. The automatic (suction) inlet valve was replaced by this cam-operated push-pull mechanism. There were detail changes in the exhaust valve support structure and in the contact breaker mechanism. The spark plug was parallel with the ground, instead of perpendicular to the bore.

(BOB FINN)

1908 Indian with optional magneto ignition. (BOB FINN)

1908 Indian. New for 1908 was the 4-hp single. The bore and stroke were 3 1/4 x 3 1/4 inches, respectively, yielding a displacement of 26.96 ci (442cc). On all 1908 models there was a knurled lever for adjusting air inlet settings. (EARL BENTLEY)

1908 Indian 4-hp single with optional magneto ignition. (EARL BENTLEY)

1908 Indian racer. Listed in the 1908 catalog was an even larger single billed as a racer. With a bore and stroke of 3 7/16 x 3 1/4 inches, the displacement was 30.16 ci (494cc). (GEORGE YAROCKI)

1908 Indian. This un-retouched picture from the Indian factory collection conveys the understated appearance of the original machines. There wasn't a lot of shiny stuff, and when there was, it was polished nickel. The engine is the new larger standard size, with a bore and stroke of 2 3/4 x 3 1/4 inches. Displacement was 19.3 ci (316cc). (EARL BENTLEY)

"Twin-Cylinder Indian:" The bore and stroke were 3 7/16 x 3 1/4 inches, and the displacement was 60.32 ci (988cc). The minimal cooling fins ensured the engine was hot enough for maximum performance in short races. Running speeds of 5 to 65 mph were claimed. The motorcycle weighed only 120 lbs., empty. The standard color was Royal Indian blue, with options of Black or Indian Red.

(GEORGE YAROCKI)

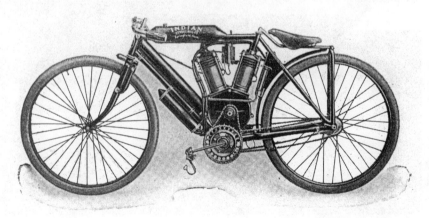

1908 Indian twin. This 38.61-ci twin was fitted with racing accessories offered by Indian: the torpedo tank, under-slung saddle and stubby exhaust pipes.

1908 Indian twin. Shown on this 5-hp twin is the new 1908 option of magneto ignition. The bore and stroke were 2 3/4 x 3 1/4 inches and the displacement was 38.61 (633cc). The rear cylinder is angled the same as on the single-cylinder engines, so as to function as part of the seat mast structure. This angle happens to be 21 degrees from the vertical. For a pleasing appearance and to achieve a horizontal inlet manifold, the front cylinder is also tilted 21 degrees from the vertical. The resulting 42-degree V-twin configuration continued throughout Indian history. (BOB FINN)

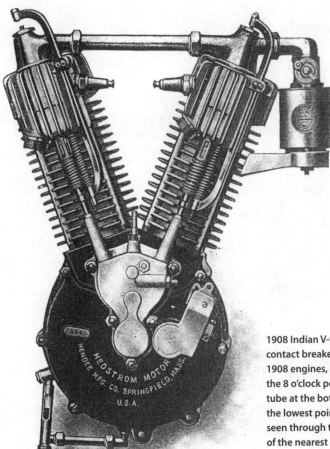

1909
First Loop Frame F-heads

The diamond frame "mopeds" had helped Indian overcome sales resistance during the earliest years. But, by 1909 the increasingly sport-oriented motorcycle public had formed a new consensus regarding the proper appearance of motorcycles. Indian, which had earlier built some loop frame racers, fell in line with the styling trend and introduced loop frame road models for the 1909 season. Diamond frame models were also continued, which not only catered to that minority taste, but also permitted Indian to use up some diamond frame stocks.

1908 Indian V-twin engine, fitted with standard contact breaker system for battery ignition. On all 1908 engines, a sight-feed tube was suspended from the 8 o'clock position of the crankcase. The horizontal tube at the bottom of the arrangement connects to the lowest point in the crankcase. The oil level can be seen through the glass window, at about the height of the nearest crankcase bolt. This layout replaced the earlier glass drain cup, which the rider monitored.

(GEORGE YAROCKI)

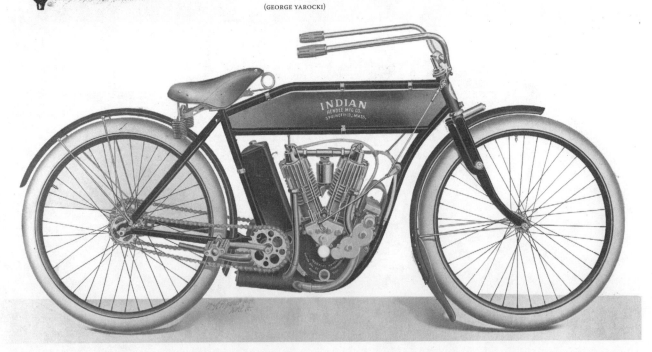

1909 "Loop Frame, Twin Cylinder Indian." The original pedal-bike style "diamond" frames had served well in earlier years, as the diamond framed Indians were user-friendly to customers moving up from pedal bikes. But by 1909, Harley-Davidson and others had set the styling pace with loop frames, which were also more suited to larger engines that were being demanded. This is the 5-hp 38.61-ci (633cc) twin. The engine differs from the 1908 version by the provision of conventional pushrods and the exhaust routing from the front cylinder. A 7-hp 60.32-ci (988cc) twin was also offered for 1909, but wasn't shown in the catalog. (BOB FINN)

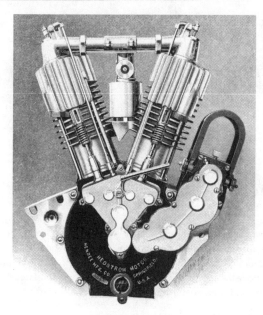

1909 Indian 3 1/2-hp 26.96 (442cc) single. On this model and the 7-hp twin, the lower third of the cylinder didn't have cooling fins. This was a stylistic move, mimicking the sparse finning of the factory racing machines. (EARL BENTLEY)

1909 V-twin engine, 38.61 ci (633cc), as used in the new loop frame. The spark plugs aren't visible because the loop-frame 1909 twins and the loop-frame 26.96-ci (442cc) single had the spark plug(s) mounted in the center of the combustion chamber. The plugs are behind the inlet manifold, and mounted parallel to the bores. In all 1909 engines, the valve timing gears were wider and bearings were larger. All loop-frame engines had larger valves. The larger exhaust valves in the loop-frame 38.61-ci twin, are evident by the newly shaped and larger exhaust ports. (GEORGE YAROCKI)

1909 Model	Engine Type, Model	Engine Data	Transmission	Features
Diamond Frame	2 3/4 hp	19.3 ci (316cc)	single-speed, all chain	battery ignition only
Diamond Frame	5 hp Twin	38.61 ci (633cc)	single-speed, all chain	battery ignition only
Loop Frame	2 3/4 hp	19.3 ci (316cc)	single-speed, all chain	battery or magneto ignition
Loop Frame	3 1/2 hp	26.96 ci (442cc)	single-speed, all chain	battery or magneto ignition
Loop Frame	4 hp	30.16 ci (494cc)	single-speed, all chain	battery or magneto ignition
Loop Frame	5 hp Twin	38.61 ci (633cc)	single-speed, all chain	battery or magneto ignition
Loop Frame	5 hp Twin Belt Dr.	38.61 ci (633cc)	single-speed, belt drive	battery or magneto ignition
Loop Frame	7 hp Twin Belt Dr	60.32 ci (988cc)	single-speed, belt drive	battery or magneto ignition

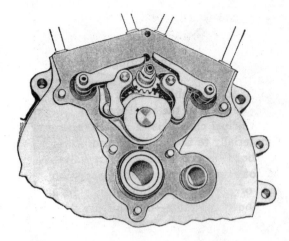

1909 Indian valve lift mechanism, showing inlet valve action. A simple, but remarkably effective, valve gear was used. Two cam lobes were on one shaft. The outer lobe operated both inlet valves through pivoting lifters, as shown in this picture. (GEORGE YAROCKI)

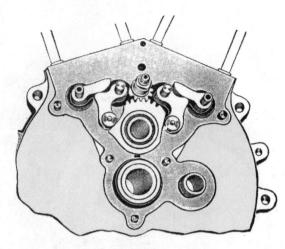

1909 Indian valve lift mechanism, showing exhaust valve action. With the cams and both inlet lifters removed, this picture shows how the inner lobe operated both exhaust valves through pivoting lifters. Note that the exhaust lifters were fitted with rollers, but the inlet lifters had no rollers. Indian justified this setup by the fact that much more force was required to lift the exhaust valves than to lift the inlet valves. (GEORGE YAROCKI)

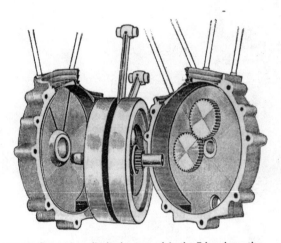

1909 Indian twin-cylinder lower end. In the F-head era, the valve drive (pinion) gear was integral with the crankpin, with the intermediary and cam gears contained within the crankcase. The intermediary gear drove the cam gear and either the contact breaker mechanism or the magneto, depending on ignition option. (GEORGE YAROCKI)

1909 Indian "Compensating Sprocket." Belt-drive manufacturers and enthusiasts claimed chain-drive was too harsh and was hard on the engine. To counter this, Indian brought out this device that consisted of mounting the driven sprocket between two friction plates.

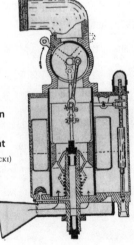

1909 Indian carburetor. A cutaway view of the unique Hedstrom concentric carburetor, as shown in the 1909 catalog. The doughnut-shaped float is evident. (GEORGE YAROCKI)

1909 Indian combustion chamber. Minus the inlet manifold, the combustion chamber reveals the new spark plug location for engines fitted in the new loop frame. The flat-roofed combustion chamber was typical of the era. (GEORGE YAROCKI)

1909 Indian. To use up stocks, Indian continued to offer the old style diamond frame models during 1909. This is the 5-hp twin, still fitted with the old-style push-pull rods instead of conventional push rods as used on the new loop frame models. On diamond-framed models, the seat mast was secured to the rear cylinder head. Hence, it wasn't possible to locate the spark plug in the center of the head. For aesthetic reasons, both spark plugs were side mounted, as in prior years. (EARL BENTLEY)

1909 38.61-ci (633cc) 5-hp belt-drive twin. From 1901 through 1908, Indian had boasted of its all-chain drive and dismissed belt-drive rivals as behind the times. But for the 1909 lineup, the company decided to cater to riders who preferred belt drive. Belt drive enthusiasts claimed the system produced a smoother running motorcycle. The spoked driven pulley was independent of the rear wheel. (EARL BENTLEY)

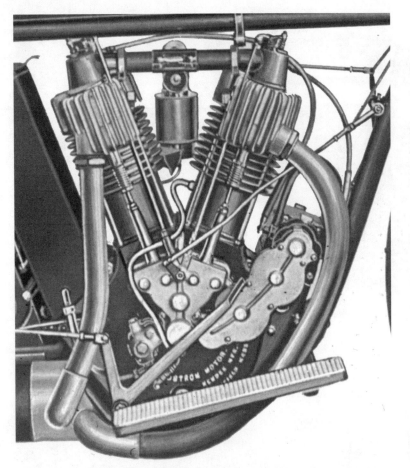

1910 Indian 7-hp twin engine. The bore was decreased from 3 7/16 to 3 1/4 inches; the stroke was increased from 3 ¼ to 3 43/64 inches; displacement was increased from 60.32 ci (988cc) to 60.92 ci (998cc). The 7- and 5-hp twins were available with either of two spark plug locations, in the center of the heads as in this example (obscured by the inlet manifold), or with the 1908 style in which the plugs were horizontally mounted in the valve area. On central-plug engines a fitting was screwed into the old-style side-mounted spark plug hole. This practice was probably used on some 1909 models, in order to avoid scrapping existing stocks. This picture is a closeup made from a 1911 catalog shot, which was identical to the corresponding 1910 catalog shot, except for minor retouching on the top frame tube (not shown here). (BOB FINN)

1910 Indian 4-hp single with belt drive. Indian added some technical novelty to the 1910 belt-drive single. Within the large driving pulley was a sun-planet gear set that restored the gear ratio of this single-speeder to about what it would have been with a conventional smaller driving pulley. Why all the bother? Because the large driving pulley was less prone to slippage than a standard pulley. (GEORGE YAROCKI)

1910

The year 1910 was one of major advances. The new "automatic" mechanical oil pump freed the rider from the concerns of lubrication management. Unknowingly, long-term history was established by Indian's new leaf spring front fork. "Unknowingly" because who could have known that the leaf spring fork would be around through 1945! The company coined an excellent term for the new front end, the "Cradle Spring Fork." Another important Indian advance was the optional two-speed transmission with "free engine" (clutch). Indian eliminated the 26.96-ci (442cc) single, but riders still had four engine choices, two each for singles and twins. For the first time, provision was made for easier installation of a headlight, via a bracket secured to the upper fork braces. During this era, acetylene lighting was favored (see section "Acetylene Lighting").

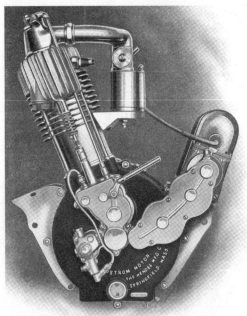

1910 Indian 30.46-ci (499cc) single. All 1910 and 1911 Indians received the mechanical oil pump, which was mounted at the 8 o'clock position of the right crankcase. The "Hedstrom Motor" legend was relocated so as not to be obscured by the pump. Indian singles were not simply "blanked off" twins, but had left and right crankcases and a cam "box" unique to the singles. Note the oil pump routing to the timing case. Early-season twins also had the oil routed to the timing case, but late-season twins had the oil routed to the front cylinder. (GEORGE YAROCKI)

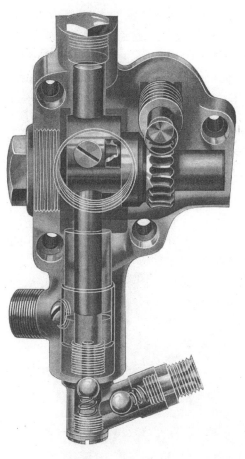

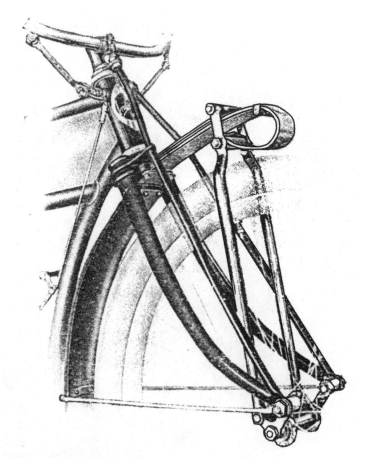

1910 Indian Cradle Spring Fork details. (GEORGE YAROCKI)

Details of the 1910 Indian oil pump. (GEORGE YAROCKI)

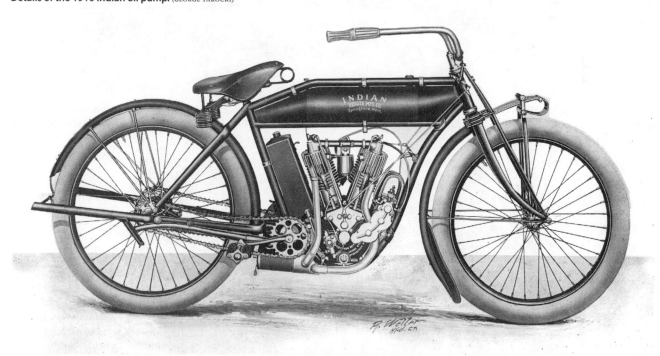

1910 Indian 5-hp twin. For 1910, Indian introduced the leaf-spring trailing-link front fork, termed the "Cradle Spring Fork." This would remain an Indian staple through 1945. The first starter was provided, consisting of a removable hand crank that was secured to the transmission. This example is a single-speed model and is fitted with the optional horizontally mounted spark plugs. Engine dimensions were unchanged. Tipping the scales at 155 lbs., the twin weighed about twice that of Indian No. 1. (BOB FINN)

1910 Model	Engine Data	Transmission	New Features
2 ¾ hp Single	19.3 ci (316cc)	all chain, single-speed or two-speed	"free engine" (clutch) with two-speed, magneto or battery ignition
4 hp Single	30.46 ci (499cc)	all chain, single-speed or two-speed	"free engine" (clutch) with two-speed, magneto or battery ignition
4 hp Single	30.46 ci (499cc)	belt, single-speed	large planet/sun gear pulley, magneto or battery ignition
5 hp Twin	38.61 ci (633cc)	all chain, single-speed or two-speed	"free engine" (clutch) with two-speed, magneto or battery ignition
7 hp Twin	60.92 ci (998cc)	all chain, single-speed or two-speed	"free engine" (clutch) with two-speed, magneto or battery ignition

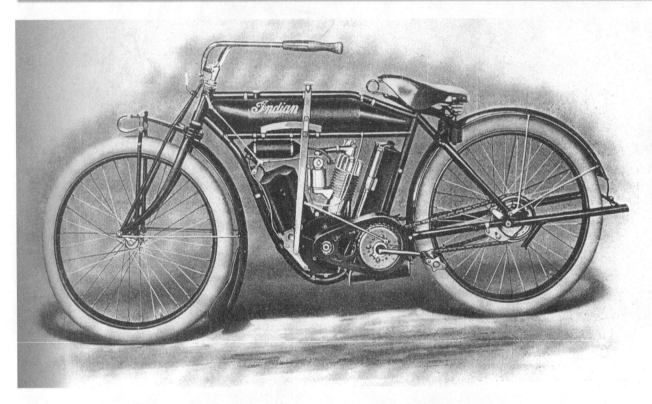

1911 Indian 2 3/4-hp single. The 19.3-ci (316cc) engine had been around since 1908. This example is fitted with battery ignition, but magneto ignition was optional at extra cost. The long lever controlled the clutch, a new feature on all 1911 Indians. The famous Indian script first appeared on some 1910 models such as this one.

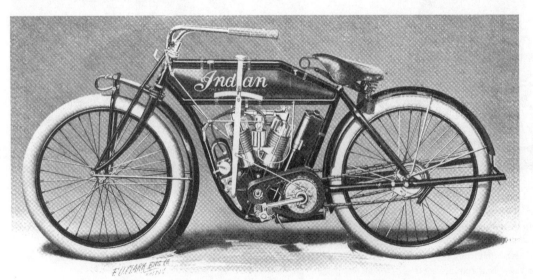

1911 Indian "5 H. P. Twin Cylinder, with Clutch." This single-speed version had a 53-inch wheelbase. Two-speed versions were 2 inches longer. The standard finish was Royal Blue, with Indian Red an option.

(EARL BENTLEY)

1911

Substantial 1911 big twin changes included new flywheels, crankshafts and connecting rods. Optional big twin cylinder heads had either the conventional spark plug disposition or horizontally mounted plugs. Some other notable firsts appeared on the 7-hp twin. The model featured the industry's first footboards, was the first road model Indian produced without the two bicycle-style pedals, and consequently was the first Indian with a single-pedal kick-starter. Long successful in racing, the company began a limited run of special overhead-valve racing twins. These weren't cataloged.

1911 Indian 4-hp belt drive single. As shown here and in the previous picture, both block and script lettering were used during 1911. (GEORGE HAYS)

1911 Indian 7-hp twin. Larger inlet valves were fitted to the 1911 7-hp engine. Indian often cut corners with its sales literature. The shift lever of this two-speeder is just forward of the saddle. The catalog picture of the 1910 two-speed 7-hp was identical except that the shift lever was midway between the two upper tank brackets. An artist simply air brushed out the earlier lever and redrew the one shown here. In fact, on the author's original print the air brush strokes can barely be seen. Actual motorcycles may have appeared slightly different from either or both of the catalog shots. This is the only archival shot in the author's collection that depicts the central spark plug location on a 1911 model. (BOB FINN)

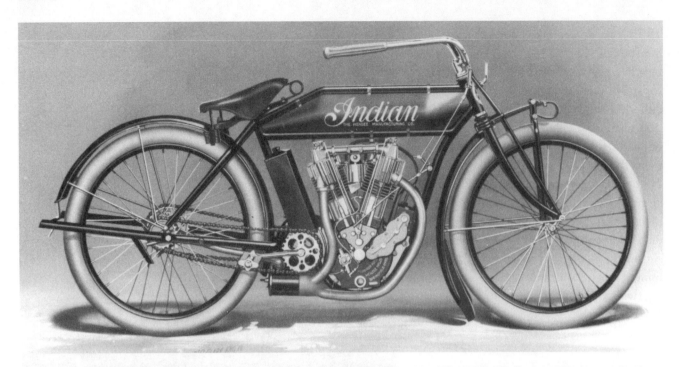

1911 Indian "Regular" (single-speed) 7-hp twin. Heavier fork connecting links (vertical rods), and heavier fork bell cranks (pivoting members) were fitted on all models. The new bell cranks included a grease cup, so the rider could lubricate the bell crank without first removing it.
(EARL BENTLEY)

1911 Indian 4-hp 30.46 ci (499cc) with conventional (small) driving pulley. This less-expensive and more reliable setup replaced the 1910-only model with the large driving pulley and integral planetary gear reduction.

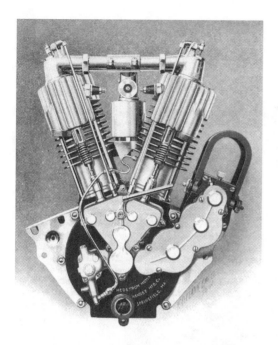

1911 Indian "4 H. P. Chain Drive." As the 30.46-ci single was essentially half of the 60.32-ci twin, Indian's biggest single shared the four-stud cylinder design of the biggest Indian twin. (EARL BENTLEY)

1911 Indian 5-hp 38.61-ci (633cc) engine. Said the catalog: "Nearly all the dirigible balloons in this country are fitted with Hedstrom motors...." Note the return to side-mounted spark plugs. (GEORGE YAROCKI)

1911 Model	Engine Data	Transmission
2 3/4 hp Single	19.3 ci (316cc)	all chain, single-speed or two-speed
4 hp Single	30.46 ci (499cc)	all chain, single-speed or two-speed
4 hp Single	30.46 ci (499cc)	belt, single-speed
5 hp Twin	38.61 ci (633cc)	all chain, single-speed or two-speed
7 hp Twin	60.92 ci (998cc)	all chain, single-speed or two-speed
"big-base" 8-Valve racer	60.92 ci (998cc)	all chain, single-speed

Note: not cataloged; a few were hand built, possibly over a -2 or 3-year period; used by favored riders only

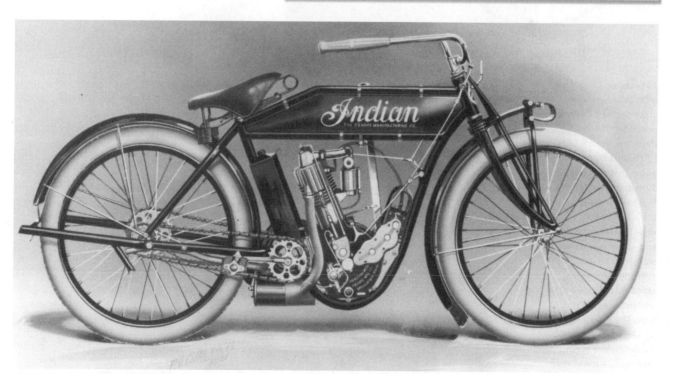

1911 Indian "4 H. P. Chain Drive." (EARL BENTLEY)

1911 Indian Isle of Man racer (above). Indian's star rider Jake DeRosier posed for this shot depicting the Isle of Man TT (Tourist Trophy) race entry. DeRosier placed 12th, but other Indians finished 1-2-3 in the world's most important road race. The two-speed team bikes were built by de-stroking the smaller standard twin (633cc) to within the 600cc class limit. The Indian sweep accelerated the trans Atlantic move toward standardization of chain drive and countershaft gear boxes. (BOB SMITH)

Circa 1911 Indian "big base" eight-valve racer. The nickname "big base" came into use a few years later when the eight-valve racer was redesigned. The engine featured four parallel valves per cylinder. The rider is Lee Humiston who, in late 1912, turned the first officially timed 100 mph on a motorcycle (but on an Excelsior). In the background is one of the dozens of wooden surfaced motordromes that were scattered across the U. S. Indian built a handful of eight-valves for favored riders to use in the popular motordrome circuit. (DAVE KINNIE COLLECTION)

Circa 1911 Indian big base eight-valve twin (at left). The unusually large crankcase, or base, housed unusually large flywheels, the purpose of which was to maintain momentum during periods when the ignition was shut off. Speed control was maintained by shuttling the ignition on and off while the fixed-wide-open carburetor ingested the mixture. Why wide open? Because the engine was "ported," meaning there were several slits near the bottom of each cylinder that vented combustion chamber pressure directly to the air. The cylinders were instantly filled with air, so a very rich carburetor mixture was essential. Fuel regulation in this unusual circumstance, was most practically achieved by a fixed-throttle setting. The rider is Ray Seymour. (DAVE KINNIE COLLECTION)

Circa 1911, typical board track "motordrome" action. These tracks were as short as 1/6 mile in circumference, though 1/4 mile was probably most common. Speeds exceeded 80 mph on the short "dromes." Night races brought the spectacle of open-ported cylinders exploding into the air stream. Thunderous noise, rumbling boards, and catchy rider nicknames like "Slivers" Boyd and "Fearless" Balke, added to the fun. Riders sometimes illegally pooled their winnings and staged artificially close contests, each taking their turn at victory. (BOB SMITH)

1912 Model	Engine Data	Transmission	Features
4 hp Single	30.46 ci (499cc)	chain drive, single-speed or two-speed	bicycle style pedals
4 hp Single	30.46 ci (499cc)	belt, single-speed	bicycle style pedals
7 hp Twin	60.92 ci (998cc)	all chain, single-speed or two-speed	bicycle style pedals
4 hp TT Model	30.46 ci (499cc)	single-speed or two-speed	kick starter, no bicycle pedals
7 hp TT Model	60.92 ci (998cc)	single-speed or two-speed	kick starter, footboards, no bicycle pedals

1912

Taking advantage of the 1-2-3 victory in the 1911 Isle of Man TT, Indian introduced two TT models for the 1912 season: a twin and a single. As to the twin, this was a styling exercise, because the production TT twin had the regular 60.92-ci (998cc) engine, whereas the actual TT winning twins were sleeved-down to 595cc (36.3-ci) motorcycles. The TT single displaced 30.46 ci (499cc). The 2 3/4-hp singles and 5-hp twins were dropped from the 1912 lineup. Indian Red became standard; Royal Blue became optional and no belt-drive model was offered.

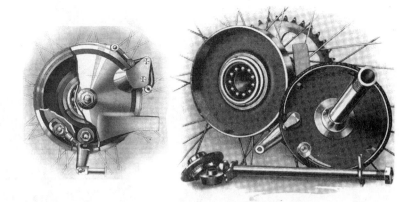

1912 Indian Double-Brake for T. T. Models. All T. T. models were equipped with a new double-brake consisting of an external contracting band and an internal expanding band. One wonders at the effectiveness of an expanding band, but the double-brake simplified export preparation, as the unit satisfied the British requirement for two brakes on all motorcycles. (GEORGE YAROCKI)

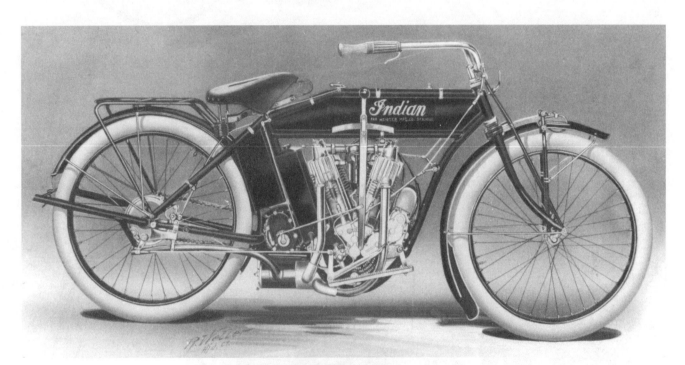

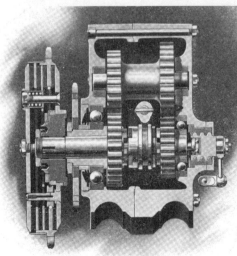

The 1912 Indian two-speed gearbox. This is a rear view. The sliding dog clutch is disengaged from the gears on either side, thus placing the machine in neutral. The unit was secured above two lower frame tubes.

(GEORGE YAROCKI)

1912 "T. T. Two Speed Model 7 H. P.—61" (above). As a styling exercise, Indian came up with T. T. models for the 1912 range. This was the first Indian to feature footboards and a kick starter (on the left side), and the first Indian without bicycle pedals. The shift lever for the two-speed box is on the top frame tube where it begins to slope downward. Other T. T. models were the single-speed twin, two-speed single and single-speed single. (EARL BENTLEY)

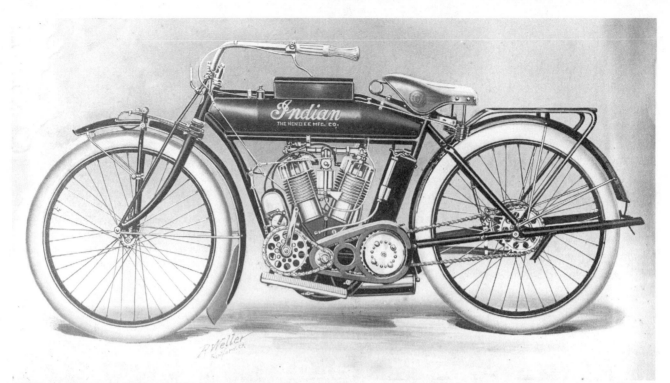

1912 Indian "T. T. Model. 7 H. P.—61. "This is the single-speed T. T. twin. Referring to the nominal displacement in cubic inches, the terms "61" and "sixty-one" had come into favor among American motorcyclists. The so-called TT models were cosmetic statements, as the winners of the famous Isle of Man race had displaced less than 36.6 ci (600cc class limit). But the road-going TT Indians ushered in several innovations: the first kick-starter, the first footboards, and the first Indian without bicycle pedals. (EARL BENTLEY)

1912 Indian "T. T. Model.
4 H. P.—30.50." This is a
single-speed version.

(GEORGE YAROCKI)

1912 Indian T. T. Model
kick-starter. The rider kicked forward—not a good idea, as one's
leg could easily hammer against
the footboard. (GEORGE YAROCKI)

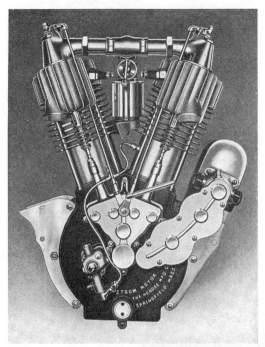

1912 Indian 60.92-ci (998cc) twin. The largest Indian twin got a new front cylinder with a downward exiting exhaust port. All 1912 Indians were equipped with side-mounted spark plugs.

(GEORGE YAROCKI)

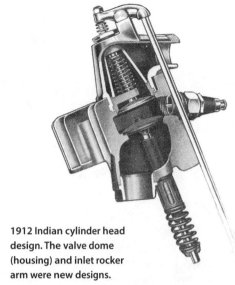

1912 Indian cylinder head design. The valve dome (housing) and inlet rocker arm were new designs.

(GEORGE YAROCKI)

1912 Indian "7 H. P.—61. Regular Model." This model was a single-speeder, with a 53-inch wheelbase—2 inches shorter than the two-speeders. All 1912 Indians got the extended front fender. Featured on all 1912 models was the "Improved Corbin-Indian Coaster Band Brake."

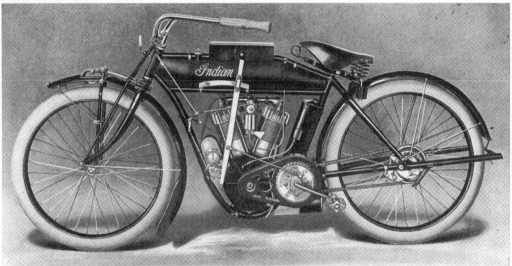

1912 Indian "4 H. P.— 30.50. Regular Model."

(GEORGE YAROCKI)

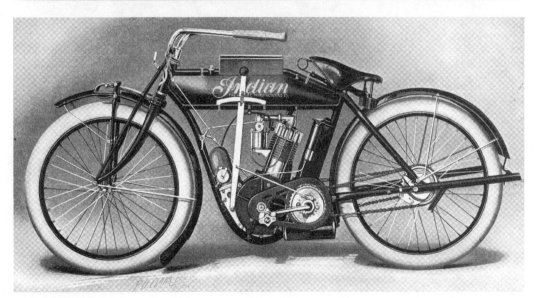

1913 Indian "7 H. P. Twin-Cylinder 61. Regular Model." The defining change was the "Cradle Spring Frame." All Indians got this feature. Tire size on all 1913 models was increased from 2 1/2 to 2 3/4 inches, with 3-inch tires optional. On all models, clearance was added between the tires and the fenders, so that tire chains could be installed for rough going. (GEORGE YAROCKI)

1913

The headline 1913 feature was the "Cradle Spring Frame," a swinging-arm suspension fitted to all models. Indian simplified its manufacturing, inventory control and spare parts operations by eliminating the belt-drive single, and by reducing engine options from four to two. Dropped from the range were the 2 3/4-hp single and the 5-hp twin. The connecting rods and rod bearings were new. The 1913 flywheels were drop forgings instead of castings. The left crankcases were wider and the drive shafts longer in order to accommodate the wider spring frame. A removable oil scoop was fitted within the left crankcase. All road models equipped with the Cradle Spring Frame, chain guard and 2 3/4-inch tires.

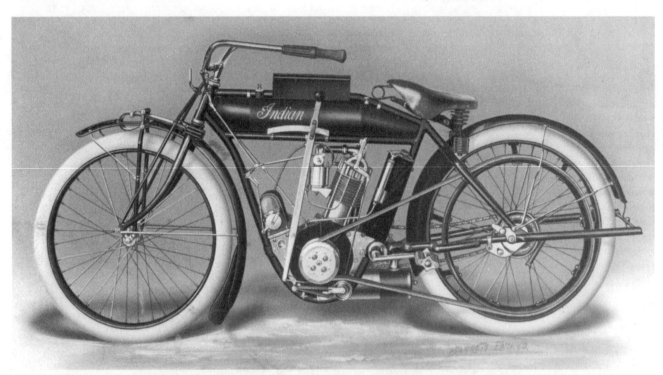

1912 Indian 4 HP-30.50 belt-drive model. A full front fender and a tank-top toolbox were new features on the belt-drive single. This was Indian's final offering of a belt-drive model.

1913 Model	Engine Data	Transmission	New Features
4 hp Single	30.46 ci (499cc)	single-speed	wider fenders
4 hp Single TT	30.46 ci (499cc)	single-speed or two-speed	wider fenders
7 hp Twin	60.92 ci (998cc)	single-speed or two-speed	wider fenders
7 hp TT Model	60.92 ci (998cc)	single-speed or two-speed	wider fenders

1913 Indian Cradle Spring Frame (above). The same frame was used throughout the range, whether the motorcycle was equipped with one-speed drive or two-speed gearbox. The two-speed transmission or the single-speed "free engine" clutch was hung beneath the channel between the front and rear sections. (GEORGE YAROCKI)

1913 Indian Cradle Spring Frame. The swinging-arm construction was about 40 years ahead of its time.

(GEORGE YAROCKI)

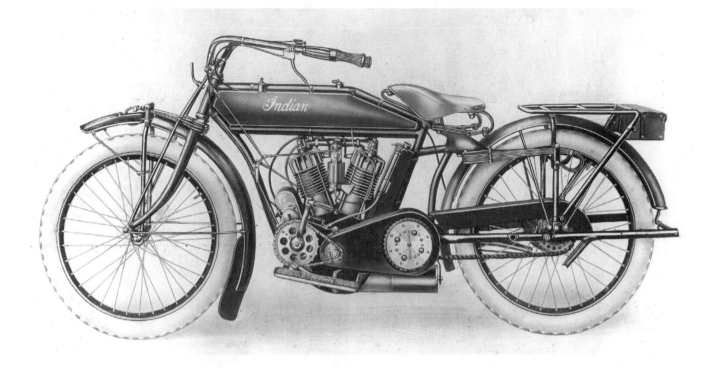

1913 Indian "7 H. P. Twin-Cylinder 61. T. T. Two-Speed Model." A more substantial primary chain guard was fitted. The kick-starter sprocket was of slightly heavier construction. The wheelbase of all 1913 models was 58 inches, 3 inches longer than the previous two-speed-ers and 5 inches longer than the previous single-speed models. For America's rough roads, the longer wheel-base would have delivered significant extra comfort even without the rear springing. (BOB FINN)

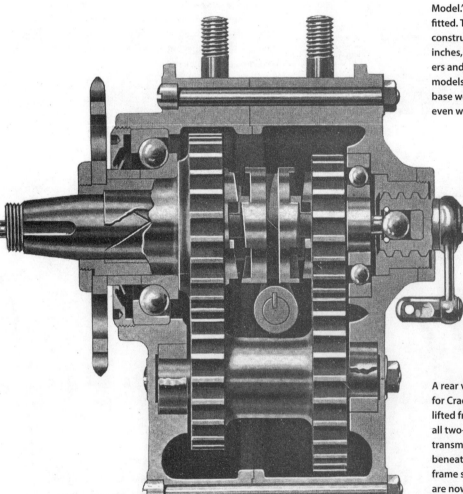

A rear view of the Indian two-speed transmission for Cradle Spring Frame. Although this picture is lifted from the 1915 catalog, the image represents all two-speed boxes for the Cradle Spring Frame. The transmission is now set up for under-slung mounting beneath the massive lower rear forging of the main frame section. The sliding dog clutch and main shaft are now above the double-gear rather than beneath.

(GEORGE YAROCKI)

1913 Indian "4 H. P. Single Cylinder 30.50. Regular Model." This mid-season catalog picture shows increased bracing for the rear luggage rack. The standard saddle for 1913 was the Mesinger Superba with leaf spring suspension. The rear chain guard made its first appearance on the 1913 models.
(GEORGE YAROCKI)

1913 Indian mid-season T. T. Single. On all 1913 models, the top frame tube sloped more sharply downward at the rear, improving the appearance and permitting a lower saddle height. The rear of the tank was narrower, adding further to the visual appeal. On all models, the muffler was 1 1/2 inches longer, and there was no cut-out as previously. (GEORGE YAROCKI)

A 1914 Indian "Two-Twenty-five Regular Model." Model names in the 1914 range indicated the retail U.S. price, in this case $225. All 1914 twins continued with the 60.92-ci (998cc) engine having a bore and stroke of 3 ¼ inches x 3 43/64 inches. (GEORGE YAROCKI)

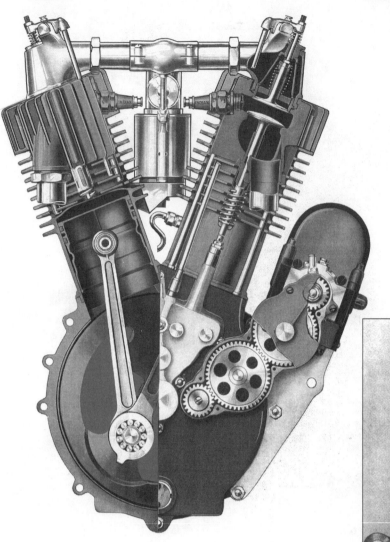

1914

The 1914 Indian range was expanded to seven models. However, only two engine types were offered: the 499cc single and the 998cc twin. A road model single joined five variations of road model twins, the twins featuring differing combinations of equipment. For the first time, some models were sold with the standard equipment of electric lights and a speedometer. All road models were equipped with the Cradle Spring Frame, chain guard and 2 3/4-inch tires.

1914 Indian "7 H. P. Twin Motor In Section Showing Internal Construction." (GEORGE YAROCKI)

The F-head Indian valve lift mechanism.

(GEORGE YAROCKI)

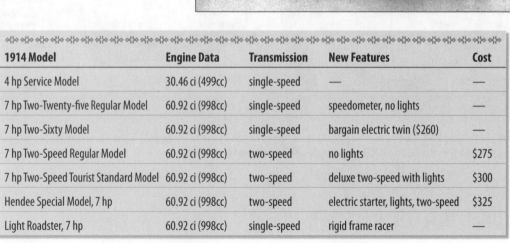

1914 Model	Engine Data	Transmission	New Features	Cost
4 hp Service Model	30.46 ci (499cc)	single-speed	—	—
7 hp Two-Twenty-five Regular Model	60.92 ci (998cc)	single-speed	speedometer, no lights	—
7 hp Two-Sixty Model	60.92 ci (998cc)	single-speed	bargain electric twin ($260)	—
7 hp Two-Speed Regular Model	60.92 ci (998cc)	two-speed	no lights	$275
7 hp Two-Speed Tourist Standard Model	60.92 ci (998cc)	two-speed	deluxe two-speed with lights	$300
Hendee Special Model, 7 hp	60.92 ci (998cc)	two-speed	electric starter, lights, two-speed	$325
Light Roadster, 7 hp	60.92 ci (998cc)	single-speed	rigid frame racer	—

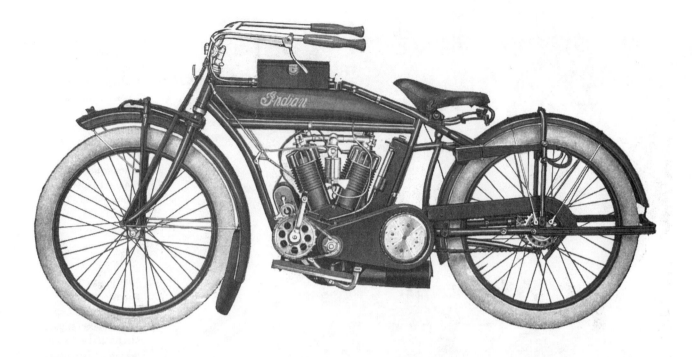

1914 Indian "Two-Speed Regular Model." Penny pinchers saved $25 by doing without lights. Price: $275. (GEORGE YAROCKI)

1914 Indian "Two-Speed Tourist Standard Model." The top of the kick-start line, this model sold for $300. (GEORGE YAROCKI)

1914 Indian "Hendee Special Model." The electric-start Hendee Special was named after company cofounder George Hendee. The model was inadequately engineered. Though it had two batteries, the combination starter motor and generator wasn't up to the task of keeping them charged. Presented as the ultimate Indian, it was the most expensive, commanding a sales price of $325.
(GEORGE YAROCKI)

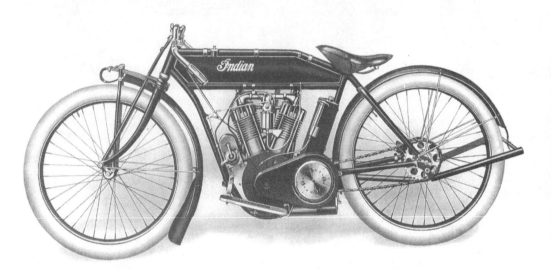

1914 Indian "Light Roadster Model." Specifications: 7 hp, 61-ci (1000cc) engine. Mechanical valves. Indian mica sparkplugs. Double-force feed system, with engine-driven pump and auxiliary hand pump. Wheelbase, 53 inches. Tires: 28 x 2 3/4 inches. Finish: Indian Red. Price: $260.
(GEORGE YAROCKI)

1914 Indian sidecar outfit. The days of sidecar outfits for practical transportation were drawing to a close because of inexpensive Ford Model T automobiles.
(GEORGE YAROCKI)

1915

A three-speed transmission was the most important advance of the 1915 lineup. The two-speed gearbox remained an option. For single-speed road models, Indian introduced the neutral countershaft which enabled the rider to start the motorcycle with the rear wheel on the ground. Indian simplified the 1915 range by cataloging all models without lights and speedometer. Twelve models consisted of varying combinations of engines and transmissions. The newest engineering was reflected in the "Little Twin." This was a scaled down 41.57-ci (681cc) version of the classic F-head "Big Twin," but with a cost-cutting rigid frame.

It was the last year of F-heads in the domestic catalog. The three-speed transmission debuted on some models. B Models were entirely new small twins. Left-over Models B and C were listed in the 1916 British catalog. Dual clutch controls (left pedal, right lever) were found on all but Model E-1. There was an extra (third) fender brace on each side. E models had optional "Japan" black hubs, spokes, and rims.

1915 Indian kick-starter. A decent rear-stroke starter finally arrived on the 1915 models. (GEORGE YAROCKI)

1915 Indian "Models B... Little Twin." For the first time since 1911, Indian offered a mid-size twin. With a bore and stroke of 2 3/4 and 3 1/2 inches, the F-head engine displaced 41.57 ci (681cc). Three variants were offered: Model B-1 Single-Speed, Model B-2 Two-Speed, and Model B-3 Three-Speed. Though the front fork looks identical to that of the big twin, the unit was of lighter construction. (GEORGE YAROCKI)

1915 Indian heavy-duty front fork, as used on the big twins.
(GEORGE YAROCKI)

1915 Indian new rear stand and rear frame structure. (GEORGE YAROCKI)

1915 Model	Engine Data	Transmission	New Features
B-1 Little Twin	41.57 ci (681cc)	1-speed	New smaller engine, rigid frame, neutral countershaft
B-2 Little Twin	41.57 ci (681cc)	2-speed	New smaller engine, rigid frame —
B-3 Little Twin	41.57 ci (681cc)	3-speed	New smaller engine, rigid frame —
C-1 Big Twin	60.92 ci (998cc)	1-speed	Neutral countershaft, tailpipe on left side
C-2 Big Twin	60.92 ci (998cc)	2-speed	Tailpipe on left side
C-3 Big Twin	60.92 ci (998cc)	3-speed	Tailpipe on left side
D-1 Speedway	60.92 ci (998cc)	1-speed	—
E-1 Service	30.46 ci (499cc)	1-speed	E-1: neutral countershaft, tailpipe on left side
E-2 Service	30.46 ci (499cc)	2-speed	—
E-3 Service	30.46 ci (499cc)	3-speed	—

1915 Indian "Models C." The 60.92-ci twin was available with single-speed, two-speed or three-speed as Models C-1, C-2 and C-3, respectively. (GEORGE YAROCKI)

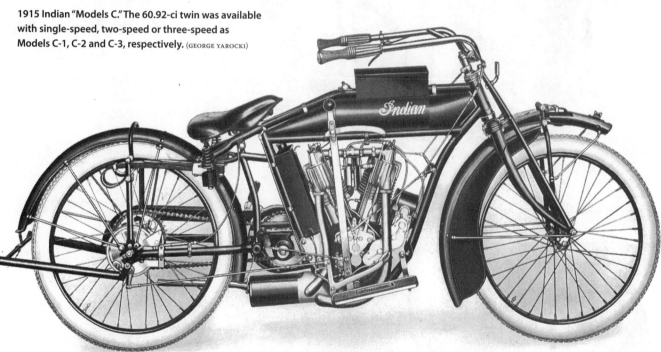

1915 Indian Model C-1, single-speed big twin.
(GEORGE YAROCKI)

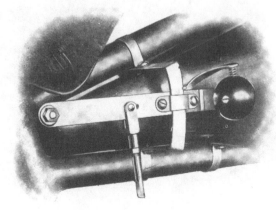

1915 Indian gear-shift mechanism.
(GEORGE YAROCKI)

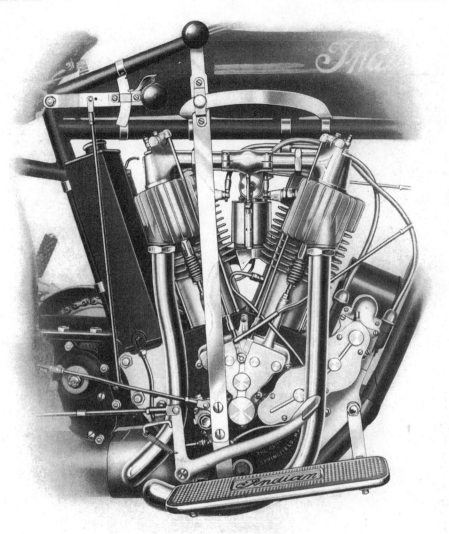

1915 Indian Model C-3, three-speed big twin. (GEORGE YAROCKI)

1915 Indian clutch components. (GEORGE YAROCKI)

1915 Indian Model C-3 with electrical lighting. (BOB FINN)

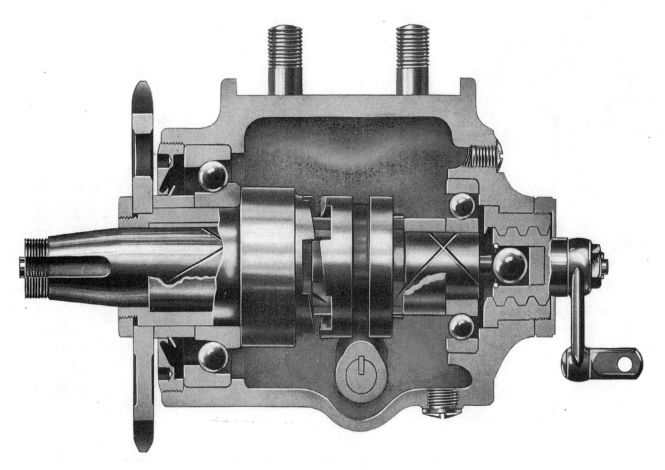

1915 Indian "Free Engine Gear" for single-speed models. For the first time the free engine gear was provided for one-speeders. Previously, one-speed models had to be pedaled either with the rear wheel lifted via the rear stand, or down the road bicycle style. The device was also termed a "neutral countershaft." (GEORGE YAROCKI)

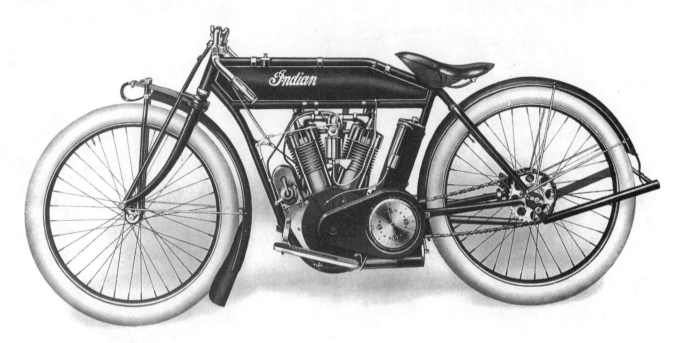

1915 Indian Model D-1 "Speedway." The identical 1914 model was termed the "Light Roadster." (GEORGE YAROCKI)

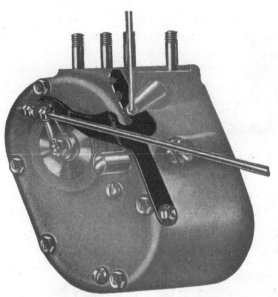

1915 Indian three-speed transmission with interlock to prevent shifting gears while the clutch engaged.

(GEORGE YAROCKI)

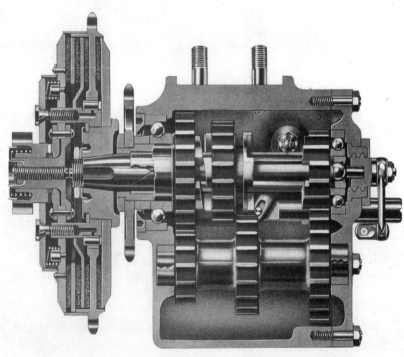

1915 Indian three-speed transmission. Note that there are shifting dogs (sometimes termed clutches) on each side of the sliding single-gear on the main (top) shaft. This would change in 1916. (GEORGE YAROCKI)

1915 Model E "Service Model" (above). In its third year of production, the Service Model was unchanged, except that the luggage rack had become an option in 1914. A new optional finish on singles was "Japan" black on hubs, spokes, and rims.

(GEORGE YAROCKI)

Comparison of standard and racing cylinder heads, circa 1915. On the left is the standard head with a flat roof. On the right is a racing head with a sloped roof. British historian Peter Hartley credits Charles B. Franklin with the sloped roof idea from about 1912. In 1914, Franklin moved to the United States and joined the Indian engineering staff. In the 1920s, British engineer Harry Ricardo patented his "squish" combustion chamber design with the sloped roof. Harley-Davidson and many automobile companies paid royalties to use the Ricardo principle. Indian never did, and was never challenged by Ricardo. (STEPHEN WRIGHT)

1915 Indian Parcel Car. Even in this era, commercial business was a marginal activity for American motorcycle companies because of automobile competition.

(GEORGE YAROCKI)

1916 Indian Spring Frame Powerplus. The 1916 big twins and big singles consisted of entirely new engines in the 1915 frame. (THE ANTIQUE MOTORCYCLE)

Perspective: 1901-1915

From 1901 through 1908, Indian promoted a pedal-bike resembling motorcycle that found ready acceptance among bicyclists. Meanwhile, Harley-Davidson and others had been advancing loop frame models with a more sporting appearance. As automobiles continued gaining in popularity, motorcycling continued evolving from a transportation alternative to a sporting outlet. With increasing emphasis on speed, ever-larger engines emphasized the handling advantage of mounting the engine lower in the frame than could be done with the pedal-bike style diamond frames. Thus, the loop frame layout came on the scene in 1909.

By 1915, American motorcycles had effectively completed the transition from a transportation option to a sporting choice. This was signified by Indian's production numbers, which saw twins account for 90 percent of the company's output.

1916 Indian Powerplus Engine. As in the F-heads, a single camshaft operated the valves. The main advantages of the side-valve configuration were cleaner and quieter running, and increased reliability. Harley-Davidson continued with F-head big twins for another 14 years, proving that the older layout was far from peaking out. But in the coming years, Indian would prove on the racetracks that the side-valve design could outrun both rival F-heads and overheads.

(THE ANTIQUE MOTORCYCLE)

1916 Indian three-speed transmission. A new feature was the sliding double-gear with shifting dogs on one side only. This replaced the previous sliding single-gear with shifting dogs on each side. In the 1915 gearbox, engagement of low (first) gear had been achieved by the harmless clunk of engaging dogs (on the right end of the upper shaft). In the 1916 gearbox, engagement of low gear was achieved by stressful teeth-to-teeth contact. Thus, the Indian clunk-into-low became part of American motorcycling.
(THE ANTIQUE MOTORCYCLE)

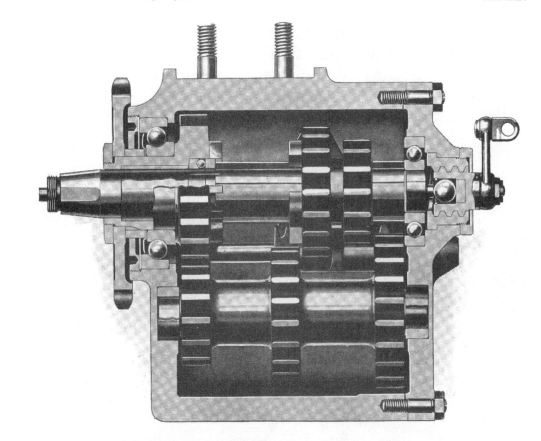

1916 Indian "Model F Cradle Spring Frame Big Twin 3 Speed." Prior to the 1916 Indian range, among American factories only Reading-Standard had built side-valve engines in large numbers. After Reading-Standard Staffer Charles Gustafson Sr. moved to Indian around 1914, he influenced the dramatic changeover.
Skeptical Indian F-head fans scornfully termed the Powerplus a Reading-Standard engine.
(THE ANTIQUE MOTORCYCLE)

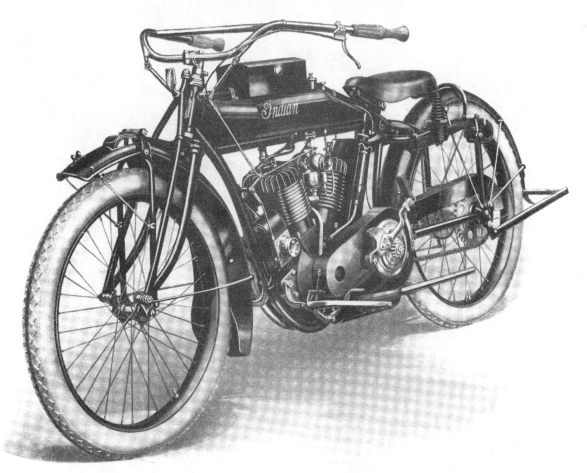

1916-1919, Early Side-Valve Motorcycles

After so much success with F-head engines, Indian abandoned them for the 1916 big twins in favor of side-valve (Flathead) power plants. Full valve enclosure made this layout attractive because there was less noise, less wear, and less grime. Period enthusiasts were surprised at the "Powerplus" name of the new genre. It seemed illogical that moving the inlet valve from the top to the side would result in a power boost. Some were disappointed enough to term the engines "Reading-Standard" units, as that company had for several years been making side-valve engines. But test rides convinced the skeptics.

The 1916 big twin was essentially the Powerplus engine in the same frame as used for 1915 F-heads. The year 1917 saw a complete makeover of the frame, which, though retaining the same general outline, featured heavier construction throughout. The years 1918 and 1919 saw only detail big twin changes as the company prepared its next big move.

1916 Highlights

"Japan" black hubs, spokes and rims became mandatory on singles and became optional on twins.

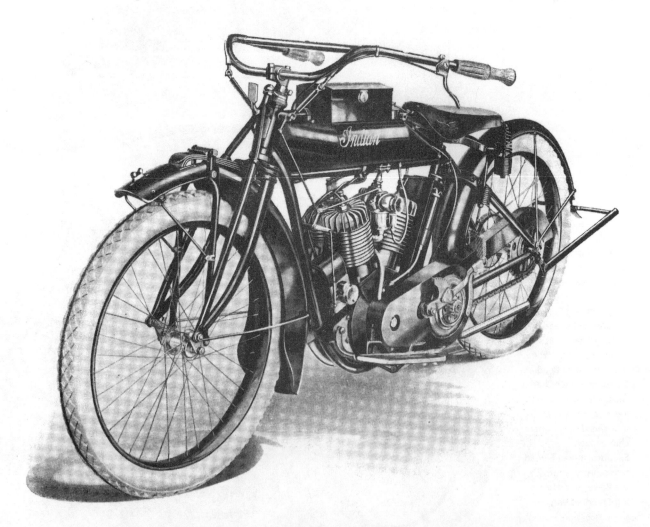

1916 Indian "Model G Regular Frame Big Twin 3 Speed." After three years of exclusive spring frame use on large models, the company decided a less expensive large model was needed. At $250, the Model G was 10-percent cheaper than the $275 Model F. (THE ANTIQUE MOTORCYCLE)

1916 Indian eight-valve racer. On each head were unequal-sized exhaust valves. The smaller of these opened slightly ahead of the larger, so as to reduce back pressure on the larger valve head. Single-cylinder versions were also built, primarily for ½-mile dirt (horse) tracks that were numerous in the Midwest. According to industry custom, displacements were rounded off to a nominal figure, 61 ci (1000cc) for the twins and 30.50 ci (500cc) for the singles. (SAM HOTTON)

1916 Indian "Cantilever Comfort Saddle."

(THE ANTIQUE MOTORCYCLE)

1916 Model	Engine Data	Transmission	Misc.
F, Powerplus twin, spring frame	60.88 ci (998cc)	3-speed	New side-valve (Flathead) engine
G, Powerplus single, rigid frame	60.88 ci (998cc)	3-speed	New side-valve (Flathead) engine.
H, overhead valve twin, 8 valves	61 ci (1000cc)	3-speed	Later termed "small base" 8-valve
H, overhead valve single, 4 valves	30.5 ci (500cc)	1-speed	Later termed "small base" 4-valve
K, two-stroke single	13.5 ci (221cc)	3-speed	Fixed ignition timing

1916 Indian Model K Featherweight engine. The outside "bacon slicer" flywheel produced maximum flywheel effect with minimum weight. The so-called keystone frame used the bolted-together engine and transmission as a stress-bearing member, and there were no frame tubes beneath the power plant.

1916 Indian eight-valve racer. Double sets of intake and exhaust valves were mounted on top of the cylinder head and mechanically operated. There were no auxiliary ports. They were built in single- and twin-cylinder types. Piston displacement: single, 30.50 cubic inches; twin, 61 cubic inches. Price: eight-valve, $350; four-valve, $300. (SAM HOTTON)

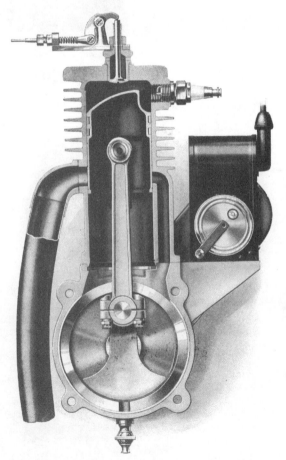

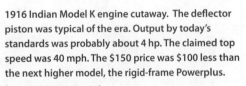

1916 Indian Model K engine cutaway. The deflector piston was typical of the era. Output by today's standards was probably about 4 hp. The claimed top speed was 40 mph. The $150 price was $100 less than the next higher model, the rigid-frame Powerplus.

(THE ANTIQUE MOTORCYCLE)

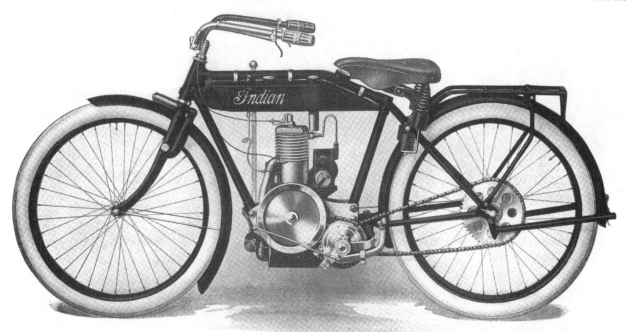

1916 Indian Model K "Featherweight." Indian hoped this lightweight user-friendly model would open up a vast market of people who were scared off by the evolution of motorcycles from their original "moped" roots to large and snorty machines. One would think that the Featherweight's weight would be proudly specified, but it wasn't. (EARL BENTLEY)

1916 Indian "Model H Overhead Valve Racing Type." The nickname "small base" was applied to these racers, to distinguish them from the earlier eight-valve twins and four-valve singles, which were nicknamed "big base." The 1916 racers had standard-sized crankcases and flywheels. The cylinders and heads were unchanged.

(THE ANTIQUE MOTORCYCLE)

1916 Indian Model K "Featherweight." The bore and stroke were 2 1/2 and 2 3/4 inches, yielding a displacement of 13.5 ci (221cc). A lever throttle was on the left handlebar. A compression release lever was on the right handlebar. The long lever is the gear shifter, situated in a four-notch arc, one each for neutral, first, second and third gears.

1916 Indian Model K transmission and kick-starter.

(THE ANTIQUE MOTORCYCLE)

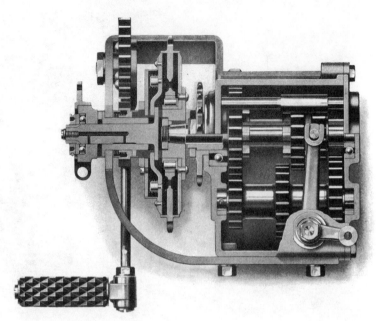

1916 Indian Model K transmission and kick-starter. The specifications were top drawer, with the transmission being a miniature version of that used on the large models. Poor sales killed the model at season's end.

(THE ANTIQUE MOTORCYCLE)

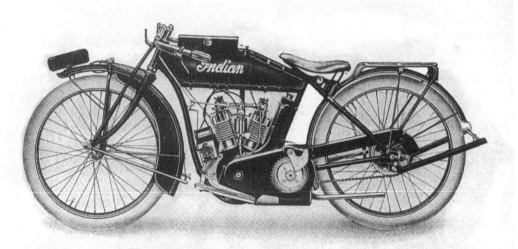

1916 Indian Model B as pictured in the British catalog. These were leftover 1915 models pulled from the warehouse. The Model B wasn't available in the United States. (GEORGE YAROCKI)

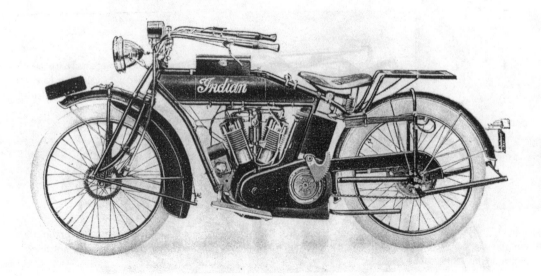

1916 Indian Model C as pictured in the British catalog. It was another 1915 leftover, rebranded as a 1916 model. This F-head wasn't available in the United States.

(GEORGE YAROCKI)

1917 Highlights

All models had three-speed transmissions, except the single-speed Model P. Powerplus bore and stroke remained 3 1/8 and 3 31/32 inches, and Powerplus displacement was: twins, 60.88 ci (998cc); singles 30.4 ci (499cc). "Japan" black was mandatory on all models' hubs, spokes and rims.

Models N, NE, P, U, V and W had the following new features: Optional olive drab finish. On olive and Indian red machines, black striping edged in gold. Valance striping on front fender. Black hubs, rims, and spokes: mandatory. New fork bell crank. New triple stem fork. Double-mounted handlebars. Old Sol headlight on NE. Webbed frame. Upper sidecar lug added to frame. Splitdorf magdyno. Simple grips replace convex "Rough Rider" style. Rounded edges on tanks. New tank filler caps. New shift lever and shifter gate. Longer clutch hand lever. Longer brake pedal. New domed exhaust valve caps. Cylinders 1/4-inch longer. Optional Schebler carburetor or Indian-built Indian Special. With Indian Special carburetor, the inlet manifold was larger. New right crankcase to accommodate new inlet and exhaust valve guides, and to work with slightly different frame geometry. New left crankcase to work with slightly different frame geometry. New footboard rear brackets. Toolbox moved under saddle. Sidecar lug added to left side of gearbox hanger section (behind and below toolbox). Larger tail pipe. New rear springs fork end connecting link. New outside operating lever of internal band brake. Additional (fourth) rear fender brace on each side. Old Sol tail light on NE. Models P, U, and V: last listed in 1917.

The O Model was a horizontally opposed twin with side-valves. It was a new model in 1917. Features included: cartridge fork, outside flywheel, fixed ignition timing.

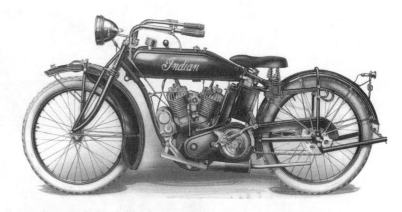

1917 Indian "Powerplus—Type N." The 1917 Powerplus got a major rework of the frame. Crankcases were new, to match up with the frame changes. More streamlined tanks with rounded edges got away from the F-head look. A gear-driven single-unit Splitdorf magdyno provided ignition and battery charging. (EARL BENTLEY)

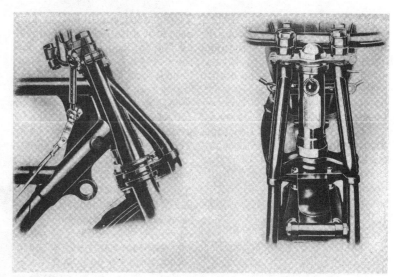

1917 Indian Powerplus frame and front fork details. Extra strength came from the webbed steering head support and larger tubing in both the frame and fork. (INDIAN SALES LITERATURE)

1917 Indian Powerplus, rider's view. (INDIAN SALES LITERATURE)

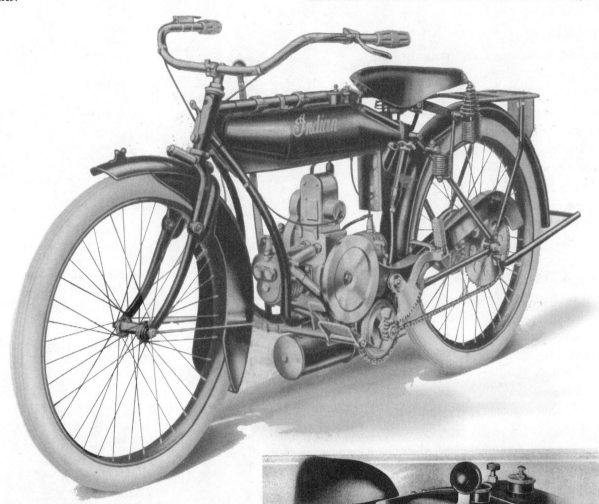

1917 Indian "Light Twin—Type O." One might think after the flop of the 1916 Model K Featherweight two-stroke, that Indian would lose its interest in "missionary" models, but they came back with a more upscale lightweight. It was, of course, more expensive, $180 versus the $150 Featherweight. A lever throttle was on the left handlebar. On the right handlebar was the magneto cutout used to stop the engine. Ignition timing was fixed at full advance, rather than rider controllable. (EARL BENTLEY)

1917 Indian Powerplus tank-mounted controls. (INDIAN SALES LITERATURE)

1917 Indian Light Twin engine. The side-mounted valves were moved by a camshaft on top of the crankcase. The angle between the valves and the combustion chamber wasn't important on this economy model, but would have been detrimental on a machine designed for sporting performance.

(INDIAN SALES LITERATURE)

1917 Indian Light Twin engine. With bore and stroke of 2 x 2 ½ inches, the displacement was 15.70 ci (257cc). The transmission was the same as used on the preceding two-stroke single. "The Light Twin is Noiseless," claimed the catalog. Indeed, these little bikes sounded and felt rather like a sewing machine.

1917 Indian factory racing team rider Gene Walker (above). Engineer Charles B. Franklin was working wonders with his side-valve racers, proceding along lines of the later and more famous British engineer Harry Ricardo. By 1920, the Franklin "Flatheads" were faster than the Indian eight-valves, the Harley-Davidson eight-valves and the Excelsior F-heads. In shorter races, where all-out speed triumphed over team strategy, rider Walker was nearly unbeatable. However, Harley-Davidson r emained the long-distance master.

(JACK ARMSTRONG)

1918 Model	Engine Data	Transmission	New Features, Misc.
N-18	60.88 ci (998cc)	3-speed	Powerplus twin, spring frame
NE-18	60.88 ci (998cc)	3-speed	Powerplus twin, spring frame, electric lights
W-18	30.4 ci (499cc)	3-speed	Powerplus single, spring frame
O-18	15.70 ci (257cc)	3-speed	Leaf-spring fork; trolley-car shifter

1918 Indian tank-mounted controls.

(GEORGE YAROCKI)

1918 Indian Type N-18. The front fork spring scroll was larger; so it extended further through the fender. The tailpipe was moved to the right side.

(EARL BENTLEY)

1918 Indian Type NE-18. A new Solar headlight was mounted to new "underslung" brackets. A separate Dixie gear-driven magneto and belt-driven Splitdorf generator replaced the previous gear-driven single-unit Splitdorf magdyno.

(EARL BENTLEY)

1918 Indian, rider's view.

1918 Indian Light Twin gear-shift control, the so-called trolley car shifter.

(GEORGE YAROCKI)

1919 Model	Transmission	Misc.
N-18 Powerplus twin, spring frame	3-speed	Optional gray finish
NE-18 Powerplus twin, spring frame, electric lights	3-speed	Optional gray finish
O-19 Light Twin	3-speed	1920-1931: low side-valve models

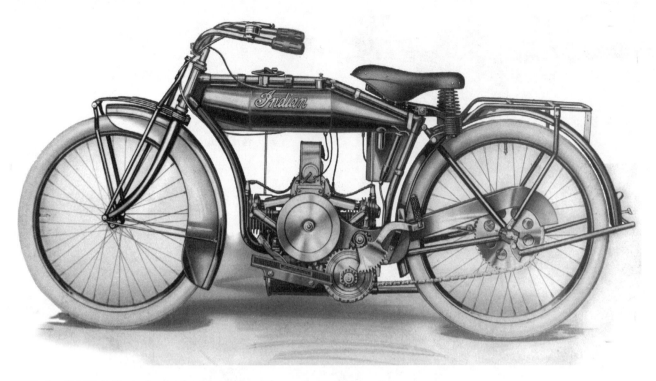

1918 Indian Light Twin. The leaf spring front fork replaced the previous cartridge unit. (EARL BENTLEY)

1919 Indian Powerplus, Type NE-19. Changes to the 1919 models were minimal due to World War I impact. The luggage rack was supplied as standard equipment, and the typically cheesy Indian catalog solution was to have an artist retouch an earlier picture. There was a new optional finish, Indian Gray with black striping edged in gold. On Indian Red models, the double gold striping did not have inboard black striping. There was a new hand-lever for the external brake. The motor base (crankcase) oil sight glass was replaced by an oil-level plug. The Model W single wasn't listed in some (or all?) catalogs, but may have been available. (EARL BENTLEY)

1920

For the 1920 season, Indian brought out the radically different 37-cubic inch (600cc) side-valve Scout V-twin. Its details and many attractions, detailed in the captions, ushered in a new era of easier handling and improved reliability. Two years later came the first Chief, which was a 61-cubic inch (1000cc) V-twin side-valve motorcycle that was basically a "big Scout" according to Indian advertisements. In 1923, the 74-cubic inch (1300cc) Big Chief debuted and immediately became the company's best seller. The year 1924 saw the last offering of the Powerplus genre, which had become very dated in appearance. The Powerplus spring frame was less than robust, causing excessive wear and, perhaps more importantly, the Powerplus didn't look "right" to American riders. In 1925 Indian introduced the 21-cubic inch (350cc) Prince single in both side-valve and overhead-valve versions.

An important exception to the Indian side-valve principle was the four-cylinder Ace. Indian bought out the Ace firm in late 1926 and in early January, 1927, offered the F-head Ace through Indian dealerships. Also joining the 1927 range was the Scout "Police Special," a 45-cubic inch (750cc) V-twin with surprising power and speed. In 1928, the Ace became the "Indian Ace." Mid-1928 saw two important developments. Along with Harley, Excelsior, and Henderson, Indian fitted a front brake to all their models. The long delay in this feature in the U.S. was in part due to the dominance of unpaved roads on the American scene. The other big news for 1928, was the introduction of the longer and lower Series 101 Scout.

In 1929, Indian pulled the plug on the Prince singles. As Harley-Davidson offered comparable models, there weren't enough sales to warrant continuing the Prince. That same year, the F-head four-cylinder was redesignated the "Indian Four." The years 1930 and 1931 saw only detailed refinements in the range.

The N-20 model had the following new Powerplus features: Heavier front fork, new fork bell cranks with screw-down lubricators, new front fender (different mounting holes) to accommodate new fork, new model Solar headlight, new headlight brackets, new integral handlebar bracket with central mount, leather control sheaths, larger (1 1/2-inch) tank filler openings, new exhaust valve lifter, gearshift and clutch levers with integral metal knob, larger exhaust ports and header pipes, new muffler to accept larger exhaust system, new left and right crankcases to accept larger mounting studs (3/8 inch), twin tail pipes: shown in parts books, mentioned in period press release (not shown in 1920 catalog), rear frame fork crown grease cups replaced oilers.

1920 Indian Powerplus Sidecar outfit. The pleated upholstery was a new feature.

(EARL BENTLEY)

1920 Model	Engine Data	Transmission
G-20 Scout, side-valve twin	36.38 ci (596cc)	3-speed
N-20 Powerplus twin, spring frame	60.88 ci (998cc)	3-speed
NE-20 Powerplus twin, spring frame with electric lights	60.88 ci (998cc)	3-speed
W-20 Commercial Powerplus single	30.49 ci (499cc)	3-speed

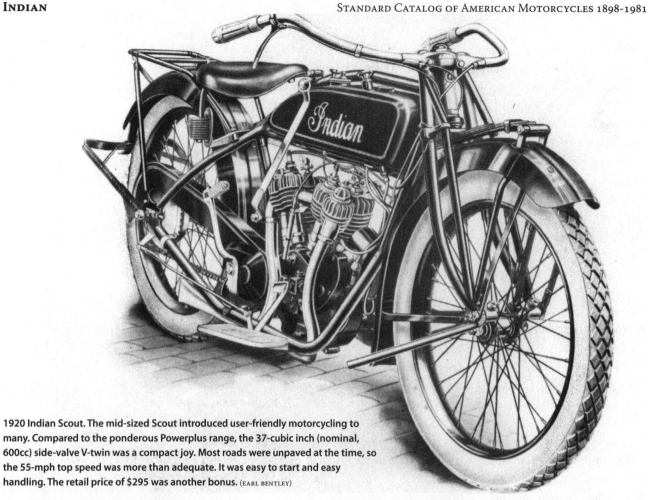

1920 Indian Scout. The mid-sized Scout introduced user-friendly motorcycling to many. Compared to the ponderous Powerplus range, the 37-cubic inch (nominal, 600cc) side-valve V-twin was a compact joy. Most roads were unpaved at the time, so the 55-mph top speed was more than adequate. It was easy to start and easy handling. The retail price of $295 was another bonus. (EARL BENTLEY)

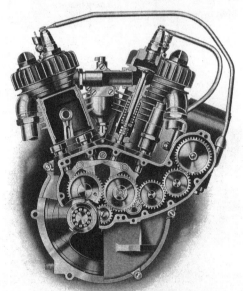

1920 Indian Scout engine. Scout valve operation was via two camshafts—one for each cylinder. For each cylinder a pair of pivoted cam-followers translated the action of a single cam lobe into inlet and exhaust valve motion. This was an update to the Powerplus method of a single camshaft having two lobes. The oil pump body (not shown) was integral with the timing case cover. (GEORGE YAROCKI)

1920 Indian Scout. The engine and three-speed transmission were bolted together. The assembled power plant was bolted on each side to the front lower frame rails, and by a single bolt beneath the transmission case. The combination of the wrap-around "cradle" frame and, effectively, unit power plant construction, fleshed out a ground-up re-thinking of the motorcycle concept. Previously, almost all motorcycles were, conceptually, enlarged pedal bikes housing an engine that was remote from the gearbox, the two being joined by chain within a sheet metal enclosure.

(EARL BENTLEY)

1920 Indian Powerplus Model NE-20 (retouched to show twin tail pipes). Some of the new features were: screw-down fork lubricator cups; new front fender and brace; new Solar model headlight; larger filler cap openings; larger inlet manifold nuts; wider rear fork crown (swing arm); and rear fork crown grease cups (replaced oilers). The 61-cubic inch (1000cc) model was listed at $390; the 74-cubic inch (1200cc) NEP-20 was listed at $415. (EARL BENTLEY)

1920 Indian Scout primary drive (below). Inside a cast-aluminum housing, a set of three helical gears spun in an oil bath. The setup was indestructible, and it wasn't long before Indian coined the phrase "You can't wear out an Indian Scout." (GEORGE YAROCKI)

1920 Indian Powerplus (below). Beware sales literature, especially Indian's! This picture was used to make the 1920 catalogs. Apart from shrunken size, half-tone production, and red coloring, the catalog picture is identical. Both images show a single tail pipe. But the press release for the October 2, 1919, *Motorcycle and Bicycle Illustrated*, extols twin tail pipes. The "referee" for such contests, is the 1920 parts book, which shows two tail pipes for the 1920 Powerplus. Conclusions: either there was a production change too late to appear in the mid-summer prepared sales literature, or the advertising department simply erred. (EARL BENTLEY)

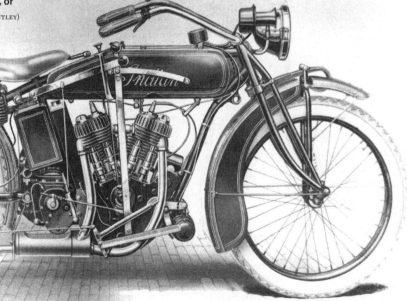

1920 Indian W-20. This was Indian's offering for commercial use. The single tail pipe is correct for one-cylinder models. The W-20 was listed at $325. This was the last year Indian offered the big singles. (EARL BENTLEY)

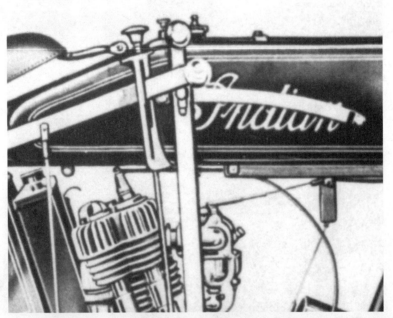

1920 Indian Powerplus. A new controls package arrived with the 1920 models. The long near-vertical lever operates the clutch, the shorter leave the transmission. The push-pull rod is the exhaust valve lifter, handy for starting, for killing the engine, and for a series of quick and easy kick-overs to clear a flooded engine. Integral knobs and levers replaced the previous aluminum levers with attached composite knobs.

(EARL BENTLEY)

1921 Model	Engine Data	Transmission	Misc.
G, Scout	36.38 ci (596cc)	3-speed	Extra braces on luggage rack.
GE, Electrically Equipped Scout	36.38 ci (596cc)	3-speed	New primary drive case with removable generator
N, Powerplus twin, spring frame	60.88 ci (998cc)	3-speed	—
NE, Powerplus twin, spring frame with electric lights	60.88 ci (998cc)	3-speed	—

1921 Indian Powerplus in export configuration. From inception through the 1930s, Indian shipped motorcycles configured to recipient nations' requirements and preferences. During the Powerplus years, this always meant the addition of a front stand and a luggage rack. The various 1921 Powerplus models were unchanged since the previous season. Some 1921 models were the last offered without electric lights.

(EARL BENTLEY)

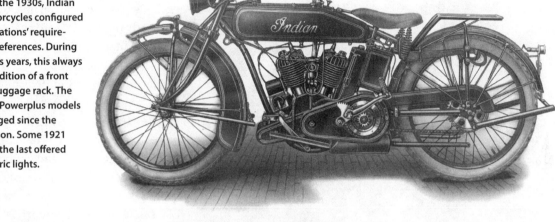

Circa 1921 Indian export model. Not appearing in any sales literature or magazine articles that have crossed the author's desk, this nevertheless appears to be a genuine export model. Or was it a contingency that didn't go any further? Though not apparent, the machine most likely was fitted with a right-side kick starter, to accommodate left-side sidecar installation in Britain. The low bars were also favored by British riders. (EARL BENTLEY)

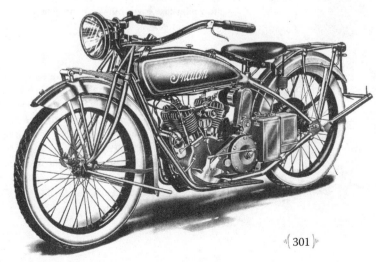

1921 Indian Scout. As electric lighting and generator were now optional, the Scout was fitted with a new primary drive case and cover. These accommodated either a generator drive, or a "blank-off" plate for unlighted models. The Mesinger Air Cushion saddle was used in 1921 only. The rear stand, semi-circular in cross section, replaced the 1920 channeled stand.

(EARL BENTLEY)

1922 Indian Chief. Destined to become one of motorcycling's longest-running hits, the 61-cubic inch (1000cc) Chief debuted in the 1922 lineup. The Chief was what advertising proclaimed it to be: a big Scout. A contemporary road test proclaimed the 61 a triumph of engineering over sheer large size, and asserted that several larger twins didn't measure up to the Chief. (EARL BENTLEY)

1922

Features for the 1922 Scout included: New headlight on GE, short trumpet Klaxon horn, Splitdorf DU-5 generator, Splitdorf S-2 magneto, switch box with ammeter, front saddle support via through-frame bolt, Persons saddle, saddle springs, 12 coils (instead of 10), seatpost springing, straight seat mast instead of curved, primary drive cover labeled "Hendee Manufacturing Co., Springfield Mass. USA," longer footboards, Powerplus style, kick-starter lug on seat mast (formerly on trans. case), new oil pump.

The Chief was an entirely new model. Bore and stroke was 3⅛ and $3^{31}/_{32}$ inches; displacement 60.88 ci (998cc). Basically, it was a larger Scout.

The name of big twins changed to "Standard." There were new front & rear fenders with crown, valances and flat braces. Other features included: Hinged rear fender. New headlight. Short trumpet Klaxon horn. Black handlebars. Splitdorf DU-5 generator. Splitdorf S-2 magneto. Switch box with ammeter. Enclosed saddle springs. Wider rear frame "horse shoe."

1922 Indian Chief oil pump. One difference from Scout layout: the Chief oil pump body wasn't integral with the timing case cover, but was entirely separate and screwed on. (GEORGE YAROCKI)

1922 Indian Chief. The left side kick-starter was due to the model's anticipated popularity as a sidecar hauler. Since American side hacks are to the right of the bikes, the left side starter kept one's leg free of sidecar struts. A benefit of the frame-mounted kicker was the ease with which it could be fitted to either side, so Britain and Commonwealth nations got a right-side kicker. As with the Scout, the double-loop frame provided some mechanical protection. (GEORGE YAROCKI)

1922 Indian Scout. New features included: new headlight, short trumpet Klaxon motor-driven horn, Splitdorf DU-5 generator, Splitdorf S-2 magneto, tank top switch box and ammeter, new front saddle support, a spring seat post (supplementing regular saddle springs), straight seat mast replaced curved mast in order to accommodate the seat post spring, kick-starter supported by the frame instead of the transmission case. (GEORGE YAROCKI)

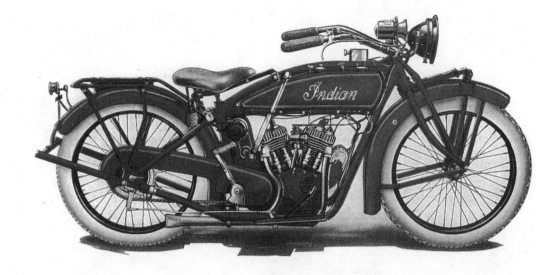

For the first time, all Indians were sold with standard equipment of electric lights and generator. The 1922 tank top switch box and ammeter were used on the Standard (Powerplus) and the Scout. (GEORGE YAROCKI)

1922 Indian Scout seat post suspension. (GEORGE YAROCKI)

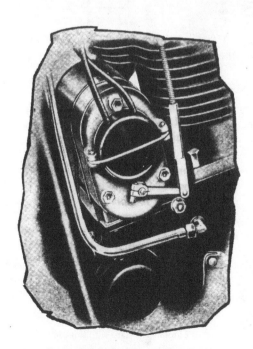

1922 Indian with Splitdorf S-2 magneto. (GEORGE YAROCKI)

1922 Indian Chief brakes. To help with the anticipated sidecar loads, as well as to comply with the British requirement for two brakes, the 1922 Chief was fitted with this "double brake." A right-side foot pedal worked the external contracting band; a left bar-mounted hand lever worked the internal brake (type not specified, either an expanding band or expanding shoes). As the brakes were cable operated, rear chain adjustment didn't require brake adjustment. (GEORGE YAROCKI)

1922 Indian Standard. The long-running spring-frame Flathead twins got a new name for 1922: "Standard." New features included: new wider front and rear fenders, flat-strip fender braces, Splitdorf DU-5 generator, Splitdorf S-2 magneto, short trumpet Klaxon motor-driven horn, new horn, tank top switch box and ammeter, enclosed seat springs, and wider rear "horseshoe" to accommodate the wider rear fender. (EARL BENTLEY)

1922 Indian Chief with sidecar. A new sidecar debuted for the 1922 season, featuring a more modern-looking fender. (EARL BENTLEY)

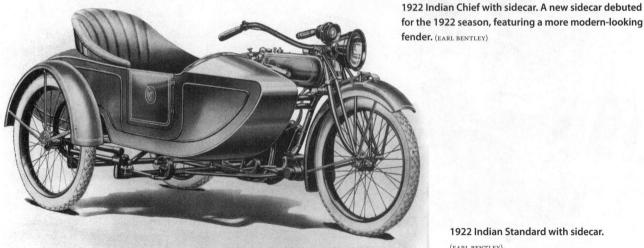

1922 Indian Standard with sidecar.

(EARL BENTLEY)

1923

Scout features included: Corcoran Victor headlight with built-in switch, ammeter without switch box, compression release moved to side of tank (previously operated by handlebar lever), long-trumpet Klaxon horn through February, Spartan horn from March, late-season oil pump body not integral with timing case cover (1924 part number; listed in 1923-1928 parts book), longer clutch operating lever (on clutch housing),

The 61-ci Chief had a longer clutch operating lever on the clutch housing. The luggage carrier was not standard equipment,

The Standard had a long-trumpet Klaxon horn through February and a Spartan horn from March.

1923 Indian Scout in export trim. The Scout got the same separate oil pump as used on the Chief and Big Chief. (EARL BENTLEY)

1923 Indian Chief and sidecar. (DOUG MITCHEL)

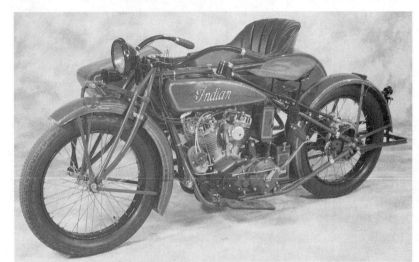

1923 Indian Chief or Big Chief. The tank-side compression release pull-rod was a new feature. The lower frame rails were made of heavier tubing, and a cross bar was fitted to the upper rear fork beneath the saddle. With raised lettering, the legend "Hendee Manufacturing Co..." was placed on the clutch cover. (EARL BENTLEY)

1924 Indian Scout, early season. New features included: larger wheel hubs (same as Chief), wider and longer handlebars, single-stripe tank trim ("running" change, i.e., during the season), front saddle support (running change, stamping instead of casting, not shown) and optional Mesinger saddle (Persons saddle remained standard). (EARL BENTLEY)

1924 Indian Chief or Big Chief. The biggest news was the "Big Chief" model, powered by an advertised 74-cubic inch (1200cc) engine. This immediately became Indian's best-selling model. The Big Chief "74" bore and stroke were 3 1/4 and 4 7/16 inches; actual displacement was 73.62 ci (1206cc). For 1924, the oil pump was enlarged. The same pump was used on Chiefs, Big Chiefs and Scouts. The shifter rod replaced the flat metal shifter on both Chiefs and Scouts. (EARL BENTLEY)

1924

1924 Scout features: a new oil pump (body not integral with timing case cover), wider and longer handlebars, split handlebar bracket, mid-season change to "pull action" front fork, with longer rockers and new front fender, and late-season primary drive legend on the clutch housing that read: "Indian Motocycle Co., Springfield Mass. USA".

1924 Chief 61 features: a new oil pump, wider and longer handlebars, split handlebar bracket, tank bracket for handlebar control wires, a mid-season change to "pull action" front forks, with longer rockers and new front fender, and late-season primary drive legend on the clutch housing that read: "Indian Motocycle Co., Springfield Mass. USA".

Big Chief, 74 features: Bore and stroke of 3 1/4 and 4 7/16 inches; displacement 73.62 ci (1206cc), wider and longer handlebars, split handlebar bracket, tank bracket for handlebar control wires, a mid-season change to "pull action" front fork, with longer rockers and new front fender, and a late-season primary drive legend on the clutch housing that read: "Indian Motocycle Co., Springfield Mass. USA".

It was the last year of the Powerplus/Standard genre. The model had a split handlebar bracket.

1924 Indian Chief or Big Chief (at right). The Chief and Big Chief got wider and longer handlebars for 1924. This is an early-season model, still with a fork that uses the "push action" principle used by Indian since 1910. Mid-season, a new fork was introduced. The company had changed its name in November, 1923, so after old primary drive covers were depleted, 1924 models bore the clutch cover legend "Indian Motocycle Company...."
(EARL BENTLEY)

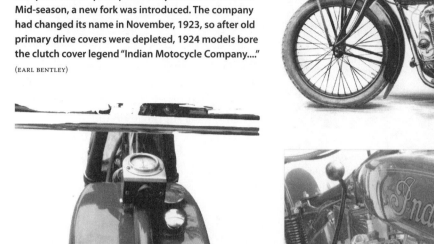

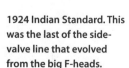

1924 Indian Chief. Rider's view. Note the "neutral" sticker on the right side of the tank.

1924 Indian Chief or Big Chief. On the cylinder tops there is a screw-on/off fitting on the opposite side from the spark plug, and the base of each sparkplug is also a screw-on/off fitting. Because the heads were integral with the cylinders, these fittings were removed to provide access to the valve heads for decarbonizing.

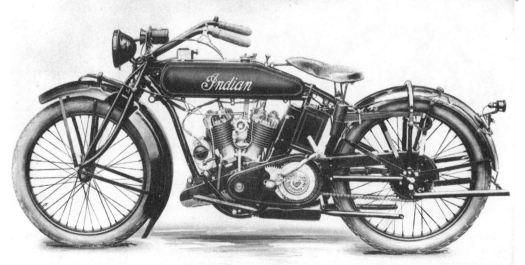

1924 Indian Standard. This was the last of the side-valve line that evolved from the big F-heads.
(EARL BENTLEY)

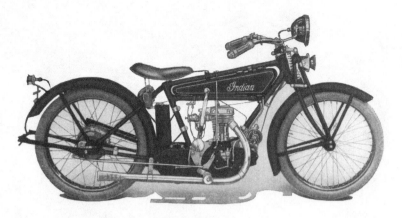

1925 Indian Prince. Indian introduced the 21-cubic inch (350cc) single-cylinder side-valve Prince for the 1925 season. The styling was inspired by British lightweights. (GEORGE YAROCKI)

1925

The Scout had removable cylinder heads, Mesinger saddle and 10 saddle springs. The Chief and Big Chief had larger "balloon" tires with new rims. The Prince was a new model with single cylinder side-valve motor, bore and stroke, of 2 3/4 x 3 37/64 inches, displacement of 21.25 ci (348cc), removable cylinder heads and clutch control by hand lever on the left handlebar.

1925 Indian Prince. Weighing about half as much as a Chief, and selling for $185 (stripped) compared to the Big Chief at $335, the Prince was designed to appeal to first-time prospects. (GEORGE YAROCKI)

1925 Indian Scout in export trim. The "pull action" fork with longer rockers was introduced as a "running" change during 1924, as was the new fender to accommodate this fork. The fork connecting links were outside the fender rather than passing through it. Removable cylinder heads were the most important additions for 1925. Indian claimed a 20-percent power increase from these heads. (EARL BENTLEY)

1925 Indian Chief or Big Chief. Larger "balloon" tires graced the 1925 big twins; larger wheel rims were accordingly fitted. (EARL BENTLEY)

1925 Indian rear stand. All models got the new channel section rear stand. (EARL BENTLEY)

1924/1925 Indian Chief fork (above). The mid-1924 "pull action" fork, as used on the Chief and Big Chief, was a "running" change during 1924. The fork rods still passed through the fender. (EARL BENTLEY)

1925 prototype overhead-cam Indian Prince. This one never got beyond the experimental stage. Again, foreign designs were inspirational, particularly the British Velocette. One reason this bike never got into production was the high cost due to extra labor. The shaft and bevel-gears layout required patient and expert assemblers to get the build-up and valve timing just right. (BOB FINN)

1926 Indian Scout and rider, showing off motorcycle accessories and clothing.

(INDIAN PHOTO)

1926

On all models, a new horn switch was a press-tab-to-handlebar unit (no switch internals).

The Scout received: larger "balloon" tires with new rims, longer and wider handlebars, new handbrake lever, ammeter with switchbox, and no seatpost. Motor numbers AG901 and up had: threaded inlet manifold and union nuts replaced unthreaded manifold and clamps, deeper cylinder head fins wrapped around exhaust ports and an accessory side stand. From Feb. 1926: there was an optional unpainted "wire brush" finish on crankcases, primary drive cases and the transmission covers.

The Chief and Big Chief received: longer and wider handlebars, new handbrake lever, new "half-pan" (stretched leather over tubular frame) Mesinger saddle, footboards moved forward and raised, new clutch footlever, and accessory side stand. From Feb. 1926 there were optional unpainted "wire brush" finishes on crankcases, primary drive case, and transmission covers.

The Prince received: a new tank, higher generator location, and chain-driven (instead of belt-driven), new frame to accommodate new tank and generator location, and optional footboards. From Feb. 1926: optional unpainted "wire brush" finish on crankcases, and transmission covers.

1926 Indian Scout. Large section "balloon" tires were the most obvious new feature for 1926 Scouts. Other changes included: slip-over exhaust headers with set screw replaced nut-secured headers, longer and wider handlebars, oil hole in chain guard above starter gears, and "running changes" of optional "brush" finish (unpainted) on crank cases, timing case cover, transmission case, and transmission case cover.

(BOB FINN)

1926 Indian Scout power plant. Cylinder head fins were made deeper for 1926, and the fins wrapped around the exhaust ports. (BOB FINN)

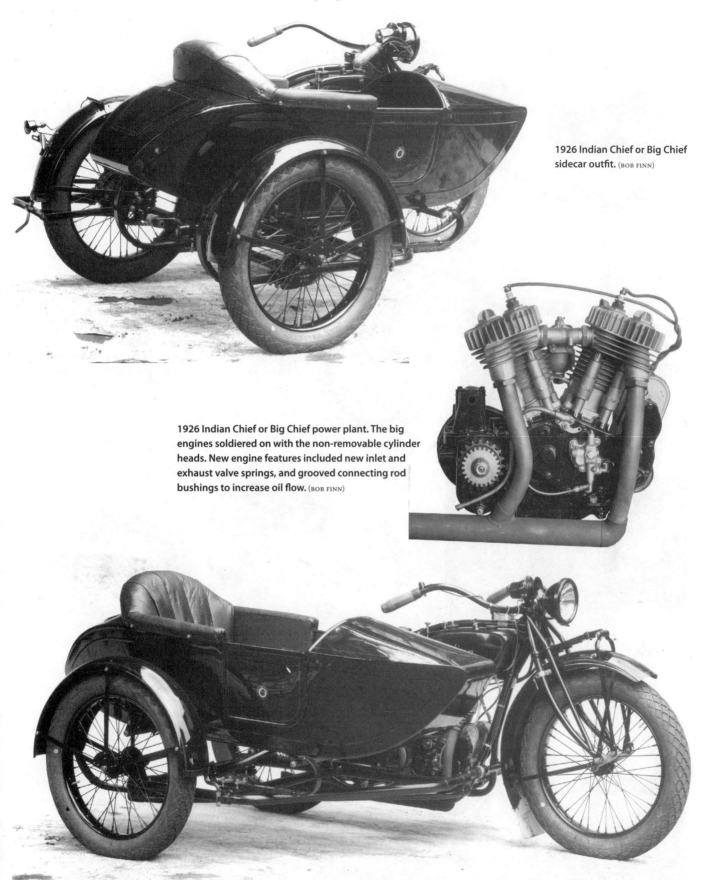

1926 Indian Chief or Big Chief sidecar outfit. (BOB FINN)

1926 Indian Chief or Big Chief power plant. The big engines soldiered on with the non-removable cylinder heads. New engine features included new inlet and exhaust valve springs, and grooved connecting rod bushings to increase oil flow. (BOB FINN)

1926 Indian Chief or Big Chief sidecar outfit. (BOB FINN)

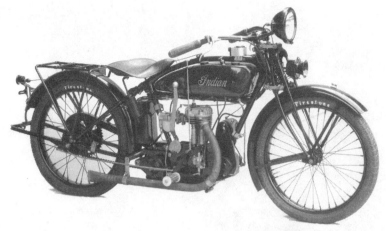

1926 Indian Prince. The 1925 trans-Atlantic styling had proven unpopular in the United States, so the wedge-shaped tank and frame gave way to traditional American shapes.

(BOB FINN)

1926 Indian Prince, as shown in the sales literature. Advertising materials didn't show the tank top switch box and ammeter, and added the tool pouch beneath the saddle. A "running change" was the optional "brush" finish (unpainted) on crank cases, timing case cover, transmission case and transmission case cover.

(BOB FINN)

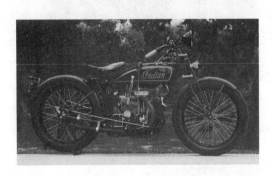

1926 Indian Prince.

(DOUG MITCHEL)

1926 Indian Prince. A Mesinger bucket saddle was fitted. The generator was relocated behind the front down tube, and the new frame front down tube angle accommodated the generator move.

(BOB FINN)

1926 Indian 45-cubic inch (750cc) flat track racer. According to oral history, this is one of only two such flat-track racers built. In 1928, these were used over a 5-mile circular course on Muroc Dry Lake, near Los Angeles. Two Indian riders were timed at over 126 mph through the wind-assisted part of the course. A total of 26 "Forty-five Overheads" were built, most being used for board track racing and hill climbing.

1926 Indian "Forty-five Over-head." The timing cover was cast bronze. Two oil pumps were fitted to some of the engines. The two camshafts ran in self-aligning ball bear-ings, and the crankshaft was also ball bearing supported. The rider braced his right leg between the foot peg and the large leather-covered knob near the front cylinder. This practice was later prohibited because severe leg injuries could result from a spill.

1926 "Forty-five Overhead." The motor number on this one is A45-26, suggesting it's the last of these specials. A 15:1 compression ratio worked with alcohol fuel. These may have been the fastest racers the factory ever built. In 2002, Australian Peter Arundel rode one of these to a two-way average of 156 mph.

Circa 1926 Indian factory racer, with four-valve head. The rider is Johnny Seymour, who set a 30.50-cubic inch (500cc) American record of 112.63 mph at Dayto-na Beach in January, 1926. Riding an eight-valve twin that was a double-up of the single, Seymour set an American record of 132 mph. At the time, the official world's record was 119 mph, but Seymour ran in one direction only and the wind, if any, wasn't specified.

(MALDWYN JONES)

1926 "Forty-five Overhead" hill climber. The motor number on this one is A45-1, suggesting it's the first of these specials. Some early examples used iron cylinder heads, so this one was refitted with aluminum heads, probably by a period hill climber.

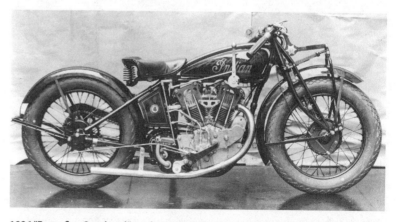

1926 Indian factory racer. Here's a closer look at the four-valve single. Note the cast-alu-minum exhaust headers.

1926 "Forty-five Overhead" road racer (at left). Nothing is known of this motorcycle, but it was presumably built for trans-Atlantic road racing because that sport had died out in the U.S. (ED KRETZ, SR.)

1927 Indian Scout, 37 cubic inches (600cc). The front fender was wider and had valanced sides. The word "Scout" was in small block letters beneath the Indian script. A buzzer horn was standard instead of a motor-driven horn. Late-1927 Scouts and Scout Forty-fives were fitted with pistons having thicker (1/8-inch) piston rings.

(EARL BENTLEY)

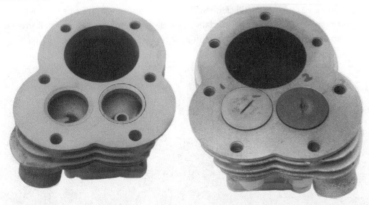

1927 Indian Scout cylinders. Sometimes, it is better to be lucky than smart. On the left, a rear head from a 37-ci Scout; on the right, a front head from a 45-ci Scout. For the new Scout 45, Indian took the quick and cheap approach, patterning the larger cylinder as closely as possible to the smaller cylinder, and simply thickening the cylinder walls. This allowed both engine sizes to use the same crankcases and timing gears. Note that this approach resulted in the 45 inlet valve being positioned very close to the bore; almost no gap remains between the valve seat and the bore. By happy accident, Indian achieved much improved breathing, and the Scout 45 quickly proved faster than most Chiefs and Harley-Davidson Seventy-fours. (GEORGE YAROCKI)

1927

The Scout, Scout 45 and Chief had a horn toggle switch (with internals); wider fenders and valance; compression release rod through a false "hole" in the tank; transition to buzzer horn and motor-driven horn became an accessory; tank lettering in small block letters "Scout," "Chief," or "Prince."

The Scout received: alemite grease fittings, optional lower "Sport" handlebars after March, longer Sport bars from June, and rear saddle supports that were part of the frame forgings instead of separate clamps.

The Scout 45 Police Special was a new model. It was a side-valve twin that featured: bore and stroke of 2 7/8 x 3 1/2 inches, displacement of 45.44 ci (745cc), alemite grease fittings optional lower "Sport" handlebars after March, longer Sport bars from June, and rear saddle supports that were part of the frame forgings instead of separate clamps.

The Chief and Big Chief had removable cylinder heads, alemite grease fittings and Splitdorf NS-2 magneto.

The Prince featured: alemite grease fittings, smaller wheels; 25 x 3.30 wheels/tires, footboards standard, footrests optional, optional foot clutch, lower generator location and horn toggle switch. The Ace was a new model, purchased from Ace company. It had an in-line four-cylinder F-head. Shipments began on April 25, 1927. Earliest shipments may have been in Sage Green, but Rolls-Royce Blue finish was soon specified. From May, Indian Red was optional.

Changes to the Ace included: pressure fed lubrication (only seven Aces previously built this way), lower saddle, new alloy pistons with larger wrist pins, new camshaft with three bearing supports, new tappet guides., and vanadium exhaust valve springs.

1927 Indian Scout "Forty-five." Indian offered an enlarged Scout "45", displacing 45 cubic inches (750cc). Power and speed exceeded expectations. Somehow, it was one of those happy combinations that seemed more than the sum of its parts. The best ones were soon outrunning both Indian and Harley-Davidson 74-cubic inch (1200cc) bikes. Alemite grease fittings were featured. The foot brake lever was larger and relocated. The compression release rod ran through a tube within the fuel tank. The tank-top switch box and ammeter, absent on 1923-1926 Scouts, was again used on this model.

(EARL BENTLEY)

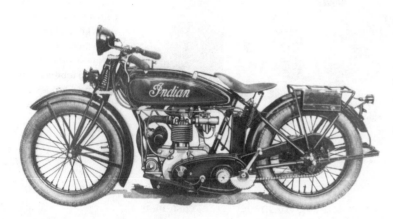

1927 Indian Prince overhead-valve model.

(EARL BENTLEY)

1927 Indian Chief. The through-the-tank compression release was fitted to the Chief and Big Chief.

(EARL BENTLEY)

1927 Indian Prince overhead-valve model.

(EARL BENTLEY)

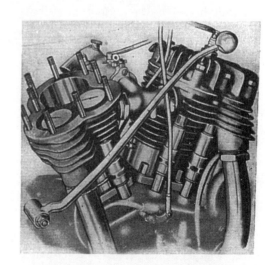

1927 Indian Chief/Big Chief engine. Running two years behind Scout design, the largest Indian engines at last were equipped with removable cylinder heads.

(GEORGE YAROCKI)

1927 Indian Scout. Since the first Scouts in 1920, the clutch pedal mounting was as shown here. Also, all Scouts to this point had a frame with the front down tubes integral with the lower (horizontal) frame tubes—in other words, one long tube was bent to form each side's down tube and lower tube.

(BOB FINN)

1928

Indian announced a policy of no annual model changes, but changes were to be incorporated as soon as practical. Motorcycles were divided into "Series."

The Scout (37 ci) and Scout 45 (45 ci) had a mid-season (about January) addition of front brake. It was a short-wheelbase model replaced by Series 101 in March, 1928. These bikes had: new 2 3/4-inch longer frames, new tanks, bullet headlights, engines moved forward 3 inches, a clutch pedal mounted directly to frame instead of special plate, and the generator moved behind the seat mast. The smaller engine was listed throughout Series 101 production, but this version was seldom advertised. Hereafter, only a single "Series 101" category will be tracked.

The Chief and Big Chief, Series 301 featured: a larger headlight had a nickel-plated rim (instead of black), new higher compression cylinder heads, new front cylinder to provide clearance for new Splitdorf DU-7 generator, a crankcase breather moved to forward edge of the left crankcase near the clutch pedal, a 16-spring-stud clutch replaced the 12-stud clutch, and new rear brakes with adjustable lower band. From mid-1928, the Chief was designated Series 301. A front brake was added, and the fork was modified to accept a telescopic brake anchor.

The Prince model, Series 201, got a mid-season (about January) addition of front brake. About March, 1928, it received a new frame and new tank and was re-designated Series 201.

The "Indian Ace" continued through July, 1928 with minimal changes.

The Series 401 had its name changed to "Four" in August, 1928. Officially termed "Series 401," it had: leaf spring fork, bullet headlight, scout-style fenders and tank, a new frame to match up with the new tank, and the Ace-style single front down tube was retained. A new combination of clutch plates reduced clutch spring pressure. A new flywheel accommodated a new clutch.

1928 Indian Scout 45. In this era, new models were traditionally announced in August and on the dealers' floors by the Labor Day holiday in the first week of September. This early-season 1928 model is representative of September 1927. A few weeks into the production schedule, the Scout 45 was cataloged with a front brake. (EARL BENTLEY)

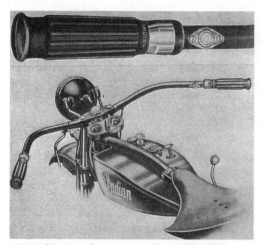

1928 Indian. New features included push-button horn operation and a handlebar-mounted instrument panel. (GEORGE YAROCKI)

1928 Indian instrument panel. The shrouded panel light was spring-loaded. To turn the light on, the rider pressed the shroud down and turned it until a button was secured in the "on" detent. (GEORGE YAROCKI)

1928 Indian Scout. Note the generator location, still in front of the seat mast. (GEORGE YAROCKI)

1928 Indian Chief (below). A new front cylinder had a slightly different exhaust port orientation in order to clear the new Splitdorf DU-7 generator.

(GEORGE HAYS)

1928 Indian Scout Series 101 (below). For the first time, the front down tubes and lower tubes were separate pieces joined by a forged "elbow." (BOB FINN)

1928 Indian Chief engine. New higher-compression cylinder heads were fitted. A 16-spring clutch replaced the 12-spring clutch. (GEORGE YAROCKI)

1928 Indian Scout Series 101. The new Series 101 Scout was a mid-season model announced in March of 1928. The frame was 2 3/4 inches longer and the engine was moved 3 inches forward. The longer wheelbase significantly softened the ride and increased stability. The engine relocation also softened the ride because the heavier forward mass reduced front end oscillation. With more weight on the front tire, handling was more sure-footed.

(GEORGE YAROCKI)

1928 Indian Scout Series 101. The generator was moved behind the seat mast. Thought not widely publicized, the 37-ci (600cc) engine was offered throughout 101 Scout production (1928-1931).

(GEORGE YAROCKI)

1928 Indian Scout Series 101 with Sweetheart sidecar (below). The lightweight "Sweetheart" sidecar was designed specifically for Scouts.

(GEORGE YAROCKI)

1928 Indian Chief with sidecar. Beginning with the 1927 Chiefs, the fork rods were outside the fender, and the fender was reshaped to accommodate this move. As this is an early-season model, it didn't have a front brake. After the front brake was added, about January of 1928, the Chief line was designated Series 301.

(GEORGE YAROCKI)

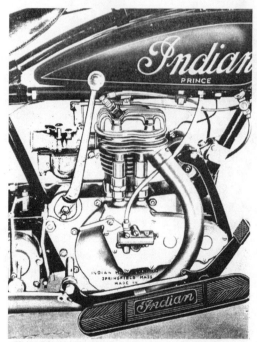

1928 Indian Prince. With the shapely 101-style tank, the Prince reached its ultimate configuration. The 1928 range was the only full year of Indian's boastful offering of singles, twins and fours.

(GEORGE YAROCKI)

1928 Indian Prince engine. With the new tank, the Prince was designated Series 201.

(GEORGE YAROCKI)

1928 Indian Ace. Taking advantage of the Ace heritage and the strength of the Indian name, the company began the transition to full Indian status with the Indian logo Ace subscript and traditional red finish. (GEORGE YAROCKI)

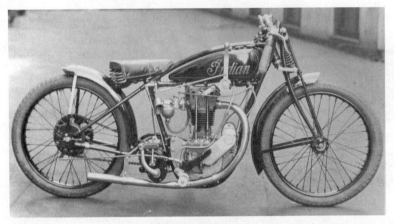

1928 Indian racer. A 30.5-ci (500cc) engine was placed in a frame normally used for 21-ci (350cc) engines. The governing racing body experimented with 30.5-ci racing, and for awhile prohibited 61-ci racing. (EMMETT MOORE)

1928 Indian racer. Star rider Jim Davis, who alternated between the Harley and Indian factory teams, raced this twin-carburetor Chief-derived racer at the 1926 Rockingham (Salem), New Hampshire, board track. Teammate Curley Fredericks turned a lap on the 11/4-mile track at a 120.3-mph pace, the all-time fastest speed recorded on a board track.

(MALDWYN JONES)

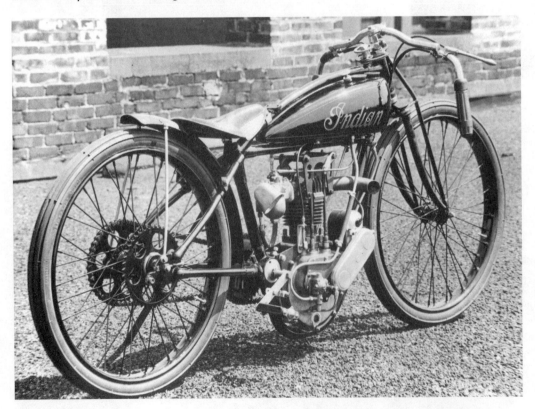

1928 Indian racer. Twenty-one cubic-inch (350cc) racing was instituted in late 1925 because the old 61-ci (1000cc) class become increasingly dangerous. Indian and Harley-Davidson built a variety of special 21-ci racers.

(EMMETT MOORE)

1929

Prince singles were discontinued in 1929. The Scout, Series 101, got drop center rims and straight-side tires replaced clincher rims and tires. A compression release rod was replaced by a toggle lever on the right crankcase.

Chief and Big Chief, Series 301, changes included: the crankcase breather moved to the timing case cover, and from July, 1929, drop center rims and straight-side tires replaced clincher rims and tires.

On the Four, Series 401, from July, 1929, drop center rims and straight-side tires replaced clincher rims and tires. From late-1929, a double front down tube frame had new engine number series starting at EA101. The Ace-style three-main-bearing crankshaft continued. A common error is terming all double-down tube Fours as Series 402; Indian didn't redesignate until the later five-main-bearing crankshaft.

The Four, Series 402, featured the five-main-bearing crankshaft (and double front down tube frame as on last Series 401s). New 1.375-inch main bearings replaced 1.25-inch bearings. New connecting rods had larger bearings. There was a larger oil sump return opening.

1929 Indian 101 Scout. The costly "through-the-tank" compression release control was replaced by a simple toggle lever on the timing case. This example was over-restored; original sand castings were quite rough compared to these.

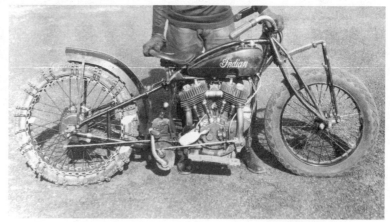

1929 Indian hillclimber. Bob Armstrong, the top amateur hill climber of 1929, campaigned on this Chief-derived special. (EMMETT MOORE)

1929 Indian 101 Scout.

1929 Indian Four. The four-cylinder transformation was completed for the 1929 season with this first Indian Four. The styling mimicked the 101 Scout. Though the Four and the Scout had the same wheelbase, 59 1/2 inches, all the Four frame tubing was larger. (GEORGE YAROCKI)

1930

1930 "models" were produced from March-April 1930 through March-April 1931. Chromium trim replaced nickel trim during 1930. Frame numbers announced Nov. 25, 1930; previously only the engine was numbered.

The Scout, Series 101, had a larger Motolamp headlight, hinged rear fender and armored taillight casing.

The Chief and Big Chief, Series 302, had: cast aluminum tanks, higher compression cylinders and new aluminum pistons. The crankcase breather returned to its 1928 location (forward edge of the left crankcase near the clutch pedal). The taillight casing was armored.

The Four, Series 402, featured: new cylinders with thicker walls, larger exhaust ports, and corner "flats" extending from base to half the height of the lowest cooling fin. From the Spring of 1930: larger spokes were found on the front wheel and sidecar wheel. Also new: armored taillight casing, heavier high and low gears with bushings, shifter gear, transmission main shaft and new transmission countershaft gear.

1930 Indian Chief. Apparently, Indian changed headlight suppliers during the 1930 season. The larger light probably replaced the smaller light; both types were larger than the 1928 bullet type.

(EARL BENTLEY)

1930 Indian Chief. The radially finned cylinder heads were used on 1927-1931 Chiefs.

(EARL BENTLEY)

1930 Indian Chief. Tank construction was changed to cast aluminum. The forward cap on the right tank accessed the oil compartment. On all models, chrome-plated small parts replaced bright nickel-plated small parts.

(EARL BENTLEY)

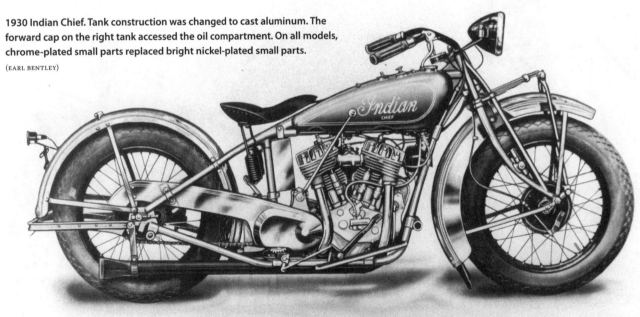

1930 Indian Chief. This was the last year for the: 1927-style front fender, 1927-style fork, Klaxon motor-driven horn, 1922-style frame with partially paralleled front down tubes and the standard left-side kick-starter. (EARL BENTLEY)

1930 Indian Four. Despite the increasingly deep economic depression, Indian continued with the expensive Four. The rider base consisted largely of police departments with continued funding, and a few more affluent riders who were not impacted by the Depression. Profits may have been minimal, but the Four's police presence and luxury specifications had a halo effect on the rest of the Indian range. (EARL BENTLEY)

1931

Among the highlights for 1931: Duco lacquer finish replaced the enamel finish for 1931 only, cadmium-plated spokes were used in lieu of black spokes, there was a center-mounted headlight and Indian-face horn mounted below the headlight, handlebars were reinforced by a crossbar, new tank transfers had smaller "Indian" script and the model name in small block letters, Auto-Lite generators replaced Splitforf units, speedometers (accessory) were gear-driven instead of cogged-wheel driven. In March 1931, Indian reinstated its traditional annual models policy.

Scout, Model 101 changes included a throttle-controlled oil pump and faster "B" motor spec's.

Chief, Model 302 features included: throttle-controlled oil pump, "solid" flywheels replacing spoked units, new alloy pistons and new cast iron pistons, new motor balancing factors for smoother fast running. At mid-season: sheet metal tanks replaced cast aluminum tanks. New larger rear brake forced a 42-teeth rear sprocket to replace 36-teeth sprocket. To achieve proper overall gear ratio, the primary drive gears were changed (larger engine-gear and smaller idler gear). A new primary drive case and cover worked with new drive gears.

Four, Model 402 features included new thicker cylinders with corner "flats" extended from the base all the way to the lowest cooling fin, and there was a new combination of clutch plates. Such clutch variations were tried almost every year of Four production and will not be further covered in detail.

1931 Indian 101 Scout. The ultimate 101 Scouts debuted for the 1931 season. Among new features were: new headlight, new Indian head horn on the front fork, new tank transfers with "Scout" subscript and new muffler. (BOB FINN)

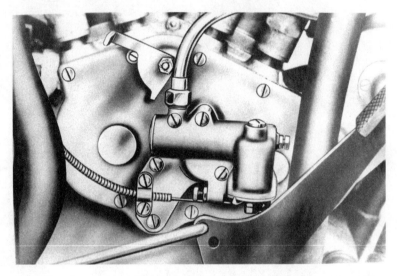

1931 Indian throttle-controlled oil pump. Most touted of all improvements was the throttle-controlled oil pump. The idea was to deliver more oil at high throttle settings independent of engine speed, for example, when going up long hills with the throttle wide open and the speed moderate.

1931 Indian Four. The new headlight and horn graced all the 1931 models. New thicker cylinders dissipated heat better. The clutch featured a new combination of plates. (EARL BENTLEY)

1932-1939, The Classic Rigid-framed Side-valves

The year 1932 introduced what amounted to a stand-alone genre of Indians. Bold new frames and tanks on both V-twins and the Four featured much longer front forks and, together with continued low saddle positions, gave riders a "sit-in-it" feel. Riders hailed the improved looks that resulted from the overall shape and from the new "saddle" fuel tanks that replaced the old between-the-rails tanks. This same aesthetic make-over was happening in Britain and Europe. Forgotten in the international styling rush, was the fact that the new shape made motorcycles heavier. This was a fact because the longer frame members necessarily had to be heavier in order to cope with the increased twisting and bending stresses that came with the extra length.

To the dismay of Series 101 Scout enthusiasts, this very popular model was dropped. In its place was a Scout consisting of the 45-cubic inch (750cc) engine in the same frame as used on the 1932 Chief. Apparently, there was too much cost pressure on the mid-sized 101 Scout to capture suffi-

cient profit margin. A new light 30.50-cubic inch (500cc) V-twin Scout Pony was built along Harley-Davidson lines with a chain primary drive covered by sheet metal and a remotely mounted gearbox.

The signal V-twin advance of 1933 was circulating lubrication—the so-called dry sump system. This cut oil consumption in half, and riders seldom had to carry extra cans of oil on trips. Dry sump lubrication prevented under-oiling and over-oiling. With over-oiling in the past, there was no longer excessive carbon build-up and frequent head removal in order to scrape out the heat generating carbon. In the 1933 lineup was a stop-gap model, a 45-cubic inch version of the little twin with the uncharacteristic name "Motoplane."

The year 1934 saw the introduction of the famous 45-cubic inch Sport Scout. Shorter and with more ground clearance than the old Series 101 Scout, the new model was ideally suited for American dirt track racing, which would soon explode in popularity. On the Chief and Scout, the indestructible helical gear primary drive was replaced by less-expensive chain drive. The oil bath principle was retained. It soon became evident that the new quieter primary drive would outlast the motorcycle.

In the 1935 lineup, Indian reached the zenith of its technical and styling advantages over Harley-Davidson. But in 1936, the arch-rival brought out the overhead-valve 61-cubic inch (1000cc) V-twin later dubbed "Knucklehead." Strangely, Indian never answered this challenge with an overhead-valve twin. Compounding Indian's troubles was the new "upside-down" Four, with side-mounted inlet valves and overhead exhaust valves. These ungainly Fours were continued in 1937.

In 1938, two years behind Harley-Davidson, styling parity was again achieved when Indian placed an integrated Harley-like instrument panel on the tanks. Indian twice established American stock motorcycle records. The hot-stuff 1938 and 1939

1932 Indian Chief. The Chief was completely restyled with a new frame, tanks, longer front fork and new front fender. The widely splayed front down tubes usually prevented frame warping in event of a spill. The "buzzer" horn replaced the motor-driven ("oogah") horn. The front fender in this publicity photo has a different lower trailing edge than the production fenders.

(EARL BENTLEY)

V-twins were termed, respectively, "Daytona" and "Bonneville" models. Since 1934 on the Sport Scout, and since 1935 on all Indians, the iron redskins had sported the war bonnet-topped Indian head transfer on tank sides, as well as attractive pen striping schemes that showed off two-color finishes with a flair. The multiplicity of standard finishes and endless extra-cost finish options reached its climax on the 1939 models with the new option of the World's Fair paint scheme joining the other three striping options that had been offered the previous four years.

The years 1934 through 1939 saw Indian winning about half the American national championship races. Since the late 1920s, the marque had been outsold by Harley-Davidson at a 2-to-1 pace, so the racing wins were tributes to both Indian design and dealer/rider enthusiasm.

1932

The 101 Scout was discontinued. The Scout, Model 232, had a 45-ci engine in the new Chief frame, with Chief tanks and front fork.

The Chief, Model 332, was Newly styled with the basic shape that continued throughout. A new frame had taller steering head, more steeply sloped top tube, widely splayed front down tubes. There were also new teardrop tanks, new cylinder heads with front-to-back finning instead of radial finning, and a late-season change to black cylinders and heads. The changes to the Model 432 Four were the same.

The Scout Pony, Model 532, was a new model. It was a side-valve twin with the following spec's; bore and stroke, 2 1/2 and 3 1/16 inches; displacement , 30.06 ci (493cc), two cam shafts, total-loss lubrication, circuit breaker (battery) ignition with wasted spark, keystone frame (engine was a stress bearing member, and no under-engine tubing) and single-row primary chain under a sheet metal cover.

1932 Indian Chief. From 1912 through 1931, all big Indians had magneto ignition and the company had constantly bragged about the superiority of Indian of this system. In 1932, Indian at last bowed to the pressure of the Great Depression. Battery ignition became standard on Scouts, Chiefs and Fours, while magneto ignition became an extra-cost option. The 1932 Scout and Chief battery ignition used the same gear drive as the magneto. (EARL BENTLEY)

A rider's view of a 1932-1934 Indian Scout or Chief. In place of the popular 101 Scout, the new namesake was essentially a 45-ci Scout engine in a Chief frame. The 232 was scorned by some dealers and riders who favored the almost mystical handling of the 101 Scouts. However, the 232 was a nimble motorcycle that felt much lighter than the companion Chief. Police departments continued to favor Scouts for easy starting and fuel economy.

1932 Indian Scout Model 232. (EARL BENTLEY)

Indian Scout base fitted with Crocker cylinders. Los Angeles Indian dealer Al Crocker jumped into the newly popular "short track" ("speedway" elsewhere in the world) racing. In 1931, Crocker manufactured racing frames for regular 101 Scout 45 side-valve engines. In 1932, he built 30.50-ci (500cc) overhead-valve engines such as this partially assembled example. Under American rules, these smaller engines raced against 45-ci Flatheads. These overhead-valve Scouts were short-lived, as in late 1933 Crocker debuted his new speedway overhead-valve singles that owed nothing to Indian design.

1932 prototype Indian Scout Pony. As with the prototype, production Scout Ponies used a wasted-spark circuit breaker battery ignition system. Driven by the rear cam, the unit was located at the 9 o'clock position of the timing case cover. (INDIAN NEWS)

1932 prototype Indian Scout Pony. Announced in June, 1932, the new little twin was a price buster at $225. This was 24 percent under the next larger model, the Scout. The keystone frame, as Indian termed it, used the engine as a stress-bearing frame member, so there was no tubing beneath the engine. (EARL BENTLEY)

1932 prototype Indian Scout Pony. To minimize cost, the primary drive system was a single-row chain under a stamped sheet metal cover, and, of course, without the benefit of running in an oil bath. Production models didn't have the auxiliary oil hand-pump as shown here. Also, production models had the instrument panel mounted to the handlebars, rather than the frame as shown here. (EARL BENTLEY)

1932 Indian Four. The Four also got the new styling with the new frame and tanks. Shown here is what amounts to an updated Ace engine in a frame that's shaped remarkably similar to 21st century designs. Though the new configuration was largely a styling statement, this "in" look paved the way for the long-travel telescopic fork 18 years later! This example was fitted with export equipment of front stand and rear **luggage rack.** (EARL BENTLEY)

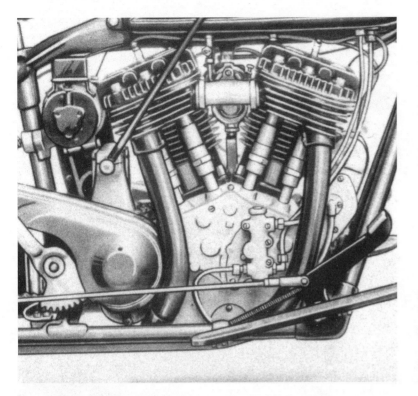

1933 Indian Chief, with magneto ignition. The old total loss, one-way system, in which oil became either carbon or smoke, was very much a hit-or-miss affair. The heart of the new dry sump (circulating) lubrication system was this new two-way oil pump. From the sump beneath the flywheels, oil was returned back to the tank. Dry sump oiling was a major improvement. For fast touring, oil mileage increased from about 200 miles per quart to about 500 miles per quart. This meant that riders seldom had to carry an extra quart of oil while traveling. (EARL BENTLEY)

1933 Indian Chief battery ignition. For the 1933 season, the standard circuit-breaker battery ignition system for Chiefs and Scouts was relocated to the timing cover, as had been done on the 1932 Scout Ponies. This required a new keyed rear camshaft to drive the circuit breaker, and a new timing case cover on which to mount the unit. These costs were more than offset by eliminating the magneto gear-train that had driven the 1932-only system for Scouts and Chiefs.

1933

On all 1933 models, pivoting lever front brake anchor replaced former telescoping tubes with a corresponding redesign of the front forks.

The Scout, Model 233 and Chief, Model 333, had: dry sump (circulating) lubrication, black cylinders and heads (also on late 1932 models), wasted-spark (no distributor) battery ignition standard, driven by magneto-gear train and optional magneto ignition.

The Four, Model 433, had: a one-year-only inlet manifold with horizontal cooling fins, black cylinders and heads (also on late 1932 models), distributor-style battery ignition standard, and magneto ignition optional.

The Scout Pony, Model 533, had dry sump (circulating) lubrication. The Motoplane, Model 633, was a new, one-year-only model with a 45-ci engine in a Scout Pony frame. It had dry sump (circulating) lubrication.

1933 Indian front end. This appeared on the Scout, Chief and Four. For 1933, Indian artists corrected the 1932 sales literature images, which had incorrectly shown a prototype front fender. In this picture, the production front fender is correctly rendered. New for 1933 was the lever brake anchor in lieu of the former telescoping unit. (EARL BENTLEY)

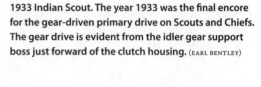

1933 Indian Scout. The year 1933 was the final encore for the gear-driven primary drive on Scouts and Chiefs. The gear drive is evident from the idler gear support boss just forward of the clutch housing. (EARL BENTLEY)

1933 Indian Scout Pony. The little twin received a new fork, plus black cylinders and cylinder heads. For the 1933 season only, Indian also offered a 45-cubic inch (750cc) version termed the "Motoplane." Except for the word "Motoplane" beneath the Indian script, the only other visible difference was one more cooling fin. (EARL BENTLEY)

In 1933, the Four was first offered as "standard" with battery ignition; magneto ignition became an extra-cost option. (INDIAN NEWS)

1933 Indian Four. For 1933 only, the distincitive horizontall finned inlet manifold was used. (EARL BENTLEY)

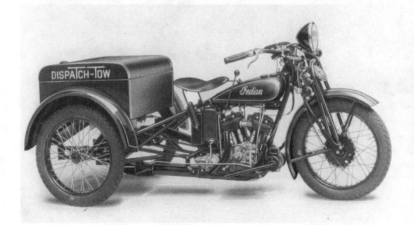

1933 Indian Dispatch Tow. Around 1930, Indian had entered the three-wheeled commercial vehicle field with a machine based on the Series 101 Scout. Harley-Davidson entered the fray in late 1932 with its 45-cubic inch (750cc) Servicar. This 1933 Indian update was based on the 45-cubic inch Motoplane. The commercial business was always "iffy" for both companies, but the Great Depression made them desperate, so that any way to sell even a few more machines was considered good business. (EARL BENTLEY)

1934

All 1934 models had optional chrome-plated rims. The Scout, Model 234, had triple-row primary drive chain replacing drive gears. The Chief, Model 334, also had triple-row primary drive chain replacing drive gears, along with standard wasted spark battery ignition, optional magneto ignition and optional aluminum heads in same pattern as iron heads. On the Four, Model 434, a 1932-and-earlier inlet manifold replaced the 1933-only manifold. The Scout Pony, Model 534, was unchanged.

The Sport Scout, Model 634, was a new side-valve twin. It's spec's included: bore and stroke, 2 7/8 and 3 1/2; displacement 45.44 ci (745cc), dry-sump lubrication, engine and transmission bolted together, belt-driven generator in front of engine, cast aluminum primary drive case, double-row primary chain, keystone frame, girder front fork, new rounded fenders, Indian-head tank transfers, wheelbase of 56 1/2 inches and a weight of 385 lbs.

1934 Sport Scout front frame section. The Sport Scout was designed along the lines of British and European sporting bikes. The then-termed "keystone" frame, once the hallmark of the defunct Excelsior, was termed a "diamond" frame across the Atlantic. Indian's use of this approach put it behind the trans-Atlantic trend, as foreign makers were at that moment discarding diamond frames for full wrap-under "cradle" frames.

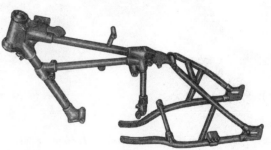

1934 Sport Scout frame, main and rear sections. The frame gave a light and racy look to the assembled motorcycle, but discarding one or two frame tubes beneath the engine could hardly have saved much weight.

(WAR DEPARTMENT TECHNICAL MANUAL 10-515, THE MOTORCYCLE)

1934 Indian Sport Scout. Bound for glory, Indian's all-new all-around middle-weight Sport Scout would carry the racing banner for the next 20 years. Note the cylindrical cover in the 9 o'clock position of the right crankcase; this housed the circuit breaker for the double-spark ("wasted" spark) ignition system. This was obligatory on the Sport Scout and Scout Pony. Chief and Four buyers could opt for the extra-cost magneto setup. The Sport Scout was a mid-season offering. (EARL BENTLEY)

Some features were unique to the 1934 Sport Scout: fork details and geometry differed from later years; the generator was belt-driven; and there was no provision for magneto operation. Lack of a magneto option is evident by the smooth clutch cover. The 1934-only double-chain primary drive and drive case were popular with racers because the 1934 setup was narrower than the later triple-row drive. As the Sport Scout was a mid-season offering, its styling features of new fenders and Indian-head transfers were not incorporated on other 1934 Indians. (EARL BENTLEY)

1934 Chief and Scout primary drive system. Indian switched from helical gear drive to four-row chain drive on the 1934 Chief and Scout. This change drew some rebuttal from Indian fans, but in fact the new setup would outlast the rest of the motorcycle, while eliminating the objectionable whine of the drive gears. These factors, plus a cost savings, spelled common sense, and the layout was still superior to Harley-Davidson's sheet-metal-covered drip-feed system.

(INDIAN PUBLICITY PHOTO)

1935

Optional tank panels appeared on all but the Model 535. New front and rear fenders appeared on the Scout, Chief and Four. Nickel-plated cylinders replaced black cylinders. Standard iron heads appeared on the Scout, Chief, and Sport Scout. The Scout was nickel-plated instead of black.

The Scout, Model 235, had optional "Y" motors with aluminum heads and larger cooling fins on cylinders and heads. Two rebound leaves were added to the top of the fork (for a total of 10).

The Chief, Model 335, had optional "Y" motors with aluminum heads and larger cooling fins on cylinders and heads. "Y" heads with "trench" between valve and piston areas. Regular-sized optional aluminum heads were discontinued. Two rebound leaves were added to the top of the fork (for a total of 10).

The Four, Model 435, had an Ace-style engine with new frame and fenders. Two rebound leaves were added to the top of the fork (for a total of 10). The Four, Model 436, was introduced in mid-1935-season (see 1936 description).

The Sport Scout, Model 635, had: a new heavier built front fork, a chain-driven generator with new left crankcase to accommodate, optional magneto ignition, a triple-row primary chain to accommodate optional magneto ignition, new primary drive case with "2 o'clock" removable plate on battery ignition models, or with take-off drive for magneto, optional "Y" motors with aluminum heads and larger cooling fins on cylinders and heads, "Y"-shaped manifolds on "Y" motors and optional compression-action seat springs.

For 1935, the Standard Scout, the Chief, and the Four all were fitted with the Indian-head tank styling made popular by the 1934 Sport Scout. In addition to the simple striping shown previously on the 1934 Sport Scout, Indian offered these two optional tank pains schemes. The top scheme was termed the "Arrow" panel; the bottom scheme was termed the "V" panel. (INDIAN NEWS)

1935 Indian Sport Scout. A triple-row primary drive chain replaced the 1934 double-row setup. The extra run drove the optional magneto. On battery ignition models, a removable panel closed off the 12 o'clock to 3 o'clock area. In 1935, Indian was at the top of its game. The tear-drop tanks and curvy fenders compared well against the somewhat slab-sided Harley-Davidson components. (EARL BENTLEY)

1935 Indian Chief. Three cylinder head options were offered: standard iron "waffle iron" heads, aluminum "waffle iron" heads, and new aluminum "Y"motor heads. See the following pictures for details. Optional on the Chief and the Scout (not the Sport Scout), was a four-speed transmission. All Harleys were still three-speeders. This prototype shows the wrong handle grips; as standard equipment, all 1935 models featured white grips in the resurrected 1917-1926 style. (EARL BENTLEY)

1935-1938 Chief cylinder head. These unusual "trench" heads with fins angled to the slip stream, and similar heads for the 45-cubic inch (750cc) models, enhanced low- and mid- range torque. Surprisingly, Indian didn't mention this improvement in any sale literature or press releases.

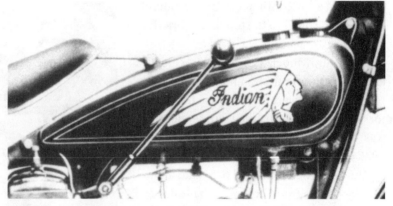

1935 Indian Scout Pony. The new tank styling applied to the little twin. (EARL BENTLEY)

1935 Indian Four. In all Indian sales literature, except 1935, the more attractive right side of the motorcycle was shown. This unusual left-side shot may mean that Indian was making more than one configuration of Four during the season, by using spare parts stock. Why is this? Because the planned 1935 "upside-down" Four was running behind schedule. (EARL BENTLEY)

1936

On all battery ignition twins, distributor ignition replaced the wasted spark system. The distributor was driven by the rear camshaft; new right crankcases accommodated this change. All models except Scout Pony had new quick-action bayonet filler caps replacing screw-on caps.

The Standard Scout, Model 236, had a name change in sales literature to highlight differences from Sport Scout. The Standard Scout and Chief, Model 336, had "T" oil lines to the valve guides. The Four, Model 436, had a new exhaust-over-inlet "upside-down" engine and new Marvel carburetor.

The Scout Pony, Model 536, got new front and rear fenders. The Sport Scout, Model 636, also got "T" oil lines to the valve guides.

1936 Indian Scout. All 1936 Indians, except the Scout Pony, were fitted with the larger "bayonet" style quick-opening tank caps, in lieu of the smaller screw-on caps used since the beginning. Note the "T" oil lines that routed breather mist to the valve guides. These were used on 1936 and 1937 Chiefs, Scouts and Sport Scouts. To accommodate the "T" lines, two-piece snap-on "clam shell" valve spring covers were fitted. (EARL BENTLEY)

1936 Indian Sport Scout. For the 1936 season, Indian introduced standard distributor ignition. This replaced the 1934-1935 standard double-spark or "wasted spark" ignition via crankcase-mounted circuit breaker. This example from sales literature is a "Y" motor with Y-shaped inlet manifold and deep aluminum head fins.

(EARL BENTLEY)

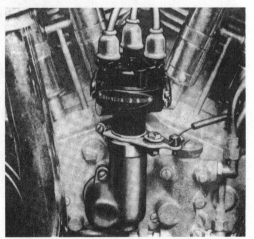

Indian distributor ignition for twins. The Auto-Lite distributor drive was taken from the rear cylinder cam. This was essentially a trouble-free system, but with the wide separation of dealerships through much of the nation, it was prudent for tourers to take along a spare capacitor and set of breaker points. Harley-Davidson made much of their claimed enhanced ignition reliability through elimination of the distributor, in their double-spark layout. (INDIAN SALES LITERATURE)

1936 Indian Sport Scout. Fitted with the optional Arrow tank panels, this restored example shows the charm of the Sport Scout. New features shown here included: center-mounted horn replaced horn with side tabs, fork without vertical horn tabs and onion-shaped gear shift knob.

1936 Sport Scout. This 1936 Sport Scout is fitted with the "Y" motor that featured a Y-shaped inlet manifold and larger head fins. (DOUG MITCHEL)

1936 Indian Chief. For the first time, a stoplight was fitted as standard equipment on the Standard Scout, Chief, Four and Sport Scout. This is another example of faulty sales literature. As in all 1936 factory-produced publicity photos, this picture shows the 1935 steering head area instead of the more substantial layout used on production 1936 Chiefs. (EARL BENTLEY)

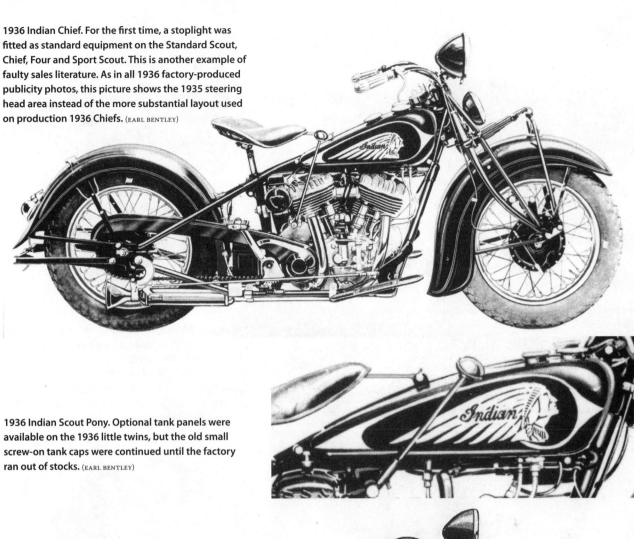

1936 Indian Scout Pony. Optional tank panels were available on the 1936 little twins, but the old small screw-on tank caps were continued until the factory ran out of stocks. (EARL BENTLEY)

1936 Model 436 Indian Four. Although announced as a late-1935 model and continued unchanged for 1936, the subtleties are today ignored and all Model 436 motorcycles are regarded as 1936 models. Indian billed this as the fastest stock motorcycle it had ever built. A 90-mph top speed was claimed. Extra power was attributed to the cooler inlet charge, made possible by the side-mounted inlet valves. The nickname was unfortunate: "Upside-Down" Four! Induction was through a new Marvel carburetor. (EARL BENTLEY)

There were four variants of the Model 436, though two of them involved only the routing of control cables. This example is one of the early-season models, with exposed exhaust valve stems and a small leg shield.

1936 Model 436 engine. Construction of these engines differed markedly from the earlier F-heads. Instead of a single top-side manifold that included four valve housings, the 436 and 437 had four separate valve "cages." The beautiful left-side finning was largely obscured by the generator and, if so equipped, even more hidden by the magneto.

Late-season Model 436 motorcycles were also fitted with a carburetor shield. The exhaust valve enclosures are evident. Non-standard features on this restored bike include: chrome plating of the valve covers, the heat shield and the carburetor shield.

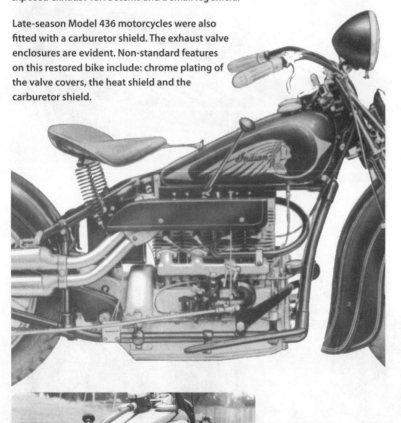

1936 Model 436 engine. Though crude in appearance, the so-called "log" manifold worked well. Differing from the earlier F-heads, the cylinders were made with a side opening instead of a top opening for a manifold. But even with this routing and the late-season heat shield, there remained concern about a rider's hot right leg.

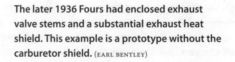

The later 1936 Fours had enclosed exhaust valve stems and a substantial exhaust heat shield. This example is a prototype without the carburetor shield. (EARL BENTLEY)

1937

All 1937 models had the gear shift lever moved forward near the steering head. Standard on the Scout, Chief and Four were interchangeable front and rear wheels.

The Standard Scout, Model 237, had chrome-plated valve spring covers and front and rear exhaust tubes. The Chief, Model 337, had chrome-plated valve spring covers and front and rear exhaust tubes, and a larger rear chain guard. The Four, Model 437, had twin Zenith carburetors with dual "Y" inlet manifolds. The Junior Scout, Model 537, had a name change, its horn was relocated below the headlight, and new quick-action bayonet filler caps replaced screw-on caps (changed a year earlier on other models). The Sport Scout, Model 637, had chrome-plated valve spring covers and front and rear exhaust tubes, and a wider front fender valance.

1937 Indian Standard Scout. This was the last season for the Chief-framed middle-sized twin. (EARL BENTLEY)

1937 Sport Scout. To cater to riders accustomed to the "backwards" action Harley-Davidson clutch, it was easy for dealers to reverse the Indian clutch action. By simply moving the clutch actuating arm 180 degrees (from 2 o'clock to 7 o'clock), the clutch was converted from automobile action to toe-to-go action. The Harley-style controls theme could be completed by using the optional left-side shifter and re-rigging the throttle for right-hand operation. (EARL BENTLEY)

1937 Indian Sport Scout. Formerly an extra-cost option, the "Y" motors were featured on all 1937 Standard Scouts, Sport Scouts and Chiefs. The most obvious change for 1937, applicable to all models, was the relocation of the gear shift lever from the "jockey" position to the forward area of the tank. Although right-side shifters remained standard, left-side shifters had been optional since 1936. (EARL BENTLEY)

The 1937 Chief, also termed the Model 337, got an increased rear fender valance (siding), and a wrap-over chain guard. The new-from-1936 steering head area is depicted. This publicity picture erroneously shows a black muffler. Standard Scouts, Chiefs and Sport Scouts were fitted with chrome exhaust headers, mufflers and valve spring covers. (EARL BENTLEY)

1937 Chief with optional cadmium-plated rims.

1937 Indian Chief. The Chief and Scout were fitted with interchangeable wheels and a cast brake drum. Riders could opt for cadmium plated wheel rims instead of the standard black rims shown here. (EARL BENTLEY)

1937 Four. The Model 437 featured twin Zenith carburetors and a forward-mounted gear shift lever. (THE ANTIQUE MOTORCYCLE)

1938

All models except the Junior Scout got new integral tank-top instrument panel. All twins had their "T" oil lines eliminated. The Standard Scout was dropped. High-performance twins were termed "Daytona" models in honor of recent stock model speed records.

Chief, Model 338, got: new cylinders with more finning in the exhaust valve area, larger valve guides, a new oil pump with takeoff drive for distributor; a new right crankcase and new wrap-around timing case cover.

The Four, Model 438, received: a new F-head engine with cylinders cast in pairs and aluminum heads cast in pairs, totally enclosed inlet rockers with air-oil mist lubrication and mandatory battery ignition.

The Junior Scout, Model 538, had an iron crankcases, transmission case and transmission case cover. The Sport Scout, Model 638, had new cylinders with more finning in the exhaust valve area, rear cylinders trimmed to clear the seat mast, and a new oil pump with takeoff drive for distributor and a new right crankcase.

Details of the front end used on Chiefs and Fours. (INDIAN PHOTO)

1938 Indian instrument panel. As well as the new instrument panel body, the 1938 model, except the little twin, were treated to a gray speedometer and ammeter with red lettering. The envisioned gray shifter knob didn't happen. (INDIAN PHOTO)

1938 Indian Chief. The rigid frame era entered its final phase with the 1938 models that included an integrated tank-top instrument panel. Concerning this feature, the company was more than a year late, as Harley-Davidson had introduced a tank-top panel in the course of the 1936 season. That was sort of a "first," as Indian had previously set the American styling pace. (PETER ARUNDEL)

1938 Indian Sport Scout. The new oil pump accommodated either the distributor shown here, or otherwise was plugged . This was a prototype engine still fitted with the old "T" oil lines; the crude retouching eliminated the "T" lines because these were not used on production models. (INDIAN PUBLICITY PHOTO)

1938 Indian Chief. The new wrap-around timing case cover cleaned up the appearance. The Sport Scout wasn't given the same treatment. The "T" oil lines were discontinued because of oil seepage. A new larger oil pump was used on the Chief and the Sport Scout. This is a magneto ignition model. (PETER ARUNDEL)

1938 Indian Four production F-head engine (at right). Just behind the rear cylinder, the push-pull rod controlled the bypass of exhaust gas upward from the middle of the header, over the inlet manifold, and downward behind the rear cylinder block and again into the header. These engines were not so prone to overheating as widely thought, largely because of the massive aluminum crankcases and aluminum heads. (BOB FINN)

1938 Indian Four. Buyers had many finish options during the 1930s. Most two-color finishes had the sides of the tanks and fenders in the same color as the frame. Some riders opted for reversing the layout, as in this example. (DOUG MITCHEL)

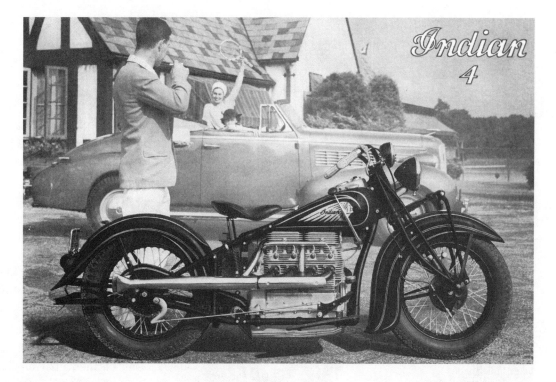

1938 Indian Four. The 1938 Four returned to F-head layout. Cylinders were cast in pairs. Enclosed inlet valves were lubricated by air-oil mist, and moved on needle bearings. Magneto ignition wasn't offered on the Model 438. On this catalog picture, the exhaust bypass (inlet manifold heating) system was improperly retouched by an artist. (INDIAN SALES LITERATURE)

1938 Indian Sport Scout. As ever, Sport Scout advertising emphasized racing victories. The top-of- the-line Sport Scouts and Chiefs were fitted with special "off-main-line" engines termed "Daytona" engines in honor of speed records set at Daytona Beach. (INDIAN SALES LITERATURE)

1939 Indian Sport Scout (above). Except for silver on police motorcycles and a few standard bikes, Indian hadn't previously offered metallic finishes. For the 1939 season, optional finishes included metallic santaupe (greenish beige) with Chinese red (shown here), and metallic Cascade blue with silver. The new hot stuff faster engines were termed "Bonneville" motors in honor of late 1938 records set on the Bonneville salt flats.

1939

All models received new standard "World's Fair" tank panels (3 panel options continued). The high-performance Chief and Sport Scout were termed "Bonneville" models in honor of recent stock model speed records.

The Chief, Model 339, featured an air cleaner to replace the air horn. A few "trench" cylinder heads were used, but this concept was phased out. This produced higher top speed at the expense of mid-range torque.

The Four, Model 439, also had a new air cleaner, and optional magneto ignition returned. The Junior Scout, Model 539, got a steering damper as standard equipment. The Sport Scout, Model 639, got the new air cleaner, a barrel-shaped fork spring and dog-bone fork stiffness adjusters replaced disk adjusters.

1939 Indian. The horizontal muffler flair was new; the bullet-shaped tail lights were first used on 1936 models. (INDIAN PHOTO)

1939 Indian Sport Scout. The "World's Fair" tank panels were a new option, in addition to the Standard, Arrow and "V" panels. During the 1938 season, the factory abandoned the "trench" heads in favor of the traditional "Ricardo" heads similar to those used for many years. This increased top speed at the expense of mid-range torque. (INDIAN PHOTO)

1939 Indian Chief. The special fast Chiefs and Sport Scouts were now termed "Bonneville" models because of new speed records set at Bonneville Salt Flats, Utah. Though Harley-Davidson held the American record for specially modified motorcycles, Indian's 1938 and 1939 records were for stock machines. The late-1938 Bonneville records were: Sport Scout, 115.126 mph; Chief, 120.747 mph.

(INDIAN PHOTO)

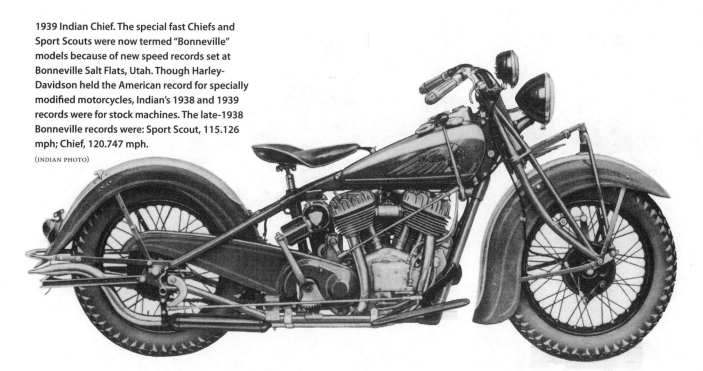

1939 Indian Chief. The 1939 models were the last of the rigid framed era for Chiefs and Fours. A new full color tank emblem was introduced during the course of the 1938 season. The fork bell cranks were angled more upward to soften the ride. This resulted in a separation of the bottom leafs from the main set.

(INDIAN PHOTO)

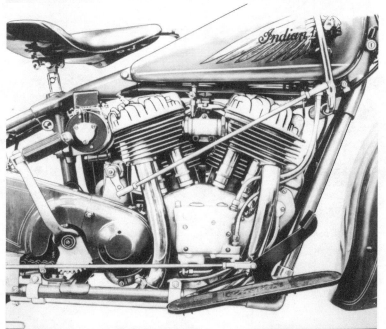

1939 Indian Chief. To improve the appearance, a sort of "hat brim" was added to the 1939 Chief and Sport Scout cylinder heads, so that the "brim" would match up with the large cylinder fins.

(BRUCE LINSDAY)

1939 Indian Junior Scout. In 1937, the little twin had been renamed "Junior Scout." Beginning with the 1938 Junior Scouts, the crankcases and transmission cases were cast iron. (INDIAN PHOTO)

1939 Indian Junior Scout. This bike sold for the rock bottom price of $215, compared to the most expensive model, the magneto ignition Four, at $465. At the time, $600 would buy a new car, so it was hard to make a good economic case with potential Junior Scout buyers.

(INDIAN PHOTO)

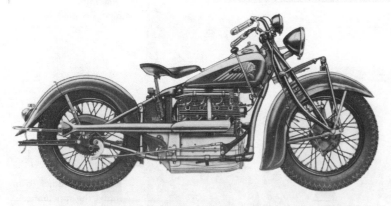

1939 Indian Four. A really good Four, with some internal polishing and spot-on tuning, would top 100 mph. (INDIAN PHOTO)

After Indian dropped the magneto option on the 1938 Fours, buyers could again opt for a magneto. Though the left side of the Four cylinders were attractive, the generator and magneto obscured the view.

(BRUCE LINSDAY)

1940-41 Streamliners

Dramatically restyled, the 1940 Indian range featured skirted fenders on all models and a plunger rear suspension "spring frame" on the Chief and Four. With a minimum of engineering design work, the decades old technology was made to look completely modern by this masterful maneuver.

Today, most enthusiasts think of skirted fenders when they think of Indians and the styling is universally revered, but in their day, the streamlined Indians were controversial, even among longtime Indian enthusiasts. You either loved them or hated them.

As with all period American motorcycles, the right side was more attractive then the left. The new Sport Scout and Chief cylinders and heads were visually stunning. The Four seemed at last to have the perfect styling blend, as the engine no longer dwarfed the rest of the machine. A year later the Sport Scout featured a spring frame, while open fenders returned to the Thirty-fifty and only detail changes applied to the Chief and Four.

Sales were brisk in these years, with Indian actually drawing even with Harley-Davidson during 1940. Although 1942 models were planned, during 1941 the defense industry bought up practically all steel and aluminum supplies in order to satisfy the needs of the Allied Powers. Consequently, very few 1942 Indians (and Harley-Davidsons) were built before the U. S. entered World War II in December of 1941. In early 1942, all civilian motor vehicle production was halted by the government.

FEATURING THE NEW SPRING FRAME

ON INDIAN FOUR AND SEVENTY-FOUR MODELS

1940

There was a spring frame on Chief and Four models and skirted fenders on all models. The Chief, Model 340, got a longer transmission main shaft to accommodate a wider frame. The Four, Model 440, got a new seat post suspension and new battery location. The Thirty-fifty, Model 540, got a name change. 1940 was also the only year for skirted fenders on this model. The Sport Scout, Model 640 had a rigid frame with skirted fenders—the only year of this combination.

The major technical improvement on the 1940 Chiefs and Fours was the new plunger rear suspension (above). The Indian spring frame looked better than it worked. Many of the early season models suffered from the stack-up of production fitting tolerances, so that the plunger units worked poorly or not at all. Looser clearances were initiated to solve the problem. Harley-Davidson responded with 5.00 x 16 low-pressure tires that delivered nearly as soft a ride even with an unsprung rear wheel. (INDIAN NEWS)

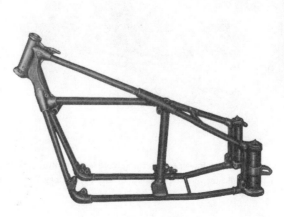

1940 Indian Chief frame. Indian frames were extremely rugged because of the heavy forgings and large diameter tubing. Except for small details, this remained the basic Chief frame through 1952. The Four spring frame was along the same lines but featured different front down-tubes and other unique details.

(WAR DEPARTMENT TECHNICAL MANUAL 10-515, THE MOTORCYCLE)

1940 Police Chief. Indian remained popular with police departments across the nation. For decades, New York City was Indian's largest police customer with some 600 Indians on patrol. (INDIAN PHOTO)

1940 Police Four. Easy starting and smooth low-speed running were features that endeared Fours to police forces. With only infrequent high-speed runs of short duration, heat build-up wasn't a problem on city police duty. The massive finned aluminum crankcase functioned as an oil cooler. (INDIAN PUBLICITY PHOTO)

1940 Indian Thirty-fifty. The lightweight Indian twin got a new name, "Thirty-fifty," denoting the 30.50-cubic inch (500cc) engine. There was no corresponding Harley-Davidson model, but Thirty-fifty sales barely justified its retention. The year 1940 was unique in the fitting of skirted fenders to the Thirty-fifty. (INDIAN SALES LITERATURE)

1940 Indian Sport Scout. Though sporting the hallmark skirted fenders, the Sport Scout continued with the rigid rear. (INDIAN SALES LITERATURE)

1940 Indian sidecar. Skirted fender sidecar styling was enhanced by a new sidecar body. (INDIAN SALES LITERATURE)

1941 Indian Chief. Beautifully restyled cylinders and heads made the new Indian V-twins look modern despite roots that reached back to 1922. Thanks to continuous attention to cooling and lubrication over the years, the performance of this 20 year old design remained up to date in America's ever faster motorcycling.

(BOB FINN),

1941

Two-color finishes (with black frame and fork) were optional on the Chief, Four, and Sport Scout. Decorative aluminum strips were placed on tank sides, except for Model 541.

The Chief, Model 341, had no significant differences from Model 340. The Four, Model 441, had no significant differences from Model 340. At mid-year, West Coast distributor Hap Alzina announced no more dealer orders for Fours would be filled, except for police use. The Thirty-fifty, Model 541, got open fenders. The Sport Scout, Model 641, got a spring frame and a longer transmission main shaft to accommodate the wider frame.

1941 Indian Chief. Throughout 1940, the Indian factory argued that 5.00 x 16 low pressure tires weren't ideal or even safe for motorcycles. But the popularity of these "car" tires on Harleys couldn't be denied. So for 1941, Indian joined Harley-Davidson in offering optional 5.00 x 16 tires. Other Chief changes were minimal. This catalog shot doesn't show the decorative tank strips that were on production models.

(BOB FINN),

1941 Indian Four. The skirted fender Fours had arguably the most beautiful right side of all period motorcycles. No detail escaped the stylists' eyes, as for instance the front down tubes which are curved to flow parallel to the front fender lines.

(BOB FINN),

1941 Indian Thirty-fifty. The little twin got open fenders for the 1941 season. (BOB FINN)

1941 Indian Four. Only in details such as the number and type of clutch plates, did the 1941 Four engine differ from the 1938 engine. Both the 1940 and 1941 Fours differed from the 1938-1939 Fours in such details as battery location, and a two-section brake rod with intermediary bell crank that allowed for rear wheel suspension travel. (BOB FINN)

1941 Indian Sport Scout (above). Pride of place in 1941 advertisements was the new spring frame Sport Scout. This prototype has a right-side speedometer cable; most production models had the cable on the left side. Increased weight diminished the model's acceleration; the 1938 model weighed 440 lbs.; the 1941 model weighed 500 lbs. Indian's reputation was enhanced by the many racing victories of Sport Scout riders, but sales never matched glory. Analysis of Indian maintenance announcements ("Contact Points") indicates the following approximate ratios for each 100 Indians built: 4 Thirty-fifties, 35 forty-five ci models (Scouts and/or Sport Scouts, as applicable), 52 Chiefs and 9 Fours. (BOB FINN)

1941 Indian Thirty-fifty engine details. This was the last year for the model. From 1938 through the end, the crankcases and transmission case were iron! (BOB FINN)

1941 Indian Sport Scout (above). Perhaps even more lovely than the long-stroke Chief engine, was the compact Sport Scout power plant. Though of side-valve design, the "rev happy" engine feels remarkably similar to modern overhead-cam units. (BOB FINN)

1942

With no sales literature, information was sketchy for 1942. By government order, no civilian vehicles were produced after February 9, 1942, because of World War II. There was limited used of chromium plating. On some motorcycles, the Indian-head metal tank emblem replaced the tear-drop emblem; other new Indians had the tear-drop emblem.

1940-1945, Military Production

Indian failed in its bid to be the major supplier of American Army motorcycles. The company satisfied the specification that called for a 30.50-cubic inch (500cc) engine, but the Army agreed with Harley-Davidson that a 45-cubic inch (750cc) engine was required, so the specifications were changed and Harley-Davidson got all the business. Part of the Army's rationale was the more modern Harley-Davidson factory, as Indian had allowed its machinery to age well past prime condition. Indian continued to sell large numbers of its Model 741 to Allied nations that traditionally had favored the 500cc size. But, as in civilian sales, Indian produced only about half as many military motorcycles as did Harley-Davidson, the respective wartime totals being about 40 thousand and 90 thousand.

The Indian factory satisfied a French order for 5,000 Chiefs with sidecars shortly before the fall of France. Otherwise, relatively minor production and sales were devoted to the Model 344 Chief, almost all going to police departments. The company captured a number of subcontracts from major defense contractors and produced many components, landing gear parts for example. Harley-Davidson also did subcontract work, but on its considerable Army motorcycle business alone was able to more efficiently operate its factory. Thus, the wartime situation postured the two American motorcycle companies for a continuation of Harley's 2-to-1 dominance in the postwar market.

1940-1945, Military Production and War

Years

Model 340M: military version of the spring frame Chief with non-skirted fenders and military specifications. About 5,000 with sidecars were sold to France. Very few others built.

640B: military version of Sport Scout; a few were used in Army test programs and some stateside base duties; not sold for combat operations.

Model 741: 30.50ci (500cc) twin, built to satisfy specification requirements of Allied nations and supposed forthcoming U. S. changeover to Allied specifications; quantity sales were limited to Allied forces, primarily Britain, Canada and Australia; more than 30,000 were sold.

Model 841: 45-ci (750cc) transverse engine, basically a "sideways" Sport Scout unit with lower compression ratio; 1,000 were built for a competitive test program against the Harley-Davidson Model XA; the army declared the XA the winner, but didn't award production contracts.

Model 344: similar to the military Chief ,but finished in civilian colors such as red, black or silver; non-skirted fenders; no chrome plating; most were sold to police departments; a few were sold to defense industry commuters.

In the summer of 1945, with the war nearly over, Army surplus Indians were purchased by Indian dealers and car dealers, and sold to civilians.

Indian Model 741. The World War II U. S. and foreign government specifications called for 30.50-ci (500cc) motorcycles, so Indian answered the call with the Model 741 that combined attributes of the civilian Thirty-fifty and Sport Scout. Harley-Davidson refused to submit bids for this size engine, and persuaded the U. S. government to up the size to 45 ci (750cc). By "cheating," Harley got all the American forces motorcycle orders, while Indian sold only to Allied nations.

(IAN CAMPBELL)

Indian Model M-1. This prototype lightweight side-valve single was designed for parachute drops, but never went into production. Of interest are the primary drive case and left-side foot-shift transmission. Apparently, designer Briggs Weaver carried over much of the detailed layout work into his postwar lightweight models discussed later. (EARL BENTLEY)

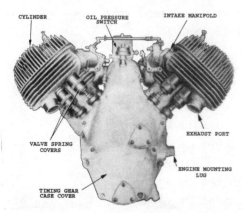

CYLINDER OIL PRESSURE SWITCH INTAKE MANIFOLD

VALVE SPRING COVERS

EXHAUST PORT

ENGINE MOUNTING LUG

TIMING GEAR CASE COVER

Indian Model 841. The smoothness of 90-degree V-twins is today well known, but in the early 1940s, the Army had to be convinced. President E. Paul du Pont first built a 90-degree Chief engine, mounted it in his three-wheeled Morgan car, and allowed Army officers to test drive the rig in order to prove the concept. The 841 was flawed by the use of a transmission along traditional Indian lines, with teeth-to-teeth engagement.

(WAR DEPARTMENT TECHNICAL MANUAL 10-515, THE MOTORCYCLE)

(Left) Indian sold about 40,000 military motorcycles during World War II, about half as many as Harley-Davidson. At war's end, surplus Models 741 enjoyed brisk sales in the transportation starved civilian market. In the decade following the war, many 741s were used in Europe. Compared to the vastness of the United States, shorter trips in populous Europe made these little bikes more practical on the Continent than in America. Almost all were "civilianized" with bright paint jobs and chrome trim, and even today a significant number have survived and entered the antique motorcycle movement. (BUTCH BAER)

Indian Model 841. One-thousand of these joined 1,000 Harley-Davidson Model XA bikes in a competitive test program for shaft-drive motorcycles. Harley-Davidson won the competition, but never got a production contract because the targeted North African desert campaign was over and the four-wheeled Jeep was succeeding. (EARL BENTLEY)

Wartime Indian Model 344. For "essential use," the U. S. government permitted Indian and Harley-Davidson to build a few new bikes during World War II. Almost all of these were sold to police departments. The open fenders were considered patriotic because the precious metal wasn't wasted on the skirted fender styling. Chrome trim was also prohibited.

(EARL BENTLEY)

Another view of the Model 344. The war years were the only ones in history in which more motorcycles were sold than passenger cars, the latter restricted to a few hundred a year for seior military officers. The Indian-head tank trim had been introduced on a few hundred civilian 1942 models built prior to American entering the world war in late 1941.

(INDIAN LITERATURE)

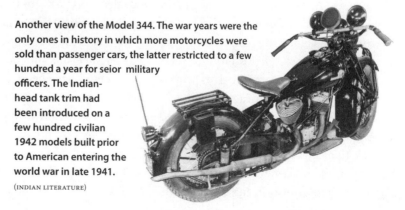

1946-53, Decline and Failure

In 1945, Indian was purchased by the Ralph Rogers group. Rogers' plan was to develop lighter and easier-handling overhead-valve models along foreign lines. Chief production was resumed in 1946 to earn money while planning for the new range, and to keep Indian dealers on the rolls for the forthcoming revolutionary lineup. The 1946 Chiefs were technically unchanged, except for a new front fork patterned after the Model 841 fork. A prototype 1947 Sport Scout was developed with the 841 style fork and Chief style belt drive generator behind the engine, but this project was cancelled. Chief production continued for the 1947 and 1948 seasons with minor changes.

Part of the long-term management program was to develop a modern one-story factory. In the spring of 1948, while machinery was being transferred from the old Indian factory, Chief production was halted so that only a handful of prototype 1949 Chiefs were built. A few dozen racing model 648 Sport Scouts were among the last Indians assembled at the old State Street "Wigwam."

In the summer of 1948, the 13.1-cubic inch overhead-valve Arrow single was launched, followed by the 26.6-cubic inch overhead-valve Scout vertical twin. In today's collector world these models are referred to as "Verticals" or "Torque models," after the name of the independent company that sold the verticals designs to Indian. The Verticals' reliability problems resulted in substantial warranty claims that bled Indian's finances. As the company struggled to resolve the engineering issues, the British government devalued the pound sterling so that prices of imported British motorcycles fell about 20 percent overnight. This proved the death knell of the Verticals.

Leftover Arrows and Scouts were offered in the 1950 range, while the new 30.50-cubic inch (500cc) Warrior and Warrior TT (off-road version) debuted. Warriors and Warrior TTs were also in the 1951 lineup.

For the 1952 season, the Warrior TT was continued and a revamped road model Warrior was advertised. Less than a dozen of these 1952 street Warriors were built before Indian pulled the plug. The last Verticals were the three-wheeled Patrol models aimed primarily at the police market during the 1952 and 1953 seasons.

From 1950 through 1953, about 500 Chiefs per year were built—though some historians believe more than 500 Chiefs were built as 1953 models. In this era, there were two versions—one for 1950-1951, and the other for 1952-1953. The 1950 Chief introduced the telescopic front fork and a slightly less valanced front fender. There was the usual ballyhoo about a new 1951 Chief, but it was identical to the 1950 model in all the important respects. For the 1952 season, further Chief cosmetic changes were made, including an engine cowling, a more abbreviated front fender and a low-mounted exhaust system. Chiefs were offered in the 1953 season with no meaningful changes.

Indian stopped domestic production effective with the 1954 season. The Indian dealer network continued through 1962, selling British bikes. Long a controversial subject, the failure of Indian was partly due to engineering and management mistakes that could have been avoided.. The key decision was "go" or "no go" regarding full-scale production of the Verticals. A more thorough test program and more gradual phase in of the Verticals might have made all the difference. The other survival plan might have been the abandonment of the

1946 Indian Chief. World War II was barely over in late 1945 when Indian announced its postwar motorcycle, the Model 346 Chief. The new double-spring girder fork was a narrower version of the unit used on the army Model 841. Production was simplified by the elimination of the short narrow trim strips that had graced the fender tops of 1940-1942 Chiefs.

(INDIAN PHOTO)

Verticals concept, but Ralph Rogers bought Indian just for that purpose. Rogers' fundamental idea was sound, that being to mine an untapped market of a new generation that was put off by the heavy prewar designs. Honda did exactly that about a dozen years later, but Honda had a great product and Rogers didn't.

Harley-Davidson was successful in selling their "Seventy-Four" big twins, despite a 30-percent higher sales price than British bikes. Riders were willing to pay the extra money to get attributes not offered by the imports. A modern overhead-valve Chief might have been equally successful, but the engineering drain of the Verticals prohibited that approach. As to the unfavorable pricing situation that arose from the action of the British government, this may have been significant enough to kill Indian even if management had crystal clear foresight and made the best possible decisions.

1946-1948

Production was never reinstated on Fours, Thirty-fifties, and Sport Scouts (road models). A girder front fork was basically a narrower version of the Model 841 fork. Chiefs were offered as three "models" depending on installed equipment. The Clubman was stripped except for black front safety guards. The Sportsman had chrome front and rear safety guards, and either a Chum-Me (buddy) seat or a deluxe solo saddle. The Roadmaster added a slightly curved accessory bar to the handlebars, a horizontal accessory bar mounted to the top of the front fork (to support a windshield), a horizontal accessory bar mounted on the fork beneath the headlight (to mount spot lights), windshield, spot lights,

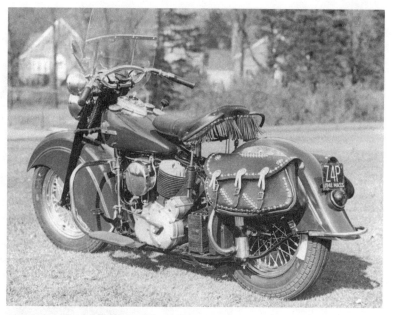

1946 Indian Chief, fully "dressed." (INDIAN PHOTO)

1946 Indian police Chief. Police sales were brisk as departments across the nation replaced well worn pre-war models.

(EARL BENTLEY)

1947 Indian Chief. Posing are Indian president Ralph B. Rogers, left, and designer G. Briggs Weaver, right. Only trim changes, such as the Indian script on the tank sides, differentiated the Model 347 from the Model 346. Behind the scenes, Indian was concentrating its engineering efforts on a radically new lineup of light and middleweight roadsters. (CLYDE EARL)

saddlebags, and a lighter luggage rack built up from aluminum pieces instead of the old cast-iron rack.

For the Chief, Model 346, it was the last year of Indian-head metal tank emblems. A late-season change oriented the ammeter face 45 degrees to the right (at full discharge, the needle was straight up). The Chief, Model 347, got Indian script metal tank emblems and "Tilted" ammeter as on late-1946 bikes.

The Chief, Model 348, had: a front wheel driven Stewart-Warner speedometer with arrow-shaped pointer, new instrument panel with warning light instead of ammeter, cast-in crankcase scrapers replacing the sump valve (except a few early season Chiefs), a new cast-aluminum gear-type oil pump, and a new forward-mounted side stand.

The Daytona Scout, Model 648, was a racer also known as a "Big Base" Scout because of a larger crankcase volume. The Rear of both crankcases had a vertical surface that, with cases mated, at the bottom provided room for the larger oil sump behind the flywheel. Engine used Model 841 flywheels. A Limited number were built; debate centers on 25 versus 50, some arguing that 25 complete motorcycles were built along with another 25 engines. Others say a few more engines were assembled after the initial deliveries. The Model 648 was assembled from spare parts stocks plus some special racing parts that were subcontracted. The complete motorcycles were sold at a loss to favored dealers and riders.

1949

A New overhead-valve "Arrow" single went on sale in the summer of 1948. Vertical twin "Scouts" were on sale in the autumn of 1948. As with postwar Chiefs, the company tried to produce the image of a multi-model overhead-valve range by offering different equipment packages.

The Arrow, Model 149, was an overhead single with the following spec's: bore and

1948 Indian Chief, fully dressed. A new front-drive speedometer is apparent from the cable passing from the tank underside to the front wheel. These were the last mass-production Indians built in the historic State Street multi-story red brick "Wigwam" that Indian had occupied since 1907. (ROBIN MARKEY)

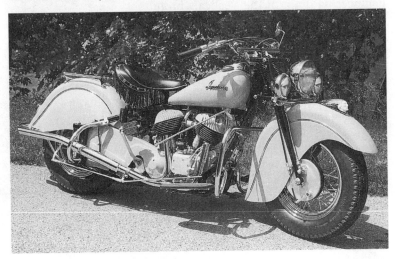

1948 Indian Chief. (DOUG MITCHEL)

1948 Indian Model 648 Daytona Scout. These were also termed "Big Base" Scouts, referring to an extension of the lower rear crankcase into a box shape that lowered crankcase pressure and reduced consequent power loss. Debates continue as to how many of these off-line race-shop built bikes were produced. The prevalent belief is that 25 complete Models 648 were assembled plus another 25 complete engines.

(MATT KEEVERS COLLECTION)

stroke, 2 3/8 and 3 inches; displacement 13.3 ci (218cc), four-speed transmission with left-side foot-shift, telescopic front fork, and standard rigid frame with plunger rear suspension optional at extra cost.

The Scout, Model 249, was an overhead-valve vertical twin with the following spec's: bore and stroke, 2 3/8 and 3 inches; displacement of 26.6 ci (436cc), four-speed transmission with left-side foot-shift, telescopic front fork and plunger rear suspension.

1949 Indian Arrow single. In the summer of 1948, Indian introduced the 13.3-ci (218cc) overhead-valve single-cylinder Arrow. Trendy features for the time were the telescopic fork and four-speed foot-shift transmission. An extra cost option was plunger rear suspension. (CLYDE EARL)

1949 Indian Scout (at right). Lacking only the Indian script tank decals, this final stage prototype represents the production configuration of the model. Seeking to mimic the historic success of the 1920 Scouts, the company chose the name "Scout" for the new 26.6-ci (436cc) overhead-valve vertical twin. Unfortunately, the engine displacement was 13 percent under the American racing limit of 30.50 ci (500cc) for overhead-valve motorcycles. (JACK ARMSTRONG)

1949 Indian Arrow. Close pitched fins and distinctive angled push rods produced a lovely engine. The carburetor isn't stock.

Prototype 1949 Indian Chief. The company advertised this foot-shift Chief for the 1949 season, but abandoned this program after only a handful of these bikes were completed in order to concentrate on production problems with the new singles and vertical twins. Veteran Indian riders and police departments howled at the loss of the long-running Chief. (EMMETT MOORE)

1950 Indian Warrior TT. In contrast to the unsuccessful road model vertical twins, the off-road Warrior TT enjoyed a good reputation among riders of dirt events. According to Indian advertising, Warrior TTs won more of these events in non-professional classes than any other marque and model. (EMMETT MOORE)

1950 Indian Chief. At last, a telescopic front fork graced the new "Blackhawk Eighty" Chief. The displacement was bumped up to 80 ci (1300cc) by increasing the stroke to a whopping 4 13/16 inches, while holding the bore at 3 1/4 inches. Fixed to the end of the crankshaft, a cam-loaded coil spring absorbed firing impulse shocks. The bulge in the forward section of the primary housing accommodated the shock absorber.

(IAN CAMPBELL)

1950 Indian Warrior. Priced above famous British 30.50-ci (500cc) vertical twins, and with the 1949 debacle well known among shoppers, the 1950 road model Warriors languished in dealer show rooms. (BOB SHINGLER)

1951 Indian Warrior. Only cosmetic changes were made to the 1951 road-going Warrior. (IAN CAMPBELL)

1951 police had roundly criticized the European riding stance required of the 1949 Scouts, so the police version satisfied the complaints via a raised saddle, high bars and footboards. Perhaps a dozen of these prototypes were finished before the company gave up on the idea. Note that the fenders are unique to this model. (EMMETT MOORE)

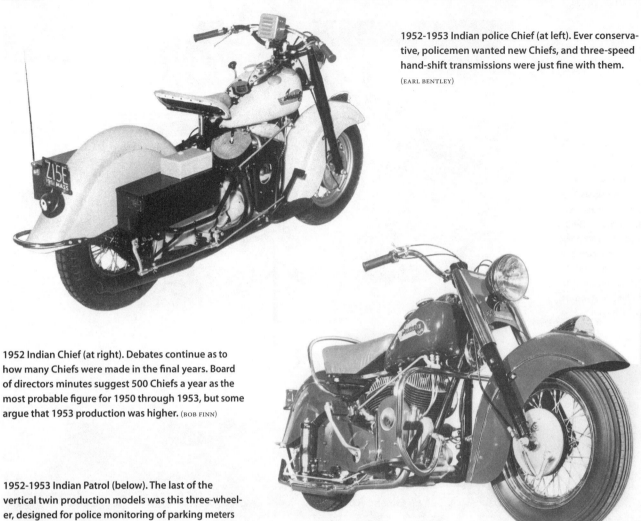

1952-1953 Indian police Chief (at left). Ever conservative, policemen wanted new Chiefs, and three-speed hand-shift transmissions were just fine with them. (EARL BENTLEY)

1952 Indian Chief (at right). Debates continue as to how many Chiefs were made in the final years. Board of directors minutes suggest 500 Chiefs a year as the most probable figure for 1950 through 1953, but some argue that 1953 production was higher. (BOB FINN)

1952-1953 Indian Patrol (below). The last of the vertical twin production models was this three-wheeler, designed for police monitoring of parking meters and for light hauling. (BOB FINN)

1952-1953 Indian Chief. Here's another 1952 advertising picture. The bench seat was in response to excessive saddle height—about 2 inches more—of the telescopic fork Chiefs. That outcome, in turn, had been caused by Indian not modifying the frame in 1950 but simply "jacking up" the front end when incorporating the 4-inch-longer telescopic forks. (BOB FINN)

1952-1953 Chief. From the 1953 sales brochure comes this picture. 1952-1953 cosmetics included the winged "Eighty" tank decals, and the skimpier front fender. The last Chiefs were a paradox. The design dated back to the 1920 Scout and the 1922 Chief. Indeed, some 1922 parts still were fitted to the 1953 model! On the other hand, excepting the BMW twins, Indian Chiefs remained as capable as any Harley-Davidson or other import in terms of reliable long-distance touring. There seemed, after all, to be merit in the age old American idiom: "There's no substitute for cubic inches." (BOB FINN)

IVER JOHNSON

The Iver Johnson Arms and Cycle Works of Fitchburg, Massachusetts, manufactured Iver Johnson motorcycles from 1907 through 1915. The motorcycles bristled with innovative features. In 1914, singles of 31 ci (510cc) and twins of 62 ci (1020cc) featured side-valve layout with unusual valve actuation by a sun and planet gear. The big V-twin had staggered crankpins so that firing impulses were evenly spaced.

1914 Iver Johnson 62 ci (1020cc) side-valve twin (at left). The leaf spring leading link front fork was of unique design. The frame was of "open" construction as the company termed it; this frame style was later termed "keystone" within the American industry. In this layout, the crankcase plugged the gap between the front and rear areas of the frame, so that the engine served as a stress-bearing member. This simplified engine removal and permitted a slightly lower placement of the power plant, which in turn increased handling stability. This example is a single-speed rigid frame model.

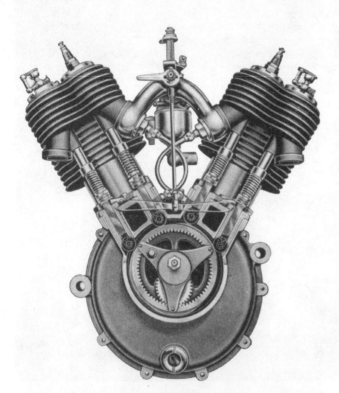

1914 Iver Johnson engine. The cam lobes are on the large geared ring. There are twice as many teeth on the large ring as on the pinion gear, so the necessary half-engine-speed resulted. At that time, the side-valve configuration was unusual in America. (GEORGE YAROCKI)

1914 Iver Johnson engine. Typical of the era, was the planetary two-speed transmission as used on the world's most popular car, the Ford Model T. Iver Johnson made their transmission distinctive by using bevel gears for the "planet" action. (GEORGE YAROCKI)

1914 Iver Johnson engine. The crankpins were offset so that the firing impulses were evenly spaced. This produced a sound like today's parallel twins rather than the popular "potato-potato-potato" sound typical of V-twins. (GEORGE YAROCKI)

1914 Iver Johnson engine. The worm-driven magneto was perhaps an extravagant feature, but typical of the company's spare-no-expense philosophy. (GEORGE YAROCKI)

1915 Iver Johnson. These motorcycles were splendidly finished with extensive polishing of the engine. (GEORGE YAROCKI)

{ J }

Jack and Heintz motorbike of the 1949-1955 period. The firm built only the motor kit.

Rather than the traditionally slippable belt drive, the Marman and Jack and Heintz used a motorcycle-style dry clutch.

JACK AND HEINTZ

The Jack and Heintz firm of Cleveland, Ohio, manufactured electrical and mechanical accessories for aircraft during World War II. After the war, a major engineering program included a prototype six-cylinder automobile and auxiliary power units for aircraft, but apparently none of these engines went into serial production. In the late forties, Jack and Heintz built components for the Marman motorbike firm of California. In 1949, Marman sold out to Jack and Heintz. The motorbikes continued in production through 1955 under the Jack and Heintz brand name. Leftovers were sold to a Long Island, New York, firm and sold as the JB Special.

JB SPECIAL

A solitary magazine ad from around 1955 provides the only data for the JB Special. These motorbikes were offered by the J. B. Special Company of Long Island, New York. These were leftovers of the Marman-designed motorbikes that Jack and Heintz had built through 1955. The only new feature appeared to be a girder front fork.

Beginning around 1959, Joseph Berliner imported Sachs-powered German lightweights and sold them as "J-Be Sachs." The Berliner corporation was located in the New York City metropolitan area. The JB Special may have been Berliner's first efforts as a national distributor.

A NEW
LIGHT
MOTORCYCLE
American Made

As easy to use as a Bicycle—the JB special is high performing, light weight and has all the qualities of a high powered motorcycle.

It has an air cooled 2 cycle 3½ H.P. engine with a cruising speed of 40 m.p.h. while getting 60 miles per gallon. The heavy duty transmission has a kick starter and chain drive. Two wheel expansion brakes insures safety.

Automotive type 6" multi plate dry disc clutch. only $250.00 FOB
Send check or M.O. F.O.B., plus tax & transportation, Long Island, N. Y.

For Free booklet & further information write:

J. B. SPECIAL Co.   42 Van Buren Street, Franklin Sq., L. I.

The JB Special. The machine is clearly a re-branded one, suggesting that it's a leftover Jack and Heintz. The line of succession seems to be: 1948-1948 Marman; 1949-1955, Jack and Heintz; circa 1955-?, JB Special.

(VINTAGE MOTOR BIKE CLUB)

JEFFERSON

The Jefferson was one of four interrelated marques. The first was the Kenzer-Waverly of Cambridge, Wisconsin. Kenzler-Waverly evolved into the Waverly Manufacturing Company, and production moved to Jefferson, Wisconsin. There, the machines were first termed "P.E.M.," after designer Perry E. Mack, then Jefferson, after the host city. See "Mack Engines."

JOHNSON MOTOR WHEEL

Louis, Harry, and Clarence Johnson of Chicago, Illinois, started building outboard motors in 1908. During World War I, the firm supplied a two-stroke horizontally opposed twin to the American Army for use in draining trenches and running generators. In 1917, the firm, now in South Bend, Indiana, began manufacturing the 154cc Johnson Motor Wheel based on the Army engine. Sales were initially brisk, but then declined through the end of production in 1921. In 1922 and 1923, the unit was built under license in England and sold in 154cc and 165cc versions as the "Economic." In 1935, the name and assets were purchased by Stephen F. Briggs and Ralph Evinrude, connected respectively to the well-known Briggs and Stratton small engine company and the Evinrude outboard motor firm.

JONAS

The Jonas was built around 1900-1903 in Milwaukee. From an advertisement: "We illustrate herewith the Jonas Motor Bicycle, lately brought out by the Jonas Cycle Co., 728 National Avenue, Milwaukee, Wis. They make them with 23 or 24 inch frame, cold drawn, seamless tubing, 28 inch wheels, tangent spokes, 1 5/8 inch single or double diameter tube tires. Motor is 2 H. P., and the machine is capable of a speed of 25 miles an hour. Weight complete, 85 pounds."

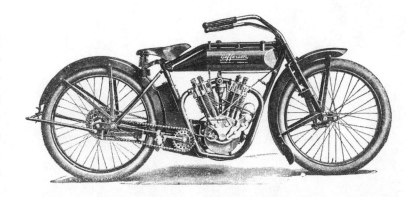

The Jefferson. After being advertised as the P.E.M. during the 1912 season, for 1913 the name was changed to Jefferson. The front and rear suspensions each consisted of a short swing-arm acting against a leaf spring set. The overhead-valve engine put the marque at the cutting edge. Displacement was approximately 61 cubic inches (1000cc). Production continued through 1914 under the Waverly name. (THE ANTIQUE MOTORCYCLE)

1919 Johnson Motor Wheel. The 154cc engine was a two-stroke horizontally opposed twin based on the engine Johnson had already been supplying to the American military for trench drainage. The engine sprocket was between the crankcase and the outside flywheel. Direct clutch-less drive was featured. The unit was built under license in England as the "Economic." (MOTORCYCLE AND BICYCLE ILUSTRATED)

A Jonas, circa 1900-03. (JIM DENNIE)

{K}

1902 Keating. Instead of a carburetor, a vaporizer was fitted under the tank. The hollow rear fender did double duty as the exhaust outlet. For 1902, single lever control replaced the 1901 arrangement of four separate levers. (JIM DENNIE)

1902 Keystone. From a period advertisement: "This motorcycle is manufactured by A. Mecky, 3535-9 Smedley Street, Philadelphia, Pa., and lists at $275. He uses a 2 1/4 H. P. De Dion motor and De Dion parts all through. It is a speedy little machine, is simply and durably built, and is an easy rider. (JIM DENNIE)

Ca 1902 Kimball. The bore and stroke of 2 1/2 and 4 inches yielded a displacement of 19.6 ci (322cc). The weight was 80 lbs. and the price was $200. (JIM DENNIE)

KEATING

The Keating was built in 1901 and 1902 by the Eisenhuth Horseless Vehicle Company, "the firm which took over the immense and magnificently equipped plant of the old Keating Bicycle Company at Middletown, Connecticut," reported *The Dealer and Repairman* in its April 1902 issue. The magazine cited the Keating bicycle as one of the leading makes.

KENZLER-WAVERLY

Engine designs of Perry E. Mack were announced in 1910 and offered for sale as proprietary engines to be put into frames and branded. The Kenzler company of Cambridge, Wisconsin, bought into the scheme and launched their Kenzler-Waverly motorcycle in 1911. This effort evolved into the Waverly Manufacturing Company. Refer to the following sections for pictures and additional information on the three other interrelated marques: Jefferson, P.E.M., and Waverly. See also "Mack Engines."

KEYSTONE

A. Mecky of Philadelphia, Pennsylvania, manufactured the Keystone motorcycle in 1902. The machine was apparently a clone of the successful Orient motorcycle.

KIMBALL

Kimball motorcycles were built around 1902 in Lynn, Massachusetts, by H L. Kimball. An unusual feature was the short wheelbase—apparently about 6 inches shorter than conventional pedal bikes.

KING AND QUICK

King and Quick motorcycles were built around 1901. A single picture in a period scrapbook is the only information found by the author.

KOKOMO

Kokomo motorcycles were built in 1911, in Kokomo, Indiana. In 1912, according to historian Stephen Wright (*The American Motorcycle 1869-1914*), Kokomo sold out to the Shaw Motor Works of Galesburg, Kansas.

Specifications cited in the May 18, 1911, Motorcycle Illustrated: "Model 1911; 3 1/2-hp engine, bore and stroke each 3 inches; mechanically operated valves; Schebler carburetor; ignition by Herz magneto; splash lubrication with sight feed; Bowden wire control by grips; V-belt transmission; reenforced loop frame. Shock absorbing fork with vanadium steel spring; wheelbase 56 inches; wheels 28 x 2 1/2 inches fitted with Kokomo studded tread tires; New Departure expanding band brake."

Circa 1901 King and Quick. (JIM DENNIE)

1911 21.2 cubic inch (347cc) Kokomo. Unusual for the era was the side-valve (Flathead) engine; almost all other motorcycles used inlet-over-exhaust (F-head) engines.
(THE ANTIQUE MOTORCYCLE)

{L}

Circa 1902 Lamson. (JIM DENNIE)

LaRay Power Cycle. Specifications: 1.9-hp Clinton four-stroke single-cylinder fan-cooled engine; automatic clutch and single-speed V-belt drive; kick-starter; LaRay girder fork with rubber band tension springing; 2-gallon fuel tank; lighting from an engine coil; front and rear brakes. (VINTAGE MOTOR BIKE CLUB)

Circa 1902 Leflem. No further data was found. With three control levers, riding it must have been a double handful!

(JIM DENNIE)

LAMSON

This picture of an early 1900s Lamson comes from a period scapbook No other information was found.

LARAY POWER CYCLE

In the mid 1940s, the LaRay Engineering and Equipment Company of Milwaukee, Wisconsin, was a small fabricator of steel tubing. In 1946 and 1947, the firm built the LaRay Power Cycle. LaRay fabricated the frames and fork, and installed the rest of the parts, which they bought from other manufacturers. These subcontractors and parts included: Clinton engines, Schwinn fenders and wheel rims, Sulky spokes and Messinger seats. Though the prototype had a Briggs and Stratton engine, the Clinton engine was chosen for production because Briggs and Stratton wouldn't put a lighting coil on its engine. The name "LaRay" was chosen because it combined the owners' first names, Larry and Ray (but the source didn't provide the last names). About 2,000 motorbikes were built. One famous outlet was New York City's Gimbel's department store, which was the arch-rival of Macy's. Near the end of 1947, LaRay went out of business due to tax problems with the Internal Revenue Service. All assets were auctioned off to settle the tax obligation.

LEFLEM

A picture in a period scrapbook is all the data uncovered on the obscure Leflem marque.

LIBERTY

The Liberty motorcycle was a standardization project of the U.S. Army, based on World War I experience. The attraction was to provide for logistics support of only one brand of motorcycle, rather than continuing to use large numbers of Indians, Harley-Davidsons and Excelsiors. A description of the motorcycle and pictures of the engine were provided in *Motorcycle and Bicycle Illustrated* for March 28, 1918. Plans called for the Liberty motorcycle to be built in the Stamford, Connecticut, factory previously used to build Schickel motorcycles. The proposed motorcycle would combine the best features of the three major American marques. Harley-Davidson was flattered by the choice of the Harley engine, with modifications, to power the Liberty. Excelsior's open-bottom "keystone" frame concept was selected for ease of engine removal and installation. Indian's contribution was unclear. When the war was over, the Liberty motorcycle was soon cancelled.

LIGHT

In 1905, the Light Manufacturing and Foundry Company of Pottstown, Pennsylvania, marketed an Indian clone it branded the "Light Thor-Bred." In 1907, the marque title was simplified to "Light," The Light was a clone of an updated Thor motorcycle that had evolved from an Indian clone to a model that was only very similar to the Indian, still with rearward sloping cylinder. In 1908, the Light company merged with Merkel, and the latter moved Merkel tooling and stocks from Milwaukee, Wisconsin, to Pottstown. The merger put into one factory the chain-driven Light and belt-driven Merkel marques.

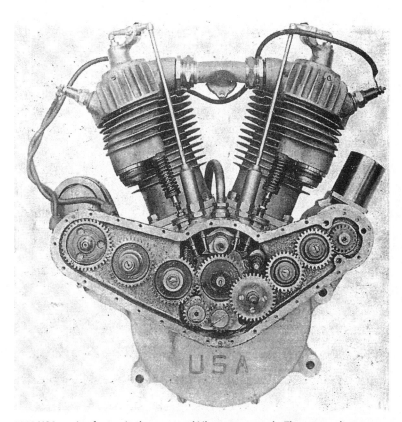

1918 USA engine for use in the proposed Liberty motorcycle. The power plant was basically a Harley-Davidson unit with two gear trains—one for the rear-mounted magneto and the other for the front-mounted generator. Although Indian supplied the large majority of motorcycles to the American army, apparently the Army had found the Harley engine to be more reliable. (GEORGE YAROCKI)

Circa 1909 Light. The so-called Thor engine is an Indian clone and appears to be the 30.46-ci (499cc) unit. For this relatively large single-cylinder engine, the frame had a straight front down tube instead of the curved tube used on smaller singles.

LIGHT THOR-BRED

One of many Indian clones, the Light Thor-bred was marketed by the Light Manufacturing & Foundry Company of Pottstown, Pennsylvania. The machines may also have been built in the Pottstown plant. Details of the arrangement between Indian and Aurora Automatic Machinery Company (Aurora, Illinois) are unknown, beyond the fact that Indian contracted its own design of engine to Aurora for manufacture, and that Aurora built their own Thor brand bikes

1905 15.85-cubic inch (260cc) Light Thor-Bred. From the April 1, 1905, *Cycle and Automobile Trade Journal*: "Made by Light Mfg. & Foundry Co., Union and Queen Streets, Pottstown, Pa. 22-inch frame; 2 x 28-inch tires; 42-inch wheelbase; single cylinder 2 19/32 (inch, bore) x 3 (inch, stroke), 1 3/4 H.P.; "Thor"motor; sight measuring lubrication; chain drive; fuel mileage 60; grip control; weight 98 lbs.; speed 30 miles per hour; price $210. Special feature: yielding and compensating sprocket; grip control of latest type." The special sprocket included two friction discs moderately tightened together, thus reducing the shock on the engine if the motorcycle suddenly stalled—a common problem when stopping in those clutch-less days.

(THE ANTIQUE MOTORCYCLE)

were initially identical to Indians. The host of Indian clones occurred because Aurora was selling all necessary components for jobbers to assemble and rebrand.

What is different about the tie-in with Light Thor-Bred is that the Pottstown firm was soon to design and build its own "Light" motorcycles, followed by its buying out of the Flying Merkel of Milwaukee, and the transfer of Merkel production to Pottstown. With these facts in mind, and the inclusion of the word "foundry" in the Pottstown company's title, one would think there were two possibilities. First, Light Manufacturing did some/all of the production jobs; second, as a minimum Light Manufacturing used its engineers to copy and refine the Indian design while planning for their own full fledged production. It was this engineering capability, however deployed with respect to the Indian clones, that ensured Light's (later, Merkel's) survival into the post Indian-clone era.

Incidentally, in this era of copycat production, there was much confusion among the public as to whether Indian or Thor had designed the most popular engine in American motorcycling. The clone companies invariably referred to these bought-in motors as "Thor" engines. Confusion must have abounded with the simultaneous existence of identical Indian, Thor, "Thor-Bred" and "Thoroughbred" motorcycles!

M-M (ALSO TERMED MARSH-METZ)

The Marsh-Metz company was created by the merger of the two independent motorcycle makers in 1906. The firm arranged to supply all their motorcycles to The American Motor Company of Brockton, Massachusetts, which sold them under the label "M-M." In 1909, singles featured a rearward-sloping cylinder forming part of the seat mast, and the crankcase also acting as a frame member. In 1910, a conventional vertical cylinder engine was fitted, but the frame was still of the open style, with the crankcase plugging the gap between the front and rear sections. In 1913, the American Motor Company sold M-M singles and 90-degree V-twins at retail outlets and wholesaled them to jobbers who sold then under various retail brand names. These included: American, Arrow, Haverford, National, and Peerless.

The 1910 M-M four hp single.

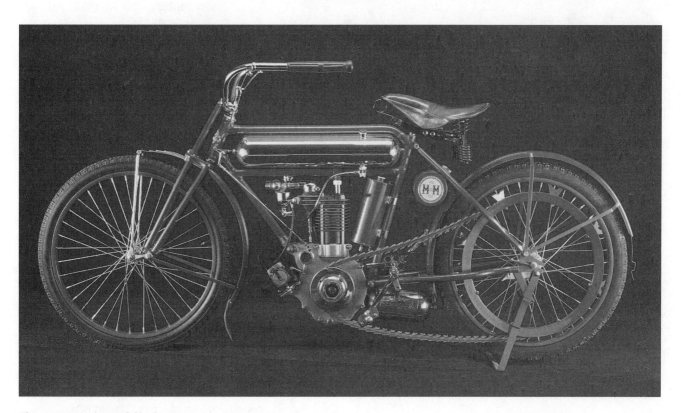

The 1910 M-M 4-hp model had a magneto ignition. (DOUG MITCHEL)

1913 M-M twin. The inherent smoothness of a 90-degree V-twin wasn't commonly understood by motorcyclists. (THE ANTIQUE MOTORCYCLE)

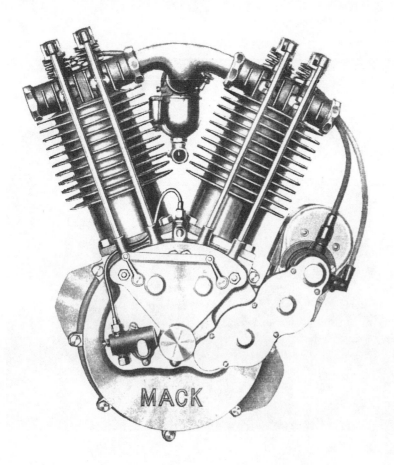

MACK ENGINES

Mack engines were designed by Perry E. Mack and used in Kenzler-Waverly, Waverly, and P. E. M. motorcycles in 1912, and in Jefferson motorcycles in 1913. All four were fundamentally the same, except for the name on the tank. These motorcycles were built in Jefferson, Wisconsin. When motorcycle production ceased at the end of 1913, the Universal Machinery Company of Milwaukee took up the manufacture and marketing of the engines, with the idea of selling them to motorcycle companies. This plan didn't succeed and the engines soon faded from the scene, like the motorcycles before them.

A Mack twin of circa 1914. Bore and stroke were 3 3/8 and 3 31/32 inches respectively, and the displacement was 60.94 ci (999cc). Companion singles were also offered, displacing 30.47 ci (499cc) and 34.95 ci (573cc). Outside of the Perry Mack designs, only Pope offered road model overheads in America during the 1910s. Harley-Davidson and Indian launched their first overhead-valve roadsters in 1936 and 1949, respectively. (THE ANTIQUE MOTORCYCLE)

MALTBY

A Maltby motorcycle was built around 1902 by F. D. Maltby of Brooklyn, New York. Whether the machine went into serial production is unknown. From the clipping in a period scrapbook: "F. D. Maltby of Brooklyn, New York, has completed a motorcycle which he offers for sale at $250 list. His motor is 1 1/4 hp, four cycle and drives a single chain and sprocket wheels. Speeds from 800 to 2200 r.p.m. are obtainable and are controlled by timing the spark or throttling mixture. The motor is attached to the seatpost and lower reach tubing by a system of locking sleeves and clamps. The sprocket wheels are moved about 3 inches backward and the crank case has backward projecting lugs, which support an eccentric sleeve with cranks and starting device. A half turn of the eccentric detaches the pedals from the motor."

Circa 1902 Maltby. (JIM DENNIE)

MANSON

Yet another Indian clone, the Manson was marketed in 1905 by the Fowler-Manson-Sherman Mfg. Company, 45-47 Fulton Street, Chicago. The company billed itself as a manufacturer, but, as noted under "Light Thor-Bred," we don't know the exact divisions of production and marketing tasks for these arrangements, which involved as a minimum the Aurora (Thor) concern, and, possibly, the Indian concern. Even if we knew the status for only one clone marque,

that wouldn't necessarily be the arrangement for another clone outfit.

What throws the subject into disarray is that Aurora was cloning the entire Indian motorcycle, not just the Indian-designed engine which it was contracted to produce for Indian. Was Aurora going it alone, or did Indian ship excess frames, forks, etc. to Aurora? Indian might even have shipped miscellaneous items to the clone companies. We just don't know. The Manson must have been short lived, as the author has found only a single 1905 reference that lists them.

From the April 1, 1905, *Cycle and Automobile Trade Journal* said of the Manson: "22 inch frame; G & J 2 inch tires; 46 inch wheelbase; single cylinder, 2 19/32 (inch, bore) x 3 (inch, stroke), 1 3/4 H.P. motor; chain drive with compensating and yielding sprocket; battery mileage 1500; fuel mileage about 75; grip control; weight 110 lbs.; speed from 5 to 50 miles an hour; price $210. Special features: made from the well known Thor parts." Apart from the weight and the peformance claimes, these specifications are identical to the same year's Light Thor-Bred, Moto-Raycycle, and Thoroughbred.

The circa 1905 Manson. (THE ANTIQUE MOTORCYCLE)

MARATHON

The Marathon was built in 1910 by L. E. Rhodes of Hartford, Connecticut. C. E. Baker and E. M. De Long collaborated on the design. Marathons featured a 27-cubic inch (443cc) two-stroke two-cylinder engine, a two-speed transmission and shaft drive. According to *The Bicycling World and Motorcycle Review*, the Marathon was the first American motorcycle to feature unit construction of the engine and transmission. Other unusual features: outside

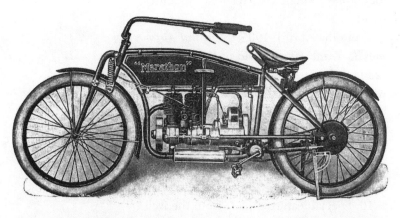

1910 Marathon. The shaft drive Marathon was powered by a two-stroke two-cylinder engine, with separate crankcase compression for each cylinder. Specifications: bore and stroke, 2 5/8 x 2 1/2 inches; displacement 27.06 cubic inches (443cc); maximum output, 7 hp; wheelbase, 60 inches; tires, 28 x 2 1/2 inches; Planhard carburetor; Bosch magneto. The two-speed sliding gear transmission linked the engine with the shaft drive through a 17-plate wet clutch. (GEORGE YAROCKI)

flywheel at the front of the engine; oil pump supply to crankshaft bearings and connecting rod big ends; muffler formed part of the lower frame and there was an exposed final drive shaft.

MARMAN

The two-stroke Marman flat-twin motorbike kit was marketed in 1947 and 1948 by the Marman Products Company of Inglewood, California. The components were designed and built by the Jack and Heintz Company of Cleveland, Ohio. According to Marman, the machine had been through a five-year development phase. Marman Products ceased operation in 1948, and production was taken up by Jack and Heintz.

A 1947 ad stated: "Positive clutch, automotive type multiple plate, dry disc clutch allows immediate pickup without pedaling and easy idling at stops. Steel cable V-belt throughout. Top pickup, cruising, and climb ability, gear ratios set to give exceptional speed, easy cruising speed of 30-35 miles per hour and superior hill climbing ability. Over 100 miles per gallon.....Profit of $32.40 on every Twin sale....National advertising in *Popular Science, Popular Mechanics*, and other selected magazines...."

1948 Marman Twin. Marman claimed it had 3 1/2 hp and a top speed of 30-35 mph.

(THE ANTIQUE MOTORCYCLIST)

MARSH

Motorcycles under the Marsh label were manufactured from 1900 through 1906 by the Motor Cycle Manufacturing Company of Brockton, Massachusetts. According to *The Dealer and Repairman* magazine of April, 1902, the Marsh company was one of the oldest in the American industry. In 1906, Marsh merged with the Metz motorcycle company to form Marsh-Metz. The motorcycles were branded "M-M" and are discussed under that heading.

1902 Marsh. Specifications: Weight, lbs.; wheelbase 45 inches; bore and stroke of 2 5/8 x 2 3/4 inches; displacement, 14.88 ci (244cc); maximum output, 2 1/4 hp. (JIM DENNIE)

W. T. Marsh on a circa 1902 racer. The engine produced up to 6 hp. The motorcycle was clocked through a 1-mile course at an average speed of 57.5 mph. (JIM DENNIE)

1903 Marsh. Obvious advances included a larger engine carried lower in the frame, and the use of the engine as a stress-bearing frame member. (JIM DENNIE)

1904 Marsh. The marque rested on its laurels in 1904. (DOUG MITCHEL)

MARVEL

Marvel motorcycles were built by a Hammondsport, New York, company founded by motorcycle and aviation pioneer Glenn Curtiss. Though Glenn was building his well-respected Curtiss marque in the same city, these were two separate factories, reports historian Stephen Wright. Marvel ads listed Hammondsport as the company location and boasted of using Curtiss components. Perhaps by this time, Glenn Curtiss was aware that aviation was his longterm future, and it would be wise to disassociate himself from the motorcycle trade. Marvels were built from 1910 through 1913.

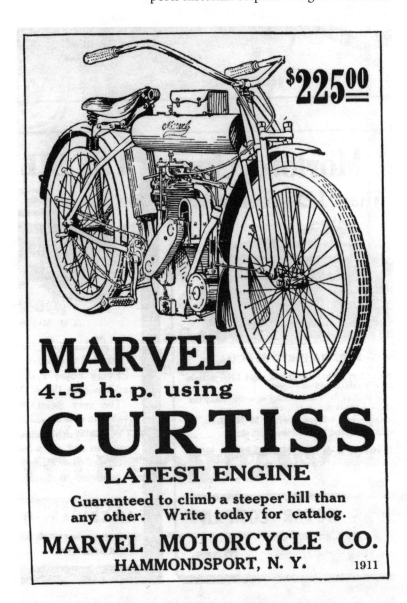

This 1912 ad makes clear the Marvel and Curtiss tie in. (BOB KAROLEVITZ)

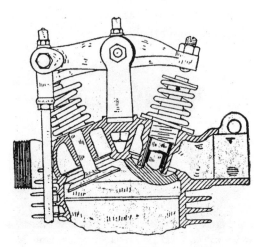

1912 Marvel engine detail. From the December 28, 1911, *Motorcycle Illustrated*: " Following Curtiss motor practice, both the Marvel and Curtiss motors use the overhead-valve construction … A single push-rod and rocker operates both valves, by an upward motion beyond a certain point for the exhaust and by downward motion for the inlet, two faces being cut on a single cam to effect this. The exhaust valve, on the right, has a cylindrical shield to protect its stem from the burned gasses as they leave the cylinder, and the seats of both valves are integral with the cylinder castings, as are also the guides. Separator roller-bearings are used in Marvel motors, and there is a ½-inch offset to the crankshaft." (MOTORCYCLE ILLUSTRATED)

MAYO

The Mayo Damper Company of Pottstown, Pennsylvania, built Mayo motorcycles from 1905 through 1908. Early models were as shown in the illustration. In 1905, a 24.5-ci (401cc) single and a 49-ci (802cc) V-twin were offered. The frame design was changed to the loop style in 1907.

M-B

M-B motorcycles were produced by the Morse-Beauregard Manufacturing Company, 460 Mount Elliot Avenue, Chicago. The machine was an inline T-head twin, with shaft drive. T-head engines featured side-mounted inverted valves, with inlet and exhaust valves on opposite sides of the combustion chamber. Production occurred for the 1912 and 1913 seasons. The 1912 M-B was a single-speeder; the 1913 M-B had a two-speed sliding-gear transmission.

MCDONALD

According to *The Encyclopedia of the Motorcycle* (Hugo Wilson), the McDonald was built around 1905 in Chicago. A period scrapbook clipping is here quoted: "A new motorcycle has recently been placed on the market by McDonald Motor Manufacturing Company, Room 310, No. 167 Dearborn St., Chicago, Illinois. This machine has a patented spring frame of their own design and 20 inches high. The wheelbase is 53 inches and 26 inches in diameter. Goodrich detachable tires 2 1/4 inch cross section are used and both wheels have steel rims. The mudguards are also of steel...."

Circa 1905 Mayo. The 24.5-ci (401cc) F-head engine was rated at 2 hp. (JIM DENNIE)

1912 M-B. Specifications: 50-cubic inch (819cc) T-head twin-cylinder engine; output, 6½-9 hp; keystone frame; wheels/tires, 28 x 2½ inches; wheelbase $275.
(MOTORCYCLE ILLUSTRATED)

1905 McDonald. Specifications: rigid front fork; swinging-arm rear suspension; Thor 2 1/4-hp Thor engine; Thor coaster brake, 1.15-gallon fuel tank sufficient to run the machine 80 miles; sufficient oil supply to run the machine 250 miles; weight, 110 lbs.; price, $210. (JIM DENNIE)

1905 Meadowbrook. From the April 1, 1905, *Cycle and Automobile Trade Journal*: "22 inch frame; 1 1/2-inch tires; wheels, 26 and 28 inches; 44-inch wheelbase; single cylinder , 2 3/16 (inch, bore) x 3 (inch, stroke), about 1 ½ H.P.; splash lubrication; belt drive; battery mileage, about 1,000; fuel mileage, 70; switch grip control; weight about 60 lbs.; speed, 30 miles; price, $150. Special feature: automatic carburetor."

(JIM DENNIE)

1917 Merkel Motor Wheel. A keynote feature of the unit was ease of installation. The entire assembly slipped right into place on a standard American bicycle. The little overhead-valve engine was ahead of its time.

(THE ANTIQUE MOTORCYCLE)

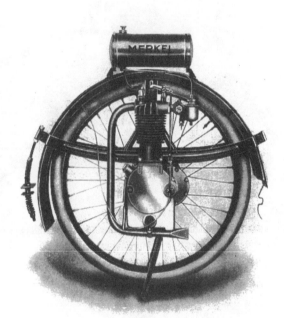

1917 Merkel Motor Wheel. The biggest drawback to the layout was difficulty in fixing flats (see text). The units sold initially for $75 and later for $85, at a time when $300 would buy a new large motorcycle. This contraption was relatively expensive.

(THE ANTIQUE MOTORCYCLE)

MEADOWBROOK

In 1905, Meadowbrook motorcycles were the product of Meadowbrook Cycle Company, Hempstead, Long Island, New York. Meadowbrooks had a distinctive design, featuring a bicycle style so-called diamond frame, but with the 9.87-cubic inch (162cc) F-head (inlet-over-exhaust) engine underslung between the two lower rear frame tubes. Production must have been brief; there was no unearthed documentation for any year but 1905. In a world full of new $210 motorcycles, the Meadowbrook concern dared to rock the boat with a sales price of only $150.

MERKEL MOTOR WHEEL

The following data comes by way of the late Jim Lucas of the Antique Motorcycle Club of America. Around 1902, Joe Merkel of Milwaukee, Wisconsin, designed a bicycle motor attachment. Pictures and information on this early effort, have not been found.

After designing Flying Merkel motorcycles, and with the end of that marque becoming obvious, in late 1916 Merkel introduced his Motor Wheel. Joe Merkel's new company was first located in Flushing, New York, and then in New York City. The factory was an assembling operation because all the components were subcontracted. Some parts were off-the-shelf items, such as the Splitdorf magneto and Eclipse wheel hubs. Merkel's goal with this motor wheel was to provide in-line thrust instead of off-center thrust as on the Smith and the Briggs & Stratton designs. He added the advancement of an overhead-valve engine. But in achieving in-line thrust, the wheel and engine became effectively inseparable so that fixing a flat required removal of the complete motor wheel assembly from the bicycle frame. To mitigate that problem, Merkel sold butt-ended inner tubes that could be removed and replaced with the wheel and tire in place.

After less than two years in operation,

the Merkel Motor Wheel company went bankrupt in late 1918. The giant Indian company purchased the assets and placed the Motor Wheel on the market around 1920. Indian modified the device to accept an external multi-disk clutch mounted to an extension of the camshaft. Production halted in 1922.

MERKEL

Merkel motorcycles were manufactured in three locations and were known by three names. From 1902 through 1908, the motorcycles were built in Milwaukee, Wisconsin. The name "Merkel" was used in press releases, advertisements and sales literature, while the tank sides displayed "The Merkel." In October, 1908, Merkel merged with the Light Manufacturing and Foundry Company of Pottstown, Pennsylvania, with the resulting trade name of "Merkel-Light."

The new company hired a team of five racing stars, including Stanley Kellog and Charles (later, "Fearless") Balke, who subsequently gained fame as Indian stars. Early 1909 models bore the legend "Merkel" on the tank sides. Perhaps during the 1909 season, the tank legend was changed to "Merkel-Light." At last, a sprung front fork was featured, which was of the leading link design. During 1909, advertising began featuring the term "Flying Merkel," but this wasn't applied to the tank sides. All 1910 models bore the double name "Merkel-Light." Merkel entered the record books when Fred Whittler rode 50 miles over a 1/3-mile Los Angeles board track, averaging 74 mph.

In May of 1911, the Miami Cycle and Manufacturing Company of Middletown, Ohio, purchased Merkel-Light and moved production to Middletown. The tank legend became "Flying Merkel." The Miami company dropped the expensive factory racing team but continued to give minor support to a couple of factory workers who were weekend warriors. One of them, Maldwyn Jones, was robbed of the 1913 200-

1902 Merkel. The F-head engine exhausted into the front down tube, a popular fashion of the time as also seen on Armac, Metz, Royal Pioneer, and Wagner motorcycles. The frame was also of standard pedal bike style, a feature shared with such makes as Mayo, Mesco and Thomas Auto-Bi. Relatively small, the engine had a bore and stroke of 2 5/8 inches and a displacement of 14.2 ci (233cc). The cooling fin surfaces, bragged Merkel, totaled 267 square inches. As the aluminum crankcase was only 3 inches thick, ordinary bicycle pedal cranks were fitted. These machines were made in lots of 25, and prompt delivery was guaranteed. (JIM DENNIE)

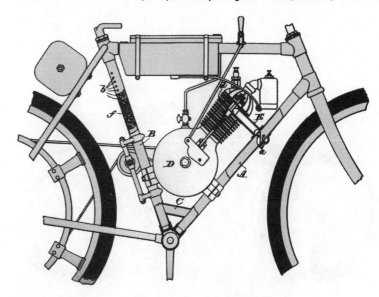

1902 Merkel. Another view of the 1902 configuration as shown in a patent application. The inlet valve was suction operated and termed "automatic." (UNITED STATES PATENT OFFICE)

1903 Merkel. Larger fuel and oil tanks, though separate, were mounted so as to present an integrated appearance. (JIM DENNIE)

1907 Merkel 2 1/4-hp model. Few, if any, substantive changes were made since 1903. Price: $155. (GEORGE YAROCKI)

mile road race National Championship by sloppy scoring; the error was later corrected, but the official results weren't changed.

The 1913 season saw the last major design improvements. Valve actuation was finally achieved by pushrods instead of cylinder suction. The frame was more robust and featured a large single spring unit for rear wheel suspension instead of the earlier twin small springs. The new fuel tank was more attractive. A spring-actuated self-starter and a two-speed planetary transmission were offered.

Flying Merkels continued in production until the plug was pulled in 1917. Only detail changes were made in the remaining years. Production stoppage was largely the result of World War I, which ended the availability of German Hess-Bright ball bearings used throughout the engine. The war also chilled the buying impulse of many potential customers and was a major factor in the disappearance of dozens of American marques at this time.

1907 Merkel-3 hp model (above). Though markedly new in appearance, this new model retained the ancient features of a rigid front fork and exhaust through the frame. Price: $185. (GEORGE YAROCKI)

1910 Merkel-Light Model A. The 2 1/4 to 2 3/4-hp Indian-designed, but Thor-branded, engine is the same 19.3 ci (316cc) unit used in the 1910 Indian range. Characteristic of this small single was the lightweight frame with curved front down tube. On all 1910 models, double-grip wire control was emphasized. The cited speed range was 5 to 40 mph. From the catalog: "Certain minor features have simply been eliminated to bring the price down to $150." Finish: Rubens Red; option, black. This was the only 1910 model with unsprung rear wheel, and the only model with the old-style leading link front fork. (GEORGE YAROCKI)

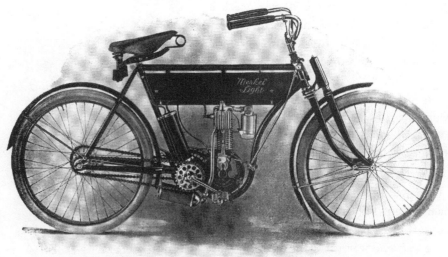

1910 Merkel-Light Racer. From the catalog: "Our two Special Models are essentially speed machines in every particular. The greatest care and skill is exercised in the designing and construction. They are built and assembled under the direct supervision of our Mr. Merkel. They are the latest and lightest possible rigid frame construction. Every ounce of superfluous weight is removed and their entire construction in every minute detail is designed to develop the greatest possible speed." (THE ANTIQUE MOTORCYCLE)

1910 Merkel Model V. Two engine sizes were offered, These were 53.92 ci (884cc) and 60.86 ci (997cc). Look closely at the front fork. At first glance, the motorcycle appears unsprung. However, the front fork was a telescopic unit and the rear wheel was a swinging-arm layout. All 1910 road model Merkels had these features except the built-to-a-price Model A. The finish was orange or optional Royal Blue. Price was $325 for the 7-hp model and $300 for the 6-hp version. (THE ANTIQUE MOTORCYCLE)

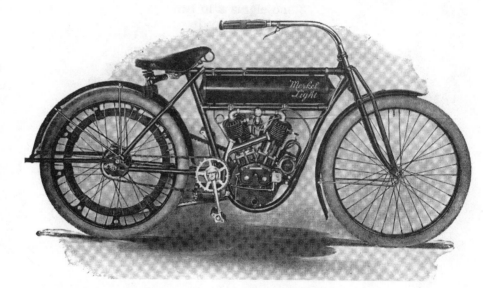

1910 Merkel valve gear. Beginning in 1908, German ball bearings were used throughout Merkel-designed engines, including the camshafts. This was the last year of the externally mounted oil pump, which was driven off the front cam gear.

(THE ANTIQUE MOTORCYCLE)

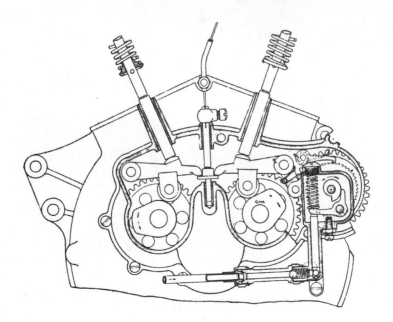

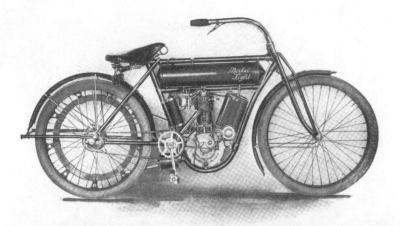

1910 Merkel Model W with battery ignition. Features included a 30.43-ci (499cc) engine, options of battery or magneto ignition and front and rear suspensions. On all 1910 road models, Merkel claimed the rear (and only) band brake was improved by the elimination of all internal components. Fuel tanks were larger on all 1910 models except the Model A.

(THE ANTIQUE MOTORCYCLE)

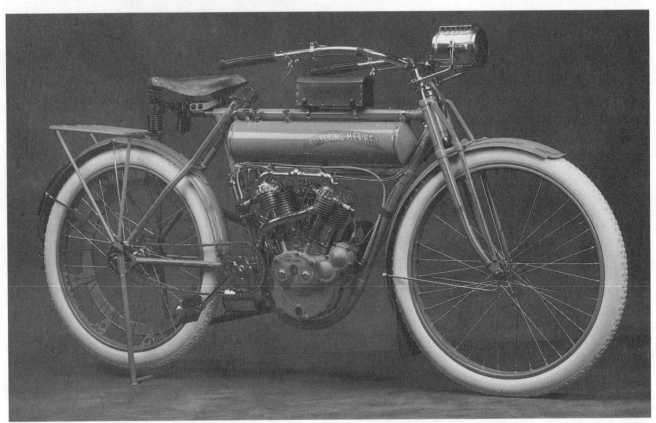

1911 Merkel Model V or VS. This view more clearly reveals the telescopic front fork. (DOUG MITCHEL)

1913 Flying Merkel "Yellow Jacket" Model. The visionary 1913 models were extensively reworked. This top of the line model was billed as the only self-starting two-speed motorcycle in the world. Since a starter was provided, the bicycle pedals were removed. (GEORGE YAROCKI)

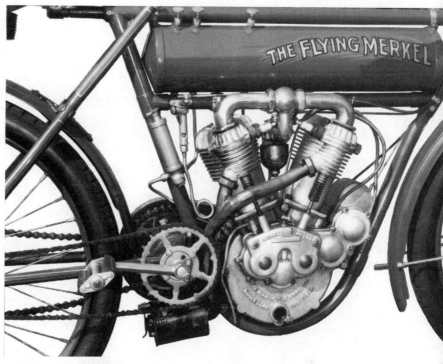

1913 Flying Merkel self-starter. The unit was basically a large scroll-style clock spring. The spring was wound tight by the first few moments of engine operation. Restarts after short stops were a snap. The rider simply pressed on the pedal to release the spring pressure. But initial starts, especially on cold days, risked depletion of the spring action before starting was achieved. For this reason, there was a removable cap so that a hand crank could be fitted for starting . There were a lot of warranty claims involving the starter, but it continued to be offered into 1915, and perhaps until the end in 1917. (PACIFIC MOTORCYCLIST)

1911 Merkel Model V or VS. In 1911, the oil pump was moved inside the cam case. Automatic inlet valves were still featured.

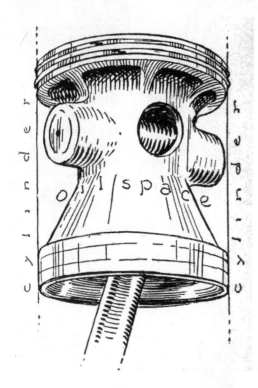

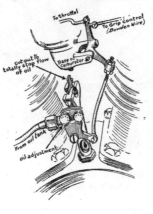

1913 Flying Merkel throttle-controlled oil pump operating mechanism. (PACIFIC MOTORCYCLIST)

1913 Flying Merkel piston. Merkel introduced this unusual "hour glass" piston to reduce friction without losing combustion pressure.

(PACIFIC MOTORCYCLIST)

1914 Flying Merkel Model 471. This is the economy single-speed chain-drive twin without the self-starter. It sold for $225. The footboards were a $5 accessory on this model. The economy single-speed belt-drive Model 470 was also priced at $225. The top-of-the-line Model 473 with self-starter and two-speed planetary transmission sold for $290. This example was apparently a late-season model, as it has the front and rear suspension rubber boots advertised as new for 1915.

(MERKEL SALES LITERATURE)

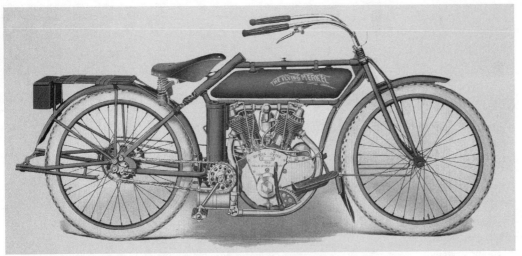

1915 Flying Merkel Model 575. For the 1915 season, as in 1914, only detail changes were applied. These included standard footboards and rubber boots for the front and rear suspensions. (MERKEL SALES LITERATURE)

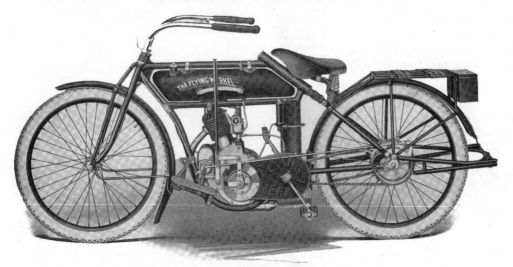

1915 Flying Merkel gear set. Many 1914 marques were available with optional two-speed planetary transmissions.

(MERKEL SALES LITERATURE)

1915 Flying Merkel Model 541. This 5 1/2-hp chain-drive single-speed model was listed at $200. Footboards were standard, but the luggage carrier was an accessory. 1915 finishes were Flying Merkel Orange and optional No. 17 National Blue. (MERKEL SALES LITERATURE)

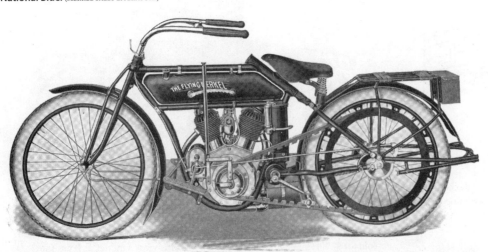

1915 Flying Merkel Model 570. The $225 belt-drive single-speed model was rated at 9 hp, complete with footboards. The luggage carrier was a $5 accessory. (MERKEL SALES LITERATURE)

MESCO

In 1905, the Motor Bicycle Equipment & Supply Company, MESCO, located at the corner of Main and Allen Streets in Buffalo, New York, offered a motorbike attachment. This was claimed to fit any pedal bicycle. No other production years have been verified. The Mesco pictured in *Cycle and Automobile Trade Journal* on April 1, 1905, was identical to prior years' Reliance motorcycles made in Addison, New York. The relationship between the two New York firms continued for several more years, culminating in MESCO taking over Reliance production when Reliance ceased operations in 1908, according to historian Stephen Wright.

1905 MESCO MOTOR BICYCLE POWER OUTFIT. From the April 1, 1905, *Cycle and Automobile Trade Journal*: "1 3/4 H.P., 2 3/4 (inch, bore) x 2 5/8 (inch, stroke) (15.6 cubic inches, 255cc); splash lubrication; chain, belt, or friction drive; gasoline and oil tank capacity, 100 miles; spark control in grip; furnished with wiring, levers, etc., to fasten to frame; weight of complete outfit, 50 lbs.; speed, 30 miles per hour; price, $75." (JIM DENNIE)

METZ

Charles Metz manufactured the Metz motorcycle in Waltham, Massachusetts, from 1902 through October, 1905, according to historian Stephen Wright. Metz's productions conveyed exceptional quality through the extensive use of polishing and bright plating. He was apparently both a skilled engineer and a visionary, as he built successful racing machines well before motorcycle racing reached its ultimate popularity. In late 1905, reported Wright, Metz merged his interest with the Marsh brothers and production was moved to Marsh headquarters in Brockton, Massachusetts. Thereafter, the motorcycles were termed "Marsh-Metz," and, later, "M-M."

1903 Metz. The general layout with the low-slung engine was ahead of its time. The exhaust pipe was routed into the front down tube; this was all the rage at that time. Other marques with this exhaust layout included Armac, Merkel, Royal Pioneer and Wagner. The large frame tubing allowed these members to do double duty. The front down tube captured the exhaust, while the seat mast housed the batteries. These two frame tubes were integral with the crankcase. The engine sprocket was carried on a shock-absorbing device. (JIM DENNIE)

1905 16.2-cubic inch (266cc) Metz Roadster. From the April 1, 1905, *Cycle and Automobile Trade Journal*: "22 inch frame; 2 1/4 x 28 inch detachable tires; 51 inch wheelbase; single cylinder 2 5/8 (inch, bore) x 3 (inch, stroke) 2 H.P. motor; force pump lubrication; direct drive by all nickel-steel chain; battery mileage, 1500; fuel mileage, 120; double grip control; weight, 110 lbs.; speed, 5 to 46 miles per hour; price, $210." (THE ANTIQUE MOTORCYCLE)

1905 32.4 cubic inch (532cc) Metz Double Cylinder Racer. From the April 1, 1905, *Cycle and Automobile Trade Journal*: "22 inch frame; 2 1/4 x 28 inch detachable tires; 51 inch wheelbase; 2 cylinder 2 5/8 (bore) x 3 (stroke) inch 4 H.P. motor; force pump lubrication; direct drive by all nickel-steel chain; battery mileage, 1500; fuel mileage, 100; double grip control; weight, 108 lbs. for racing, 120 for road; speed, 60 miles per hour; price, $275. (THE ANTIQUE MOTORCYCLE)

1915 Miami Motor Bicycle. The Motor Bicycle was designed from the ground up. Although featuring pedals for ease of starting and perhaps to suggest docility to skeptical parents, the little job was in reality a small motorcycle. The name "Motor Bicycle" was probably an attempt to suggest safety. Apart from the listed weight of 125 lbs. and the obvious side-valve engine, no other data has been found. (THE ANTIQUE MOTORCYCLE)

MIAMI MOTOR BICYCLE

The Miami Motor Bicycle was a product of the same Middletown, Ohio, company that manufactured the Flying Merkel Motorcycle. The machine was a complete functioning unit, rather than a motor attachment. The product line was launched at the January, 1915, New York City motorcycle show. The Miami Cycle and Manufacturing Company left the motorcycle business in 1917 and the Motor Bicycle probably expired at the same time.

Circa 1902 Michigan. (JIM DENNIE)

MICHAELSON

Michaelson motorcycles were built from 1913 through 1915 by the Shapiro-Michaelson Motorcycle Company of Minneapolis, Minnesota. Designer Joe Michaelson had designed Minneapolis motorcycles from 1908 through 1913. Michaelson singles were similar to the better-known Minneapolis models. Michaelsons had a forward-sloping cylinder, whereas Minneapolis singles had a vertical cylinder. Both featured unit construction of engine and transmission. A Michaelson V-twin appeared to use Spacke proprietary cylinders and inlet manifold. The engine was mounted "backwards," so that the inlet and exhaust manifolds were on the left side of the motorcycle.

MICHIGAN

The Michigan was built around 1902. No data has been found, other than a single picture in a period scrapbook.

MILITAIRE (ALSO MILITOR)

The Militaire marque claimed to be an automobile rather than a motorcycle! This tied in with the design of the machine which was that of a purely sidecar arrangement. The single-cylinder machine was previewed in 1910 and launched in 1911 with the marque title of "Militor." For 1912, the cooling system was changed from forced air to circulating water.

In 1913, the concept was radically reworked, with power coming from an inline 68-ci (1114cc) four-cylinder F-head engine. The lower crankcase did double duty as the frame! The design was licensed to The Champion Motor Car Company of Saint Louis, Missouri, and the firm sold the machine for a few months under the name Champion.

When the Champion company ceased production, Mr. N. R. Sinclair of Buffalo, New York, purchased the rights and assets, and set up the Militaire Autocycle Company. The design was improved by a more shapely fuel tank and the mounting of the saddle on a telescoping tube that permitted a wide variation in saddle height. The Buffalo company went bankrupt in 1917.

The cause was next taken up by the Militor Corporation of New Jersey, which may have based its hopes on army business now that America had entered World War I. Army trials weren't impressive and only a few Militors were purchased. In 1919, the New Jersey firm sold out to automobile makers Knox Motors of Springfield, Massachusetts. One suspects that Knox never got production going, because rights and assets were sold in 1920 to the Bullard Machine Tool Company, where the final stage of production began in the Bridgeport, Connecticut, factory. In the roughly 10 years of the concept, five different manufacturing firms had taken turns losing money!

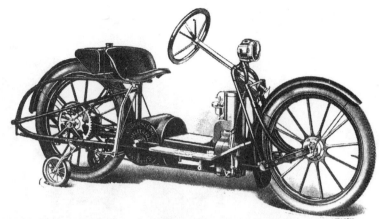

1910 prototype Militor. This fanciful vehicle appeared in a December 1910 advertisement. The picture represents the company philosophy, which was to build a unique vehicle that wouldn't be confused with conventional motorcycles. Hub center steering, front and rear suspension, chain drive and small balancing wheels are obvious. The single-cylinder 29-ci (480cc) F-head engine was air cooled by a fan. Magneto ignition was featured. Friction drive linked the drive shaft and drive sprocket. Other technical details are unknown. (BOB KAROLEVITZ)

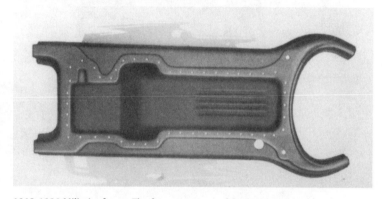

1913-1920 Militaire frame. The frame was part of the lower crankcase. (BRUCE LINSDAY)

1913 Champion (later, Militaire). The four-cylinder F-head engine displaced 68 ci (1114cc). Full shaft drive replaced the earlier combination shaft and chain arrangement. Drive was through a three-speed transmission. The price was $300. (BOB KAROLEVITZ)

Circa 1920 Militor. The new name arrived in 1917 after manufacturing was taken up by a fourth company! Engine size had grown to 80 ci (1306cc) in the 1913-1919 era, and then to 87.5 ci (1434cc).

Circa 1920 Militor. With the larger engine size came the new overhead-valve configuration.

1909 Minneapolis twin. Power was delivered through a two-speed countershaft transmission. The marque was one of the first American motorcles—perhaps the first—with this feature. (BRUCE LINSDAY)

MINNEAPOLIS

Minneapolis motorcycles were manufactured from 1908 through 1915 in Minneapolis, Minnesota. The firm was connected to the Michaelson marque of 1913-1915 in that both were designs of Joe Michaelson. Later Minneapolis singles featured a vertical cylinder; Michaelson singles had a forward-sloping cylinder. Initially, Minneapolis bikes were clones of the 1908 Thor, including the girder fork. In 1909, Minneapolis introduced a two-speed countershaft transmission, the first ever offered on an American motorcycle. Another new 1909 Minneapolis feature was a leading link front fork. In either 1910 or 1911, Minneapolis brought out side-valve engines, making them one of the few American marques to use this layout. The innovation continued with the 1911 introduction of the first unit construction motorcycles built in America.

1911 Minneapolis power plant. This was the first American motorcycle with unit construction of the engine and transmission. Minneapolis was also among the earliest American side-valve motorcycles, preceded only by Reading-Standard, Pierce and Reliance. Minneapolis defied styling convention by placing the valves on the left side of the engine.

(THE ANTIQUE MOTORCYCLE)

1909 Minneapolis twin. The engine was built by Thor. Minneapolis added the styling touch of situating the engine in the conventional manner, as opposed to the Thor arrangement of a sloping front cylinder and vertical rear cylinder. In 1909, Minneapolis introduced this leading link fork. (BRUCE LINSDAY)

1911 Minneapolis Model N "Big 5." The name signi-fied the maximum rated output of 5 hp. The bore and stroke were 3 1/2 and 3 3/4 inches, yielding a displace-ment of 36.08 ci (591cc). The price was $300. (THE AN-TIQUE MOTORCYCLE)

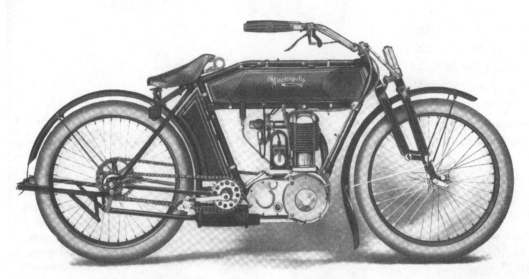

1911 Minneapolis Model NB. At $265, this was the firm's economy model single-speed bike.
(THE ANTIQUE MOTORCYCLE)

1915 Minneapolis commercial delivery outfit. Most American motorcycle firms had little success marketing motorcycles for business use, but in the increasingly competitive industry, even such small sales were important to factories. (DOUG MITCHEL)

MITCHELL

The Mitchell was manufactured from 1901 through 1906, first by the Wisconsin Wheel Works, then by the Mitchell Motor Car Company of Racine, Wisconsin. On August 22, 1902, in Chicago, Mitchell rider A. A. Hansen covered 634 1/4 miles on the Garfield Park Track for the first American 24-hour record. From the April 1, 1905, *Cycle and Automobile Trade Journal*: "22 inch frame; 2 inch tires; wheelbase 55 inches; single cylinder, 3 1/2 (inch, bore) x 4 (inch, stroke) 3 1/2 H.P. motor; gravity feed lubrication; belt drive; battery mileage, 1000; fuel mileage, 60; spark control; weight, 160 lbs.; speed, 60 miles per hour; price, $175. Special features: Grip control, chain washer belt; 10 gauge frame; long wheel base."

MOHS

The Mohs Seaplane Corporation of Madison, Wisconsin, built a small motorcycle in the 1960s. The name was "Model 95 Ultra-lite." The exact production span wasn't found by the author, but 1964 sales lit-

erature was located. Sometime thereafter, Mohs sold the rights to Atchison Products of Crystal Lake, Illinois. Atchison marketed the machine as the Starlite.

Mohs was an unusual firm, to put it politely. One of their products was a sidecar that did double-duty as a canoe. An article in Hemmings Motor News said that the Mohs designed Ostentatienne—your guess is as good as mine—Opera Sedan was the ugliest car ever built. It came with a naugahyde exterior covering. One can't help wondering if their seaplanes would fly. Or float.

1905 38.48-cubic inch (630cc) Mitchell. This motorcycle was also sold by Geer as the Blue Bird model, differing only in the fuel tank, oil tank, and ignition coil.
(THE ANTIQUE MOTORCYCLE)

1964 Mohs Model 95 Ultra-lite. It had Chrysler two-stroke single-cylinder 98cc (6 ci) engine, needle and ball bearings throughout and pull-cord starter (no pedals). According to the company: "40 mph top speed, 0-30 mph acceleration in less than 10 seconds with 200-lb. rider. Thread traffic effortlessly. Fan cooled engine allows indefinite idling periods."

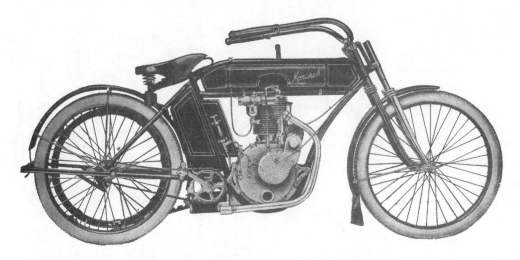

Circa 1912-15 Monarch. From the unusually large engine, and the then hefty output claim of 5 hp, the engine capacity was probably about 37 ci (600cc). (BOB KAROLEVITZ)

Circa 1949 Monark Super Twin. The two-stroke twin was predictably smooth. However, lack of low- and mid-range torque made it less capable on hills than the rival four-stroke single-cylinder Whizzers.

(GEORGE STRATTON)

Circa 1949 Monark Super Twin. Similar in concept to the Marman (Jack and Heintz), the two-stroke twin Monark differed in one important aspect: Monark, already a builder of bicycles, offered the complete Monark motorbike ready to ride.

(GEORGE STRATTON)

MONARCH *(Chicago, Westfield)*

The Pope family of motorcycles included the Monarch brand. These machines were initially Indian clones. The cloned Monarch line was offered around 1905. The motorcycle family was sold under various names already in use by Pope's bicycle empire. These variously labeled machines were built in Chicago and Westfield, Connecticut, according to regional brand significance. Refer to the Crescent entry for a picture.

MONARCH *(Oswego)*

The Ives Motorcycle Corporation manufactured Monarch motorcycles from 1912 through 1915. These were actually rebranded Reliance motorcycles, that make having gone under in 1910. Singles of 30.50 (500cc) and 37 ci (600cc) and twins of 61 ci (1000cc) constituted the lineup.

MONARK

Monark motorbikes were manufactured by the Monark Bicycle Company of Chicago, 1949-1954. The engines were subcontracted to Power Products.

MOORE

Only a single picture has surfaced of the oddball Moore. The late Jim Lucas, historian and literature collector, wrote about the Moore in the Spring, 1989, The Antique Motorcycle. Lucas is the source of all data. The Moore was built in Cleveland, Ohio, in 1910 only. As Cleveland was later the home of the equally odd Militor, Lucas opined that there might be some connection between the two, even if the Moore was only an inspiration for the later marque.

Circa 1902 Morgan. Looking quite similar to a number of marques such as the Lamson, the Stratton, and the Thomas, the Morgan got lost in the shuffle. Of this "family," only the Thomas lasted more than a year or two. (JIM DENNIE)

MORGAN

The Morgan Motor Company of Brooklyn, New York, made motorcycles around 1902. Morgan also sold engines separately. Two models were offered, delivering 1 1/2 hp and 2 1/4 hp. The April, 1902, issue of *The Dealer and Repairman* termed the Morgan one of the leading makes.

MORRIS AND COCKHILL

One picture from a period scrapbook, is all the data uncovered on this obscure marque.

Circa 1902 Morris and Cockhill "Racing Bicycle." (JIM DENNIE)

1910 Moore. The horizontally disposed cylinders were water cooled. The windshield as standard equipment may have been a first. Outrigger wheels were also unique.

(CYCLE)

1947 Mustang Colt. A Mustang designed leading-link fork and 4.00 x 8.00 inch tires were fitted. The 4 hp 122cc Villiers two-stroke didn't give the Mustang a clearly unique market approach as Gladden Products envisioned. A little over 200 of these were sold before the next-generation Mustang debuted. (VINTAGE MOTOR BIKE CLUB)

1948 Mustang Model 2. This is the bike that carved out the marque's unique American market, that of a peppy lightweight. The 9 1/2-hp 19.4-ci (318cc) side-valve single was designed by nearby Kinner Motors, which had been using them for other applications. Twelve-inch disk wheels, Mustang's own undamped telescopic fork, lighting from an extra coil on the magneto and a British-built Burman three-speed foot-shift transmission completed the package. (MUSTANG SALES LITERATURE)

1950 Mustang Model 4 "Standard." The 9 ½-hp engine was turned around so as to have both valves on the front. (MUSTANG SALES LITERATURE)

MUSTANG

During World War II, Gladden Products of Glendale, California, built aircraft components. With the War's end, the company decided to take up motorcycle manufacture to replace the lost business. This would be a natural fit for them, as Gladden had sufficient facilities and skilled machinists to launch the new product.

To minimize risk and hold down costs, the company decided to buy British Villiers motorcycle power plants, consisting of a two-stroke single in unit with a three-speed transmission. Gladden ordered 100 of the 12-ci (197cc) units, but Villiers was completely occupied supplying several British companies that were enjoying a booming postwar business. So the first Mustang "Colt" models were powered by the Villiers 7 1/2-ci (122cc) engine. Setting a precedent, the power plants were fitted to Gladden's own design of frame and running gear, including 12-inch disk wheels and a Gladden designed leading link fork. Gladden found that the 122cc engine, at 4 hp, was only half as potent as the desired 197cc. The Colt didn't measure up to their concept of a unique peppy light-weight—Cushman, Whizzer, and Servi-Cycle were already crowding the low-power field, so Gladden wanted something in a class by itself.

During 1946 and 1947, while a little over 200 of the Colts were being sold, Gladden was searching for a replacement engine and transmission. It got the package by dealing with the Burman transmission company of England, and by purchasing the nearby Kinner Motors Company. Kinner had been building the 19.4-ci (318cc) side-valve single-cylinder "Bumble Bee" for aircraft generator and industrial applications. Only a few modifications were required to make the Bumble Bee motor ready for Mustang use. The running gear included 12-inch disk wheels, but the front fork was changed to a Gladden designed undamped telescopic unit.

As the unusual Mustang engine size

didn't fit into America's traditional motorcycle racing classes, racing was not a mainstay of company strategy. But an important exception was Mustang test rider Walt Fulton, who enjoyed much success in scrambles racing, the precursor of today's motocross. Fulton and his Mustang won or placed well in many scrambles races against larger machines, due both to the Mustang's quick handling and Fulton's riding skills. These venues included the famous Big Bear Hare and Hound involving hundreds of desert riders, and the Catalina (Island) Grand National road race 14 miles off the Los Angeles Coast. At Catalina, other well-known racers, like Jimmy Phillips and Ed Kretz Jr., placed well.

Business was good throughout the 1940s and 1950s, but in the '60s, Japanese motorcycles took over the lightweight field in the U.S. as they were doing in Britain and Europe. The new 1960 spring-frame Thoroughbred failed to stem the tide, and Mustang ceased production during 1966.

1956-1958 Colt. The "Colt" name was brought back for this single-speed automatic clutch model built down to a price, $325, which compared to about $400 for the two-speed Cushman Eagle. The new Colt was out of the Mustang mainstream and not a good seller. (CLYDE EARL)

1957 Mustang Standard. Mustangs looked good from any angle. Handling was surprisingly good. Also offered that year was the 10 1/2-hp "Special" with high-rise exhaust pipe and front wheel brake. From 1959 through 1965, the rigid-frame four-speed Stallion was offered with standard wire wheels. (MUSTANG SALES LITERATURE)

1950 Mustang engine.
(MUSTANG SALES LITERATURE)

Mustang Delivery Cycle. The three-wheeler was offered in 1949 with the backwards engine of the Model 2, and in this form for the years 1950-1956 and 1963-1965. The interconnected Mustang fuel tanks blended into a very attractive package. These were popular among period customizers of both Harleys and British bikes.
(CLYDE EARL)

Circa 1963 Mustang Trail Machine. This bike was functional, but genuinely ugly. By this time, Japanese manufacturers were offering more sophisticated trail bikes. (VINTAGE MOTOR BIKE CLUB)

1960 Mustang Thoroughbred. Mustang claimed the weight was 220 lbs., only 5 lbs. more than the rigid-framed line. The nifty wire wheels were introduced on the 1959 rigid framed Stallion models. Though functionally improved over the rigid-frame layout, the Thoroughbred lacked the dynamite good looks of the Stallion and similar models. (VINTAGE MOTOR BIKE CLUB)

1920 Neracar. Although always the target of builders of "everyman" models, motorcycle business commuters were always too few and far between to rely on. (BRUCE LINSDAY)

NERACAR

Neracar motorcycles were the product of the Neracar Corporation of Syracuse, New York. The name "Neracar" was a unique near-pun, as it both conveyed the vehicle's near-car qualities and was almost the same as the designer's name—Carl Neracher.

Domestic production was in the years 1920-1923. Manufacturing rights were sold to the Sheffield Simplex Limited of England, which built the machine from 1924 through 1927 using both the original two-stroke single-cylinder engine and a larger British four-stroke single-cylinder engine. The Neracar's relatively good weather protection drew praise from British riders who often road over rain-slicked roads.

Steering was through the hub-center principal, like an automobile. Handling was claimed to be superb, and riders were fond of showing how extremely slow a Neracar

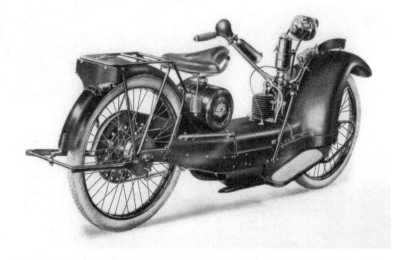

1920 Neracar. The 12.9-ci (211cc) two-stroke single suffered from erratic carburetion according to one period expert. (BRUCE LINSDAY)

could be ridden. On the other hand, the author knew the late Maldwyn Jones, Schebler carburetor's traveling trouble-shooter. Jones' sojourns included a trip to the Neracar factory to iron out carburetor problems. Jones, an ex-racer, said that Neracar handling was awful because of the sloppy excessive play through the various joints between the handlebars and the front wheel. Take your pick. Jones also said that the carburetion was "hopeless" because of the long uphill route the mixture took from the low-slung carberetor.

Racing was out of the question, but good publicity was achieved when the famous Erwin "Cannonball" Baker rode a Neracar from New York to Los Angeles in late 1922.

He averaged 19.3 mph, not so slow as it sounds because of the poor roads over much of the route. Fuel and oil consumption were 74.76 mpg and 150 miles per quart.

NEW ERA

New Era motorcycles were manufactured from 1909 through 1913 by the New Era Autocycle Company of Dayton, Ohio. The unorthodox design featured an open frame in front of the rider. With a double-wide footboard, only the narrow backbone tube had to be avoided, so that the riding position was similar to that of a motorscooter. Engine placement kept the rider's legs away from the grime that inevitably built up on motorcycles of the dirt-road days.

1912 New Era. The bore and stroke of the F-head engine were 3.215 and 3.75 inches, yielding a displacement of 30.4 ci (499cc). The connecting rod and crankshaft were mounted on German Hess-Bright ball bearings. A two-speed planetary transmission was mounted on the left side of the crankcase. For 1912, a mechanically operated inlet valve replaced the previous automatic (suction) inlet valve. Ignition was by Bosch magneto, which was claimed to produce a sufficient spark running as slow as 55 rpm. An automatic drip-feed oiling system could be assisted by an auxiliary hand pump for heavy going, such as fast speeds or running through deep sand or uphill.

ORIENT

The Orient motorcycle was made from 1900 through 1905 by the Waltham Manufacturing Company of Waltham, Massachusetts. Some sources claim the Orient was the first American-made motorcycle; others cite the Thomas Auto-Bi. The debate could hinge on the definition of an American marque, because the 1900-1902 Orients used a proprietary French built Aster engine. Indeed, the marque was sometimes listed as the "Orient-Aster." On July 31, 1900, Albert Champion (later, of Champion and AC sparkplugs) rode an Orient 5 miles in 7 minutes, 1.25 seconds over Boston's Charles River race track in the first motorcycle speed performance (not a race) in the U.S. On May 30, 1902, Orient rider W. T. Green won the first motorcycle road race in the U.S.

For 1903, Orient brought out its own engine design. At 160 lbs., the motorcycle was relatively heavy; Orient claimed this was an advantage because the machine absorbed more vibration. Orient ceased motorcycle production in 1905 in order to concentrate on automobiles.

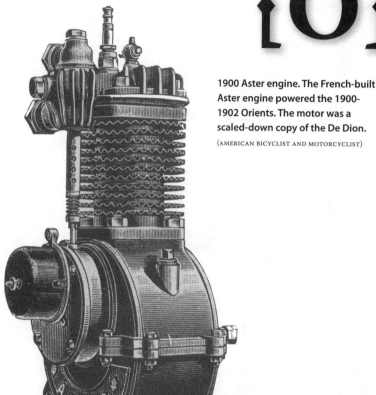

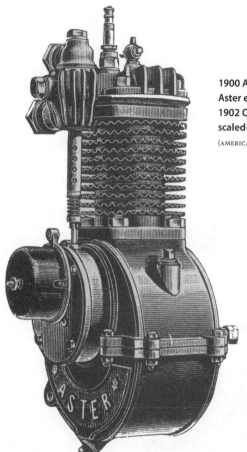

1900 Aster engine. The French-built Aster engine powered the 1900-1902 Orients. The motor was a scaled-down copy of the De Dion.
(AMERICAN BICYCLIST AND MOTORCYCLIST)

1903 Orient. According to the April, 1902, *The Dealer and Repairman*, the marque had the largest and most powerful engine used in a motorcycle. The magazine also stated the Orient was "...almost in a class by itself." Five quarts of fuel would propel the Orient 75 to 100 miles. (BRUCE LINSDAY)

[P]

1901 Patee. The F-head engine appears to have been a De Dion clone.

(SCIENTIFIC AMERICAN)

PATEE

The Patee was advertised throughout 1901 in *Scientific American*, so it wasn't a one-off prototype. However, no technical details were provided. According to *Encyclopedia of the Motorcycle* (Hugo Wilson), the obscure marque was built in Indianapolis, Indiana. Apparently, production didn't continue long into 1902.

PEERLESS

The Peerless was a clone of the M-M (sometimes termed Marsh-Metz). In 1913, the American Motor Company of Brockton, Massachusetts, wholesaled M-M motorcycles to jobbers who rebranded them. These included Arrow, Haverford, National, and Peerless. The latter firm was located in Boston, Massachusetts.

1913 Peerless twin. A clone of the M-M, the Peerless twin had a bore and stroke of 3 1/4 x 4 inches, yielding a displacement of 66.36 ci (1088cc). This was a single-speeder with the so-called "free engine" (clutch) control by a lever on the left side of the tank. The finish was Peerless steel gray.

(BRUCE LINSDAY)

1913 Peerless "5" single. An M-M clone, the F-head (inlet-over-exhaust) engine had a bore 3 1/4 inches, a stroke 4 inches and displacement of 33.18 cubic inches (544cc). As shown, this was a single-speed bike. Speeds of 5 to 55 mph were cited.

(BRUCE LINSDAY)

P. E. M.

The P. E. M. marque was one of four that differed only in the name on the tank. The others were the Waverly, the Kenzler-Waverly and the Jefferson The order of succession was: Kenzler-Waverly, Waverly, P.E.M, and Jefferson. Adding further confusion, engines were stamped either "Waverly" or "Mack," the latter in recognition of designer Perry E. Mack. The P. E. M. name was chosen after the company reorganized and moved from Milwaukee to Jefferson, Wisconsin, in 1911. Another name change came in 1913, this time "Jefferson" was chosen in honor of the place of manufacture. See also "Mack Engines."

1911 P. E. M. The motorcycle was identical to the single-cylinder 1910 Waverly (shown elsewhere) and the single-cylinder 1913 Jefferson. (BOB KAROLEVTIZ)

PIERCE

From 1909 through 1913, the Pierce Cycle Company of Buffalo, New York, made Pierce single-cylinder and four-cylinder motorcycles. In the 1912 catalog, Pierce announced, "The Pierce Cycle Company does not propose to compete in price with products of other companies." That philosophy was inherited from the parent Pierce Arrow Motor Car Company, builders of luxurious automobiles.

The birth of the motorcycle line goes back to 1908. Perry Pierce, only son of George Pierce, owner of the Pierce Arrow car company, was given the Pierce Cycle (bicycles) Company. Perry also was given the old Pierce Arrow car factory in downtown Buffalo.

Both the Pierce singles and fours featured a frame made from 4-inch-diameter tubing. The single was a belt-drive job; the four had shaft drive. Engine styles differed too, the single being an F-head and the four being a T-head. The latter configuration was seldom used. The "T" designation came from the fact that the inlet and exhaust valves were on opposite sides of the bore.

The 1909 lineup featured only the four. This was a clutch-less single-speeder, but the 1910-1913 fours had a clutch and a two-speed transmission.

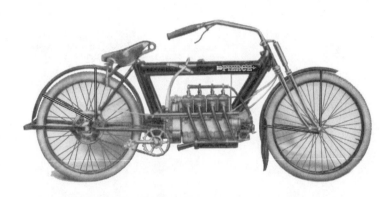

1912 Pierce Four-Cylinder Model. An outside flywheel and shaft drive were featured, along with a two-speed transmission. The bore and stroke of 2 3/16 and 2 1/4 inches yielded a displacement of 33.8 ci (554cc). (BRUCE LINSDAY)

1912 Pierce Four. The marque was inspired by the Belgian FN four in terms of the size, the four cylinders and the underslung engine. However, the FN was an F-head machine and the Pierce was a T-head.

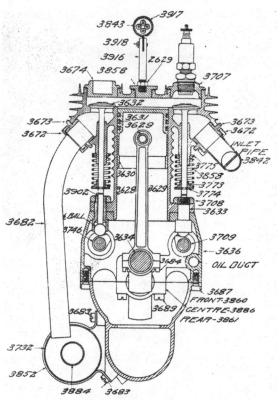

1912 Pierce Four-Cylinder Model engine. The "T-head" configuration is apparent. One could easily imagine that this layout would be superior to the side-valve design that would ultimately dominate the American scene. But in the U.S., the only long-term adherent to T-head design was the American La France fire engine. (BRUCE LINSDAY)

The side-valve single was introduced in the 1910 range as a 36.08-ci (591cc) mount, with bore and stroke of 3½ and 3¾ inches. Previously, among American marques, only Reading Standard had built side-valve engines. 1911 valve action was from a single cam. In 1911, the stroke was increased to 4 inches, bumping up the size to 38.48 ci (630cc). In 1912, the single's valve gear was changed to a two-cam arrangement, and the crankcase was strengthened.

The Pierce company erred in its belief that it could turn a profit by offering motorcycles in which cost was no object. The marque shut down before the 1914 season.

PIRATE

From 1913 to 1915, the Milwaukee Motorcycle Company built Pirate motorcycles, in Milwaukee, Wisconsin. These machines bore a striking resemblance to Yale motorcycles, which were last offered for the 1913 season. They were, in fact, clones except that the Pirate used conventional cylinder finning instead of the unique Yale finning.

1912 Pierce Model 12B. Billed as the "Hill-Climbing Single," the engine had a bore and stroke of 3½ and 4 inches, yielding a displacement of 38.48 ci (630cc). Pierce introduced side-valve singles in 1910, joining Reading Standard and Reliance as the only American builders of this configuration. (BRUCE LINSDAY)

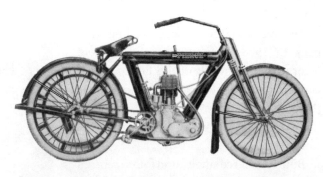

1912 Pierce Model 12A "Runabout." This was described as lighter and less powerful than the other Pierce singles. The Runabout continued with the 1920-style single-cam valve gear. Engine dimensions weren't provided by the catalog, but the capacity was probably about 25 ci (410cc). (BRUCE LINSDAY)

1913 Pirate. Except for the conventional cylinder finning on the Pirate, the Milwaukee design is identical to the Yale. Refer to the Yale section for identical Pirate specifications. (BOB KAROLEVITZ)

PONY CYCLE

In the 1940s, the Hawk Tool and Engineering Company of Clarkstown Michigan, was a manufacturer of stamping dies and tooling fixtures for the automobile industry. The firm also produced various parts for the federal government. In 1948, Hawk bought the rights to the lightweight "Powerbike" motorcycle. The machine had come to the company's attention because the designer worked for one of its customers. From 1949 through 1953, the company built prototypes, started production tooling, and set up a marketing network. Hawk settled on the name "Pony Cycle," and launched its little motorcycle in 1954.

Initially, sales were brisk, partly because the Pony Cycle fell into its own niche. The 7.95-ci (130cc) four-stroke single-cylinder Continental Red Seal engine was about half the size used by Cushman, the dominant motorscooter in the market. On the other hand, much of the performance difference was made up by the Pony Cycle's 185-lb. weight, as compared to the Cushman Eagle's 271 lbs.. Continental engines were good sellers and were used to power a variety of machines such as lawn mowers, air compressors, generator sets, etc., so customers were confident that spare parts would be available.

Hawk then designed a less-expensive ($189.50) step-through model called the "Pony Scooter." The giant retail marketer Montgomery-Ward retailer soon awarded Hawk a production contract for the motorscooter, which was sold as a "Montgomery-Ward." "Wards," as it was casually called, was also Sears-Roebucks' longtime national rival in the mail-order field. People in the great rural midwest could do much of their shopping via the Wards or Sears catalogs.

Unfortunately, after a year and a half, Hawk couldn't meet Ward's production quotas, so Wards terminated the agreement. This was a severe blow, because Hawk had built up a large inventory of components. Hawk tried, unsuccessfully, to secure a Postal Department contract. In 1958, the firm stopped production. All remaining inventories were sold to other manufacturers for use in other products. Hawk returned to its original focus, the tool and die business.

1955 Pony Cycle. One problem Hawk solved neatly was how to build a low-cost fuel tank. It did this by soldiering together two belt guard stampings. Specifications: 3-hp 7.95-ci (130cc) blower-cooled Continental Red Seal four-stroke side-valve single-cylinder engine, optional 5 1/2-hp engine (size and price unknown), pull-cord starter, automatic centrifugally controlled variable pulley V-belt drive, Hawk trailing link front fork, built-in splash shield and 4.00 x 12-inch tires.

1911 Pope Model H. This was Pope's price leader, a 30.45-ci (499cc) belt-drive single-speeder without a clutch. (BRUCE LINSDAY)

1911 Pope Model H drive system (at right). The simple clutch-less single-speed drive was still popular despite the availability of clutch devices on other Pope models and other marques. (BRUCE LINSDAY)

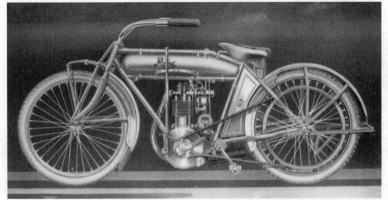

POPE

One of America's technical leaders was the Pope. Built from 1911 through 1918, the motorcycles were a product of the West field, Massachusetts plant. The parent company was the Pope Manufacturing Company of Hartford, Connecticut, builders of Pope cars in Hartford and Toledo, Ohio. Prior to the establishment of the Pope motorcycle marque, the parent firm had built and sold a variety of marques named after several popular pedal bikes they manufactured, including: American, Columbia, Cleveland, Crescent, Imperial, Monarch, Rambler and Tribune. These differed only in the name on the tank sides.

Only single-cylinder Popes were offered in 1911, these with a Breeze carburetor. The first Pope V-twin arrived in the 1912 range, and it was at the leading edge of technology with its overhead-valve configuration. This was the first use of overhead-valves by a prominent American maker. Another hallmark feature was plunger rear suspension, predating this trend by nearly 40 years. Other new offerings for 1912 included: Schebler carburetors, choice of high or low handlebars, and an optional Eclipse "free engine" (clutch).

Pope design matured in the 1914 range, when a two-speed countershaft transmission was offered. It took only one season to reveal the difficulties of a heavy rear hub in an unsprung frame moving over the very rough roads of the era. Alas, Pope management and finances weren't up to the task of efficiently building and wisely marketing motorcycles, so the marque was absent from the 1919 scene.

1913 Pope Model K. With basically the same engine as the Model H price cutter, the K added a "free engine" clutch control. It's the long handle on the left side of the tank. (BRUCE LINSDAY)

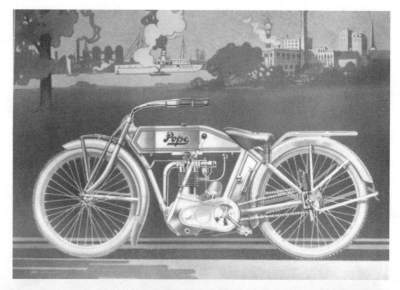

1913 Pope Model M. Fiv- hp was all the rage, with some marques offering a "5" or a "Big 5" model to signify their largest singles. The 5-hp Pope Model M featured a bore and stroke of 3 5/8 and 3 11/16 inches, and a displacement of 38.06 ci (624cc), which was a typical size for the 5-hp class. Model M buyers also got the more up to date styling as used on the twins.

(BRUCE LINSDAY)

1913 Pope Model L. Painted gray with blue striping and with numerous brightly plated nickel parts, these were handsome machines. All 1913 and earlier Popes were single-speeders. In 1914, Pope offered a counter-shaft two-speed transmission.

(BRUCE LINSDAY)

1913 Pope Model L engine. These advanced engines debuted in the 1912 lineup. The bore and stroke were 3 21/64 and 3 1/2 inches, yielding a displacement of 60.90 ci (998cc). These engines won many a street "war" and forced Harley-Davidson, Indian and Excelsior to increase the power of their F-head twins.

1913 Pope Model K engine. Workmanship was first class. (BRUCE LINSDAY)

1913 Pope rear suspension (left). Introduced in 1912, the plunger spring units were about four decades ahead of common use.

1916 Pope Model T-16 (below). The two long hand levers arrived on the 1914 two-speeders. The lever at the 1 o'clock position is the clutch control; the lever at the 11 o'clock position is the gear shift. Subsequent design changes were minimal. (THE ANTIQUE MOTORCYCLE)

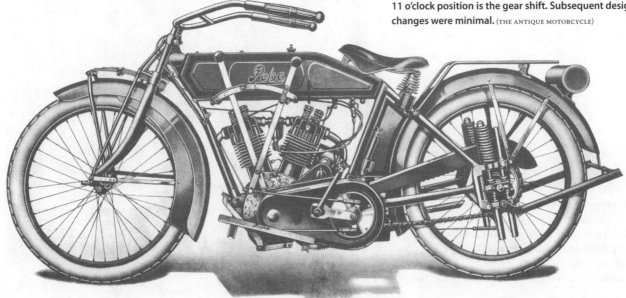

1918 Pope twin. This was the last production year. Popes were not significantly changed after 1914. (CYCLE)

POW-WOW

Power Wheel Incorporated, of Chicago, Illinois, produced the Pow Wow motorbike attachment in 1948. From an ad in the May, 1948, *American Bicyclist and Motorcyclist*: "All cast aluminum construction, no steel to rust, no enamel to chip. All shafts in sealed ball bearings pre-lubricated for life. Powered by the Power Products Model 1000 Engine (50,000 in use on lawn mowers, etc.) that gives 100 effortless miles per gallon...."

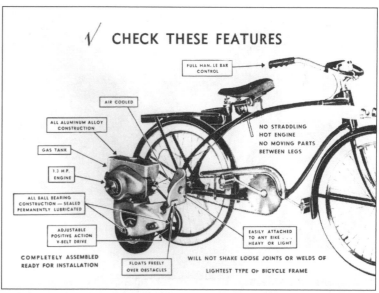

1948 Pow Wow. This was an old idea in a new package. The genre goes back to the Smith Motor Wheel and the Dayton Motor Bicycle of pre-World War I days. All-aluminum construction was touted. The size of the 1.3-hp engine wasn't stated. (VINTAGE MOTOR BIKE CLUB)

1941 Powell Aviate, or Model A-V8. Specifications: fan-cooled side-valve (Flat-head) single-cylinder engine, bore 3 1/16 inch, stroke 2 7/8 inches, displacement 21.18 cubic inches (347cc), maximum output, 5 hp, "engine contains parts from popular low-priced car;" battery ignition, automobile generator, single-speed transmission with automatic centrifugal clutch, tires 16 x 4 inches, speed, 50 mph, fuel consumption 90 mpg. The history has been lost, but this machine is so nearly identical to the 1948 Cyclone Motorcycle Scooter that there must have been a connection. (MOTORCYCLIST)

1949 Powell P-81. Specifications: side-valve (Flat-head) engine, bore 3 1/16 inch, stroke 3 1/4 inch, displacement 23.94 cubic inches, maximum output 8 hp at 3200 rpm, magneto ignition; die-cast wheels; dry-sump lubrication, 196 lbs., cruising speed 45 mph, top speed over 60 mph, black finish, price $247. The large cover over the crankcase conceals the automatic centrifugal clutch. (MOTORCYCLIST)

POWELL

The Powell Manufacturing Company of Compton, California, began making motorscooters in the 1930s. Its first motorcycle-styled, but small-wheeled, creation was the 1940-1942 Aviate, cutely designated the Model A-V-8. The airplane designations were used because the public was excited about recent years' tremendous progress in airplane design. After World War II ended in 1945, the company again offered step-through scooters. In 1949, Powell returned to the theme of a motorcycle-styled, but scooter-wheeled vehicle, with the Model P-81. Again, the name was aviation connected, as America's first prominent jet fighter was the Lockheed P-80.

The Powell P-81 was a uniquely styled little motorcycle, and pleasing to 1949 eyes. The bars upswept dramatically from the top of the front fork, then down swept with equal drama, so that the handle grips were angled sharply down toward the ground. This look was all the rage with California custom bikes and, just three years later, the same general shape was applied to the bars of the 1952 Harley-Davidson Model K middleweight. Harley also offered such "spaghetti bars," as an accessory on Harley's two-stroke lightweights.

Another styling touch included the bulbous flat-bottomed fuel tank, which was reminiscent of the British built Triumph. There was a bit of the Harley springer fork look to the 1949-1950 telescopic P-81 fork, for at the top were twin exposed coil springs. The 1951 models had a conventional telescopic fork, which may have worked better with the springs enclosed, but with this fork and conventional handlebars the Powell lost some of its original styling flare. Throughout production, the engine had the motorcycle look, as there was no cooling fan and shroud as on conventional motorscooters.

With a rated 8 hp, the 23.9-cubic inch (392cc) P-81 was a very peppy putt. The Powell had lots more acceleration and top speed than the 14-cubic inch (230cc), and

1949 Powell P-81. Note the filler cap behind the steering head. The 2-inch-diameter frame tube served as the oil reservoir for the dry-sump lubrication system. (POWELL SALES LITERATURE)

later 17cubic inch (280cc), Cushman motorscooters, that were sweeping the nation.

The performance and styling, so pleasing to the motorcycle crowd, were probably part of Powell's undoing. Parents (like the author's) felt their kids would be safer on a slower and more timidly styled step-through. Parental votes for chuffing Cushmans was made easier by the P-81's thumping motorcycle staccato. Meanwhile, the California-built Mustang was taking the P-81 idea and executing it better by providing a foot-shift British gearbox and one of the most beautiful fuel tanks ever built. The motorcycle crowd fell for Mustangs and the Powell P-81 had nowhere to go. P-81 sales continued through 1951.

POWERBIKE

The Powerbike was produced by Sagninaw Products Corporation around 1950. Other than an ad.,no other data was found by the author. The company is still in business but efforts to learn of their history proved fruitless.

PRATT

Pratt motorcycles were produced briefly—no records have been found other than from 1911. The firm's name shows just how dramatically the times were changing. Pratts were built by the Elkhart Carriage & Harness Manufacturing Company, of Elkhart, Indiana. Only a single model, the Pratt-4, was offered. This 30.46-cubic inch (499cc) single was almost identical to the 1911 Yale

SMART NEW

POWERBIKE

gets you there safely and economically

The motor is in the rear, mounted low to aid balance and handling. No grease to rub off on your legs, no hot fumes blowing in your face. 100 miles per gallon, 30 MPH. 1½ HP fan cooled engine, kick starter, automatic clutch, fits any man's or woman's balloon-tire bike. See your dealer or write direct. TERRITORIES AVAILABLE.

SAGINAW PRODUCTS CORP. • SAGINAW. MICHIGAN

SAY YOU SAW IT IN POPULAR MECHANICS

Circa 1950 Powerbike. The Powerbike was typical of the post-World War II motorbike genre. It was the stuff of boyhood dreams, when a youngster longed for motoring, but was too young to get a car driving license. (VINTAGE MOTOR BIKE CLUB)

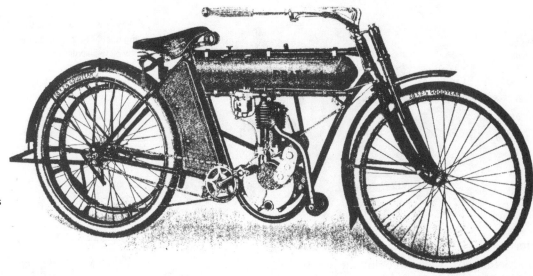

1911 "Pratt-4." The Elkhart company concentrated on marketing. It figured that by offering only a single medium-sized model, management problems would be minimized and efficiencies would be reaped. Compare this picture with that of the 1911 Yale single and it's apparent the machines are nearly identical. Apparently, Yale was wholesaling these machines to Pratt. (MOTORCYCLE ILLUSTRATED)

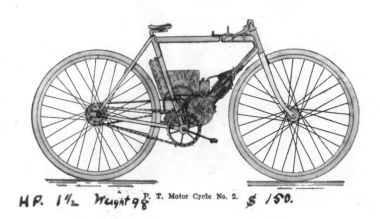

Circa 1902 P. T. Model 2. (JIM DENNIE)

Circa 1902 P. T. Model 3. (JIM DENNIE)

single. The frames differed only in the front down tube, while the tanks, fork, fenders, battery box and handlebars were identical. Even the cylinder appears identical. The timing covers differed, but this would have been a relatively simple thing to alter if one were either pirating a design or selling one's own. Something was going on, that's for sure.

The following specifications are from the 1911 catalog: "Motor, 4 H.P. accepted four-cycle type; bore 3 1/4 x 3 4/64-inch stroke; enclosed flywheels weighing 31 pounds, perfectly balanced; ... ignition, Hera High Tension Auto Type Magneto; ... Finish, French gray enamel, beautifully striped...."

P. T.

Pictures from a period scrapbook are the only data found by the author. As the illustrations are line drawings, these may have been concept definitions that never turned into hard metal.

RACYCLE (ALSO MOTO RACYCLE)

The Racycle began as an Indian clone. Briefly, this meant that the Thor company built engines for Indian and was permitted to copy the Indian design both for its own Thor motorcycles, and for machines wholesaled to jobbers and rebranded. Though sometimes termed the Moto Racycle in advertisements, the bikes were always labeled simply "Racycle."

Historically, the Racycle is most significant for being marketed by the Miami Cycle & Manufacturing Company, Grand Avenue, Middletown, Ohio. This firm was destined to buy out the Merkel, later termed Flying Merkel, one of the more advanced motorcycles of the pre-World War I era.

By 1907, the Racycle had taken on some Thor fitments such as the tanks, which also were seen on the Reading-Standard and other Indian clones. By 1913, the Racycle had no apparent Thor and Indian routes. By this time, the Racycle was a low-priced line marketed alongside the more costly and prestigious Flying Merkel. Thus, when Merkel folded in 1917, so did Racycle.

THE MOTO-RACYCLE. PRICE $210.

Circa 1905 Racycle, 15.85 cubic inch (260 cc). From the April 1, 1905, *Cycle and Automobile Trade Journal*: "22 inch frame; 2 inch G & J tires; 46 inch wheelbase; single cylinder 2 19/32 (inch, bore) x 3 (inch, stroke) 1 3/4 H.P. motor; automatic lubrication; chain drive; batter mileage, about 1500; fuel mileage about 75; grip control; weight 110 lbs.; speed, 8 to 37 miles per hour; price $210." (THE ANTIQUE MOTORCYCLE)

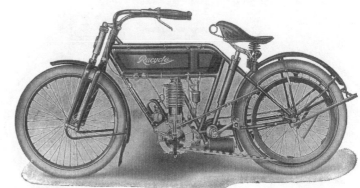

1913 Racycle (above). The heavy-duty front fork was completely different from that of the companion marque, the Flying Merkel. A major cost cutter was the single-speed drive. Seat post suspension and a "free engine" clutch added touches of class to an otherwise built-to-a-price machine. The clutch was controlled by a hand lever on the left handlebar.

(GEORGE YAROCKI)

1907 Racycle. Thor, as the wholesaler, was beginning to make detail changes from its original Indian clone status. These changes, such as different tanks, began to be incorporated on the cloned bikes, such as this one.

(GEORGE YAROCKI)

Rambler, Crescent, Monarch, Imperial

All the Improved Features

PRICE, $225.00
Pope Product

From the April 1, 1905, *Cycle and Automobile Trade Journal:* "The Rambler Motor Cycle, Price $210. 22 inch frame; 2 inch G. & J. tires; 46 inch wheelbase; single cylinder, 2 19/32 (inch, bore) x 3 (inch, stroke) "Thor" motor, 1 3/4 H.P.; splash lubrication; sight feel oiler; drive by 1/4 inch nickel steel chain; battery mileage 1000 miles; fuel mileage 75; single lever control spark and throttle; weight 105 lbs.; price $210. Special features: Spring front fork; friction sprocket; guard over engine chain; full steel mudguards." (THE ANTIQUE MOTORCYCLE)

1903 Reading Standard. Except for the name on the tank, this motorcycle was identical to the period Indian. This happened because engine-builder Thor supplied both Indian and itself, and sold off excess engines and frames to other companies. The clover-leaf sprocket was shown earlier on a 1901-1902 Indian. The engine size was approximately 13.7 ci (225cc). (BRUCE LINSDAY)

RAMBLER

Along with one of the "American" marques, the early Cleveland marque, the Crescent, and the Tribune, the Rambler was one of Colonel Alfred Pope's brands. As listed in 1905, the Rambler was an Indian clone. The 15.85-cubic inch (260cc) Rambler used the so-called "Thor" engine, an Indian-designed unit build under license by the Aurora Automatic Machinery Company of Aurora, Illinois. This buy-in approach avoided the need to establish and sustain a motorcycle engineering department. Not surprisingly, the design wasn't updated and by 1905 it was becoming dated. Production ceased in 1906; however, the parent company continued and eventually built Pope motorcycles through 1918.

READING STANDARD (ALSO R-S)

Most of early American motorcycle history concerns the so-called "Big Three," Harley-Davidson, Indian and the Excelsior firm that built both Excelsiors and Hendersons. Of all the lesser marques, the Reading Standard was produced longest. Starting in 1903, Reading Standard was the only non-Big-Three builder of large motorcycles to survive the World War I economic stress. Half of the marque name was derived from the factory location in mountainous Reading, Pennsylvania. The "Standard" part of the name came from the popular idea that production motorcycles should incorporate proven industry standards. With all the hills and mountains around the area, the marque slogan throughout its history was: "Built and tested in the mountains."

1904 Reading Standard. Again, the model is almost identical to the same year Indian in every respect but the name. Minor differences were the leaf-spring saddle suspension and the pedal sprocket. These kinds of small details may have been changed during the course of the production year by either or both companies, and in the case of the saddle may reflect an accessory offering by Reading Standard. (BRUCE LINSDAY)

Detractors countered with: "Built in the mountains and tested downhill."

Reading Standard's most significant historical contribution was its pioneering of the side-valve (Flathead) engine configuration in American motorcycling. After Reading Standard staffer Charles Gustafson left to work at Indian, he is believed to have been instrumental in convincing Indian to change its large models from F-head to side-valve configuration. Upon the announcement of the 1916 Indian side-valve twins, some traditionalists disdainfully referred to the new Indians as "Reading Standards."

The best business years were 1917, 1918 and 1919, with about 1,700 Reading Standards being built and sold each year. Though a small force nationally, the marque enjoyed pockets of success such as, of course, Reading. The city's Pierce and Ardis C. Hettinger were the nation's biggest Reading Standard dealer, selling about 100 motorcycles a year. Portland, Oregon, was another success story, with almost all postmen riding Reading-Standards on their routes.

Following some wins in local area races during 1919, the company advertised: "When an R-S wins you know it is a stock machine. We build no specials." However, in 1921 the Reading Standard name was placed on a special racer powered by a Cyclone engine. Notable rider Ray Creviston got the jockey job, but he won no races against top competition.

Production in Reading Pennsylvania came to an end in 1923. However, the assets were purchased by the Cleveland motorcycle company, which sold the Reading Standard "Greyhound" during the 1924 season before pulling the plug. From the sudden drop in the 1924 prices, it appears that the Cleveland company was assembling machines from stock and had no intention of resuming real production. In production for 21 years, Reading Standard had made a valiant effort.

1905 Reading Standard. During this season the name on the tank changed to "Thoroughbred." A play on words, this name clouded the Indian-clone issue—Thor and Light Thor-Bred motorcycles were also identical to the Indian. From the catalog: "First American machine to use a combination gasoline and oil tank with oil force pump, within diamond of frame, together with standard dry cells obtainable everywhere. Single grip control. Spring fork." With new tanks, the marque was beginning to look more like the current year Thor, but Thor, Thoroughbred and the rest of the Thor-based bikes were mechanically identical to the Indian. (BRUCE LINSDAY)

1906 Reading Standard. The intermingling of Thor ideas with the basic Indian design continued. For instance, this 1906 Reading Standard closely resembles the 1907 Racycle shown earlier, and the 1909 Thor Model 8. Reading Standard won its biggest competition victory this year, the Pike's Peak climb. This win was publicized for many years afterwards. (BRUCE LINSDAY)

1907 Reading Standard. The 1907 model introduced side-valve configuration to the American scene. From the catalog: "Exclusive adoption of mechanical intake valve integral with motor. Independent chain adjustment, adoption 5/8 in. roller chain. Re-arrangement of batteries, coil, and improved oiling device, leaving space over rear wheel clear for low saddle position, luggage carrier or tandem attachment."

(BRUCE LINSDAY)

1908 Reading Standard. From the catalog: "R-S compensating sprocket with enlarged friction surface, indestructible. Refinements in entire machine..."

(BRUCE LINSDAY)

1908 Reading Standard. This motorcycle built for two wasn't unique. The Wagner marque also offered such a machine. (GEORGE YAROCKI)

1909 Reading Standard. The leading link front fork debuted. From the catalog: "The big wheel for 1909, full view of new, advanced, and practical features. The result of seven years of actual test and practical experience ..." (BRUCE LINSDAY)

1909 Reading Standard racer. Rider Ray Seymour raced this motorcycle at the Los Angeles Coliseum during the 1910 season. The coliseum is shown in the background. The unusual F-head twin was brought out in 1908. The front and rear cylinders are identical, which required both left and right side cams that operated, respectively, the front and rear cylinders. The company claimed better cooling resulted. The big twin probably had something to do with a new slogan appearing in ads: "No limit to speed but the law." (MOTORCYCLE ILLUSTRATED)

1909 Reading Standard
three-wheeler. Now in
its third production year,
the side-valve Reading
Standard layout preceded
Indian's side-valve con-
version by seven years,
and Harley-Davidson's by
20 years!

1911 Reading
Standard belt-drive
single (below). That year,
a two-speed rear hub
was offered.

(THE ANTIQUE MOTORCYCLE)

1911 Reading Standard belt-drive single. The spring seat post softened the ride. (GEORGE YAROCKI)

1914 Reading Standard. The new frame positioned the saddle 2 inches lower and presented a more pleasing appearance. A larger cone clutch was fitted. The horizontal frame tube was removable, to provide more room for engine work, especially with the tank also removed. With this arrangement, the cylinders could easily be removed. The first Reading Standard two-speed was offered, a move that kept the marque abreast of Harley-Davidson, Indian and Excelsior, which also brought out two-speeders that year. (MOTORCYCLE ILLUSTRATED)

1915 Reading Standard. As in 1914, a new frame was featured. During the seasons of 1913 and 1914, the standard finish was brown as it had been for several previous years, and the optional finish was green. In 1915, all motorcycles were finished in brown.

(BOB KAROLEVITZ)

1917 Reading Standard Model 17-T. A heavier frame, a rounded fuel tank, and a new braking system highlighted the 1917 models. From the catalog: "The R-S has a distinguished appearance. Its lines are strong and bold, but dignified, and are dictated by the strength of the mechanical parts." Price was $275.

(GEORGE YAROCKI)

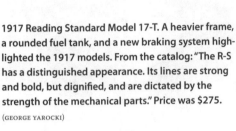

1917 Reading Standard engine. Enclosed valve lifters were brought out in 1917, and the magneto was moved forward of the engine. The new cylinders had notably different exhaust port locations and angles. Specifications: bore and stroke, 3 3/8 x 3 3/4 inches; displacement, 67.09 ci (1100 cc); valve actuation via two cams. (GEORGE YAROCKI)

1917 Reading Standard Model 17-T-E. From the catalog: "The 1917 R-S is unquestionably the motorcycle of quality and refinement for those who desire the very best obtainable." Price: $315. (GEORGE YAROCKI)

1918 Reading Standard. The separate oil tank was new, as was the olive drab finish that was also used on Harley-Davidsons, Indians and Excelsiors. (GEORGE YAROCKI)

1920 Reading Standard Model 20TE. The stroke was increased from 3 3/4 inches to 4 inches, and with the continued bore of 3 3/8 inches, this increased the displacement to 71.57 ci (1173 cc). Valves were increased from 1 5/8 inches to 1 3/4 inches. Cams were reduced and rocker levers (lifter arms) were made longer, which was said to reduce rocker wear and improve acceleration. For the first time, there were no single-cylinder models in the range. (BRUCE LINSDAY)

1920 Reading Standard Model 20T. The separate oil tank was eliminated, and the oil supply was again carried in a compartment within the main tanks. Apparently, this was done so that an auxiliary hand pump could be easily used. Flat strip fender braces replaced the previous rod braces. (BRUCE LINSDAY)

1920 Reading Standard engine. Cylinder head finning and exhaust ports were new 1920 features. Unfortunately, there was insufficient metal between the valve seats and the bore. This resulted in heat buildup and cracked ports. (GEORGE YAROCKI)

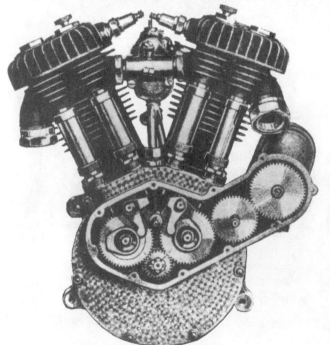

1923 Reading Standard. This picture was included in the February 1, 1923, issue of *Motorcycle and Bicycle Illustrated*. The article announced the purchase of Reading Standard by the Cleveland Motorcycle Manufacturing Company. In the October, 4, 1923, issue, Cleveland announced the 1924 Reading Standard Greyhound finished in "rich ordnance" grey (battleship grey), striped in blue. Other changes to the Greyhound included: no valance on the front fender; front fender slots through which the fork passed; and rear fender trimmed to end shortly below the 10 o'clock positioned lower fender brace.

(MOTORCYCLE AND BICYCLE ILLUSTRATED)

REGAS

The Regas Vehicle Company of Rochester, New York, built the Regas motorcycle in 1903.

RELIANCE

Reliance motorcycles were built from 1903 through 1908 by the Reliance Motor Cycle Company of Addison, New York. By 1908, the company was wholesaling motorcycles to the MESCO mail order company, which rebranded the motorcycles "Erie." According to Stephen Wright, MESCO took over Reliance production in 1909, and this seems clear from the 1909 catalog, which stated the company was in Oswego, New York, which was the home of MESCO.

1903 Regas (above). This single-speeder was powered by a De Dion 2 1/4-hp F-head single-cylinder engine. Unusually small wheels (16 inches) and large-diameter tires (4 inches) were fitted. The operating range was 75 miles. (JIM DENNIE)

1905 Reliance (left). This machine differed from the 1903 model in that the earlier Reliance had a friction drive. Specifications: 21 1/2-inch frame; 1 3/4 to 2-inch tires; 50-inch wheel base; bore and stroke of 2 3/4 and 3 inches; displacement of 17.8 ci (292 cc); rated output of 1 3/4 to 2 hp; sight feed oiler; battery mileage about 1,000; fuel mileage 75-plus; grip control optional; weight 95 lbs.; speed 5 to 40 mph; price $135 to $150. (THE ANTIQUE MOTORCYCLE)

1907 Reliance. This motorcycle differed from the 1909 Erie Light-weight model in only two details. The Reliance had a rigid front fork; the Erie had a sprung fork. The Reliance had a small belt idler pulley that permitted the belt to be slipped in the manner of a clutch, but the Erie had a simple direct belt drive. The F-head engine had an unspecified capacity. However, industry standards equated displacement and output, so the cited 2 1/2 hp signified about 15 ci (250cc). (BRUCE LINSDAY)

1909 Reliance Model C. Of interest is the side-valve (Flat-head) engine, then being offered by only one other American marque, Reading Standard. Specifications: 3 1/2-hp side-valve engine; bore and stroke of 3 1/8 x 3 3/8 inches; displacement 25.9 ci (424cc); double grip control; Eclipse or Corbin brake; 2.5-gal. fuel tank; sight-feed lubrication; weight 140 lbs.; speeds of 6 to 50 mph; finish of crimson, orange, and black; price $200. (BRUCE LINSDAY)

1909 Reliance Model D. This small F-head twin was asserted to be lighter than most singles on the market. Specifications: 5-hp F-head engine; bore and stroke of 2 9/16 x 3 inches; displacement of 30.9 ci (507cc); wheelbase 56 inches; height 19 inches; wheels 26 or 28 inches; double grip control; Eclipse or Corbin brake; speed 6 to 60 mph; weight 140 lbs.; finish of crimson, orange, and black; price $225. (BRUCE LINSDAY)

1909 Reliance Model E. The top of the line was this 7-hp side-valve twin. Bore and stroke of 3 1/8 and 3 3/8 inches yielded a displacement of 51.8 ci (848cc). Wheelbase was 56 inches; height 19 inches; weight 160 lbs.; price $250. Other specifications were the same as the Model D. (BRUCE LINSDAY)

Aluminum Bike Motor Weighs 32 lb., Delivers 35 m.p.h. Speed

Now comes a 2-hp. aluminum gasoline engine for the bicyclist who wants a change from pedaling. Capable of speeds up to 35 m.p.h., it is said to provide smooth riding without the shimmy sometimes caused by heavier engines. Weighing only 32 lb., the unit is light enough to permit easy handling when the bike has to be lifted up curbs.

The motor is mounted in an inverted position behind the saddle with a direct friction drive on the rear wheel. It is a two-cycle engine of the mechanical-valve type and is designed to fit all standard-make bicycles. The gasoline tank over the engine is flat on top and might provide space, if desired, for strapping on packages. Reynolds Metals Co., of Louisville, Ky., makes it.

Inverted installation just behind the saddle provides direct friction drive on the top of the rear wheel itself.

Circa 1950 Reynolds motorbike attachment.

(VINTAGE MOTOR BIKE CLUB)

REYNOLDS

The Reynolds Metals Company of Louisville, Kentucky, built the Reynolds motorbike attachment. The production span is unknown, but the period ad has a 1950s look.

ROKON

During the early 1970s, the Rokon company of Keen, New Hampshire, was building the Rokon Trail-Breaker. Since the tanks were labeled "Trail-Breaker," these unique two-wheeled-drive motorcycles are discussed later under that title. During the late 1970s, the company built various conventional off-road Rokon bikes that featured foreign Maico and Sachs engine components. Hence, these do not fall under this book's definition of American motorcycles. During this era, the name "Rokon" appeared on the tank sides of the two-wheeled drive motorcycle; however, these bikes were powered by a foreign Sachs engine and, likewise, do not meet this book's definition of American motorcycles.

ROLLAWAY

From 1919 through 1921, the Rollaway Company of Toledo, Ohio, manufactured the Rollaway motorbike attachment. There were three different street addresses within one month!

Two-stroke single cylinder engine; friction drive via a 2 3/4-inch-diameter rubber-covered wheel mounted directly on the crankshaft.

(THE ANTIQUE MOTORCYCLE)

ROYAL

Royal motorcycles were built from 1901 through 1908 by the Royal Motor Works of Worcester, Massachusetts. The company was founded by Emil Hafelfinger, whose 1901 engine design was closely copied by Indian designer Oscar Hedstrom. In turn, through the Thor company's operations, Indian clones sported perhaps a dozen marque names. Hafelfinger's influence was

Circa 1902 Royal. The product of Emil Hafelfinger's fertile brain, this motorcycle may not look impressive now, but Hafelfinger's influence spread over the entire American industry. Most likely, the engine size was close to that of the Indian, which would be about 14 ci (230cc). (JIM DENNIE)

1909 Royal Pioneer. The engine featured overhead valves and a hemispherical combustion chamber. But the combustion chamber must have been quite roomy to accommodate the horizontal valve disposition. Also, the long and heavy L-shaped rockers must have greatly reduced maximum revolutions. Small wonder that the marque lasted only two years. For some reason, many designers of the era were in love with the idea of routing the exhaust through the frame. Royal Pioneer was perhaps the last to use this approach.

(THE ANTIQUE MOTORCYCLE)

1909 Royal Pioneer. The brass fuel tank was described as double-ended and seamless. The overall quality of the finish was above average.
(DOUG MITCHEL)

as profound then as his anonymity is now. Hafelfinger partnered with Charles Persons, whose bicycle and motorcycle saddle business became one of the more successful in the industry. In 1909, the marque name was changed to "Royal Pioneer."

ROYAL PIONEER

The "Royal" marque name was replaced by "Royal Pioneer" for the 1909 season by the Royal Motor Works of Worcester, Massachusetts (see Royal section). The machines featured an unorthodox single-cylinder overhead-valve engine, which, despite being mounted vertically, had the valves horizontally disposed! The 1910 models had no visible changes, and production ceased at season's end.

[S]

The S & J. From a period scrapbook comes this picture of an S & J motorcycle. Based on the large engine, the low position of the engine and the loop frame, the S & J appears to be circa 1905. (JIM DENNIE)

1914 Schickle Big Six. The two-stroke single had a bore and stroke of 4 and 3 3/8 inches, yielding a displacement of 42.4 ci (695cc). The name "Big Six" came from the horsepower rating, which by industry standard was assigned based strictly on engine size. A companion 5-hp model had both the bore and stroke sized at 3 3/8 inches, and a displacement of 30.2 ci (495cc). Both chain- and belt-drive versions were offered. (BRUCE LINSDAY)

S & J

The S & J "motor cycle" was built in 1902 by Sylvester and Jones of East Weymouth, Massachusetts. The firm had earlier built the S & J bicycle. The unusual F-head engine had two exhaust ports. A conventional port worked with a mechanically operated valve. An additional two-stroke-style piston port was opened when the piston neared bottom-dead-center, allowing the exhaust to flow through a pipe and into the muffler. Maximum output was 3 hp at 1000 rpm, and the engine could run as slow as 200 rpm. A 3 1/2-inch stroke was cited, but the bore wasn't specified. The piston was 3 3/4 inches high, and the company thought this dimension was advantageous because it was greater than the stroke. The connecting rod was solid bronze.

From a period ad: "Every live agent who is awake to the opportunity we offer him will write without delay for full particulars. We devoted much time to experimenting before we placed our machine on the market. When we seek agents, it is with the intention of giving them a motor cycle which will be a source of pleasure and not annoyance to their customers. We have done the experimenting; now you can do the selling. That is, if you are looking for an easy money-maker."

SCHICKEL

The Schickel marque had an unusual split history. From 1912 through 1918, these lightweight two-stroke singles were built in Stamford, Connecticut, by the Schickel Motor Company. The firm was among the world's earliest makers of large two-

1914 Schickle Big Six. The flywheel, crankpin and crankshaft were combined in one piece. Though single-speeders in standard trim, a two-speed transmission was available on special order. A new feature was the spring seat post with shock absorber. The finish was grey and black. (BRUCE LINSDAY)

stroke singles, its 1914 effort being a 42.4 ci (695cc) edition. Schickel claimed a big advantage was the ability of their engines to run on kerosine (in Britain, "paraffin") in areas where gasoline (in Britain, "petrol") was difficult to obtain. On that point, it's worth noting that the first drive-in filling station didn't arrive in the U. S. A. until 1913. Previously, gasoline and kerosine were sold from barrels, often on the back door side of hardware stores. Kerosine was more widely distributed than gasoline because it was the pre-electric age and kerosine was universally used for household lamps. Thus, the touted Schickel advantage of kerosine running.

In 1918, the factory was turned over to the government for the intended purpose of building the "U.S.A." engine of the proposed Liberty Army motorcycle that was to combine the best features of Harley-Davison, Indian and Excelsior. The Schickel was reintroduced at the 1920 Chicago, Illinois, motorcycle show. Production then continued through 1924.

1922 Schickel Model T. The two-speed transmission consisted of a primary drive crankshaft gear and a driven gear, acting through two independent clutches to produce low-and high-speed ratios. The literature bragged about no sliding gears. (BRUCE LINSDAY)

1922 Schickel Model T. The two-stroke single had a bore and stroke of 3 x 3 inches, and a displacement of 16.7 ci (290 cc). The finish was black with gold trim. (BRUCE LINSDAY)

1913 Sears Magneto model. In addition to the more expensive magneto ignition, this model featured the "new improved cushion pneumatic" front fork, which was another Thor component. Otherwise, the specifications were the same as for the Leader model. The price, complete with Free Engine Pulley was $179. Thus, the comparably equipped magneto and battery ignition models were priced only $17 apart. In that era, the $17 investment was well worth it because of the unreliability of batteries in rough-riding motorcycles. (THE ANTIQUE MOTORCYCLE)

SEARS

The famous Sears-Roebuck mail-order business added motorcycles to its 1913 line. These, of course, were rebranded machines because Sears was strictly a retail sales business. Sears offered Thor clones in 1913 and Spacke powered models. These Spacke powered bikes were probably built by the Excelsior Cycle Company of Chicago, Illinois. However, as startling as this may sound, this wasn't Chicago's famous Excelsior Motor Manufacturing and Supply Company that built Excelsiors and Henderson. In 1914, Spacke singles and twins were offered.

After years of selling foreign motorcycles under the Allstate label, in the late 1960s, Sears again sold bikes that bore the Sears name on the tank sides. However, these were Italian built Gilera motorcycles.

1913-1914 Sears Leader. This rebranded Thor was offered for the 1913 and 1914 seasons, with no changes made for the latter year. Specifications: F-head single with bore and stroke of 3 1/4 x 3.60 inches; displacement 29.9 ci (489cc); battery ignition; Brown and Barlow carburetor; wheelbase, 56 inches; weight 185 lbs.; Brooks saddle; 28 x 2 1/2-inch tires; Sears spring fork (same as on 1908 Thor); 4-gal. fuel tank; 2-qt. oil compartment in tank. Finish: light French gray striped in red and green. Price, standard: $150. Price, with accessory Eclipse free engine (clutch) pulley, as shown: $162.50. (DOUG MITCHEL)

1913 Sears twin. These came in two variants. A 60.92-ci (998 cc) Invincible Seven had a bore and stroke of 3.25 and 3.67 inches. A 70.62 ci (1157 cc) Dreadnaught Nine had a bore and stroke of 3.50 and 3.67 inches. The "Seven" and "Nine" referred to the cited horsepower by industry standard that equated output to engine size with no questions asked. The term "Dreadnaught" was in fashion for the latest battleships of the worlds' navies. The engine was built by Spacke and is discussed later as a separate marque. (THE ANTIQUE MOTORCYCLE)

1913 Sears twin. Specifications: leaf spring front fork; Spacke engine (see section "Spacke"); magneto ignition; Eclipse Free Engine (clutch) Pulley; single-speed; tires, 28 x 2 3/4 inches; wheelbase 57 inches; weight 250 lbs.; rich cherry red and ivory white finish. Prices: Invincible Seven, $225; Dreadnaught Nine, $250. (THE ANTIQUE MOTORCYCLE)

1914 Sears DeLuxe Big Five. Spacke singles first entered the lineup in 1913. The actual displacement was 35.3 ci (578 cc). The wheelbase was 57 inches, and the machine weighed 220 lbs. A top speed of 50 mph was claimed. The price was $220. (DOUG MITCHEL)

SERVI-CYCLE

Servi-Cycle lightweight motorcycles were built from 1935 through 1951 by the Simplex Manufacturing Corporation of New Orleans, Louisiana. From 1952 through 1960, this line and various step-through scooters and mini-bikes were continued with the name "Simplex." The company was founded by J. Paul Treen, a Harley-Davidson dealer who saw the need for a lightweight machine. One is tempted to term the Servi-Cycle and its follow-on Simplex as "motorbikes," owing to the light construction which, on the earliest models, included regular bicycle balloon tires. But these were uniquely designed complete units without pedals. Apart from the earliest tires, and the handlebars with supporting stem, there were no other pedal bike components.

Only detail changes were made during this era. Some examples: a bulbous tank in 1936; larger brakes in 1936; a change from roller-ball bearings to tapered roller bearings in 1936; a change from lever throttle to twist-grip throttle in 1936; a change from 7/8-inch frame tubing to 1-inch tubing in 1938; compression release built into the throttle grip in 1938; foot-clutch in 1940; longer stroke in 1940 (advertised, 2 1/2 inches; actual 2.462 inches), which increased displacement to a claimed 125cc (actual, 127cc); kickstarter in 1947; front brake became optional (instead of standard) in 1948; iron-lined aluminum cylinders in 1949, etc. Such refinements continued through 1951, at which time the little motorcycles were renamed "Simplex." The Simplex era is covered later.

1935 Servi-Cycle. There was no clutch and no kick-starter. The rider squeezed the right grip to engage the compression release, then pushed off. A smooth stop required the compression release. The left-bar lever was the front brake; a left-side pedal worked the rear brake. Specifications: engine, two-stroke single, bore 2 1/4 inches, stroke 1 5/8 inches, displacement 7.06 cubic inches (116 cc), Eiseman LE-71 magneto; single-speed; top speed 30 mph; price $137.50. Note: Although this is a 1936 advertising picture, it shows the 1935 flat-sided tank and there were other significant changes. (MOTORCYCLIST)

SHAW

Shaw motorbikes and motorcycles were built from 1903 through 1917 by the Shaw Manufacturing Company of Galesburg, Kansas, founded by W. Shaw. The firm built only motor attachments through 1910. In 1911, Shaw purchased the Kokomo Motorcycle Company of Kokomo, Indiana, then sold an updated version of the Kokomo design as a complete lightweight motorcycle from 1912 through 1914. The main change to the Kokomo design was a larger cylinder. Shaw continued making the motorbike attachment through this period.

In 1914, Mr. Shaw discontinued the Shaw motorcycle in order to build a light two-passenger car known as the Shaw Speedster. The company continued making the motorbike attachment and added a complete motorbike with the engine in a standard bicycle frame.

The new complete motorbike was powered by a four-stroke 2 1/2-hp single-cylinder engine. In 1915, the motorbike primary and final drives were changed from belt to chain, and the cooling fins were enlarged. Magneto ignition was also introduced. Incidentally, from 1913 through 1917, Mr. Shinzo Morita of Osaka, Japan, had a standing order for 18 Shaw motorbike attachments per month. In 1917, Shaw stopped building both the motorbike attachment and the complete motorbike. The company continued in business through 1962, building Model T Ford tractor attachments, small farm tractors, and the Shaw Du-All garden tractor. During World War II, the company built aircraft and machine gun parts. In 1962, Mr. Shaw sold his business to Brush Hog, a manufacturer of rotary lawnmowers.

1914 Shaw motorbike attachment Model B. This was the battery ignition outfit installed in an ordinary pedal bicycle. A similar belt-drive Model M kit had magneto ignition. Both included a four-stroke 2 1/2-hp engine.

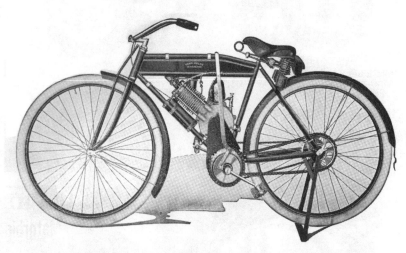

1915 Shaw complete motorbike Model H "Motorbicycle." This magneto ignition motorbike was similar to the Model M attachment kit, but the drive system was changed from a belt to primary and final drive chains. (THE ANTIQUE MOTORCYCLE)

Mid-fifties Simplex Compact. (CYCLE)

SIMPLEX

From 1935 through 1951, lightweight Servi-Cycles had been built by the Simplex Manufacturing Company of New Orleans, Louisiana. From 1952 through 1960, this line was continued under the name "Simplex." In 1953, an automatic centrifugal clutch was introduced on the "Automatic" model. Twin tailpipes became standard in 1954. Production of the traditional motorbike ceased in 1960 because of competition from imported lightweights. The firm carried on for awhile with various small-wheeled designs, one of which was a genuine small motorcycle and at least two of which were dangerously small machines that today might be termed micro motorcycles. The motorcycle was offered either with a Clinton engine, as pictured, or a British built Villiers 250cc two-stroke with four-speed foot-shift.

1956 Simplex Automatic. The 129 cc engine featured an "overhung" crank, meaning the crankshaft was supported on the drive (left) side only. This made for easy inspection and, if necessary, replacement of the connecting rod big end. Rated became optional equipment in 1948. Evident is the kickstarter, which had been introduced on the 1947 Servi-Cycles. (SIMPLEX PUBLICITY PHOTO)

Mid-1950s Simplex motorcycle. Specifications: 7-hp Continental Red Seal side-valve single-cylinder engine; tires, 4.80/4.00 x 12 inches (20-inch outer diameter); undamped telescopic front fork; undamped swinging-arm rear suspension; red and silver finish. Price $298, front brake $10 extra, kick-starter $10 extra (otherwise, pull-cord starting). (VINTAGE MOTOR BIKE CLUB)

1972 Simplex. Specifications: 4.9-hp Continental side-valve single-cylinder engine; tires, 5.30 x 6 inch (14-inch outer diameter); undamped telescopic front fork; unsprung rear wheel; red and silver finish. Price, standard, $229, front brake $10 extra, kick-starter $10 extra (otherwise, pull-cord starting). (VINTAGE MOTOR BIKE CLUB)

Snell California Motor Cycle

1904 Snell-California. Except for the name, these bikes were identical to the Yale-California machines built in the same factory. The F-head engine displaced 17.8 cubic inches (292cc), bore and stroke were 2 3/4 x 3 inches. The single-speed power was transmitted by a three-ply belt. Speeds of 4 to 50 mph were claimed.
(BRUCE LINSDAY)

SNELL-CALIFORNIA

The Snell-California was one of four interconnected marques. The first of these was the California motorcycle built in San Francisco. Refer to the earlier section on California and Yale-California for additional information.

The production of Snell-California motorcycles was undertaken in 1904 by the newly formed Consolidated Manufacturing Company of Toledo, Ohio. Snell-California and Yale-California motorcycles were built in the same factory and were identical except for the names. The "Snell" and "Yale" names were already in use on the company's bicycles. In 1905, the Snell-California name was dropped in favor of the Yale-California name. In 1909, the name was shortened to "Yale." The balance of the company's history is told in the later "Yale" section.

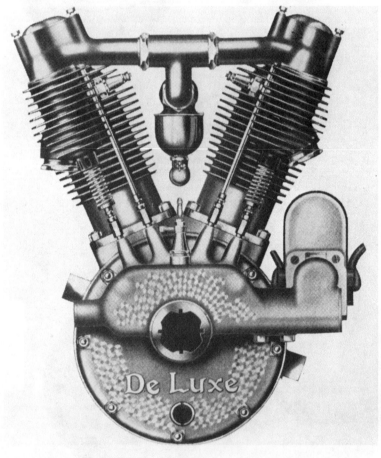

1913 Spacke twin. With its machine-turned finish and compact layout, the F-head Spacke engines were attractive. These were fitted to such makes as: Crawford, Dayton, DeLuxe and Sears. These were made in two sizes, 60.92 ci (998cc) and 70.62 ci (1157cc). Bores on the two engines were 3.25 and 2.50 inches; identical strokes were 3.67 inches. A companion 30.46-ci (499cc) single was also offered.
(THE ANTIQUE MOTORCYCLE)

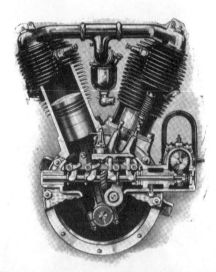

1913 Spacke twin. From 1913 through 1915, full enclosure of the overhead valves gave the De Luxe engine an important advantage over the engines of Harley-Davidson, Indian, and Excelsior. The rest of the Spacke design seems a wasteful exercise in technical bravado. The cost of making the gear-driven camshaft and gear-driven magneto might have been better spent elsewhere, as there was no need for being so elaborate. (THE ANTIQUE MOTORCYCLE)

SPACKE ENGINES

The F. W. Spacke Machine Company of Indianapolis, Indiana, built proprietary De Luxe engines from about 1913 through

1917. These uniquely designed single-cylinder and V-twin engines were used on a number of American marques—a situation made possible by the availability of standard frame tubing and frame components from Standard Welding of Cleveland, Ohio, according to historian Stephen Wright.

STAHL

Stahl motorcycles, also known as CVS, were built from 1902 through 1912 by the Home Manufacturing Company of Philadelphia, Pennsylvania. Early examples featured a pedal-bike style so-called "diamond" frame. Later machines had a loop frame. F-head singles of 27 ci (442cc) and F-head twins of 57 ci (934cc) were among later offerings.

STARLITE

In the mid-1960s, Atchison Products of Crystal Lake, Illinois, purchased the patents and manufacturing rights for the Model 95 Ultra-lite motorcycle from the Mohs Seaplane Corporation. Starlite advertising data differed slightly from that issued under the Mohs trade name. The Starlite-cited 8 hp was surely an error; the engine was realistically listed as 5 hp in a Mohs ad. The Mohs ad stated engine size of 98cc; the Starlite ad cited 95cc.

STEARNS

Little is known of the Stearns. This example was built to pace racing bicyclist Jimmy Michael in his efforts to set speed records. This Stearns racer could run up to 50 mph on the wooden bicycle tracks called velodromes. An article in the December 21, 1901, *Scientific American* mentioned that the low saddle height was for the purpose of getting the machine's rider directly in front of the bicyclist who was trying for speed or distance records.

Specifications: fan-cooled 8-hp 95cc Chrysler engine; pull-cord starter (no pedals); spring-controlled engine mount; heavy-duty 0.108-gauge wheel spokes; top speed 40 mph; weight under 90 lbs.; price $269. (VINTAGE MOTOR BIKE CLUB)

1901 Stearns racer. Specifications: 3 3/4 hp (about 21 ci or 350 cc) DeDion F-head single-cylinder engine; engine speeds of 600 to 2000 rpm; weight 165 lbs. (SCIENTIFIC AMERICAN)

STEFFEY

The Steffey Manufacturing Company of Philadelphia, Pennsylvania, claimed to be the nation's first builder of motorcycle engines. The firm produced complete motorcycles from 1901 through about 1904. These single-cylinder bikes were offered either with air cooling or water cooling. Steffey also built at least one steam-powered motorcycle. From the April, 1902, *The Dealer and Repairman*: "The Steffey Mfg. Co. ... was one of the earliest, if not the first, builders of motor bicycles in this country,

Circa 1902 Steffey. Water cooling was unique for this American era. Steffey also built air-cooled models. The various engines offered ranged from 1 1/4 to 3 hp. (JIM DENNIE)

Circa 1902 Stratton. The era included builders of proprietary engines, frames and attachments. In its engine layout, this circa 1902 Stratton looks identical to the period Lamson. (JIM DENNIE)

and it bears the further distinction of being the only maker of a motor bicycle with water cooled motor ... The Steffey company furnishes complete motor sets, finished motors, motor castings, and various factors in the line of carburetors, ignition apparatus, mufflers, etc."

Teen-aged E. Paul du Pont built his own motorcycle from one of the Steffey kits. About 30 years later, he gained control of the Indian motorcycle company.

STRATTON

According to *The Encyclopedia of the Motorcycle* (Hugo Wilson), the Stratton was made in New York City. Aside from this and a picture from a period scrapbook, no other data were found by the author.

SUDDARD

The strange motorcycle shown in the accompanying drawing was the brainchild of William A. Studdard, who submitted the drawing with a patent application. The patent was effective January 26, 1904. The saddle appears to be suspended on a combination of coil springs (H) and leaf springs (G). The steering wheel appears too close to the saddle for practical use. No other information has been discovered on a "Suddard" motorcycle, so the marque may have been stillborn.

SYCAMORE

The Sycamore was built along the lines of the Pope family of early motorcycles ,such as the Columbia. Early Bradley models also featured the cylinder behind the seat mast. No information was found on the Sycamore, other than this picture from a period scrapbook.

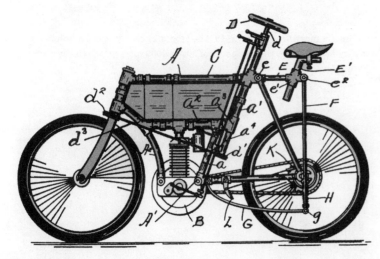

1904 Suddard. (UNITED STATES PATENT OFFICE)

Circa 1903 Sycamore. (JIM DENNIE)

THIEM

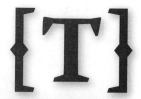

The Joerns-Thiem company began in 1900 as a maker of motorcycle engines and complete motorcycles, which were marketed under other names. One of these Thiem clones was the 1911 American (Chicago) Model 51. Sears also sold a Thiem clone. In 1912 and 1913, the company sold motorcycles under its own Thiem brand. These motorcycles were among the earliest American machines with side-valve (Flathead) engines. The last motorcycles with "Thiem" on the tank sides, were the 1913 models. In that year, the company launched a follow-on marque, the illustrious Cyclone overhead-cam models.

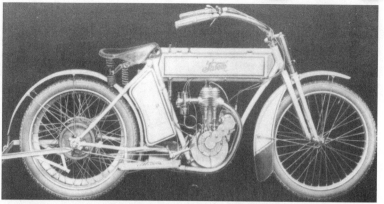

1912 Thiem 5-horsepower Model E with chain drive and two-speed rear hub. The side-valve engine had a bore and stroke of 3 1/4 and 3 47/64 inches, and a displacement of 31 ci (50 cc). Other specifications: leading link fork; loop frame; Troxel saddle; choice of single-speed chain drive, two-speed rear hub with chain drive, or single-speed belt drive; wheelbase 56 inches; silver gray with light green striping. Price $235. (BRUCE LINSDAY)

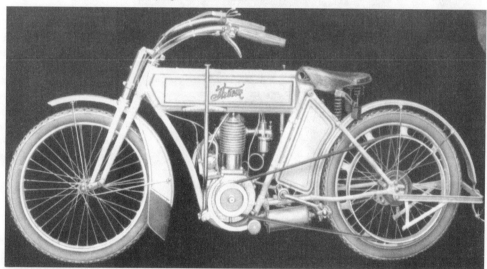

1912 Thiem 5-hp Model E with flat belt drive. The price was $200. (BRUCE LINSDAY)

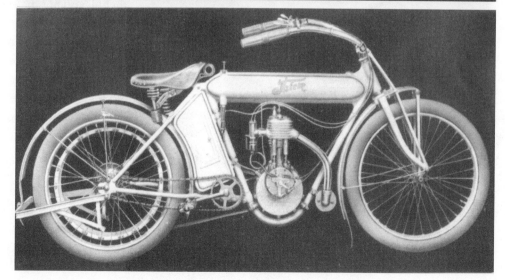

1912 Thiem 4-hp Model G. The capacity wasn't cited in the literature, but by industry convention a 4-hp engine displaced about 24 ci (400cc). Price, $145.

(BRUCE LINSDAY)

1903 Thomas Auto-Bi. Now entering its fourth production year, Thomas built a motorcycle with a pivoted sprung fork and a swinging-arm rear suspension. The small coil springs for these systems are seen just below and forward of the handlebars, and just below and aft of the saddle. The engine was rated at 2 1/2 hp. (SCIENTIFIC AMERICAN)

1904 Thomas Auto-Bi. The catalog billed this one as the "1904 Thomas Model 36 Motor Bicycle," and the name on the tanks sides was "Thomas." Yet, the term "Thomas Auto-Bi" was used in the catalog text. In the 1904 model, we see the natural progression toward more enclosure and increasingly stylistic lines.

(BRUCE LINSDAY)

1907 Thomas Auto-Bi. In 1909, this model became the Greyhound Model 48. (GEORGE YAROCKI)

THOMAS AUTO-BI (ALSO, AUTO-BI)

Because most sources found by the author use the term "Thomas Auto-Bi," this section includes all but the earliest information and picture. Refer to the section "Auto-Bi" for discussion of the marque's earliest days and a picture representing the first motorcycle configuration. The marque debuted in 1900. In the April, 1902, issue of *The Dealer and Repairman*, the company claimed to have built the first successful commercially produced motorcycle in the United States. Other also sources also credit the marque with this distinction. In 1909, the Thomas family sold out, the company was reorganized and the name was changed to the Greyhound Motor Works. Production continued through 1912.

THOROUGHBRED

Just in case buyers weren't confused enough from the Indian clones situation, along came the Thoroughbred about 1905. Confusing? Yes, because there was the Thor, the Thor-Bred, and the Thoroughbred, all direct copies of the Indian! The name "Thoroughbred" was the only thing distinctive about this Indian clone, but the marketing company, Reading-Standard, later pioneered the side-valve engine in the American industry. Thoroughbred production may have been confined to the year 1905 only, but was brief in any case. Subsequent bikes from this factory were produced as the Reading-Standard marque.

Specifications from the April 1, 1905, *Cycle and Automobile Trade Journal*: "22 inch frame; 28 x 2 inch tires; 46 inch wheelbase; single cylinder 2 19/32 (inch, bore) x 3 (inch, stroke) 1 3/4 H.P. motor; automatic lubrication; chain drive; battery mileage 1500 to 2000; fuel 60 to 80 miles, according to roads; grip control; weight 110 lbs.; speed 6 to 35 miles per hour; price $210. Special features: Extra fine finish and workmanship; spring hub; air outlet for oil cup; stopcock for draining gasoline tank."

TIGER AUTO-BIKE

The Tiger Auto-Bike was built in 1915 and 1916 by the Tiger Auto-Bike Company of Chicago.

TORPEDO

The Hornecker Motor Manufacturing Company of Whiting, Indiana, built Torpedo motorcycles from 1906 through 1908. Production continued in 1909 after the factory was moved to Geneseo, Illinois, according to historian Stephen Wright.

1909 Torpedo Model F. Rated output was 5 hp, and the sales price was $275. The engine and bizarre inlet manifold are the same as the 1909 Thor twin, except that the Thor might have been slightly larger because of its 6-hp rating. (BRUCE LINSDAY)

Thoroughbred Motor Cycle
Made by Reading Standard Cycle Mfg. Co., Reading, Pa.

1905 15.85-cubic inch (260cc) Thoroughbred.
(THE ANTIQUE MOTORCYCLE)

1915 Tiger Auto-Bike. The engine was a 14.7-ci (241cc) two-stroke single built by the Fredrickson company. The Tiger weighed 112.5 lbs. and sold for $112.50. (BOB KAROLEVITZ)

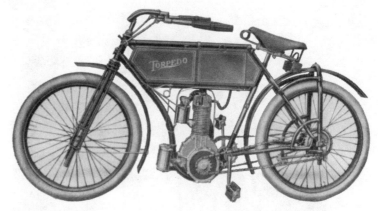

1909 Torpedo Model G. "The highest grade and most improved Motorcycle built in the United States," claimed the catalog. Noteworthy were the telescopic front fork and the plunger rear suspension. The bike sold for $225. The Model C cost $225 and was identical, except for a rigid frame. (BRUCE LINSDAY)

1906 Tourist. The bike was 56 inches long and weighed 150 lbs., both typical figures for the era. From the press release: "A spring prevents the pedals from revolving while the feet are on the footrest. Power is transmitted by a leather belt .. and no idler is found necessary. The manufacturer, however, supplies an idler if desired...."
(JIM DENNIE)

The unique two-wheeled drive Trail-Breaker. (VINTAGE MOTOR BIKE CLUB)

TOURIST

The Tourist was built in 1906 and 1907 by the Breeze Motor Manufacturing Company of Newark, New Jersey. The F-head single-cylinder engines were typical, but Tourist was one of the few 1906 marques with a loop frame—the most notable exponent of which was Harley-Davidson. Tourist was also among the first—perhaps the very first—to feature statically mounted footrests.

TRAIL-BREAKER

Although referred to in period magazine test articles as the "Rokon" or "Rokon Trail-Breaker," the name on the tank was "Trail-Breaker," hence the marque is discussed here. The motorcycle originated from an African hunting expedition of wealthy J. B. Nethercutt, owner of Merle Norman Cosmentics. A one-off two-wheel-drive bike was created by J. B. and his two sons to get them to places where their four-wheel-drive Land Rover couldn't go.

From 1959 through 1963, about 1,000 bikes were built in Sylmar, California, before production ceased. These bikes were powered by a 146cc (8.9-ci) air-cooled Chrysler four-stroke single-cylinder engine originally designed for marine use. Drive was through a three-speed hand-shifted transmission.

In 1965, investors bought the company, moved it to Wilmington, Vermont, and changed the company name to Rokon, which was derived from their motel "On The Rocks." An improved drive system was featured that incorporated a limited-slip mechanism that improved handling during turns. In 1967, production was moved to Keene, New Hampshire. At this time, the three-speed hand-shift transmission was replaced with a torque-converter. Production continued through 1978, when the firm went bankrupt.

During the Keene operations, Rokon began building conventional off-road bikes that featured foreign Maico and Sachs engine components; these do not meet this book's definition of American motorcycles. Likewise, the name "Rokon" was placed on the tank sides of the two-wheeled drive motorcycles, but the engines were imported from Sachs, so these models do not meet this book's definition of American motorcycles. Production of these American-Foreign Rokon Trail-Breakers continues into the 21st century.

Travis Motor Bike. The makers, or distributors if this was a licensed Velo Solex copy, claimed the unit could be mounted on any bicycle in less than 30 minutes. The 1 1/5- horsepower Travis weighed only 17 lbs. The price was $79.95. (VINTAGE MOTOR BIKE CLUB)

TRAVIS BIKE MOTOR

The Travis Bike Motor was manufactured by the Starbrand Corporation of Indianapolis, Indiana, around 1955. Previously, this motorbike attachment was sold by Travis Products as the Dyno-Mite. These units appeared much like the French designed Velo Solex, yet look slightly different in shape and don't have the long engage/disengage hand-lever of the French unit.

TRIBUNE

The early 20th century American industry was full of clones, most of them offshoots of the Indian marque though manufactured by Thor. Another set was the product of the Pope family of companies. Identical motorcycles, apart from the names, were established in parallel to popular pedal bikes of the time that were marketed by the Pope-owned entities. Among these were America, Columbia, Cleveland and Tribune. Refer to the section "American (Connecticut)" for a picture representative of the Tribune.

TRIUMPH

The Triumph Manufacturing Company of Detroit, Michigan, built Triumph motorcycles in 1912 and 1913. This firm had no connection with the world famous Triumph company of England. In 1912, a single-speed single-cylinder Model A was offered. In 1913, the Model B with two-speed planetary gearbox arrived. The 1913 plans also called for a three-speed Model C. However, production ceased in late 1912, shortly after the announced 1913 lineup. Whether or not any 1913 models were actually produced is anybody's guess.

1913 Triumph Model B. A counter-shaft mounted two-speed planetary transmission was featured. Specifications weren't discovered by the author, but the engine appears to be about 600cc (37 ci), which had become a popular size in other marques' models termed "Six" or "Big Six." (THE ANTIQUE MOTORCYCLE)

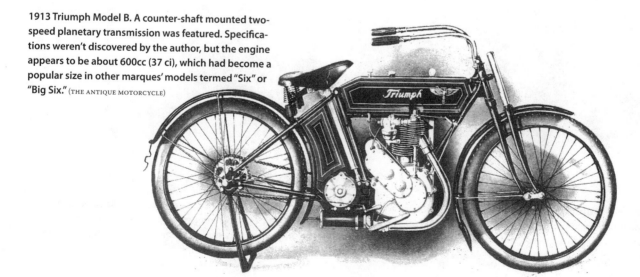

{V}

VARD

Vard Inc., of Pasadena, California, was one of thousands of small firms that did subcontracting work for major defense industry companies during World War II. Following the war, Vard built several prototype motorcycles. One of these, a 21.35ci (350cc) side-valve single, was pictured and described in the October 19, 1944, issue of *Motor Cycling* (a British magazine). Pictures and captions detail this prototype. For whatever reasons, Vard wasn't satisfied with this motorcycle. The company then designed a 15.2-ci (250cc) sleeve-valve single for motorcycle use.

Vard decided not to produce a motorcycle, but the firm did play a significant role in postwar American motorcycling. Vard designed and, from 1946 through 1949, manufactured the first American telescopic fork since the long-gone Flying Merkel. The Vard fork was a popular modification, especially in motorcycle-happy California, where the fork made a night-and-day difference in popular off-road riding. This business came to an end in 1949 when Harley-Davidson and Indian both started building bikes with telescopic forks.

1944 Vard prototype. Specifications: "Light weight of 350 pounds, with 4 gallons as and 2 quarts oil. Top speed of 65 mph. Gas consumption—60 miles per gallon. Spring frame. Telescopic front fork, hydraulically controlled and completely enclosed. Rear shock absorber units hydraulically controlled and completely enclosed. No frame lubrication required. Rubber mounted handlebars...."
(BRUCE LINSDAY)

1944 Vard prototype. Specifications, continued: "....Sealed beam headlamp and speedometer mounted in shroud. Short wheelbase of 53 inches for maneuverability. Hand-controlled clutch. Four-speed progressive foot-shift transmission. Engine of rugged, unit-type construction, with dry sump and totally enclosed valves. Carburetor of the sleeve throttle type. Only two gears in the entire engine. Aluminum alloy head, piston, and connecting rod. All engine bearings are plain and pressure-fed at 60-120 pounds oil pressure." (BRUCE LINSDAY)

WAGNER

The Wagner Motorcycle Company of Saint Paul, Minnesota, built Wagners from 1901 through 1914. During this period, about 8,500 Wagners were built and sold. Wagner was one of the first American manufacturers to situate the engine low in the frame. The 1905 models combined a more or less diamond (pedal bike) frame with the low engine mounting.

At the time, most American motorcycles situated the engine higher in a diamond frame, either as Indians or Indian clones or as mimickers. Engine size grew from about 15 cubic inches in 1904, to 17.8 in 1905, to 26.96 on the 1909 Semi-Racer, to 26.96 on all 1910 models, to 29.0 on 1911 models, which continued unchanged through the end in 1914.

A period advertisement read: "Why buy anything but the best? Money placed in a

1905 Wagner. From the April 1, 1905, *Cycle and Automobile Trade Journal:* "20 inch frame; 2 1/4 inch tires; 52 inch wheelbase; single cylinder, 2 3/4 (inch, bore) x 3 (inch, stroke) 3 H.P. motor; splash lubrication; drive by V-belt; battery mileage, 1000; fuel mileage, 125; improved grip control; weight 110 lbs.; speed 3 to 40 miles; price, $200. Special features: Patented loop frame and twin-forks; gears made integral with shafts; simplified carburetor." (JIM DENNIE)

1909 Wagner Model 6. This was the basic configuration for most bikes produced from 1905 through 1914. The engine specifications had not changed since 1905. The price was $200. (BRUCE LINSDAY)

1909 Wagner Ladies Drop Frame Model. Company head George Wagner had an enthusiastic riding daughter, Clara. This probably was a factor in the introduction of this ladies' model. Clara entered the 1910 Federation of American Motorcyclists Western Endurance Run of 365 miles on this kind of Wagner. She scored a perfect 1,000 points. The price was $210. (BRUCE LINSDAY)

1909 Wagner Semi-Racing Model. A larger engine was fitted, with bore and stroke of 3 1/4 inches, the displacement being 26.96 cubic inches (442cc). The price was $210. (BRUCE LINSDAY)

1909 Wagner Two-Engine Tandem. Two 2 1/2-hp engines were the motive force. Wagner also built a 1909 single-engine tandem, with the engine in the front position. Speeds of 4 to 30 mph were achievable. (GEORGE YAROCKI)

1909 Wagner. The low mounted engine was a great idea, good enough to impress many in the 1905-1909 era, but the company seemed to rest on its laurels thereafter. Other marques left it behind in the technology race.

Circa 1911 Waverly engine. The Perry E. Mack proprietary engines didn't catch on in the industry. Though some Kenzler-Waverly and Waverly motorcycles used engines stamped "Waverly," these were identical to the Mack engines. (THE ANTIQUE MOTORCYCLE)

good Motor Cycle is an investment. But money placed in a poor motorcycle is a loss ... We have spent three years perfecting a Motor Cycle to offer the public ..."

WAVERLY

The Waverly was one of four interrelated marques, each differing from the other only in the name. The first was the Kenzler-Waverly built in Cambridge, Wisconsin. This marque evolved into the Waverly, also built at Cambridge. After production moved to Jefferson, Wisconsin, the motorcycles were renamed "P.E.M.," after designer Perry E. Mack, and were subsequently renamed again as "Jefferson" in honor of the home city. See "Mack Engines."

Circa 1911 Waverly. Power was from the Mack engine designed by Perry E. Mack. (THE ANTIQUE MOTORCYCLE)

WHIPPLE

Whipple motorcycles were manufactured by the Whipple Cycle Company, 260 West Jackson Boulevard, Chicago, Illinois, from 1904 through 1906.

From a turn-of-the-century scrapbook came the following: "...Whipple Cycle Company... offer a $120 motorcycle which will no doubt meet with large sale ... It is capable of traveling at speeds up to 25 miles per hour, and will climb any hill in that neighborhood on its low gear ..."

1904 Whipple. A new feature for 1904 was a "two speed friction clutch," which, actually, was a simple transmission. (JIM DENNIE)

WILLIAMSON

Thomas G. Williamson of Philadelphia, Pennsylvania, built his motorcycles around 1902. The motor was described as being an "Americanized French design," and weighed 30 lbs. Instead of a carburetor, the "Little Giant Vaporizer" was fitted and offered for sale separately to the trade. Vaporizers were already distinctly out of date. These devices dripped fuel into an absorbing material, a wick, so to speak, and the fumes were inhaled by the engine. It was very crude stuff and out of date by 1900.

Circa 1902 Williamson. (JIM DENNIE)

The mid-'50s Wizard motorbike was a Simplex sold through the nationwide Western Auto stores.

WIZARD

In the mid-1950s, the nationwide Western Auto stores sold Simplex lightweight motorcycles that differed only in the brand name "Wizard" applied to the fuel tank. "Wizard" was a brand name used on a variety of Western Auto products.

WYSE-CYCLE

During World War II, Wyse Laboratories of Dayton, Ohio, built various items for nearby Wright Field, later known as Wright-Patterson Air Force Base. Wright Field was the center for aeronautical research. Wyse products included scale model aircraft, aircraft equipment, test equipment, and instruments. After the war, the firm designed the Wyse-Cycle, including the engine. Wyse advertised the Wyse-Cycle during 1946 and 1947. Production levels are unknown, and it's even possible that the project never got past prototype stage. Wyse Laboratories was succeeded in 1947 by GAD-JETS Incorporated, which concentrated on manufacturing military spare parts. The Wyse-Cycle was dropped at that time.

In 1951, a section of the company sprouted its own corporate wings as Projects Unlimited. In 1960, Projects Unlimited experimented with an updated version of the Wyse-Cycle, known as the Skat-Kat, then went into production with the Skat-Kitty, which was what today would be termed a minibike.

1946 specifications: Side-valve single-cylinder Wyse developed 4-hp engine; wheelbase, 48 inches; weight, 245 lbs.; tires, 18 x 5.50 inches; speeds up to 40 mph; fuel mileage, 50 to 70 mpg; transmission, non-shifting Centraulic Speedset; drive, roller chain; ignition, battery; tank capacity, 2 gal.; generator, Wyse Recto-charge; Colors, Storm Red, Goldenrod, Hickory Brown, Dawn Blue, Forest Green; retail price, "approximately $275." That last tidbit suggests at the time of the source advertisement, the Wyse-Cycle had not gone into full-scale production. The lack of anyplace to put one's feet, also suggests prototype status.

1946 Wyse-Cycle.

(VINTAGE MOTOR BIKE CLUB)

Bibliography

The American Motorcycle 1869-1914, by Stephen Wright.

The Antique Motorcycle; Summer 1968, Winter 1969, and all issues from 1970 through 2005. *The Complete Illustrated Encyclopedia of American Motorcycles*, by Todd Rafferty. Cycle, all issues from 1950 through 1961.

Cycle World, all issues from 1962 through 2005.

The Dealer and Repairman, April, 1902. *The Encyclopedia of the Motorcycle*, by Hugo Wilson. *Golden Age of the Fours*, by T. A. Hodgdon. *Motorcycles and Sidecars*, by Victor W. Page. *Motorcycle Illustrated* and succeeding titles, all issues from 1906 through *American Bicyclist and Motorcyclist*, December 1931.

Motorcycling and Bicycling and succeeding title *Motorcycling* including *The Bicycling World*, various issues, 1919 through 1928.

Motorcyclist, most issues from 1936 through 1948. *Scientific American*, some issues from 1901 and 1902.

A Treasury of Motorcycles of the World, by Floyd Clymer.

Vintage Motor Bike Club, all issues from 1987 through 2005.

The World's Motorcycles 1894-1963, by Erwin Tragatsch.

Yesterday's Motorcycles, by Bob Karolevitz.

AUTHOR'S NOTE: Sales literature, ads, press releases, and a period scrapbook are cited as applicable to each marque.